W9-AGY-378

THE HARMONY GUIDE TO
CROCHETING

THE HARMONY GUIDE TO

CROCHETING

Techniques and Stitches

Edited by Debra Mountford

Harmony Books/New York

Copyright © 1986, 1992 by Lyric Books Limited

All rights reserved. No part of this book may be reproduced or transmitted in any form or by any means, electronic or mechanical, including photocopying, recording, or by any information storage and retrieval system, without permission in writing from the publisher.

Published by Harmony Books, a division of Crown Publishers, Inc., 201 East 50th Street, New York, New York 10022. Member of the Crown Publishing Group.

Random House, Inc. New York, Toronto, London, Sydney, Auckland

Originally published in two separate volumes as *The Harmony Guide to Crochet Stitches* and *The Harmony Guide to 100's More Crochet Stitches*.

Harmony and colophon are trademarks of Crown Publishers, Inc.

Manufactured in Belgium

Library of Congress Cataloging-in-Publication Data

The Harmony guide to crocheting : techniques and stitches / edited by
  Debra Mountford. — 1st ed.
    "Originally published in two separate volumes as the Harmony guide
  to crochet stitches and the Harmony guide to 100's more crochet
  stitches"—
    Includes index.
    1. Crocheting. I. Mountford, Debra. II. Harmony Books (Firm)
  III. Harmony guide to crochet stitches. IV. Harmony guide to 100's
  more crochet stitches.
  TT820.H272 1993
  746.43'4—dc20   92-45594
                                            CIP

ISBN 0-517-88074-1
10 9 8 7 6 5 4 3 2 1
First Edition

CONTENTS

Introduction   4

Basic Stitches   16

Stitch Variations   17

Clusters   19

Patterns for Texture and Color   22

All-over Patterns   52

Openwork and Lace Patterns   64

Filet Crochet   89

Motifs   102

Irish Style Crochet   137

Edgings and Trimmings   150

Afghan (Tunisian Crochet)   161

Index   173

Introduction

About Crochet

Traditionally crochet was worked almost exclusively in very fine cotton yarn to create or embellish household items such as curtains, table cloths or place mats. Crochet was often added as decoration or trimming on collars and fine lawn handkerchiefs. The frill on the front of a man's shirt was often crochet work.

With the increase in the availability of yarn in a wide variety of textures and colours we are no longer limited to just these articles when we consider ways to use the craft of crochet. The samples in this book were worked in a fine mercerised cotton, but may take on a totally different appearance if different yarns are used. The lacier stitches probably look their best in these smooth threads, but some of the all-over stitches and many of the Afghan (Tunisian) stitches can be more interesting when worked in tweedy or textured yarns.

Equipment

Crochet Hooks

Crochet hooks are usually made from steel, aluminium or plastic in a range of sizes according to their diameter. As each crochet stitch is worked separately until only one loop remains on the hook, space is not needed to hold stitches and the hooks are made to a standard convenient length.

Holding the Hook and Yarn

There are no hard and fast rules as to the best way to hold the hook and yarn. The diagrams below show just one method, but choose whichever way you find the most comfortable.

Due to the restrictions of space it is not possible to show diagrams for both right and left handed people. Left handers may find it easier to trace the diagrams and then turn the tracing paper over, thus reversing the image, alternatively reflect the diagrams in the mirror. Read left for right and right for left where applicable.

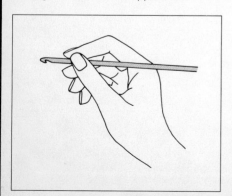

The hook is held in the right hand as if holding a pencil.

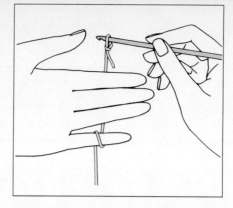

To maintain the slight tension in the yarn necessary for easy, even working, it can help to arrange the yarn around the fingers of the left hand in this way.

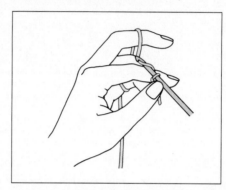

The left hand holds the work and at the same time controls the yarn supply. The left hand middle finger is used to manipulate the yarn, while the index finger and thumb hold on to the work.

To Start

Almost all crochet begins with a base or starting chain, which is a series of chain stitches, beginning with a slip knot.

Slip Knot

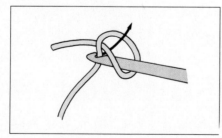

Make a loop then hook another loop through it. Tighten gently and slide the knot up to the hook.

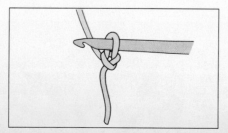

Yarn Over (yo)

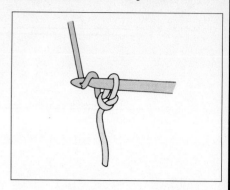

Wrap the yarn from back to front over the hook (or hold the yarn still and manoeuvre the hook). This movement of the yarn over the hook is used over and over again in crochet and is usually called 'yarn over', abbreviated as 'yo'.

Chain Stitch (ch ○)

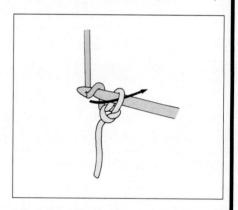

Yarn over and draw the yarn through to form a new loop without tightening up the previous one.

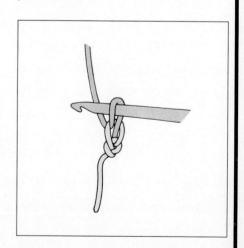

Repeat to form as many chains as required. Do not count the slip knot as a stitch.

Note: Unless otherwise stated. when working into the starting chain always work under two strands of chain loops as shown in the diagram.

Basic Stitches

All the crochet patterns in this book are produced using combinations of the following basic stitches. They are shown in the diagrams worked into a starting chain but the method is the same whatever part of the work the stitch is worked into.

Slip Stitch (sl st ●)

This is the shortest of crochet stitches and unlike other stitches is not used on its own to produce a fabric. It is used for joining, shaping and where necessary carrying the yarn to another part of the fabric for the next stage.

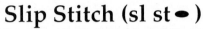

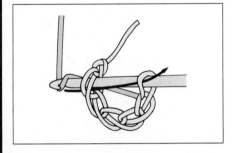

Insert the hook into the work (second chain from hook in diagram), yarn over and draw the yarn through both the work and loop on the hook in one movement.

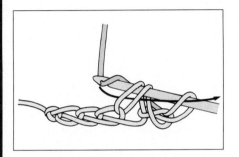

To join a chain ring with a slip stitch, then insert hook into first chain, yarn over and draw through the work and the yarn on the hook.

Single Crochet (sc +)

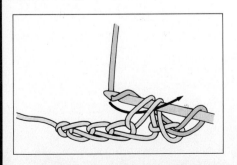

1. Insert the hook into the work (second chain from hook on starting chain), *yarn over and draw yarn through the work only.

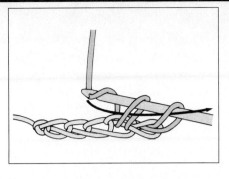

2. Yarn over again and draw the yarn through both loops on the hook.

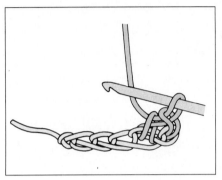

3. 1sc made. Insert hook into next stitch; repeat from * in step 1.

Half Double Crochet (hdc ⊤)

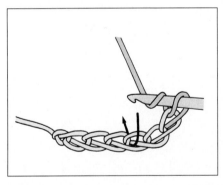

1. Yarn over and insert the hook into the work (third chain from hook on starting chain).

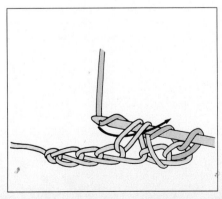

2. *Yarn over and draw through the work only.

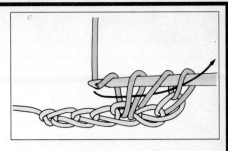

3. Yarn over again and draw through all three loops on the hook.

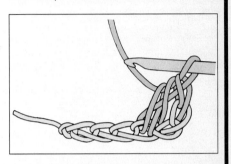

4. 1hdc made. Yarn over, insert hook into next stitch; repeat from * in step 2.

Double Crochet (dc ⊤)

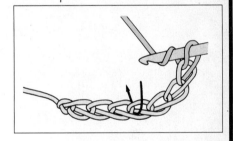

1. Yarn over and insert the hook into the work (fourth chain from hook on starting chain).

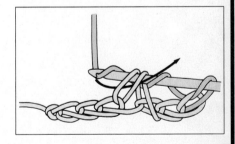

2. *Yarn over and draw through the work only.

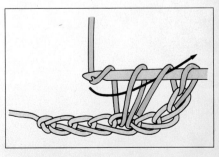

3. Yarn over and draw through the first two loops only.

Making Crochet Fabric

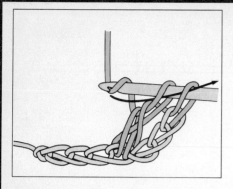

4. Yarn over and draw through the last two loops on the hook.

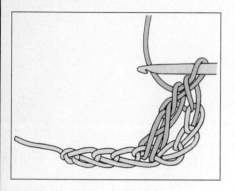

5. 1dc made. Yarn over, insert hook into next stitch; repeat from * in step 2.

Treble (tr)

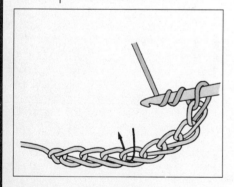

1. Yarn over twice, insert the hook into the work (fifth chain from hook on starting chain).

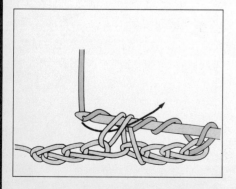

2. *Yarn over and draw through the work only.

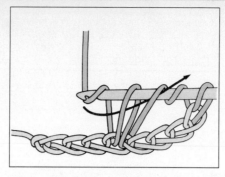

3. Yarn over again and draw through the first two loops only.

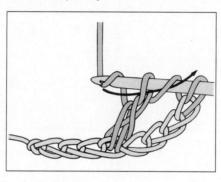

4. Yarn over again and draw through the next two loops only.

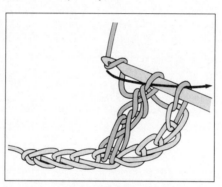

5. Yarn over again and draw through the last two loops on the hook.

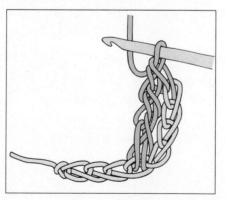

6. 1tr made. Yarn over twice, insert hook into next stitch; repeat from * in step 2.

Longer Basic Stitches

Double treble (dtr), triple treble (ttr), quadruple treble (quadtr) etc. are made by wrapping the yarn over three, four, five times etc. at the beginning and finishing as for a treble, repeating step 4 until two loops remain on hook, finish with step 5.

Making Crochet Fabric

These are the basic procedures for making crochet fabrics.

Starting Chain

To make a flat fabric worked in rows you must begin with a starting chain. The length of the starting chain is the number of stitches needed for the first row of fabric plus the number of chain needed to get to the correct height of the stitches to be used in the first row. All the patterns in this book indicate the length of starting chain required to work one repeat of the design. See 'Starting Chains and Pattern Repeats' on page 11.

TIP

When working a large piece it is sensible to start with more chain than necessary as it is simple to undo the extra chain if you have miscounted.

Working in Rows

A flat fabric can be produced by turning the work at the end of each row. Right handers work from right to left and left handers from left to right. One or more chain must be worked at the beginning of each row to bring the hook up to the height of the first stitch in the row. The number of chain used for turning depends upon the height of the stitch they are to match as follows:

single crochet = 1 chain
half double crochet = 2 chain
double crochet = 3 chain
treble = 4 chain

When working half double crochet or longer stitches the turning chain takes the place of the first stitch. Where one chain is worked at the beginning of a row starting with single crochet it is usually for height only and is in addition to the first stitch.

Basic Dc Fabric

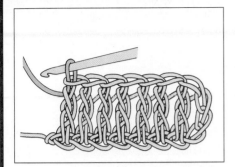

Make a starting chain of the required length plus two chain. Work one double crochet into fourth chain from hook. The three chain at the beginning of the row form the first double crochet. Work one double crochet into the next and every chain to the end of the row.

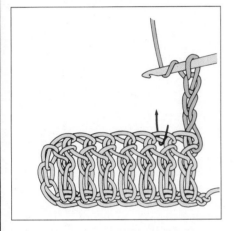

At the end of each row turn the work so that another row can be worked across the top of the previous one. It does not matter which way the work is turned but be consistent. Make three chain for turning. These turning chain will count as the first double crochet.

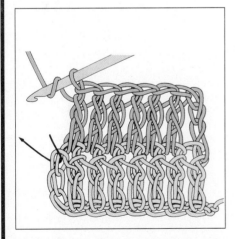

Skip the first double crochet in the previous row, work a double crochet into the top of the next and every double crochet including the last double crochet in row, then work a double crochet into third of three chain at the beginning of the previous row.

Note: Unless otherwise stated when working into the top of a stitch, always work under two strands as shown in diagram.

Fastening Off

To fasten off the yarn permanently break off the yarn about 5cm (2 ins) away from the work (longer if you need to sew pieces together). Draw the end through the loop on hook and tighten gently.

Joining in New Yarn and Changing Color

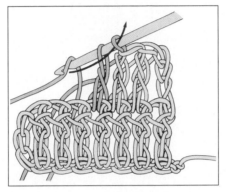

When joining in new yarn or changing color, work in the old yarn until two loops of the last stitch remain in the old yarn or color. Use the new color or yarn to complete the stitch.

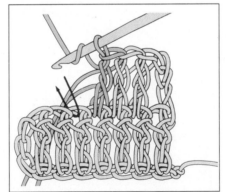

Continue to work the following stitches in the new color or yarn, as before.

If you are working whole rows in different colors, make the change during the last stitch in the previous row, so the new color for the next row is ready to work the turning chain.

Do not cut off any yarns which will be needed again later at the same edge, but continue to use them as required, leaving an unbroken 'float' thread up the side of the fabric.

If, at the end of a row, the pattern requires you to return to the beginning of the same row without turning and to work another row in a different color in the same direction, complete the first row in the old color and fasten off by lengthening the final loop on the hook, passing the whole ball through it and gently tighten again. That yarn is now available if you need to rejoin it later at this edge (if not, cut it).

Stitch Variations

Most crochet stitch patterns, however elaborate, are made using combinations of basic stitches. Different effects can be created by small variations in the stitch making procedure or by varying the position and manner of inserting the hook into the fabric. The following techniques are used frequently to build up crochet fabric.

Note: Terms such as 'group', 'cluster', 'picot', 'shell', 'fan', 'flower', 'petal', 'leaf' and 'bobble' do not denote a fixed arrangement of stitches. Exactly what they mean may be different for each pattern. The procedure is therefore always given at the beginning of each set of instructions as a Special Abbreviation.

Groups or Shells

These consist of several complete stitches worked into the same place. They can be worked as part of a pattern or as a method of increasing.

Five Double Crochet Group

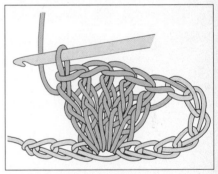

Work five double crochet into one stitch.

Summary of Common Groups or Shells

On diagrams the point at the base of the group will be positioned above the space or stitch where the hook is to be inserted.

2, 3 and 4 half double crochet group

Work 2(3,4) half double crochet into same place.

2, 3, 4 and 5 double crochet group

Work 2(3,4,5) double crochet into same place.

2, 3, 4 and 5 treble group

Work 2(3,4,5) treble into same place.

Stitch Variations

Clusters

Any combination of stitches may be joined into a cluster by leaving the last loop of each temporarily on the hook until they are worked off together at the end. Working stitches together in this way can also be a method of decreasing.

It is important to be sure exactly how and where the hook is to be inserted for each 'leg' of the cluster. The 'legs' may be worked over adjacent stitches, or stitches may be skipped between 'legs'.

Three Dc Cluster

(Worked over adjacent stitches).

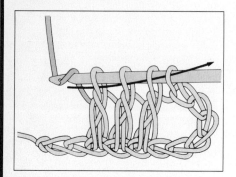

Work a double crochet into each of the next three stitches leaving the last loop of each double crochet on the hook.

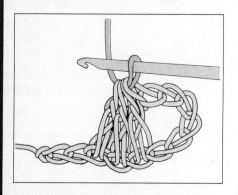

Yarn over and draw through all four loops on the hook.

Summary of Common Clusters

(Worked over adjacent stitches).
On diagrams each 'leg' of the cluster will be positioned above the stitch where the hook is to be inserted.

3, 4 and 5 double crochet cluster

Work a double crochet into each of the next 3(4,5) stitches leaving the last loop of each on the hook. Yarn over and draw through all loops on hook.

3, 4 and 5 treble cluster

Work a treble into each of the next 3(4,5) stitches leaving the last loop of each on the hook. Yarn over and draw through all loops on hook.

Bobbles

When a cluster is worked into one stitch it forms a bobble.

Five Dc Bobble

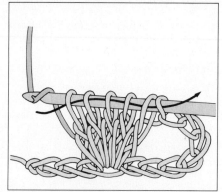

1. Work five double crochet into one stitch leaving the last loop of each on the hook.

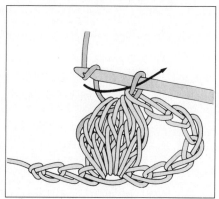

2. Yarn over and draw through all the loops on the hook.

More bulky bobbles can be secured with an extra chain stitch. If this is necessary it would be indicated within the pattern.

Summary of Common Bobbles

Follow instructions as if working a cluster but for each 'leg' insert the hook into the same stitch or space.

3, 4 and 5 double crochet bobble

4, 5, 6 and 7 treble bobble

Popcorns

Popcorns are groups of complete stitches usually worked into the same place, folded and closed at the top. An extra chain can be worked to secure the popcorn.

Five Dc Popcorn

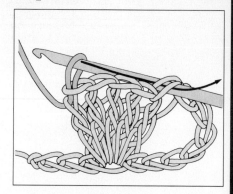

1. Work five double crochet into one stitch. Take the hook out of the working loop and insert it into the top of the first double crochet made, from front to back.

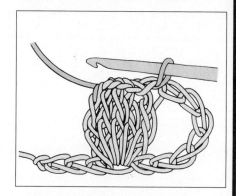

2. Pick up the working loop and draw this through to close the popcorn. If required work one chain to secure the popcorn.

Summary of Common Popcorns

On diagrams the point at the base of the popcorn will be positioned above the space or stitch where it is to be worked.

3 and 4 half double crochet popcorn

Work 3(4) half double crochet into the same place, drop loop off hook, insert hook into first half double crochet, pick up dropped loop and draw through.

3, 4 and 5 double crochet popcorn

Work 3(4,5) double crochet into the same place, drop loop off hook, insert hook into first double crochet, pick up dropped loop and draw through.

3, 4 and 5 treble popcorn

Work 3(4,5) treble into the same place, drop loop off hook, insert hook into first treble, pick up dropped loop and draw through.

Puff Stitches

These are similar to bobbles but worked using half double crochet, into the same stitch or space. However because half double crochet cannot be worked until one loop remains on the hook, the stitches are not closed until the required number have been worked.

Three Half Double Crochet Puff Stitch

(Worked into one stitch).

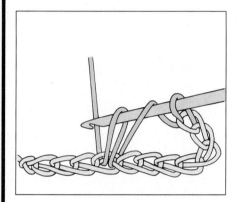

1. Yarn over, insert the hook, yarn over again and draw a loop through (three loops on the hook).

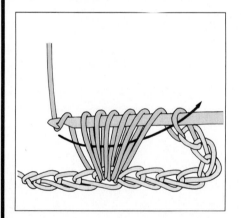

2. Repeat this step twice more, inserting the hook into the same stitch (seven loops on the hook); yarn over and draw through all the loops on the hook.

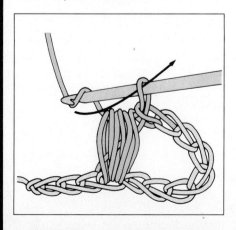

3. As with popcorns and bulky bobbles an extra chain stitch is often used to secure the puff stitch firmly. This will be indicated within the pattern if necessary.

A **cluster** of half double crochet stitches is worked in the same way as a puff stitch but each 'leg' is worked where indicated.

Picots

A picot is normally a chain loop formed into a closed ring by a slip stitch or single crochet. The number of chains in a picot can vary.

Four Chain Picot

(Closed with a slip stitch).

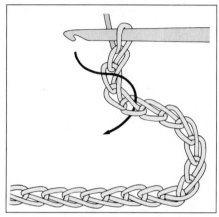

1. Work four chain.

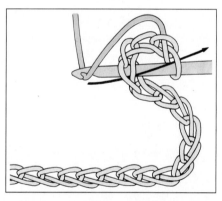

2. Into fourth chain from hook work a slip stitch to close.

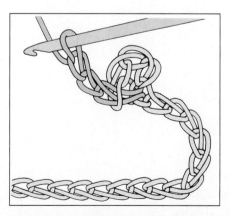

3. Continue working chain or required stitch.

Note: When working a picot closed with a slip stitch at the top of a chain arch, the picot will not appear central unless an extra chain is worked after the slip stitch.

Crossed Stitches

This method produces stitches that are not entangled with each other and so maintain a clear 'X' shape.

Crossed Treble

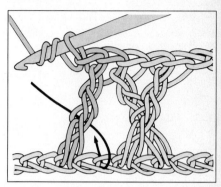

Skip two stitches and work the first treble into next stitch. Work one chain then work second treble into first of skipped stitches taking the hook behind the first treble before inserting.

See individual pattern instructions for variations on crossed stitch.

'X', 'Y' and 'λ' Shapes

In lacy stitch patterns long stitches are sometimes made into 'X' and 'Y' shapes without crossing them.

Treble 'λ' and 'X' Shapes

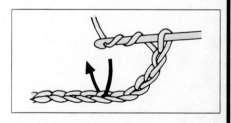

1. Wrap the yarn round the hook twice, insert the hook as required to make the lower part of the first 'leg'.

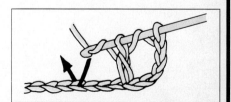

2. Wrap the yarn, draw a loop through, wrap the yarn and draw through 2 loops (3 loops on the hook); wrap the yarn once more and insert the hook again as required to make the lower part of the second 'leg'.

Stitch Variations

3. Wrap the yarn, draw a loop through, wrap the yarn and draw through 2 loops to complete both lower 'legs'.

4. Wrap the yarn and draw through 2 loops; repeat this last step twice more to complete the first 'arm' - note that at this stage you have completed a 'λ' shape.

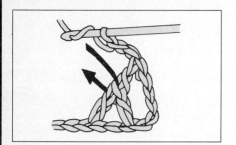

5. Make chains as required to take the hook to the top of the second 'arm', wrap the yarn once, insert the hook into the center of the cluster just completed, picking up 2 threads at the left-hand side, and draw a loop through.

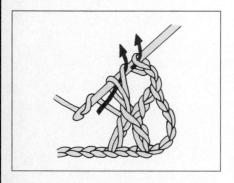

6. Wrap the yarn and draw through 2 loops.

7. Repeat this last step to complete the second 'arm' and the whole 'X' shape.

Double Treble 'Y' Shape

1. Work one complete double treble stitch for the lower 'leg' and first 'arm'.

2. Make some chains as required to take the hook to the top of the second 'arm' and work 1 double crochet into the center of the double treble to complete the second 'arm' and whole 'Y' shape in the same way as for the 'X' shape above.

Loop (Fur) Stitch

Loop stitch is a variation of single crochet and is usually worked on 'wrong side' rows because the loops form at the back of the fabric.

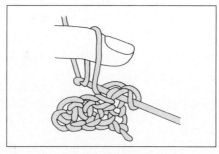

1. Using the left-hand finger to control the loop size insert the hook, pick up both threads of the loop and draw these through; wrap the supply yarn over the hook.

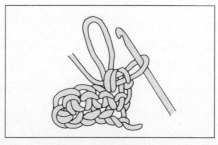

2. Draw through all the loops on the hook to complete.

Note: When each loop is cut afterwards the texture of the fabric resembles fur.

Bullion Stitch

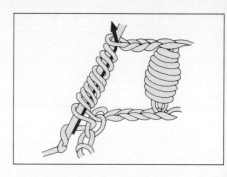

Wrap the yarn over the hook as many times as specified (usually 7 to 10 times); insert the hook as required; wrap the yarn once again and draw a loop through; wrap the yarn again and draw through all the loops on the hook, picking them off one at a time, if necessary; work a chain to complete the bullion stitch.

Lace Loops

Lace loops are most often used either as a decorative edging or for the kind of fabric making sometimes called 'broomstick' crochet.

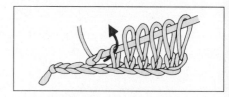

1. Insert the hook, wrap the yarn over the hook and draw a loop through; wrap the yarn again, draw another loop through the first and lengthen this as required; repeat this procedure, keeping each loop on the hook.

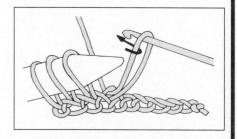

2. To help keep larger loops even in size, work from left to right and transfer each loop to a large size knitting needle (or 'broomstick').

3. 2 or more lace loops can be made into clusters in various ways as an alternative to basic stitches.

Soloman's Knot

A Soloman's Knot is a lengthened chain stitch locked with a single crochet stitch worked into its back loop.

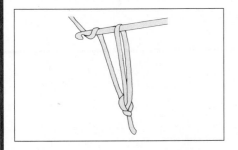

1. Make 1 chain and lengthen the loop as required; wrap the yarn over the hook.

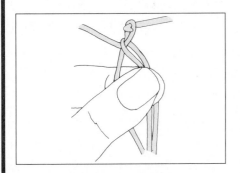

2. Draw through the loop on the hook, keeping the single back thread of this long chain separate from the 2 front threads.

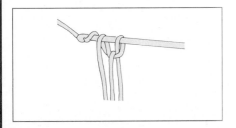

3. Insert the hook under this single back thread and wrap the yarn again.

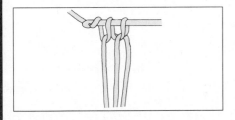

4. Draw a loop through and wrap again.

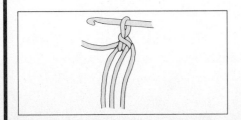

5. Draw through both loops on the hook to complete.

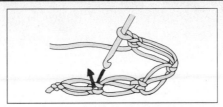

6. It is necessary to work back into the 'knots' between the lengthened chains in order to make the classic Soloman's Knot fabric, see page 83.

Placement of Stitches

All crochet stitches (except chains) require the hook to be inserted into existing work. It has already been shown how to work into a chain and into the top of a stitch, however stitches can also be worked into the following places.

Working into Chain Spaces

When a stitch, group, shell, cluster or bobble etc. is positioned over a chain or chains, the hook is often inserted into the space under the chain.

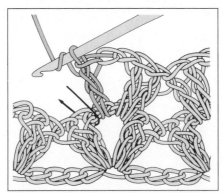

It is important to notice, however, if the pattern instructions stipulate working **into** a particular chain as this will change the appearance of the design.

If necessary information of this kind has been given as notes with the diagram.

A bobble, popcorn or cluster that is worked into a chain space is shown in the diagram spread out more than one worked **into** a stitch, therefore on the diagrams they will not be closed at the base.

5dc bobble into a stitch or space

Working Around the Stem of a Stitch

Inserting the hook round the whole stem of a stitch creates raised or relief effects.

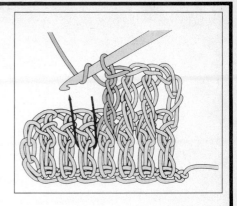

Working around the front of stem gives a stitch that lies on the front of the work.

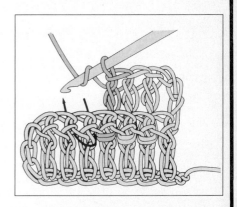

Working around the back of stem gives a stitch that lies on the back of the work.

Working Under the Front or Back Loop Only

Inserting the hook under one loop at the top of the stitch leaves the other loop as a horizontal bar.

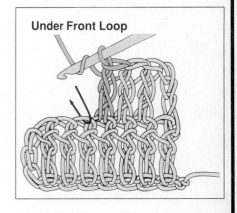

Under Front Loop

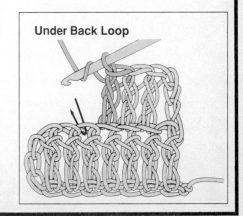

Under Back Loop

Stitch Variations

Working in Rows

If you work consistently into the front loop only you will make a series of ridges alternately on the back and front of the work. Working into the back loop only makes the ridges appear alternately on the front and back of the work.

If however you work alternately into the front loop only on one row and then the back loop only on the next row, the horizontal bars will all appear on the same side of the fabric.

Working in Rounds

Working always into the front loop only will form a bar on the back of the work, and vice versa.

Working Between Stitches

Inserting the hook between the stems of the stitches produces an open effect.

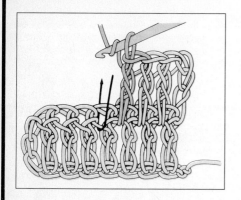

Ensure the number of stitches remains constant after each row.

Marguerites (Stars)

A popular form of 'spiked' cluster - often called a 'Marguerite' or 'Star' - is formed by inserting the hook 3, 4, 5, or perhaps even more times, partly into the side of the previous stitch and partly into the next few stitches in the previous row.

4 'Spike' Marguerites

1st Marguerite

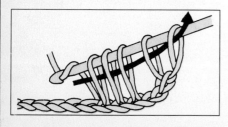

1. Insert the hook into the 2nd chain from the hook, wrap the yarn round the hook and draw a loop through; repeat this step 3 more times into the 4th, 5th and 6th chains from the hook, (5 loops on the hook); wrap the yarn and draw through all the loops.

2. Make one chain firmly to close the Marguerite.

2nd and subsequent Marguerites

3. Insert the hook, wrap the yarn and draw loops through as follows: into the loop which closed the previous Marguerite; into the same place as the previous Marguerite finished; and into each of the next 2 stitches (5 loops on the hook).

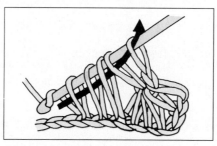

4. Wrap the yarn, draw through all the loops on the hook and make a chain firmly to close the Marguerite.

Spikes

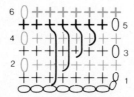

'Spikes' are made by inserting the hook further down into the fabric than usual, either below the next stitch, or to one side of it.

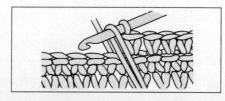

1. A loop is drawn through and up to the height of the current row.

2. The stitch is then completed normally.

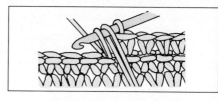

3. Spikes can be worked singly, in sequences, or in clusters by inserting the hook in different places, drawing a loop through each and finishing by drawing a loop through all the loops so collected. They add interest to fabric texture, but are most dramatic when worked in contrasting colours.

Note: It is important to work 'spike' loops loosely enough to avoid squashing the fabric, but with sufficient tension to maintain the stability of the fabric. When a whole sequence of stitches is 'spiked', it may help to work each one as a 'twin' cluster together with a stitch worked normally under the top 2 loops of the stitch as follows:

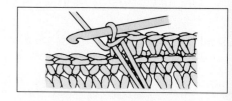

4. Insert the hook as indicated for the 'Spike' wrap the yarn around the hook and draw a loop through and up to the height of the current row; insert the hook under the top 2 loops of the next stitch, wrap the yarn and draw a loop through, (3 loops on the hook).

5. Wrap the yarn and draw through all the loops on the hook to complete.

Corded or Reversed Single Crochet

Corded single crochet is used as a decorative texture (Corded Rib), or edging (Corded Edge). It consists of working single crochet stitches in the 'wrong' direction, ie from left to right for right-handers.

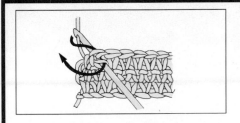

1. After a right side row do not turn. Always starting with the hook facing downwards insert the hook back into the next stitch to the right. Pull the yarn through twisting the hook to face upwards at the same time.

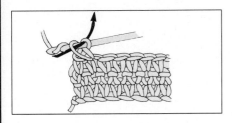

2. Wrap the yarn and draw through to finish off the single crochet as normally.

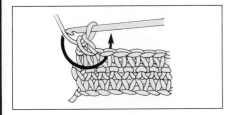

3. Insert the hook ready for the next stitch.

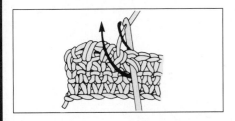

4. The direction of working causes the stitches to twist and create the decorative effect.

Linked Stitches

The stems of all basic stitches, except single crochet, may be linked to each other in the middle. This gives the resulting fabric greater firmness and stability.

Linked Trebles

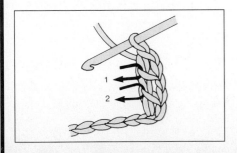

1. Insert the hook down through the upper of 2 horizontal loops round the stem of the

previous stitch, wrap the yarn over the hook and draw a loop through; insert the hook down through the lower horizontal loop of the same stitch, wrap the yarn and draw another loop through.

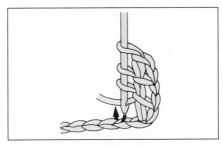

2. Treat these 2 loops as the wrappings which are required for an ordinary treble and complete the stitch in the normal way.

To make the first linked treble following the turning chain, insert the hook into the 2nd then the 4th chains from the hook in order to pick up the 2 preliminary loops.

Both double crochet and longer stitches are made in the same way with the appropriate number of preliminary linked and wrapped loops.

Pattern Instructions

In order to follow crochet instructions you should know how to make the basic stitches and to be familiar with basic fabric-making procedures.

Any unusual stitches or combinations of stitches have been given as a Special Abbreviation with the particular pattern.

Any specific techniques - for example working with padding threads - are given at the start of the relevant section, in this case Irish Style Crochet.

All the patterns in this book have been given in the form of both written instructions and diagrams, so that you can choose to follow either method.

However, if you are more used to written instructions it is still a good idea to look at the diagram to get an overall picture of how the design has been put together.

Diagram followers may find it helpful to refer to the written instructions to confirm their interpretation of the diagram.

Working from a Diagram

Diagrams should be read exactly as the crochet is worked. For example, motifs are worked from the center outwards and all-over patterns from the bottom to the top. Where the direction of work, within a design, is not obvious an extra line drawing or arrows are given to show where the direction changes (for example Curved Fan Stitch on page 43). Each stitch is

represented by a symbol that has been drawn to resemble its crocheted equivalent. The position of the symbol shows where the stitch should be worked.

Stitch symbols are drawn and laid out as realistically as possible but there are times when they have to be distorted for the sake of clarity. For example stitches may look extra long to show clearly where they are to be placed, but you should not try to make artificially long stitches. This distortion is particularly apparent on diagrams that represent fabrics not intended to lie flat (for example Tooth Stitch on page 45). Sometimes it has been necessary to use a colored arrow to indicate where particular stitches should be worked. This occurs most often in the Irish Style Crochet section, because many of the designs are three-dimensional.

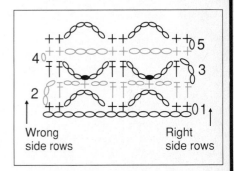

Wrong side rows / Right side rows

Right Side and Wrong Side Rows

Where the work is turned after each row only alternate rows are worked with the right side of the work facing. These 'right side rows' are printed in black on stitch diagrams and read from right to left. Wrong side rows are printed in blue and read from left to right. Row numbers are shown at the side of the diagrams at the **beginning** of the row.

Patterns worked in rounds have the right side rows facing on every round. To make them easier to follow we have printed alternate rounds in black and blue.

Starting Chains and Pattern Repeats

The number of starting chain required is given with each pattern. It may be given in the form of a multiple, for example:-
Starting chain: Multiple of 7 sts + 3.
This means you can make any length of chain that is a multiple of 7 + 3, such as 14 + 3ch, 21 + 3ch, 28 + 3ch etc.

In the written instructions the stitches that should be repeated are contained within brackets [ ] or follow an asterisk *. These stitches are repeated across the row or round the required number of times. On the diagrams the stitches that have to be repeated can be easily visualised. The

Pattern Instructions

extra stitches not included in the pattern repeat are there to balance the row or make it symmetrical and are only worked once. Obviously turning chains are only worked at the beginning of each row. Some diagrams consist of more than one pattern repeat so that you can see more clearly how the design is worked.

Working in Color

Capital letters A, B, C etc. are used to indicate different yarn colors in both written instructions and diagrams. They do not refer to any particular color. See page 7 for instructions on changing color within a pattern.

Tension (or Gauge)

This refers to the number of stitches and rows in a given area. When following a pattern for a garment or other article the instructions will include a specified tension. If you do not produce fabric with the same number of stitches and rows as indicated, your work will not come to the measurements given.

To ensure that you achieve the correct tension work a tension sample or swatch before starting the main part of the crochet. The hook size quoted in the pattern is a suggestion only. You must use whichever hook gives you the correct tension.

If you are going to use a stitch pattern from this book to design an article of your own, it is still important to work a tension sample in order to calculate the number of stitches you will require. It is worth experimenting with different hook sizes so that you find the best tension for your chosen pattern and yarn. Some stitches look and feel better worked loosely and others need to be worked more firmly to be at their best.

Shaping

If you are working crochet to make something which requires shaping, such as decreasing for the neckline of a garment or increasing to add width for a sleeve, you need to know something about shaping.

Increasing is generally achieved by working two or more stitches in the pattern where there would normally be one stitch. Conversely, decreasing is achieved by working two or more stitches together, or missing one or more stitches. However it can be difficult to know exactly where these adjustments are best made, and a visual guide would make the work easier!

On the diagrams at right we show you some examples of shapings which cover a variety of possibilities. We recommend that you use this method yourself when planning a project. First pencil trace the diagram given with the stitch. If necessary repeat the tracing to match the repeat

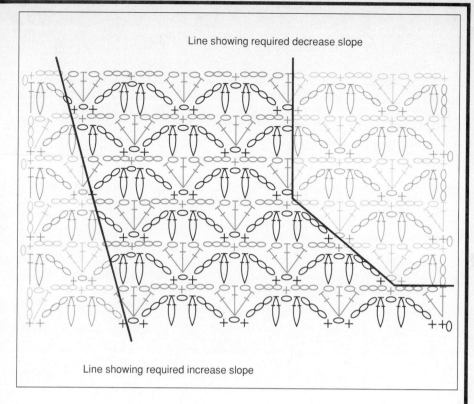

Line showing required decrease slope

Line showing required increase slope

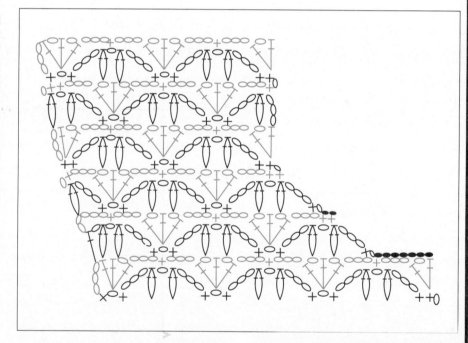

of the pattern until you have a large enough area to give you the shape you require. Once this is correct **ink it in** so that you can draw over it in pencil without destroying it. Now draw over this the shaping you require matching as near as possible the style of the particular pattern you are using.

Joining Seams

Various methods can be used to join pieces of crochet. The use of the item will often dictate the method used, the seam could be invisible or decorative. Below are a few suggestions for joining pieces of crochet.

To join with an invisible sewn seam, place

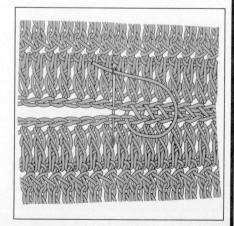

pieces edge to edge with the wrong sides uppermost and whip stitch together.

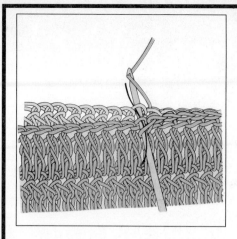

To join invisibly using a crochet hook, place right sides of pieces together and slip stitch through one loop of each piece as illustrated.

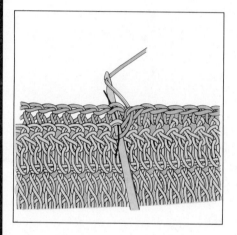

To create a decorative ridged seam on the right side of the work, place wrong sides together and join with single crochet working under two strands of each piece as illustrated.

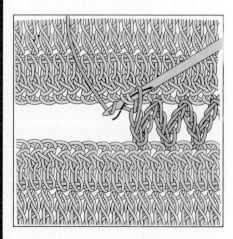

Alternatively with the right side of both pieces uppermost they can be joined with a row of fancy openwork chains.

Pressing and Finishing

The methods you use to finish your crochet depend largely on what you are using it for and what yarn you have used.

Cotton

Cotton yarns benefit from being wetted or thoroughly steamed. If you are using household starch (as opposed to spray starch) now is the time to apply it, either by immersing the crocheted piece or dabbing the wet starch on to the material. Pin out very near to the edge, at very close intervals, stretching or easing the material to ensure that it is even. Picots, bobbles or other intrinsic features should be carefully placed with a pin at this stage. Having satisfied yourself that the shape is correct, the work can now be pressed using a hot iron. Do not allow the full weight of the iron to rest on the work especially where interesting textures are involved. Remove the pins and if required make fine adjustments to the edges of the material to ensure that they are straight. Now leave until the work is **thoroughly** dry.

Motifs and Irish Style Pieces

Work as given above but leave the pins in position until the work is **thoroughly** dry. Ensure that all three-dimensional features show to their best advantage.

Other Yarns

In principal the methods given for working with cotton yarns apply, but you must read the finishing or pressing information usually included with your yarn. Not every yarn will be suitable for or require starching and some yarns cannot be pressed with a hot iron.

Abbreviations and Symbols

Listed below are the standard abbreviations and symbols that have been used for pages 15 to 160 of this book. Refer to pages 4 to 15 for more detailed instructions of these and other stitch variations. If a pattern contains an unusual combinations of stitches these are explained in the Special Abbreviation at the beginning of that pattern.

Separate abbreviations and symbols have been used for the Afghan (Tunisian) stitches in this book and these have been given at the beginning of that section on pages 161 to 172.

Abbreviations

Alt = alternate, **beg** = begin(ning), **ch(s)** = chain(s), **ch sp** = chain space, **cm** = centimetre(s), **dec** = decrease, **dc** = double crochet, **dtr** = double treble, **hdc** = half double crochet, **inc** = increase, **ins** = inches, **quadtr** = quadruple treble, **rep** = repeat, **sc** = single crochet, **sl st** = slip stitch, **sp(s)** = space(s), **st(s)** = stitch(es), **tog** = together, **tr** = treble, **ttr** = triple treble, **yo** = yarn over.

sc2(3)tog
insert hook as indicated, yo, draw loop through = 3(4) loops on hook.

hdc2(3/4)tog
yo, insert hook as indicated, yo, draw loop through = 5(7/9) loops on hook.

dc2(3/4/5)tog
yo, insert hook as indicated, yo, draw loop through, yo, draw through 2 loops = 3(4/5/6) loops on hook.

tr2(3/4/5)tog
yo twice, insert hook as indicated, yo, draw loop through, (yo, draw through 2 loops) twice = 3(4/5/6) loops on hook.

dtr2(3/4/5/etc)tog
yo 3 times, insert hook as indicated, yo, draw loop through, (yo, draw through 2 loops) 3 times = 3(4/5/6/etc) loops on hook.

Basic Symbols used in Diagrams

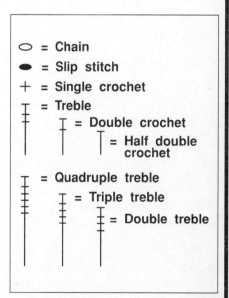

⬭ = **Chain**

⬬ = **Slip stitch**

+ = **Single crochet**

┬ = **Treble**

   ┬ = **Double crochet**

    ┌ = **Half double crochet**

= **Quadruple treble**

   = **Triple treble**

    = **Double treble**

The number of strokes crossing the stems of stitches longer than a half double crochet represents the number of times the yarn is wrapped over the hook **before** the hook is inserted into the work.

Basic Stitches

Basic Single Crochet

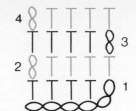

Any number of sts.
(add 1 for base chain)

1st row: Skip 2ch (count as 1sc), 1sc into next and each ch to end, turn.

2nd row: 1ch (counts as 1sc), skip 1 st, 1sc into next and each st to end working last st into tch, turn.

Rep 2nd row.

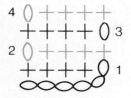

Hint: In some patterns the turning chain does **not** count as a stitch when working single crochet. In these cases the first sc is worked into the second ch from hook on the first row, and thereafter into the first sc of the previous row.

Basic Double Crochet

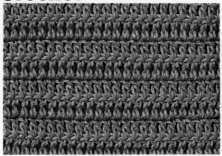

Any number of sts.
(add 2 for base chain)

1st row: Skip 3ch (count as 1dc), 1dc into next and each ch to end, turn.

2nd row: 3ch (count as 1dc), skip 1 st, 1dc into next and each st to end working last st into top of tch, turn.

Rep 2nd row.

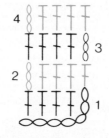

Basic Half Double Crochet

Any number of sts.
(add 1 for base chain)

1st row: Skip 2ch (count as 1hdc), 1hdc into next and each ch to end, turn.

2nd row: 2ch (count as 1hdc), skip 1 st, 1hdc into next and each st to end working last st into top of tch, turn.

Rep 2nd row.

Basic Trebles

Any number of sts.
(add 3 for base chain)

1st row: Skip 4ch (count as 1tr), 1tr into next and each ch to end, turn.

2nd row: 4ch (count as 1tr), skip 1 st, 1tr into next and each st to end, working last st into top of tch, turn.

Rep 2nd row.

Back Loop Single Crochet

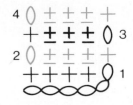

Worked as Basic Single Crochet except from 2nd row insert hook into back loop only of each st.

Front Loop Single Crochet

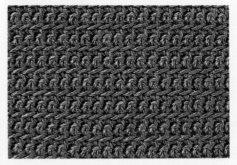

Worked as Basic Single Crochet except from 2nd row insert hook into front loop only of each st.

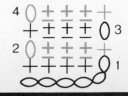

16

Stitch Variations, Abbreviations and Symbols on pages 7 to 15

Back and Front Loop Single Crochet

Multiple of 2 sts.
(add 1 for base chain)
1st row: Skip 2ch (count as 1sc), 1sc into next and each ch to end, turn.
2nd row: 1ch (counts as 1sc), skip 1 st, *1sc into back loop only of next st, 1sc into front loop only of next st; rep from * ending 1sc into top of tch, turn.
Rep 2nd row.

Shallow Single Crochet

Worked as Basic Single Crochet except from 2nd row insert hook low into body of each st below 3 horizontal loops and between 2 vertical threads.

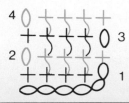

Back Loop Half Double Crochet

Worked as Basic Half Double Crochet except from 2nd row insert hook into back loop only of each st.

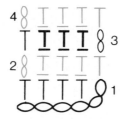

Back and Front Loop Half Double Crochet

Multiple of 2 sts.
(add 1 for base chain)
1st row: Skip 2ch (count as 1hdc), 1hdc into next and each ch to end, turn.
2nd row: 2ch (count as 1hdc), skip 1 st, *1hdc into back loop only of next st, 1hdc into front loop only of next st; rep from * ending 1hdc into top of tch, turn.
Rep 2nd row.

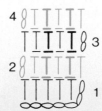

Linked Half DCs

Any number of sts.
(add 1 for base chain)
Special Abbreviation
Ỿ Lhdc (Linked Half Double Crochet) = insert hook into single vertical thread at left-hand side of previous st, yo, draw loop through, insert hook normally into next st, yo, draw loop through st, yo, draw through all 3 loops on hook.
Note: To make first Lhdc at beg of row treat 2nd ch from hook as a single vertical thread.
1st row: 1Lhdc into 3rd ch from hook (picking up loop through 2nd ch from hook), 1Lhdc into next and each ch to end, turn.
2nd row: 2ch (count as 1hdc), skip 1 st, 1Lhdc into next and each st to end, working last st into top of tch, turn.
Rep 2nd row.

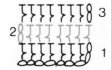

Herringbone Half Double Crochet

Any number of sts.
(add 1 for base chain)
Special Abbreviation
Ỳ HBhdc (Herringbone Half Double Crochet) = yo, insert hook, yo, draw through st and first loop on hook, yo, draw through both loops on hook.
1st row: Skip 2ch (count as 1hdc), 1HBhdc into next and each ch to end, turn.
2nd row: 2ch (count as 1hdc), skip 1 st, 1HBhdc into next and each st to end working last st into top of tch, turn.
Rep 2nd row.

Stitch Variations

Wide Doubles

Worked as Basic Double Crochets but after 1st row insert hook between stems and below all horizontal threads connecting sts.

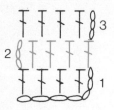

Note: Base chain should be worked loosely to accommodate extra width.

Herringbone Double Crochets

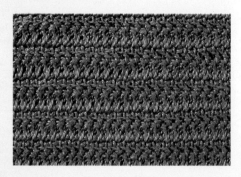

Any number of sts.
(add 2 for base chain)

Special Abbreviation

⅄ **HBdc (Herringbone Double Crochet)** = yo, insert hook, yo, draw through st and first loop on hook, yo, draw through 1 loop, yo, draw through both loops on hook.

1st row: Skip 3ch (count as 1dc), 1HBdc into next and each ch to end, turn.

2nd row: 3ch (count as 1dc), skip 1 st, 1HBdc into next and each st to end, working last st into top of tch, turn.

Rep 2nd row.

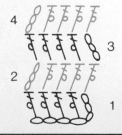

Alternative Doubles

Any number of sts.
(add 2 for base chain)

Special Abbreviation

ȶ **Alt dc (Alternative Double Crochet)** = yo, insert hook, yo, draw loop through, yo, draw through 1 loop only, yo, draw through all 3 loops on hook.

1st row: Skip 3ch (count as 1dc), 1dc into next and each ch to end, turn.

2nd row: 3ch (count as 1dc), skip 1 st, work 1 Alt dc into next and each st to end, working last st into top of tch, turn.

Rep 2nd row.

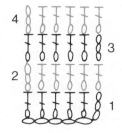

Linked Trebles

Any number of sts.
(add 3 for base chain)

Special Abbreviation

ᵮ **Ltr (Linked Treble)** = insert hook down through upper of 2 horizontal loops round stem of last st made, yo, draw loop through, insert hook down through lower horizontal loop of same st, yo, draw loop through, insert hook normally into next st, yo, draw loop through st, (4 loops on hook), [yo, draw through 2 loops] 3 times

Note: To make first Ltr (at beg of row), treat

2nd and 4th chs from hook as upper and lower horizontal loops.

1st row: 1Ltr into 5th ch from hook (picking up loops through 2nd and 4th chs from hook), 1Ltr into next and each ch to end, turn.

2nd row: 4ch (count as 1tr), skip 1 st, 1Ltr into next and each st to end, working last st into top of tch, turn.

Rep 2nd row.

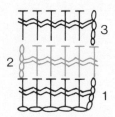

Singles and Doubles

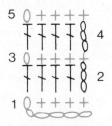

Any number of sts.
(add 1 for base chain)

1st row (wrong side): Skip 2ch (count as 1sc), 1sc into next and each ch to end, turn.

2nd row: 3ch (counts as 1dc), skip 1 st, 1dc into next and each st to end, working last st into top of tch, turn.

3rd row: 1ch (counts as 1sc), skip 1 st, 1sc into next and each st to end, working last st into top of tch, turn.

Rep 2nd and 3rd rows.

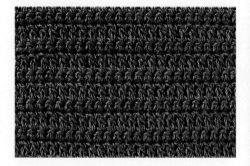

Hint: This is one of the simplest and most effective combination stitch patterns. It is also one of the easiest to get wrong! Concentration is required as you work the ends of the rows to avoid increasing or decreasing, or working two rows of the same stitch running by mistake.

Track Stitch

Any number of sts.
(add 1 for base chain)

1st row (wrong side): Skip 2ch (count as 1sc), 1sc into next and each ch to end, turn.
2nd row: 5ch (count as 1dtr), skip 1 st, 1dtr into next and each st to end, working last st into top of tch, turn.
3rd, 4th and 5th rows: 1ch (counts as 1sc), skip 1 st, 1sc into next and each st to end, working last st into top of tch, turn.
Rep 2nd to 5th rows.

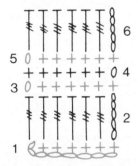

Single Crochet Cluster Stitch I

Multiple of 2 sts + 1.
(add 1 for base chain)

1st row (wrong side): 1sc into 2nd ch from hook, *1ch, skip 1ch, 1sc into next ch; rep from * to end, turn.
2nd row: 1ch, 1sc into first st, 1ch, sc2tog inserting hook into each of next 2 ch sps, 1ch, *sc2tog inserting hook first into same ch sp as previous st then into next ch sp, 1ch; rep from * ending 1sc into last st, skip tch, turn.
3rd row: 1ch, 1sc into first st, *1ch, skip 1ch, 1sc into next st; rep from * to end, skip tch, turn.

Rep 2nd and 3rd rows.

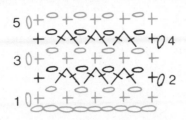

Single Crochet Cluster Stitch II

Multiple of 2 sts + 1.
(add 1 for base chain)

1st row: Skip 1ch, *sc2tog inserting hook into each of next 2ch, 1ch; rep from * ending 1sc into last ch, turn.
2nd row: 1ch, sc2tog inserting hook into first st then into next ch sp, 1ch, *sc2tog inserting hook first before and then after the vertical thread between the next 2 clusters, 1ch; rep from * ending 1sc into last sc, skip tch, turn.
Rep 2nd row.

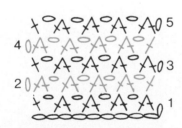

Single Crochet Cluster Stitch III

Multiple of 2 sts.
(add 1 for base chain)

1st row: Skip 2ch (count as 1hdc), *sc2tog inserting hook into each of next 2ch, 1ch; rep from * ending with 1hdc into last ch, turn.
2nd row: 2ch (count as 1hdc), skip 1 st, *sc2tog inserting hook into back loop only of next ch then into back loop only of next st, 1ch; rep from * ending with 1hdc into top of tch, turn.
Rep 2nd row.

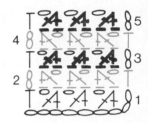

Single Crochet Cluster Stitch IV

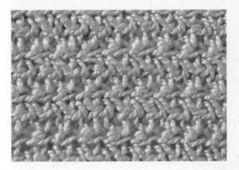

Multiple of 2 sts + 1.
(add 1 for base chain)

Special Abbreviation
SC (Slip Cluster) = insert hook into ch or st as indicated, yo, draw loop through, insert hook again as indicated, yo, draw loop through st and through next loop on hook, yo, draw through last 2 loops on hook.

1st row: 1SC inserting hook into 2nd and then 3rd ch from hook, 1ch; *1SC inserting hook into each of next 2ch, 1ch; rep from * ending 1sc into last ch, turn.
2nd row: 1ch (counts as 1sc), skip 1 st, *1SC inserting hook into front loop only of next ch then front loop only of next st, 1ch; rep from * ending 1sc into top of tch, turn.
Rep 2nd row.

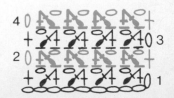

Clusters

Trinity Stitch I

Multiple of 2 sts + 1.
(add 1 for base chain)

1st row: 1sc into 2nd ch from hook, sc3tog inserting hook first into same ch as previous sc, then into each of next 2ch, *1ch, sc3tog inserting hook first into same ch as 3rd leg of previous cluster, then into each of next 2ch; rep from * to last ch, 1sc into same ch as 3rd leg of previous cluster, turn.

2nd row: 1ch, 1sc into first st, sc3tog inserting hook first into same place as previous sc, then into top of next cluster, then into next ch sp, *1ch, sc3tog inserting hook first into same ch sp as 3rd leg of previous cluster, then into top of next cluster, then into next ch sp; rep from * to end working 3rd leg of last cluster into last sc, 1sc into same place, skip tch, turn.

Rep 2nd row.

Trinity Stitch II

Worked as Trinity Stitch I.
Work 1 row each in colors A, B and C throughout.

Hint: Normally the maximum number of stitches which may be worked together into a single crochet cluster is 3. (Longer stitches may have more).
Remember that working stitches together into clusters is often the best way to decrease.

Half Double Crochet Cluster Stitch I

Any number of sts.
(add 1 for base chain)

1st row: Skip 2ch (count as 1hdc), *hdc2tog all into next ch; rep from * to end, turn.

2nd row: 2ch (count as 1hdc), skip 1 st, hdc2tog all into next and each st, ending with hdc2tog into top of tch, turn.

Rep 2nd row.

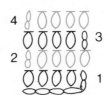

Half Double Crochet Cluster Stitch II

Any number of sts.
(add 2 for base chain)

1st row: Skip 2ch (count as 1hdc), hdc2tog inserting hook into each of next 2ch, *hdc2tog inserting hook first into same ch as previous cluster then into next ch; rep from * until 1ch remains, 1hdc into last ch, turn.

2nd row: 2ch (count as 1hdc), hdc2tog inserting hook first into first st then into next st, *hdc2tog inserting hook first into same st as previous cluster then into next st; rep from * ending 1hdc into top of tch, turn.

Rep 2nd row.

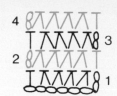

Half Double Crochet Cluster Stitch III

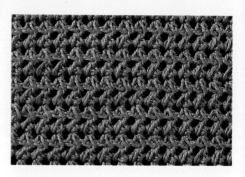

Multiple of 2 sts.
(add 1 for base chain)

1st row: Skip 2ch (count as 1hdc), *hdc2tog inserting hook into each of next 2ch, 1ch; rep from * ending 1hdc into last ch, turn.

2nd row: 2ch (count as 1hdc), skip 1 st, *hdc2tog inserting hook into next ch sp then into next st, 1ch; rep from * ending 1hdc into top of tch, turn.

Rep 2nd row.

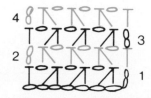

Forked Cluster Stitch

Any number of sts.
(add 2 for base chain)

Stitch Variations, Abbreviations and Symbols on pages 7 to 15

Clusters

Special Abbreviation

FC (Forked Cluster) = [yo, insert hook into ch or st as indicated, yo, draw loop through] twice (5 loops on hook), [yo, draw through 3 loops] twice.

1st row: Skip 2ch (count as 1dc), work 1FC inserting hook into each of next 2ch, *work 1FC inserting hook into same ch as previous FC then into next ch; rep from * until 1ch remains, 1dc into last ch, turn.

2nd row: 3ch (count as 1dc), 1FC inserting hook into each of first 2 sts, *1FC inserting hook into same st as previous FC then into next st; rep from * ending 1dc into top of tch, turn.

Rep 2nd row.

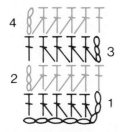

Odd Forked Cluster Stitch

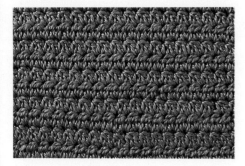

Any number of sts.
(add 2 for base chain)
Special Abbreviation
OFC (Odd Forked Cluster) = yo, insert hook into ch or st as indicated, yo, draw loop through, yo, draw through 2 loops, insert hook into next ch or st, yo, draw loop through, yo, draw through all 3 loops on hook.

1st row: Skip 2ch (count as 1hdc), 1OFC inserting hook first into 3rd then 4th ch from hook, *1OFC inserting hook first into same ch as previous OFC then into next ch; rep from * until 1ch remains, 1hdc into last ch, turn.

2nd row: 2ch (count as 1hdc), 1OFC inserting hook into first st then into next st, *1OFC inserting hook into same st as previous OFC then into next st; rep from * ending 1hdc into top of tch, turn.

Rep 2nd row.

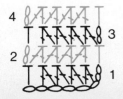

Mixed Cluster Stitch

Multiple of 2 sts + 1.
(add 1 for base chain)
Special Abbreviation
MC (Mixed Cluster) = yo, insert hook into first st as indicated, yo, draw loop through, yo, draw through 2 loops, skip 1 st, [yo, insert hook into next st, yo, draw loop through] twice all into same st, (6 loops on hook), yo, draw through all loops on hook.

1st row (wrong side): Skip 2ch (count as 1sc), 1sc into next and each ch to end, turn.

2nd row: 2ch (count as 1hdc), 1MC inserting hook into first then 3rd st, *1ch, 1MC inserting hook first into same st as previous MC; rep from * ending last rep in top of tch, 1hdc into same place, turn.

3rd row: 1ch (counts as 1sc), skip 1 st, 1sc into next and each st to end, working last st into top of tch, turn.

Rep 2nd and 3rd rows.

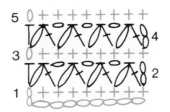

Double Crochet Cluster Stitch I

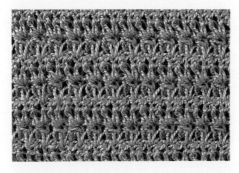

Multiple of 2 sts.
(add 2 for base chain)
Special Abbreviation
DcC (Double Crochet Cluster) = *yo, insert hook into ch or st as indicated, yo, draw loop through, yo, draw through 2 loops*, skip 1 ch or st, rep from * to * into next st, yo, draw through all 3 loops on hook.

1st row: Skip 2ch (count as 1dc), work 1DcC inserting hook first into 3rd ch, 1ch, *work 1DcC inserting hook first into same ch as previous DcC, 1ch; rep from * ending 1dc into last ch, turn.

2nd row: 3ch (counts as 1dc), 1DcC inserting hook first into first st, 1ch, *1DcC inserting hook first into same st as previous DcC, 1ch; rep from * ending 1dc into top of tch, turn.

Rep 2nd row.

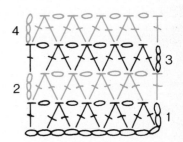

Double Crochet Cluster Stitch II

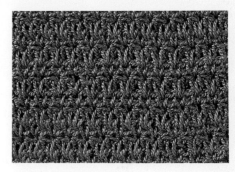

Multiple of 2 sts.
(add 2 for base chain)
Special Abbreviation
DcC (Double Crochet Cluster) worked as under Double Crochet Cluster Stitch I.

1st row (right side): Skip 2ch (count as 1dc), work 1DcC inserting hook into 3rd ch then 5th ch, 1ch, *work 1DcC inserting hook first into same ch as previous DcC, 1ch; rep from * ending 1dc into last ch, turn.

2nd row: 1ch (counts as 1sc), skip 1 st, *1sc into next ch sp, 1ch, skip 1 st; rep from * ending 1sc into top of tch, turn.

3rd row: 3ch (count as 1dc), 1DcC inserting hook first into first st, 1ch, *1DcC inserting hook first into same st as previous DcC, 1ch; rep from * ending 1dc into top of tch, turn.

Rep 2nd and 3rd rows.

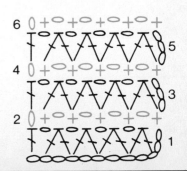

Patterns for Texture and Color

Double Crochet Cluster Stitch III

Any number of sts.
(add 2 for base chain)

1st row: Skip 3ch (count as 1dc), work dc2tog into next and each ch until 1ch remains, 1dc into last ch, turn.

2nd row: 3ch (count as 1dc), dc2tog between first dc and next cluster, *dc2tog between next 2 clusters; rep from * ending 1dc into top of tch, turn.

Rep 2nd row.

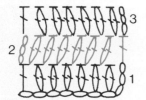

Crunch Stitch

Multiple of 2 sts.
(add 1 for base chain)

1st row: Skip 2ch (count as 1hdc), *sl st into next ch, 1hdc into next ch; rep from * ending sl st into last ch, turn.

2nd row: 2ch (count as 1hdc), skip 1 st, *sl st into next hdc, 1hdc into next sl st; rep from * ending sl st into top of tch, turn.

Rep 2nd row.

Floret Stitch I

Multiple of 2 sts + 1.
(add 2 for base chain)

1st row (right side): Skip 3ch (count as 1dc), 1dc into next and each ch to end, turn.

2nd row: 1ch, skip 1 st, *1dc into next st, sl st into next st; rep from * ending last rep into top of tch, turn.

3rd row: 3ch (count as 1dc), skip 1 st, *1dc into next dc, 1dc into next sl st; rep from * ending last rep into tch, turn.

Rep 2nd and 3rd rows.

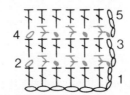

Floret Stitch II

Worked as Floret Stitch I.
Work 1 row each in colors A and B alternately throughout.

Floret Stitch III

Worked as Floret Stitch I.
Work 1 row each in colors A, B and C throughout.

Griddle Stitch

Multiple of 2 sts.
(add 2 for base chain)

1st row: Skip 3ch (count as 1dc), *1sc into next ch, 1dc into next ch; rep from * ending 1sc into last ch, turn.

2nd row: 3ch (count as 1dc), skip 1 st, *1sc into next dc, 1dc into next sc; rep from * ending 1sc into top of tch, turn.

Rep 2nd row.

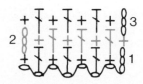

Crumpled Griddle Stitch

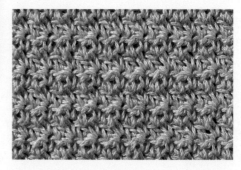

Multiple of 2 sts + 1.
(add 2 for base chain)

1st row: Skip 3ch (count as 1dc), *1sc into next ch, 1dc into next ch; rep from * to end, turn.

2nd row: 3ch (count as 1dc), skip 1 st, *1sc into next sc, 1dc into next dc; rep from * ending last rep into top of tch, turn.

Rep 2nd row.

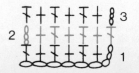

Stitch Variations, Abbreviations and Symbols on pages 7 to 15

Patterns for Texture and Color

Solid Shell Stitch

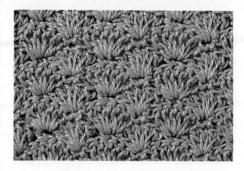

Multiple of 6 sts + 1.
(add 1 for base chain)

1st row: 1sc into 2nd ch from hook, *skip 2ch, 5dc into next ch, skip 2ch, 1sc into next ch; rep from * to end, turn.

2nd row: 3ch (count as 1dc), 2dc into first st, *skip 2dc, 1sc into next dc, skip 2dc, 5dc into next sc; rep from * ending last rep with 3dc into last sc, skip tch, turn.

3rd row: 1ch, 1sc into first st, *skip 2dc, 5dc into next sc, skip 2dc, 1sc into next dc; rep from * ending last rep with 1sc into top of tch, turn.

Rep 2nd and 3rd rows.

1sc into each of last 4 sc, skip tch, turn.

4th row: 1ch, 1sc into first st, 1sc into next and each st to end, skip tch, turn.

5th row: 3ch (count as 1dc), 3dc into first st, *skip 3 sts, 1sc into each of next 7 sts, skip 3 sts, 7dc into next st; rep from * ending last rep with 4dc into last sc, skip tch, turn.

Rep 2nd, 3rd, 4th and 5th rows.

Wavy Shell Stitch II

Worked as Wavy Shell Stitch I.
Work 1 row each in colors A, B and C throughout.

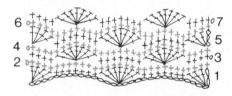

Wavy Shell Stitch I

Multiple of 14 sts + 1.
(add 2 for base chain)
Note: See Wavy Shell Stitch II for stitch diagram.

1st row (right side): Skip 2ch (count as 1dc), 3dc into next ch, *skip 3ch, 1sc into each of next 7ch, skip 3ch, 7dc into next ch; rep from * ending last rep with 4dc into last ch, turn.

2nd row: 1ch, 1sc into first st, 1sc into each st to end, finishing with 1sc into top of tch, turn.

3rd row: 1ch, 1sc into each of first 4 sts, *skip 3 sts, 7dc into next st, skip 3 sts, 1sc into each of next 7 sts; rep from * to last 11 sts, skip 3 sts, 7dc into next st, skip 3 sts,

Catherine Wheel I

Multiple of 10 sts + 6.
(add 1 for base chain)
Special Abbreviation

CL (Cluster) = work [yo, insert hook, yo, draw loop through, yo, draw through 2 loops] over the number of sts indicated, yo, draw through all loops on hook

1st row (wrong side): 1sc into 2nd ch from hook, 1sc into next ch, *skip 3ch, 7dc into next ch, skip 3ch, 1sc into each of next 3ch; rep from * to last 4 ch, skip 3 ch, 4dc into last ch, turn.

2nd row: 1ch, 1sc into first st, 1sc into next st, *3ch, 1CL over next 7 sts, 3ch, 1sc into

each of next 3 sts; rep from * to last 4 sts, 3ch, 1CL over last 4 sts, skip tch, turn.

3rd row: 3ch (count as 1dc), 3dc into first st, *skip 3ch, 1sc into each of next 3sc, skip 3ch, 7dc into loop which closed next CL; rep from * to end finishing with skip 3ch, 1sc into each of last 2sc, skip tch, turn.

4th row: 3ch (count as 1dc), skip first st, 1CL over next 3 sts, *3ch, 1sc into each of next 3 sts, 3ch, 1CL over next 7 sts; rep from * finishing with 3ch, 1sc into next st, 1sc into top of tch, turn.

5th row: 1ch, 1sc into each of first 2sc, *skip 3ch, 7dc into loop which closed next CL, skip 3ch, 1sc into each of next 3sc; rep from * ending skip 3ch, 4dc into top of tch, turn.

Rep 2nd, 3rd, 4th and 5th rows.

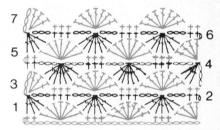

Catherine Wheel II

Worked as Catherine Wheel I.
Make base chain and work first row in color A. Thereafter work 2 rows each in color B and color A.

Catherine Wheel III

Worked as Catherine Wheel I.
Work 1 row each in colors A, B and C throughout.

Patterns for Texture and Color

Catherine Wheel IV

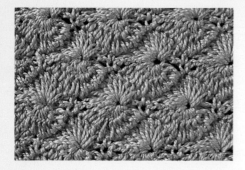

Multiple of 8 sts + 1.
(add 1 for base chain)

Special Abbreviation

CL (Cluster) worked as under Catherine Wheel I.

1st row (right side): 1sc into 2nd ch from hook, *skip 3ch, 9dc into next ch, skip 3ch, 1sc into next ch; rep from * to end, turn.

2nd row: 3ch (count as 1dc), skip first st, 1CL over next 4 sts, *3ch, 1sc into next st, 3ch, 1CL over next 9 sts; rep from * ending last rep with 1CL over last 5 sts, skip tch, turn.

3rd row: 3ch (count as 1dc), 4dc into first st, *skip 3ch, 1sc into next sc, skip 3ch, 9dc into loop which closed next CL; rep from * ending last rep with 5dc into top of tch, turn.

4th row: 1ch, 1sc into first st, *3ch, 1CL over next 9 sts, 3ch, 1sc into next st; rep from * ending last rep with 1sc into top of tch, turn.

5th row: 1ch, 1sc into first st, *skip 3ch, 9dc into loop which closed next CL, skip 3ch, 1sc into next sc; rep from * to end, skip tch, turn.
Rep 2nd, 3rd, 4th and 5th rows.

1st row (right side): Skip 3ch (count as 1dc), 1dc into next and each ch to end, turn.

2nd row: 1ch (counts as 1sc), 2dc into first st, *skip 2 sts, work [1sc, 2dc] into next st; rep from * to last 3 sts, skip 2 sts, 1sc into top of tch, turn.

3rd row: 3ch (count as 1dc), skip 1 st, 1dc into next and each st to end, working last st into top of tch, turn.
Rep 2nd and 3rd rows.

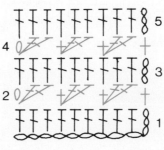

Silt Stitch

Multiple of 3 sts + 1.
(add 2 for base chain)

Hexagon Stitch

Multiple of 8 sts + 4.
(add 1 for base chain)

Special Abbreviations

CL (Cluster) = work [yo, insert hook, yo, draw loop through loosely] over number and position of sts indicated, ending yo, draw through all loops, 1ch tightly to close Cluster.

Picot = 5ch, 1sc into 2nd ch from hook, 1sc into each of next 3ch.

1st row (wrong side): 1sc into 2nd ch from hook, 1sc into each of next 3ch (counts as Picot), skip 3ch, 3dc into next ch, skip 3ch, 1sc into next ch, *skip 3ch, into next ch work [3dc, 1 Picot, 3dc], skip 3ch, 1sc into next ch; rep from * to end, turn.

2nd row: 4ch (count as 1tr), 1CL over each of first 8 sts, 3ch, 1sc into top of Picot, *3ch, 1CL over next 15 sts inserting hook into underside of each of 4ch of Picot, into next 3dc, 1sc, 3dc and 4sc of next Picot, then 3ch, 1sc into top of Picot; rep from * to end, turn.

3rd row: 1ch, 1sc into first st, *skip 3ch, into loop which closed next CL work [3dc, 1 Picot, 3dc], skip 3ch, 1sc into next sc; rep from * ending skip 3ch, 4dc into loop which closed last CL, skip tch, turn.

4th row: 7ch (count as 1tr and 3ch), starting into 5th ch from hook work 1CL over next 15 sts as before, *3ch, 1sc into top of Picot,

3ch, 1CL over next 15 sts; rep from * ending last rep with 1CL over last 8 sts, skip tch, turn.

5th row: 8ch, 1sc into 2nd ch from hook, 1sc into each of next 3ch (counts as 1dc and 1 Picot), 3dc into first st, skip 3ch, 1sc into next sc, *skip 3ch, into loop which closed next CL work [3dc, 1 Picot, 3dc], skip 3ch, 1sc into next sc; rep from * ending last rep with 1sc into 4th ch of tch, turn.
Rep 2nd, 3rd, 4th and 5th rows.

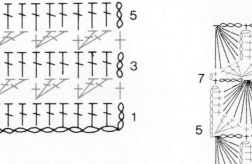

Grit Stitch I

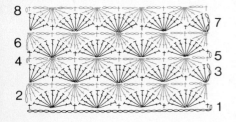

Multiple of 2 sts + 1.
(add 2 for base chain)

1st row: Skip 2ch (count as 1sc), 1sc into next ch, *skip 1ch, 2sc into next ch; rep from * to last 2ch, skip 1ch, 1sc into last ch, turn.

2nd row: 1ch (counts as 1sc), 1sc into first st, *skip 1sc, 2sc into next sc; rep from * to last 2 sts, skip 1sc, 1sc into top of tch, turn.
Rep 2nd row.

Stitch Variations, Abbreviations and Symbols on pages 7 to 15

Patterns for Texture and Color

Grit Stitch II

Multiple of 2 sts + 1.
(add 2 for base chain)

1st row: Skip 2ch (count as 1sc), 1dc into next ch, *skip 1ch, work [1sc and 1dc] into next ch; rep from * to last 2ch, skip 1ch, 1sc into last ch, turn.

2nd row: 1ch (counts as 1sc), 1dc into first st, *skip 1dc, work [1sc and 1dc] into next sc; rep from * to last 2 sts, skip 1dc, 1sc into top of tch, turn.

Rep 2nd row.

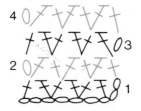

Sedge Stitch II

Multiple of 3 sts + 1.
(add 2 for base chain)

1st row: Skip 2ch (count as 1sc), 2dc into next ch, *skip 2ch, [1sc, 2dc] into next ch; rep from * to last 3ch, skip 2ch, 1sc into last ch, turn.

2nd row: 1ch (counts as 1 sc), 2dc into first st, *skip 2dc, [1sc, 2dc] into next sc; rep from * to last 3 sts, skip 2dc, 1sc into top of tch, turn.

Rep 2nd row.

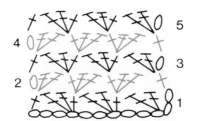

Wedge Stitch I

Multiple of 6 sts + 1.
(add 1 for base chain)

Special Abbreviation

WP (Wedge Picot) = work 6ch, 1sc into 2nd ch from hook, 1hdc into next ch, 1dc into next ch, 1tr into next ch, 1dtr into next ch.

1st row (wrong side): 1sc into 2nd ch from hook, *1WP, skip 5ch, 1sc into next ch; rep from * to end, turn.

2nd row: 5ch (count as 1dtr), *1sc into top of WP, over next 5ch at underside of WP work 1sc into next ch, 1hdc into next ch, 1dc into next ch, 1tr into next ch, 1dtr into next ch, skip next sc; rep from * omitting 1dtr at end of last rep when 2 sts remain, **[yo] 3 times, insert hook into last ch at underside of WP, yo, draw loop through, [yo, draw through 2 loops] 3 times, rep from ** into next sc, yo, draw through all 3 loops on hook, skip tch, turn.

3rd row: 1ch, 1sc into first st, *1WP, skip next 5 sts, 1sc into next st; rep from * ending last rep with 1sc into top of tch, turn.

Rep 2nd and 3rd rows.

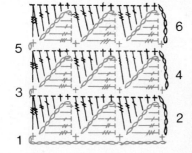

Sedge Stitch I

Multiple of 3 sts + 1.
(add 2 for base chain)

1st row: Skip 2ch (count as 1sc), work [1hdc, 1dc] into next ch, *skip 2ch, work [1sc, 1hdc, 1dc] into next ch; rep from * to last 3ch, skip 2ch, 1sc into last ch, turn.

2nd row: 1ch (counts as 1sc), work [1hdc, 1dc] into first st, *skip [1dc and 1hdc], work [1sc, 1hdc, 1dc] into next sc; rep from * to last 3 sts, skip [1dc and 1hdc], 1sc into top of tch, turn.

Rep 2nd row.

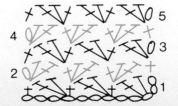

Wattle Stitch

Multiple of 3 sts + 2.
(add 1 for base chain)

1st row: Skip 2ch (count as 1sc), *work [1sc, 1ch, 1dc] into next ch, skip 2ch; rep from * ending 1sc into last ch, turn.

2nd row: 1ch (counts as 1sc), skip first sc and next dc, *work [1sc, 1ch, 1dc] into next ch sp, skip 1sc and 1dc; rep from * ending with [1sc, 1ch, 1dc] into last ch sp, skip next sc, 1sc into top of tch, turn.

Rep 2nd row.

Wedge Stitch II

Worked as Wedge Stitch I.
Make base chain and work first row in color A. Thereafter work 2 rows each in color B and color A.

Patterns for Texture and Color

Crosshatch Stitch I

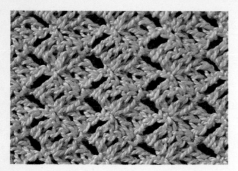

Multiple of 7 sts + 4.
(add 3 for base chain)

1st row: Skip 2ch (count as 1dc), 2dc into next ch, *skip 3ch, 1sc into next ch, 3ch, 1dc into each of next 3ch; rep from * to last 4ch, skip 3ch, 1sc into last ch, turn.

2nd row: 3ch (count as 1dc), 2dc into first sc, *skip 3dc, 1sc into first of 3ch, 3ch, 1dc into each of next 2ch, 1dc into next sc; rep from * ending skip 2dc, 1sc into top of tch, turn.

Rep 2nd row.

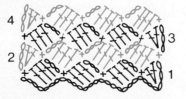

Crosshatch Stitch II

Worked as Crosshatch Stitch I.
Work 1 row each in colors A, B and C throughout.

Ridged Chevron Stitch

Multiple of 12 sts.
(add 3 for base chain)

1st row: Skip 3ch (count as 1dc), 1dc into next ch, *1dc into each of next 3ch, [over next 2ch work dc2tog] twice, 1dc into each of next 3ch, [2dc into next ch] twice; rep from * ending last rep with 2dc once only into last ch, turn.

2nd row: 3ch (count as 1dc), 1dc into first st, always inserting hook into back loop only of each st *1dc into each of next 3 sts, [over next 2 sts work dc2tog] twice, 1dc into each of next 3 sts, [2dc into next st] twice; rep from * ending last rep with 2dc once only into top of tch, turn.

Rep 2nd row.

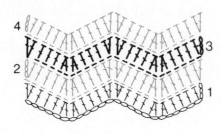

Sharp Chevron Stitch

Multiple of 14 sts.
(add 2 for base chain)

1st row: Skip 2ch (count as 1dc), 2dc into next ch, *1dc into each of next 3ch, [over next 3ch work dc3tog] twice, 1dc into each of next 3ch, [3dc into next st] twice; rep from * ending last rep with 3dc once only into last ch, turn.

2nd row: 3ch (count as 1dc), 2dc into first st, *1dc into each of next 3 sts, [over next 3 sts work dc3tog] twice, 1dc into each of next 3 sts, [3dc into next st] twice; rep from * ending last rep with 3dc once only into top of tch, turn.

Rep 2nd row.

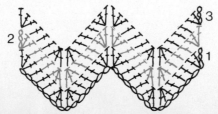

Close Chevron Stitch

Multiple of 11 sts + 1.
(add 1 for base chain)
Work 4 rows each in colors A and B alternately throughout.

1st row (right side): 2sc into 2nd ch from hook, *1sc into each of next 4ch, skip 2ch, 1sc into each of next 4ch, 3sc into next ch; rep from * ending last rep with 2sc only into last ch, turn.

2nd row: 1ch, 2sc into first st, *1sc into each of next 4 sts, skip 2 sts, 1sc into each of next 4 sts, 3sc into next st; rep from * ending last rep with 2sc only into last st, skip tch, turn.

Rep 2nd row.

Peephole Chevron Stitch

Multiple of 10 sts.
(add 2 for base chain)

1st row: Skip 2ch (count as 1dc), 1dc into each of next 4ch, *skip 2ch, 1dc into each of next 4ch, 2ch, 1dc into each of next 4ch; rep from * to last 6ch, skip 2ch, 1dc into each of next 3ch, 2dc into last ch, turn.

2nd row: 3ch (count as 1dc), 1dc into first st, 1dc into each of next 3 sts, *skip 2 sts, 1dc into each of next 3 sts, [1dc, 2ch, 1dc] into 2ch sp, 1dc into each of next 3 sts; rep from * to last 6 sts, skip 2 sts, 1dc into each of next 3 sts, 2dc into top of tch, turn. Rep 2nd row.

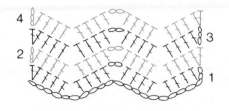

Crunchy Chevron Stitch

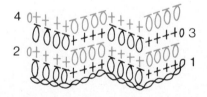

Multiple of 8 sts.
(add 1 for base chain)

Work 1 row each in colors A, B, C, D and E throughout.

1st row: 1sc into 2nd ch from hook, 1sc into each of next 3ch, *hdc2tog all into each of next 4ch, 1sc into each of next 4ch; rep from * to last 4ch, hdc2tog all into each of last 4ch, turn.

2nd row: 1ch, then starting in first st. *1sc into each of next 4 sts, hdc2tog all into each of next 4sc; rep from * to end, skip tch, turn.

Rep 2nd row.

Simple Chevron Stitch

Multiple of 10 sts + 1.
(add 2 for base chain)

1st row: Skip 2ch (count as 1dc), 1dc into next ch, *1dc into each of next 3ch, over next 3ch work dc3tog, 1dc into each of next 3ch, 3dc into next ch; rep from * ending last rep with 2dc into last ch, turn.

2nd row: 3ch (count as 1dc), 1dc into first st, *1dc into each of next 3dc, over next 3 sts work dc3tog, 1dc into each of next 3dc, 3dc into next dc; rep from * ending last rep with 2dc into top of tch, turn.

Rep 2nd row.

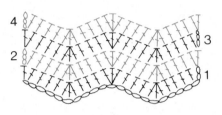

Textured Wave Stitch

Multiple of 20 sts.
(add 1 for base chain)
Special Abbreviation
2Cdc (2 crossed double crochets) = skip next st, 1dc into next st, 1dc into skipped st working over previous dc.

Work 2 rows each in colors A and B alternately throughout.

1st base row (right side): Skip 2ch (count as 1sc), 1sc into next and each ch to end, turn.

2nd base row: 1ch (counts as 1sc), skip 1 st, 1sc into next and each st to end working last st into tch, turn.

Commence Pattern
1st row: 3ch (count as 1dc), skip 1 st, over next 4 sts work [2Cdc] twice, *1sc into each of next 10 sts, over next 10 sts work [2Cdc] 5 times; rep from * to last 15 sts, 1sc into each of next 10 sts, over next 4 sts work [2Cdc] twice, 1dc into tch, turn.

2nd row: As 1st row.

3rd and 4th rows: As 2nd base row.

5th row: 1ch (counts as 1sc), skip 1 st, 1sc into each of next 4 sts, *over next 10 sts work [2Cdc] 5 times, 1sc into each of next 10 sts; rep from * to last 15 sts, over next 10 sts work [2Cdc] 5 times, 1sc into each

of last 5 sts working last st into tch, turn.
6th row: As 5th row.
7th and 8th rows: As 2nd base row.
Rep these 8 rows.

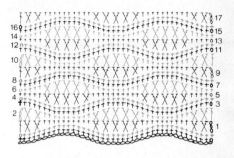

2 rows each in colors A and B

Long Wave Stitch

Multiple of 14 sts + 1.
(add 1 for base chain)
Special Abbreviations
Gr (Group) (worked over 14 sts) = 1sc into next st, [1hdc into next st] twice, [1dc into next st] twice, [1tr into next st] 3 times, [1dc into next st] twice, [1hdc into next st] twice, [1sc into next st] twice.

Rev Gr (Reverse Group) (worked over 14 sts) = 1tr into next st, [1dc into next st] twice, [1hdc into next st] twice, [1sc into next st] 3 times, [1hdc into next st] twice, [1dc into next st] twice, [1tr into next st] twice.

Work 2 rows each in colors A and B alternately throughout.

1st row (right side): Skip 2ch (count as 1sc), *1Gr over next 14ch; rep from * to end, turn.

2nd row: 1ch (counts as 1sc), skip first st, 1sc into next and each st to end working last st into top of tch, turn.

3rd row: 4ch (count as 1tr), skip first st, *1 Rev Gr over next 14 sts; rep from * ending last rep in tch, turn.

4th row: As 2nd row.

5th row: 1ch (counts as 1sc), skip first st, *1Gr over next 14 sts; rep from * ending last rep in tch, turn.

6th row: As 2nd row.

Rep 3rd, 4th, 5th and 6th rows.

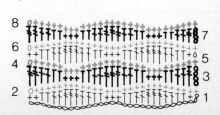

Patterns for Texture and Color

Smooth Wave Stitch

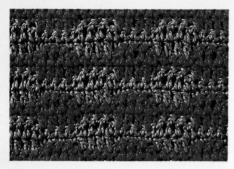

Multiple of 8 sts + 4.
(add 1 for base chain)

Work 2 rows each in colors A and B alternately throughout.

1st row (right side): Skip 2ch (count as 1sc), 1sc into each of next 3ch, *1dc into each of next 4ch, 1sc into each of next 4ch; rep from * to end, turn.

2nd row: 1ch (counts as 1sc), skip first st, 1sc into each of next 3 sts, *1dc into each of next 4 sts, 1sc into each of next 4 sts; rep from * to end working last st into top of tch, turn.

3rd row: 3ch (count as 1dc), skip first st, 1dc into each of next 3 sts, *1sc into each of next 4 sts, 1dc into each of next 4 sts; rep from * to end working last st into top of tch, turn.

4th row: As 3rd row.

5th and 6th rows: As 2nd row.
Rep 3rd, 4th, 5th and 6th rows.

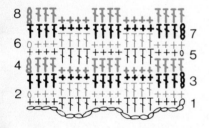

Wave and Chevron Stitch

Multiple of 6 sts + 1.
(add 1 for base chain)

Work 2 rows each in colors A, B, C and D throughout.

Base row: (right side): Skip 2ch (count as 1sc), 1sc into next and each ch to end, turn.

Commence Pattern

1st row: 1ch (counts as 1sc), skip 1 st, *1hdc into next st, 1dc into next st, 3tr into next st, 1dc into next st, 1hdc into next st, 1sc into next st; rep from * to end, turn.

2nd row: 1ch, skip 1 st, 1sc into next st (counts as sc2tog), 1sc into each of next 2 sts, *3sc into next st, 1sc into each of next 2 sts, over next 3 sts work sc3tog, 1sc into each of next 2 sts; rep from * to last 5 sts, 3sc into next st, 1sc into each of next 2 sts, over last 2 sts work sc2tog, skip tch, turn.

3rd row: As 2nd row.

4th row: 4ch, skip 1 st, 1tr into next st (counts as tr2tog), *1dc into next st, 1hdc into next st, 1sc into next st, 1hdc into next st, 1dc into next st**, over next 3 sts work tr3tog; rep from * ending last rep at **, over last 2 sts work tr2tog, skip tch, turn.

5th row: 1ch (counts as 1sc), skip 1 st, 1sc into next and each st to end, turn.

6th row: As 5th row.
Rep these 6 rows.

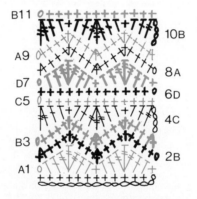

Crossed Double Crochet Stitch

Multiple of 2 sts.
(add 2 for base chain)

Special Abbreviation

2Cdc (2 crossed double crochets) worked as under Textured Wave Stitch

1st row (right side): Skip 3ch (count as 1dc), *2Cdc over next 2ch; rep from * ending 1dc into last ch, turn.

2nd row: 1ch (counts as 1sc), skip 1 st, 1sc into next and each st to end, working last st into top of tch, turn.

3rd row: 3ch (count as 1dc), skip 1 st, *work 2Cdc over next 2 sts; rep from * ending 1dc into tch, turn.

Rep 2nd and 3rd rows.

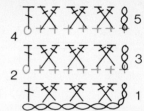

Woven Shell Stitch

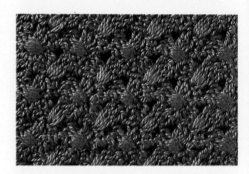

Multiple of 6 sts + 1.
(add 2 for base chain)

Special Abbreviation

CGr (Crossed Group) = skip 3dc and next st, 3dc into 2nd of next 3dc, 3ch, 3dc into 2nd of 3dc just skipped working back over last 3dc made.

1st row: Skip 3ch (count as 1dc), *skip next 3ch, 3dc into next ch, 3ch, 3dc into 2nd of 3ch just skipped working back over last 3dc made, skip 1ch, 1dc into next ch; rep from * to end, turn.

2nd row: 3ch (count as 1dc), 3dc into first st, 1sc into next 3ch arch, *1CGr, 1sc into next 3ch arch; rep from * ending 4dc into top of tch, turn.

3rd row: 3ch (count as 1dc), skip 1 st, 1CGr, *1sc into next 3ch loop, 1CGr; rep from * ending 1dc into top of tch, turn.

Rep 2nd and 3rd rows.

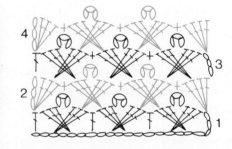

Crossbill Stitch

Stitch Variations, Abbreviations and Symbols on pages 7 to 15

Patterns for Texture and Color

Multiple of 4 sts + 1.
(add 2 for base chain)

Special Abbreviation
2Cdc (2 crossed double crochets) = skip 2 sts, 1dc into next st, 1ch, 1dc into first of 2 sts just skipped working back over last dc made

1st row: Skip 3ch (count as 1dc), *work 2Cdc over next 3ch, 1dc into next ch; rep from * to end, turn.
2nd row: 3ch (count as 1dc), 1dc into first st, skip 1dc, *1dc into next ch, work 2Cdc over next 3dc, rep from * ending 1dc into last ch, skip 1dc, 2dc into top of tch, turn.
3rd row: 3ch (count as 1dc), skip 1 st, *work 2Cdc over next 3dc, 1dc into next ch; rep from * ending last rep into top of tch, turn.
Rep 2nd and 3rd rows.

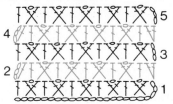

Sidesaddle Cluster Stitch

Multiple of 5 sts + 1.
(add 1 for base chain)

1st row: 1sc into 2nd ch from hook, *3ch, dc4tog over next 4ch, 1ch, 1sc into next ch; rep from * to end, turn.
2nd row: 5ch, 1sc into next cluster, *3ch, dc4tog all into next 3ch arch, 1ch, 1sc into next cluster; rep from * ending 3ch, dc4tog all into next 3ch arch, 1dc into last sc, skip tch, turn.
3rd row: 1ch, skip 1 st, 1sc into next CL, *3ch, 1CL into next 3ch arch, 1ch, 1sc into next CL; rep from * ending last rep with 1sc into tch arch, turn.
Rep 2nd and 3rd rows.

Crossed Cluster Stitch

Multiple of 8 sts + 4.
(add 1 for base chain)

Special Abbreviation
2CC (2 crossed clusters) = skip 1 st, into next st work *[yo, insert hook, yo, draw loop through] twice, yo, draw through all 5 loops on hook; rep from * into st just skipped working over previous cluster.

1st row (wrong side): Skip 2ch (count as 1sc), 1sc into next and each ch to end, turn.
2nd row: 3ch (count as 1dc), skip 1 st, *2CC over next 2 sts, 1dc into each of next 6 sts, rep from * to last 3 sts, 2CC over next 2 sts, 1dc into tch, turn.
3rd row: 1ch (counts as 1sc), skip 1 st, 1sc into next and each st to end, working last st into top of tch, turn.
4th row: 3ch (counts as 1dc), skip 1 st, 1dc into each of next 4 sts, *2CC over next 2 sts, 1dc into each of next 6 sts; rep from * to last 7 sts, 2CC over next 2 sts, 1dc into each of last 5 sts, working last st into tch, turn.
5th row: As 3rd row.
Rep 2nd, 3rd, 4th and 5th rows.

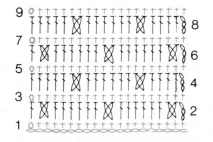

Diagonal Shell Stitch

Multiple of 4 sts + 1.
(add 1 for base chain)

Special Abbreviation
Shell = [1sc, 3ch, 4dc] all into same st.

1st row (right side): Work 1 shell into 2nd ch from hook, *skip 3ch, 1 shell into next ch; rep from * to last 4ch, skip 3ch, 1sc into last ch, turn.
2nd row: 3ch (count as 1dc), skip 1 st, *skip 1dc, over next 2 sts work dc2tog, 3ch, skip 1dc, 1sc into top of 3ch; rep from * to end, turn.
3rd row: 1ch, 1 shell into first st, *skip 3ch and next st, 1 shell into next sc; rep from * ending skip 3ch and next st, 1sc into top of tch, turn.
Rep 2nd and 3rd rows.

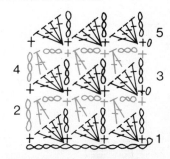

Sidesaddle Shell Stitch

Multiple of 6 sts + 1.
(add 3 for base chain)

Special Abbreviation
Shell = 3dc, 1ch, [1sc, 1hdc, 1dc] all into side of last of 3dc just made.

1st row (wrong side): Skip 3ch (count as 1dc), 3dc into next ch, skip 2ch, 1sc into next ch, *skip 2ch, Shell into next ch, skip 2ch, 1sc into next ch; rep from * to last 3ch, skip 2ch, 4dc into last ch, turn.
2nd row: 1ch (counts as 1sc), skip 1 st, *skip next 3 sts, Shell into next sc, skip 3 sts, 1sc into next ch sp; rep from * ending last rep with 1sc into top of tch, turn.
3rd row: 3ch (count as 1dc), 3dc into first st, skip 3 sts, 1sc into next ch sp, *skip 3 sts, Shell into next sc, skip 3 sts, 1sc into next ch sp; rep from * ending skip 3 sts, 4dc into tch, turn.
Rep 2nd and 3rd rows.

Patterns for Texture and Color

Interlocking Block Stitch I

Multiple of 6 sts + 3.
(add 2 for base chain)

Special Abbreviation
Sdc (Spike double crochet) = work dc over ch sp by inserting hook into top of next row below (or base chain).
Work 1 row each in colors A, B and C throughout.

1st row: Skip 3ch (count as 1dc), 1dc into each of next 2ch, *3ch, skip 3ch, 1dc into each of next 3ch; rep from * to end, turn.
2nd row: *3ch, skip 3 sts, 1Sdc over each of next 3 sts; rep from * to last 3 sts, 2ch, skip 2 sts, sl st into top of tch, turn.
3rd row: 3ch (count as 1Sdc), skip 1 st, 1Sdc over each of next 2 sts, *3ch, skip 3 sts, 1Sdc over each of next 3 sts; rep from * to end, turn.
Rep 2nd and 3rd rows.

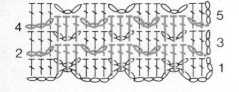

Interlocking Block Stitch II

Worked as Interlocking Block Stitch I.
Work 1 row each in colors A and B alternately throughout. Do not break yarn when changing color, but begin row at same end as color.

Diagonal Spike Stitch

Multiple of 4 sts + 2.
(add 2 for base chain)

Special Abbreviation
Sdc (Spike double crochet) = yo insert hook into same place that first dc of previous 3dc block was worked, yo, draw loop through and up so as not to crush 3dc block, [yo, draw through 2 loops] twice.

1st row: Skip 3ch (count as 1dc), *1dc into each of next 3ch, skip next ch and work 1Sdc over it instead; rep from * ending 1dc into last ch, turn.
2nd row: 3ch (count as 1dc), skip 1 st, *1dc into each of next 3 sts, skip next st and work 1Sdc over it instead; rep from * ending 1dc into top of tch, turn.
Rep 2nd row.

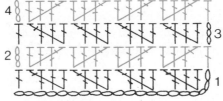

Alternating Spike Stitch I

Multiple of 2 sts.
(add 1 for base chain)

Special Abbreviation
Ssc (Spike single crochet) = insert hook below next st 1 row down (i.e. into same place as that st was worked), yo, draw loop

through and up to height of present row, yo, draw through both loops on hook

1st row: Skip 2ch (count as 1sc), 1sc into next and each ch to end, turn.
2nd row: 1ch (counts as 1sc), skip 1 st, *1sc into next st, 1Ssc over next st; rep from * ending 1sc into tch, turn.
Rep 2nd row.

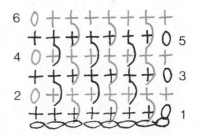

Alternating Spike Stitch II

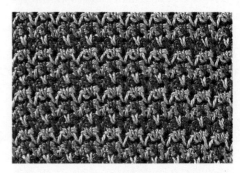

Worked as Alternating Spike Stitch I.
Work 1 row each in colors A, B and C throughout.

Arrowhead Spike Stitch

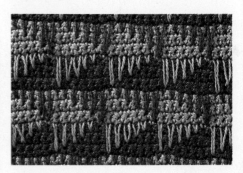

Multiple of 6 sts + 2.
(add 1 for base chain)

Special Abbreviation
Ssc (Spike single crochet) = insert hook below next st 1 or more rows down (indicated thus: Ssc1, Ssc2, Ssc3, etc), yo, draw loop through and up to height of current row,

Stitch Variations, Abbreviations and Symbols on pages 7 to 15

Patterns for Texture and Color

yo, draw through both loops on hook

Work 6 rows each in colors A and B alternately throughout.

Base row (right side): Using A 1sc into 2nd ch from hook. 1sc into each ch to end, turn.

Commence Pattern

1st row: 1ch, 1sc into first and each st to end, skip tch, turn.

Work 4 rows as 1st row.

6th row: Using B 1ch, 1sc into first st, *1sc into next st, 1Ssc1 over next st, 1Ssc2 over next st, 1Ssc3 over next st, 1Ssc4 over next st, 1Ssc5 over next st; rep from * ending 1sc into last st, skip tch, turn.

Work 5 rows as 1st row.

12th row: Using A 1ch, 1sc into first st, *1Ssc5 over next st, 1Ssc4 over next st, 1Ssc3 over next st, 1Ssc2 over next st, 1Ssc1 over next st, 1sc into next st; rep from * ending 1sc into last st, skip tch, turn.

Rep these 12 rows.

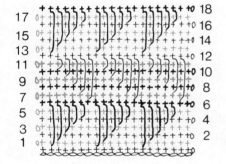

Spiked Squares

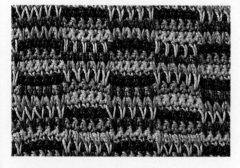

Multiple of 10 sts + 1.
(add 1 for base chain)

Special Abbreviation

Ssc (Spike single crochet) worked as under Arrowhead Spike Stitch. Note: when working Sscs over previous Sscs be careful to insert hook in centers of previous Sscs.

Work 2 rows each in colors A, B and C throughout.

Base row (right side): 1sc into 2nd ch from hook, 1sc into next and each ch to end, turn.

Commence Pattern

1st row: 1ch, 1sc into first and each st to end, skip tch, turn.

2nd row: 1ch, 1sc into first st, *1Ssc2 over each of next 5 sts, 1sc into each of next 5

sts; rep from * ending 1sc into last sc, skip tch, turn.

Rep the last 2 rows 3 times more.

9th row: As 1st row.

10th row: 1ch, 1sc into first st, *1sc into each of next 5 sts, 1Ssc2 over each of next 5 sts; rep from * ending 1sc into last sc, skip tch, turn.

Rep the last 2 rows 3 times more.

Rep these 16 rows.

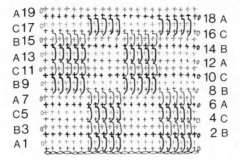

Spike Cluster Stitch

Multiple of 8 sts + 5.
(add 1 for base chain)

Special Abbreviation

SPC (Spike Cluster) = over next st pick up 5 spike loops by inserting hook as follows: 2 sts to right of next st and 1 row down; 1 st to right and 2 rows down; directly below and 3 rows down; 1 st to left and 2 rows down; 2 sts to left and 1 row down, (6 loops on hook); now insert hook into top of next st itself, yo, draw loop through, yo, draw through all 7 loops on hook

Work 4 rows each in colors A and B alternately throughout.

Base row (right side): 1sc into 2nd ch from hook, 1sc into each ch to end, turn.

Commence Pattern

1st row: 1ch, 1sc into first and each st to end, skip tch, turn.

2nd and 3rd rows: As 1st row.

4th row: 1ch, 1sc into each of first 4 sts, *1SPC over next st, 1sc into each of next 7 sts (Hint: be careful not to pick up any of the spikes of the previous SPC); rep from * ending 1sc into last st, skip tch, turn.

5th, 6th and 7th rows: As 1st row.

8th row: 1ch, 1sc into each of first 8 sts, *1SPC over next st, 1sc into each of next 7 sts; rep from * to last 5 sts, 1SPC over next st, 1sc into each of last 4 sts, skip tch, turn.

Rep these 8 rows.

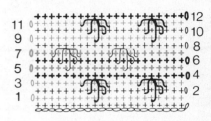

5-Star Marguerite Stitch

Multiple of 2 sts + 1.
(add 1 for base chain)

Special Abbreviation

M5C (Marguerite Cluster with 5 spike loops) = pick up spike loops (ie: yo and draw through) inserting hook as follows: into loop which closed previous M5C, under 2 threads of last spike loop of same M5C, into same place that last spike loop of same M5C was worked, into each of next 2 sts (6 loops on hook), yo, draw through all loops on hook

1st row (wrong side): 1sc into 2nd ch from hook, 1sc into next and each ch to end, turn.

2nd row: 3ch, 1M5C inserting hook into 2nd and 3rd chs from hook and then first 3 sts to pick up 5 spike loops, *1ch, 1M5C; rep from * to end, skip tch, turn.

3rd row: 1ch, 1sc into loop which closed last M5C, *1sc into next ch, 1sc into loop which closed next M5C; rep from * ending 1sc into each of next 2ch of tch, turn.

Rep 2nd and 3rd rows.

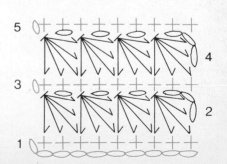

Patterns for Texture and Color

Simple Marguerite Stitch

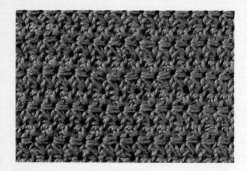

Multiple of 2 sts + 1.
(add 2 for base chain)

Special Abbreviation

↖ **M3C (Marguerite Cluster with 3 spike loops)**

1st row: Make a spike loop (i.e. yo and draw through) into 2nd, 3rd and 5th chs from hook, yo and through all 4 loops (1M3C made), *1ch, make 1M3C picking up 1 loop in ch which closed previous M3C, 2nd loop in same place as last spike of previous M3C, skip 1ch, then last loop in next ch, yo and through all 4 loops; rep from * to end, turn.

2nd row: 3ch, make 1M3C picking up loops in 2nd and 3rd ch from hook and in ch which closed 2nd M3C on previous row, *1ch, work 1M3C picking up first loop in ch which closed previous M3C, 2nd loop in same place as last spike of previous M3C and last loop in ch which closed next M3C on previous row; rep from * to end, picking up final loop in top of ch at beg of previous row.
Rep 2nd row.

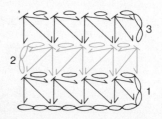

Granule Stitch

Multiple of 4 sts + 1.
(add 1 for base chain)

Special Abbreviation

Psc (Picot single crochet) = insert hook, yo, draw loop through, [yo, draw through 1 loop] 3 times to make 3ch, yo, draw through both loops on hook. Note: draw picot chain

loops to the back (right side) of fabric.

1st row (right side): 1sc into 2nd ch from hook, 1sc into each ch to end, turn.

2nd row: 1ch, 1sc into first st, *1Psc into next st, 1sc into next st; rep from * to end, skip tch, turn.

3rd row: 1ch, 1sc into first and each st to end, skip tch, turn. Hint: Hold down the picot chains at the front and you will see the top 2 loops of the Psc where you are to insert the hook.

4th row: 1ch, 1sc into each of first 2 sts, *1Psc into next st, 1sc into next st; rep from * to last st, 1sc into last st, skip tch, turn.

5th row: As 3rd row.

Rep 2nd, 3rd, 4th and 5th rows.

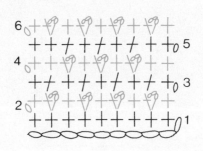

Relief Arch Stitch

Multiple of 8 sts + 1.
(add 1 for base chain)

1st row (wrong side): 1sc into 2nd ch from hook, 1sc into each of next 2ch, *7ch, skip 3ch, 1sc into each of next 5ch; rep from * to last 6ch, 7ch, skip 3ch, 1sc into each of last 3ch, turn.

2nd row: 3ch (count as 1dc), skip 1 st, 1dc into each of next 2 sts, *going behind 7ch loop work 1tr into each of next 3 base ch**, 1dc into each of next 5sc; rep from * ending last rep at ** when 3 sts remain, 1dc into each of last 3 sts, skip tch, turn.

3rd row: 1ch, 1sc into first st, *7ch, skip 3 sts, 1sc into next st at same time catching in center of 7ch loop of last-but-one row, 7ch, skip 3 sts, 1sc into next st; rep from * to end, turn.

4th row: 3ch (count as 1dc), skip 1 st, *going behind 7ch loop of last row work 1tr into each of next 3 sts of last-but-one row, 1dc into next sc; rep from * to end, skip tch, turn.

5th row: 1ch, 1sc into each of first 2 sts, *1sc into next st at same time catching in center of 7ch loop of last-but-one row, 7ch, skip 3 sts, 1sc into next st at same time catching in center of 7ch loop of last-but-one

row**, 1sc into each of next 3 sts; rep from * ending last rep at ** when 2 sts remain, 1sc into each of last 2 sts, turn.

6th row: As 2nd row working trs into last-but-one row.

Rep 3rd, 4th, 5th and 6th rows.

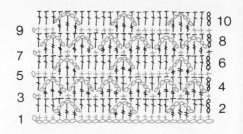

Thistle Pattern

Multiple of 10 sts + 1.
(add 1 for base chain)

Special Abbreviation

Catch Loop = Catch 10ch loop of Thistle by inserting hook under ch at tip of loop **at the same time** as under the next st.

Base row (wrong side): Skip 2ch (count as 1sc), 1sc into each of next 4ch, *into next st work a Thistle of 1sc, [10ch, 1sc] 3 times**, 1sc into each of next 9ch; rep from * ending last rep at **, 1sc into each of last 5sc, turn.

Commence Pattern

Note: Hold loops of Thistle down at front of work on right side rows.

1st row: 1ch (count as 1sc), skip 1sc, 1sc into each of next 4sc, *skip 1sc of Thistle, work sc2tog over next 2sc, skip last sc of Thistle**, work 1sc into each of next 9 sts; rep from * ending last rep at **, 1sc into each of next 4sc, 1sc into tch, turn.

2nd, 4th, 8th and 10th rows: 1ch, skip 1 st, 1sc into each st to end, turn.

3rd row: 1ch, skip 1 st, 1sc into next sc, *catch first loop of Thistle in next sc, 1sc into each of next 5sc, skip center loop of Thistle, catch 3rd loop in next st**, 1sc into each of next 3sc; rep from * ending last rep at **, 1sc into each of last 2 sts, turn.

5th row: 1ch, skip 1 st, 1sc into each of next 4sc, *work 6dc into next sc and at the same time catch center loop**, 1sc into each of next 9sc; rep from * ending last rep at **, 1sc into each of last 5 sts, turn.

6th row: 1ch, skip 1 st, 1sc into each of first 4sc, *1ch, skip 6dc, 1sc into each of next 4sc**, work a Thistle into next sc, 1sc into each of next 4sc; rep from * ending last rep

Stitch Variations, Abbreviations and Symbols on pages 7 to 15

Patterns for Texture and Color

at **, 1sc into last st, turn.

7th row: 1ch, skip 1 st, 1sc into each of next 9 sts, *work sc2tog over center 2 of next 4sc, skip 1sc, 1sc into each of next 9 sts; rep from * to last st, 1sc into last st, turn.

9th row: 1ch, skip 1 st, 1sc into each of next 6sc, *catch first loop into next sc, 1sc into each of next 5sc, catch 3rd loop into next sc**, 1sc into each of next 3sc; rep from * ending last rep at **, 1sc into each st to end, turn.

11th row: 1ch, skip 1 st, 1sc into each of next 9 sts, *work 6dc into next sc and catch center loop at the same time, 1sc into each of next 9sc; rep from * to last st, 1sc in last st, turn.

12th row: 1ch, skip 1 st, 1sc into each of next 4sc, *work a Thistle into next sc, 1sc into each of next 4sc**, 1ch, skip 6dc, 1sc into each of next 4sc; rep from * ending last rep at **, 1sc into last st, turn.

Rep these 12 rows.

Corded Ridge Stitch

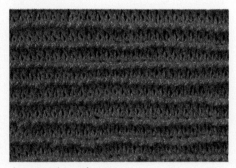

Any number of sts.
(add 2 for base chain)

Note: work all rows with right side facing, i.e. work even numbered rows from left to right

1st row (right side): Skip 3ch (count as 1dc), 1dc into next and each ch to end. Do not turn.

2nd row: 1ch, 1sc into front loop only of last dc made, *1sc into front loop only of next dc to right; rep from * ending sl st into top of tch at beginning of row. Do not turn.

3rd row: 3ch (count as 1dc), skip 1 st, 1dc into back loop only of next and each st of last-but-one row to end. Do not turn.

Rep 2nd and 3rd rows.

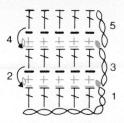

Astrakhan Stitch

Any number of sts.
(add 2 for base chain)

Note: work all rows with right side facing, i.e. work even numbered rows from left to right.

1st row (right side): Skip 3ch (count as 1dc), 1dc into each ch to end. Do not turn.

2nd row: *7ch, sl st into front loop only of next dc to right; rep from * ending 7ch, sl st into top of tch at beginning of row. Do not turn.

3rd row: 3ch (count as 1dc), skip 1 st, 1dc into back loop only of next and each st of last-but-one row to end. Do not turn.

Rep 2nd and 3rd rows.

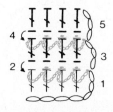

Embossed Roundels

Multiple of 8 sts + 5.
(add 2 for base chain)

Special Abbreviation

ERd (Embossed Roundel) = work [1dc, 2ch] 9 times all into same st, remove hook from working loop, insert hook from back through top of first dc of Roundel and, keeping sts of Roundel at back of fabric, pick up working loop again and draw through to close Roundel.

1st row (right side): Skip 3ch (count as 1dc), 1dc into next and each ch to end, turn.

2nd row: 3ch (count as 1dc), skip 1 st, 1dc into each of next 3 sts, *1ERd into next st, 1dc into each of next 7 sts; rep from * ending 1dc into top of tch, turn.

3rd row: 3ch (count as 1dc), skip 1 st, 1dc into next and each st to end, working last st into top of tch, turn.

4th row: 3ch (count as 1dc), skip 1 st, *1dc into each of next 7 sts, 1ERd into next st; rep from * to last 4 sts, 1dc into each of last 4 sts, turn.

5th row: As 3rd row.

Rep 2nd, 3rd, 4th and 5th rows.

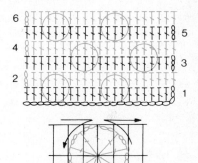

Embossed Pockets

Multiple of 3 sts + 1.
(add 2 for base chain)

Special Abbreviation

PGr (Pocket Group) = work [1sc, 1hdc, 3dc] round stem of indicated st.

1st row (wrong side): Skip 3ch (count as 1dc), 1dc into each ch to end, turn.

2nd row: 1PGr round first st, skip 2 sts, sl st into top of next st, *1PGr round same st as sl st, skip 2 sts, sl st into top of next st; rep from * to end, turn.

3rd row: 3ch (count as 1dc), skip 1 st, 1dc into each st to end, turn.

Rep 2nd and 3rd rows.

Patterns for Texture and Color

Single Rib

Multiple of 2 sts.
(add 2 for base chain)

1st row (wrong side): Skip 3ch (count as 1dc), 1dc into next and each ch to end, turn.
2nd row: 2ch (count as 1dc), skip first st, *1dc/rf round next st, 1dc/rb round next st; rep from * ending 1dc into top of tch, turn.
Rep 2nd row.

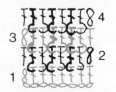

Zig-Zag Rib

Multiple of 4 sts + 2.
(add 2 for base chain)

Base row (wrong side): Skip 3ch (count as 1dc), 1dc into next and each ch to end, turn.
Commence Pattern
1st row: 2ch (count as 1dc), skip first st, *1dc/rf round each of next 2 sts, 1dc/rb round each of next 2 sts; rep from * ending 1dc into top of tch, turn.
2nd row: 2ch (count as 1dc), skip first st, 1dc/rb round next st, *1dc/rf round each of next 2 sts**, 1dc/rb round each of next 2 sts; rep from * ending last rep at ** when 2 sts remain, 1dc/rb round next st, 1dc into top of tch, turn.
3rd row: 2ch (count as 1dc), skip first st, *1dc/rb round each of next 2 sts, 1dc/rf round each of next 2 sts; rep from * ending 1dc into top of tch, turn.

4th row: 2ch (count as 1dc), miss first st, 1dc/rb round next st, *1dc/rb round each of next 2 sts**, 1dc/rf round each of next 2 sts; rep from * ending last rep at ** when 2 sts remain, 1dc/rf round next st, 1dc into top of tch, turn.
5th row: As 3rd row.
6th row: As 2nd row.
7th row: As 1st row.
8th row: As 4th row.
Rep these 8 rows.

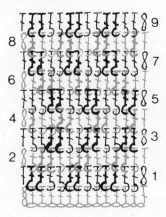

Ripple Stitch I

Multiple of 2 sts + 1.
(add 2 for base chain)

1st row (right side): Skip 3ch (count as 1dc), 1dc into each ch to end, turn.
2nd row: 1ch (counts as 1sc), skip first st, 1sc into each st to end, working last st into top of tch, turn.
3rd row: 3ch (count as 1dc), skip first st, *1tr/rf round dc below next st, 1dc into next st; rep from * to end, turn.
4th row: As 2nd row.
5th row: 3ch (count as 1dc), skip first st, *1dc into next st, 1tr/rf round dc below next st; rep from * to last 2 sts, 1dc into each of last 2 sts, turn.
Rep 2nd, 3rd, 4th and 5th rows.

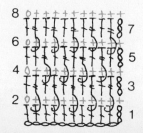

Ripple Stitch II

Worked as Ripple Stitch I.
Work 2 rows each in colors A and B alternately throughout.

Basketweave Stitch

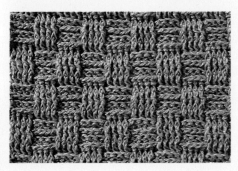

Multiple of 8 sts + 2.
(add 2 for base chain)

Base row (wrong side): Skip 3ch (count as 1dc), 1dc into next and each ch to end, turn.
Commence Pattern
1st row: 2ch (count as 1dc), skip first st, *1dc/rf round each of next 4 sts, 1dc/rb round each of next 4 sts; rep from * ending 1dc into top of tch, turn.
Rep the last row 3 times.
5th row: 2ch (count as 1dc), skip first st, *1dc/rb round each of next 4 sts, 1dc/rf round each of next 4 sts; rep from * ending 1dc into top of tch, turn.
Rep the last row 3 times.
Rep these 8 rows.

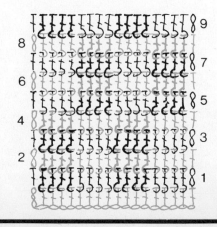

Stitch Variations, Abbreviations and Symbols on pages 7 to 15

Patterns for Texture and Color

Raised Chevron Stitch

Multiple of 16 sts + 1.
(add 2 for base chain)

1st row (right side): Skip 3ch, dc2tog over next 2ch (counts as dc3tog), *1dc into each of next 5ch, [2dc, 1ch, 2dc] into next ch, 1dc into each of next 5ch**, dc5tog over next 5ch; rep from * ending last rep at ** when 3ch remain, dc3tog, turn.

2nd row: 3ch, skip first st, dc/rb2tog over next 2 sts (all counts as dc/rb3tog), *1dc/rf round each of next 5 sts, [2dc, 1ch, 2dc] into next ch sp, 1dc/rf round each of next 5 sts**, dc/rb5tog over next 5 sts; rep from * ending last rep at ** when 3 sts remain, dc/rb3tog, turn.

3rd row: 3ch, skip first st, dc/rf2tog over next 2 sts (all counts as dc/rf3tog), *1dc/rb round each of next 5 sts, [2dc, 1ch, 2dc] into next ch sp, 1dc/rb round each of next 5 sts**, dc/rf5tog over next 5 sts; rep from * ending last rep at ** when 3 sts remain, dc/rf3tog, turn.

Rep 2nd and 3rd rows.

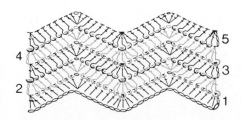

Crinkle Stitch I

Multiple of 2 sts.
(add 1 for base chain)

1st row (wrong side): Skip 2ch (count as 1hdc), 1hdc into each ch to end, turn.

2nd row: 1ch, 1sc into first st, *1sc/rf round next st, 1sc/rb round next st; rep from * ending 1sc into top of tch, turn.

3rd row: 2ch (count as 1hdc), skip first st, 1hdc into next and each st to end, skip tch, turn.

4th row: 1ch, 1sc into first st, *1sc/rb round next st, 1sc/rf round next st; rep from * ending 1sc into top of tch, turn.

5th row: As 3rd row.

Rep 2nd, 3rd, 4th and 5th rows.

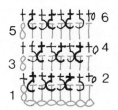

Crinkle Stitch II

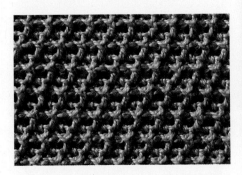

Worked as Crinkle Stitch I, but using wrong side of fabric as right side.

Crossed Ripple Stitch

Multiple of 3 sts + 2.
(add 1 for base chain)

1st base row (wrong side): 1sc into 2nd ch from hook, 1sc into each ch to end, turn.

2nd base row: 3ch (count as 1dc), skip first st, *skip next 2 sts, 1dc into next st, 1ch, 1dc back into first of 2 sts just skipped — called Crossed Pair; rep from * ending 1dc into last st, skip tch, turn.

Commence Pattern

1st row: 1 ch, 1sc into first st, 1sc into next and each st and each ch sp to end working last st into top of tch, turn.

2nd row: As 2nd base row, except as 2nd st of each Crossed Pair work 1dc/rf loosely round first st of corresponding Crossed Pair 2 rows below.

Rep these 2 rows.

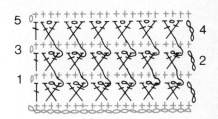

Leafhopper Stitch

Multiple of 4 sts + 1.
(add 2 for base chain)

Special Abbreviation

LCL (Leafhopper Cluster) = *[yo, insert hook at front and from right to left behind stem of st before next st, yo, draw loop through and up to height of hdc] twice, yo, draw through 4 loops**, skip next st, rep from * to ** round stem of next st, ending yo, draw through all 3 loops on hook.

1st row (wrong side): Skip 3ch (count as 1dc), 1dc into next and each ch to end, turn.

2nd row: 3ch (count as 1dc), skip first st, 1dc into next st, *1LCL over next st, 1dc into each of next 3 sts; rep from * omitting 1dc from end of last rep, turn.

3rd row: 3ch (count as 1dc), skip first st, 1dc into next and each st to end, working last st into top of tch, turn.

4th row: 3ch (count as 1dc), skip first st, *1dc into each of next 3 sts, 1LCL over next st; rep from * ending 1dc into each of last 4 sts, working last st into top of tch, turn.

5th row: As 3rd row.

Rep 2nd, 3rd, 4th and 5th rows.

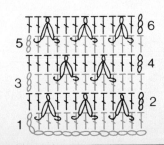

Patterns for Texture and Color

Gwenyth's Cable

Worked over 19 sts on a background of basic double crochets with any number of sts.

1st row (right side): 1tr/rf round first st, 1dc into next st, skip next 3 sts, 1dtr into each of next 3 sts, going behind last 3dtrs work 1dtr into each of 3 sts just skipped, 1dc into next st, 1tr/rf round next st, 1dc into next st, skip next 3 sts, 1dtr into each of next 3 sts, going in front of last 3dtrs but not catching them work 1dtr into each of 3 sts just skipped, 1dc into next st, 1tr/rf round next st.

2nd row: As 1st row, except work 1tr/rb instead of rf over first, 10th and 19th sts to keep raised ridges on right side of fabric.

Rep 1st and 2nd rows.

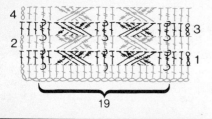

Dots and Diamonds

Multiple of 4 sts + 3.
(add 1 for base chain)

Special Abbreviation

Psc (Picot single crochet) = insert hook, yo, draw loop through, [yo, draw through 1 loop] 3 times, yo, draw through both loops on hook. Note: draw picot ch loops to front (right side) of fabric.

Base row (right side): 1sc into 2nd ch from hook, 1sc into each of next 2ch, *psc into next ch, 1sc into each of next 3ch; rep from * to end, turn.

Commence Pattern

1st row: 3ch (count as 1dc), skip first st, 1dc into each st to end, skip tch, turn.

2nd row: 1ch, 1sc into first st, *psc into next st, 1sc into next st**, tr/rf2tog over next st inserting hook round 2nd sc in last-but-one row for first leg and round following 4th sc for 2nd leg (skipping 3 sts between), 1sc into next st; rep from * ending last rep at ** in top of tch, turn.

3rd row: As 1st row.

4th row: 1ch, 1sc into first st, 1tr/rf over next st inserting hook round top of first raised cluster 2 rows below, *1sc into next st, psc into next st, 1sc into next st**, tr/rf2tog over next st inserting hook round same cluster as last raised st for first leg and round top of next raised cluster for 2nd leg; rep from * ending last rep at ** when 2 sts remain, 1tr/rf over next st inserting hook round top of same cluster as last raised st, 1sc into top of tch, turn.

5th row: As 1st row.

6th row: As 2nd row, except to make new raised clusters insert hook round previous raised clusters instead of scs.

Rep 3rd, 4th, 5th and 6th rows.

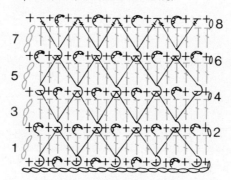

Crossed Puff Cables

Worked over 11 sts on a background of basic double crochets with any number of sts.

1st row (right side): 1dc into each st.

2nd row: *1tr/rb round next st, work a Puff st of hdc5tog all into next st, 1tr/rb round next st**, 1dc into next st; rep from * once and from * to ** again.

3rd row: *Leaving last loop of each st on hook work [1dc into next st, skip Puff st, work 1tr/rf round next st] ending yo, draw through all 3 loops on hook, 1dc into top of Puff st, leaving last loop of each st on hook work

[1tr/rf round st before same Puff st and 1dc into top of st after Puff st] ending yo, draw through all 3 loops on hook**, 1dc into next st; rep from * once and from * to ** again.

4th row: As 2nd row, but make new tr/rbs by inserting hook under raised stems only of previous sts.

Rep 3rd and 4th rows.

Tulip Cable

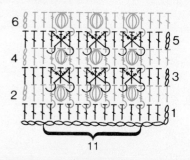

Worked over 15 sts on a background of basic double crochets with any number of sts.

Special Abbreviations

FCL (Forward Cluster) = leaving last loop of each st on hook work 1dc into next st and 1tr/rf or rb (see Note below) round next st after that, ending yo, draw through all 3 loops on hook.

BCL (Backward Cluster) = leaving last loop of each st on hook work 1tr/rf or rb round st below dc just made and 1dc into next st.

Note: Raised legs of these clusters are to be worked at front (rf) on right side rows and at back (rb) on wrong side rows as indicated in the text thus: FCL/rf, FCL/rb, BCL/rf, BCL/rb.

TCL (Triple Cluster) = leaving last loop of each st on hook work 1tr/rf round st below dc just made, 1dc/rf round next Puff st, and 1tr/rf round next st, ending yo, draw through all 4 loops on hook.

1st row: (right side): 1tr/rf round next st, 1dc into next st, 1tr/rf round next st, 1dc into each of next 2 sts, [1FCL/rf] twice, 1dc into next st, [1BCL/rf] twice, 1dc into each of next 2 sts, 1tr/rf round next st, 1dc into next st, 1tr/rf round next st.

2nd row: [1tr/rb round next st, 1dc into next st] twice, [1FCL/rb] twice, 1dc into each of next 3 sts, [1BCL/rb] twice, [1dc into next st, 1tr/rb round next st] twice.

3rd row: [1tr/rf round next st, 1dc into next st] twice, 1tr/rf round each of next 2 sts, 1dc into each of next 3 sts, 1tr/rf round each of

Stitch Variations, Abbreviations and Symbols on pages 7 to 15

next 2 sts, [1dc into next st, 1tr/rf round next st] twice.

4th row: 1tr/rb round next st, 1dc into next st, 1tr/rb round next st, 1dc into each of next 2 sts, [1BCL/rb] twice, work a Puff st of hdc5tog all into next st, [1FCL/rb] twice, 1dc into each of next 2 sts, 1tr/rb round next st, 1dc into next st, 1tr/rb round next st.

5th row: 1tr/rf round next st, 1dc into next st, 1tr/rf round next st, 1dc into each of next 3 sts, 1BCL/rf, 1TCL, 1FCL/rf, 1dc into each of next 3 sts, 1tr/rf round next st, 1dc into next st, 1tr/rf round next st.

6th row: *1tr/rb round next st, 1dc into next st, 1tr/rb round next st**, 1dc into each of next 9 sts, rep from * to **.

Rep these 6 rows.

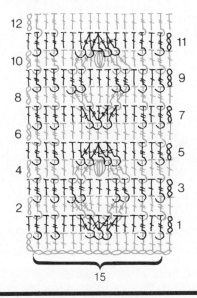

Puff Stitch Plaits

Multiple of 8 sts + 1.
(add 1 for base chain)

1st row (right side): Skip 2ch (count as 1hdc), 1hdc into each of next 2ch, *1ch, skip 1ch, hdc3tog all into next ch, 1ch, skip 1ch**, 1hdc into each of next 5ch; rep from * ending last rep at ** when 3ch remain, 1hdc into each of last 3ch, turn.

2nd row: 2ch (count as 1hdc), skip first st, 1hdc into each of next 2 sts, *hdc3tog into next ch sp, 1ch, skip 1 st, hdc3tog into next ch sp**, 1hdc into each of next 5 sts; rep from * ending last rep at ** when 3 sts remain including tch, 1hdc into each of last 3 sts, turn.

3rd row: 2ch (count as 1hdc), skip first st, 1hdc into each of next 2 sts, *1ch, skip 1 st, hdc3tog into next ch sp, 1ch, skip 1 st**, 1hdc into each of next 5 sts; rep from * end-

ing last rep at ** when 3 sts remain including tch, 1hdc into each of last 3 sts, turn.
Rep 2nd and 3rd rows.

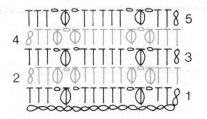

Aligned Puff Stitch

Multiple of 2 sts + 1.
(add 1 for base chain)

1st row (right side): 1sc into 2nd ch from hook, *1ch, skip 1ch, 1sc into next ch; rep from * to end, turn.

2nd row: 2ch (count as 1hdc), skip first st, *hdc4tog all into next ch sp, 1ch, skip 1sc; rep from * ending hdc4tog into last ch sp, 1hdc into last sc, skip tch, turn.

3rd row: 1ch, 1sc into first st, *1ch, skip 1 st, 1sc into next ch sp; rep from * ending in top of tch, turn.
Rep 2nd and 3rd rows.

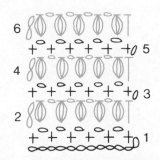

Boxed Puff Stitch

Multiple of 3 sts + 1.
(add 4 for base chain)
Special Abbreviation
Puff Stitch = hdc4tog all into same st and closed with 1ch drawn tightly.

1st row (right side): Puff st into 5th ch from hook, *skip 2ch, [1dc, 2ch, puff st] all into next ch; rep from * ending skip 2ch, 1dc into last ch, turn.

2nd row: 1ch, skip first st, *work 1dc loosely over next row into first of 2 skipped sts in row below, 1sc into puff st, 1sc into next 2ch sp; rep from * ending 1sc into 3rd ch of tch, turn.

3rd row: 5ch (count as 1dc and 2ch), puff st into first st, *skip 2sc, [1dc, 2ch, puff st] all into next dc; rep from * ending skip 2sc, 1dc into last dc, skip tch, turn.

Rep 2nd and 3rd rows.

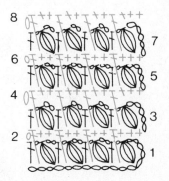

Aligned Cobble Stitch

Multiple of 2 sts + 1.
(add 1 for base chain)
1st row (right side): 1sc into 2nd ch from hook, 1sc into each ch to end, turn.

2nd row: 1ch, 1sc into first st, *1tr into next st, 1sc into next st; rep from * to end, skip tch, turn.

3rd row: 1ch, 1sc into first st, 1sc into next and each st to end, skip tch, turn.
Rep 2nd and 3rd rows.

37

Patterns for Texture and Color

Wavy Puff Stitch Sprays

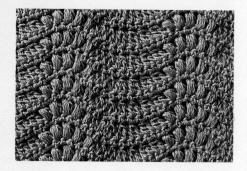

Multiple of 17 sts.
(add 2 for base chain)

1st row (right side): 1dc into 4th ch from hook (counts as dc2tog), [dc2tog over next 2ch] twice, *[1ch, work hdc4tog into next ch] 5 times, 1ch**, [dc2tog over next 2ch] 6 times; rep from * ending last rep at ** when 6ch remain, [dc2tog over next 2ch] 3 times, turn.

2nd row: 1ch, 1sc into first st and then into each st and each ch sp to end excluding tch, turn.

3rd row: 3ch, skip first st, 1dc into next st (counts as dc2tog), [dc2tog over next 2 sts] twice, *[1ch, work hdc4tog into next st] 5 times, 1ch**, [dc2tog over next 2 sts] 6 times; rep from * ending last rep at ** when 6 sts remain, [dc2tog over next 2 sts] 3 times, skip tch, turn.
Rep 2nd and 3rd rows.

V-Twin Popcorn Stitch

Multiple of 11 sts + 3.
(add 2 for base chain)

1st row (right side): Skip 3ch (count as 1dc), 1dc into each of next 2ch, *2ch, skip 3ch, 5dc popcorn into next ch, 1ch, 5dc popcorn into next ch, 1ch, skip 2ch, 1dc into each of next 3ch; rep from * to end, turn.

2nd row: 3ch (count as 1dc), skip first st, 1tr/rb round next st, 1dc into next st, *3ch, skip 1ch and 1 popcorn, 2sc into next ch sp, 3ch, skip 1 popcorn and 2ch, 1dc into next st, 1tr/rb round next st, 1dc into next st; rep from * ending last rep in top of tch, turn.

3rd row: 3ch (count as 1dc), skip first st, 1tr/rf round next st, 1dc into next st, *2ch, skip 3ch, 5dc popcorn into next sc, 1ch, 5dc popcorn into next sc, 1ch, skip 3ch, 1dc into next st, 1tr/rf round next st, 1dc into next st; rep from * ending last rep in top of tch, turn.
Rep 2nd and 3rd rows.

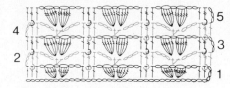

Blackberry Salad Stitch

Multiple of 4 sts + 1.
(add 2 for base chain)

1st row (right side): Skip 3ch (count as 1dc), 1dc into each ch to end, turn.

2nd row: 1ch, 1sc into each of first 2 sts, *work dc5tog into next st, 1sc into each of next 3 sts; rep from * to last 3 sts, work dc5tog into next st, 1sc into each of last 2 sts (including top of tch), turn.

3rd row: 3ch (count as 1dc), skip first st, 1dc into each st to end, skip tch, turn.

4th row: 1ch, 1sc into each of first 4 sts, *work dc5tog into next st, 1sc into each of next 3 sts; rep from * ending 1sc into top of tch, turn.

5th row: As 3rd row.
Rep 2nd, 3rd, 4th and 5th rows.

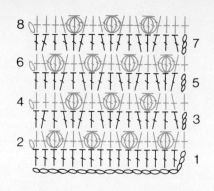

Bullion Diagonals

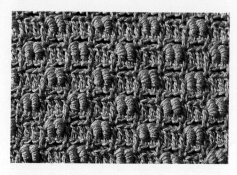

Multiple of 6 sts + 2.
(add 1 for base chain)

1st row (wrong side): 1sc into 2nd ch from hook, 1ch, skip 1ch, 1sc into next ch, *2ch, skip 2ch, 1sc into next ch; rep from * to last 2ch, 1ch, skip 1ch, 1sc into last ch, turn.

2nd row: 3ch (count as 1dc), skip first st, 1dc into next ch sp, *1dc into next sc, 1 Bullion st into each of next 2ch, 1dc into next sc**, 1dc into each of next 2ch; rep from * ending last rep at ** when 1 ch sp remains, 1dc into next ch, 1dc into last sc, skip tch, turn.

3rd row: 1ch, 1sc into first st, 1ch, skip 1 st, 1sc into next st, *2ch, skip 2 sts, 1sc into next st; rep from * to last 2 sts, 1ch, skip 1 st, 1sc into top of tch, turn.

4th row: 3ch (count as 1dc), skip first st, 1 Bullion st into next ch sp, *1dc into next sc, 1dc into each of next 2ch, 1dc into next sc**, 1 Bullion st into each of next 2ch; rep from * ending last rep at ** when 1ch sp remains, 1 Bullion st into next sp, 1dc into last sc, skip tch, turn.

5th row: As 3rd row.
Rep 2nd, 3rd, 4th and 5th rows.

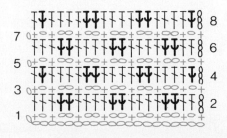

Diagram Note
┬ Bullion Stitch with [yo] 7 times.

Stitch Variations, Abbreviations and Symbols on pages 7 to 15

Popcorn Waffle Stitch

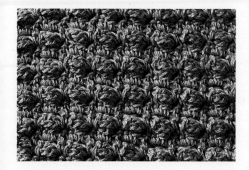

Multiple of 4 sts + 1.
(add 1 for base chain)

1st row (right side): 1sc into 2nd ch from hook, *3ch, 5dc popcorn into same place as previous sc, skip 3ch, 1sc into next ch; rep from * to end, turn.

2nd row: 3ch (count as 1dc), skip first st, *1sc into each of next 2ch, 1hdc into next ch, 1dc into next sc; rep from * to end, skip tch, turn.

3rd row: 1ch, 1sc into first st, *3ch, 5dc popcorn into same place as previous sc, skip next 3 sts, 1sc into next dc; rep from * ending last rep in top of tch, turn.

Rep 2nd and 3rd rows.

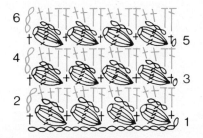

Diagonal Trip Stitch

Multiple of 6 sts + 2.
(add 1 for base chain)

1st row (right side): 1sc into 2nd ch from hook, 1sc into each ch to end, turn.

2nd row: 1ch, 1sc into first st, *1tr into next

st, 1sc into next st, 1tr into next st, 1sc into each of next 3 sts; rep from * ending 1sc into last sc, skip tch, turn.

3rd row: 1ch, 1sc into first st, 1sc into next and each st to end, skip tch, turn.

4th row: 1 ch, 1sc into each of first 2 sts, *1tr into next st, 1sc into next st, 1tr into next st, 1sc into each of next 3 sts; rep from * to end, skip tch, turn.

5th row: As 3rd row.

6th row: 1 ch, 1sc into each of first 3 sts, *1tr into next st, 1sc into next st, 1tr into next st, 1sc into each of next 3 sts; rep from * to end, omitting 1sc at end of last rep, skip tch, turn.

Continue in this way, working the pairs of tr 1 st further to the left on every wrong side row.

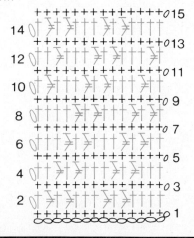

Bobble Braid Stitch

Worked over 13 sts on a background of any number of sts worked in basic double crochet on right side rows and single crochet on wrong side rows.

1st row (right side): 1dc into each of first 4 sts, [1ch, skip 1 st, 1dc into next st] 3 times, 1dc into each of last 3 sts.

2nd row: 1sc into each of first 4 sts, work dc5tog into next ch sp, 1sc into next dc, 1sc into next sp, 1sc into next dc, dc5tog into next sp, 1sc into each of last 4 sts.

3rd row: 1tr/rf round first st 2 rows below (ie: 1st row), 1dc into next st on previous (ie: 2nd) row, 1tr/rf round next st 2 rows below,

[1ch, skip 1 st, 1dc into next st on previous row] 3 times, 1ch, skip 1 st, 1tr/rf round next st 2 rows below, 1dc into next st on previous row, 1tr/rf round next st 2 rows below.

4th row: 1sc into each of first 6 sts, work dc5tog into next st, 1sc into each of last 6 sts.

5th row: [1tr/rf round corresponding raised st 2 rows below, 1dc into next st] twice, [1ch, skip 1 st, 1dc into next st] 3 times, 1tr/rf round corresponding raised st 2 rows below, 1dc into next st, 1tr/rf round corresponding raised st 2 rows below.

Continue as set on 2nd, 3rd, 4th and 5th rows.

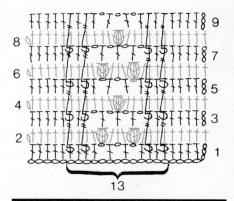

Loop or Fur Stitch

Multiple of 8 sts.
(add 2 for base chain)

1st row (right side): Skip 3ch (count as 1dc), 1dc into next and each ch to end, turn.

2nd row: 1ch, 1sc into each of first 2 sts, *1 Loop st into each of next 4 sts**, 1sc into each of next 4 sts; rep from * ending last rep at **, 1sc into each of last 2 sts including top of tch, turn.

3rd row: 3ch (count as 1dc), skip 1 st, 1dc into next and each st to end, skip tch, turn.

Rep 2nd and 3rd rows.

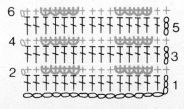

Diagram Note
⊎ Sc Loop Stitch

Patterns for Texture and Color

Interweave Stitch

Multiple of 2 sts + 1.
(add 2 for base chain)

Work 1 row each in colors A, B and C throughout.

1st row (right side): Skip 3ch (count as 1dc), 1dc into next and each ch to end, turn.
2nd row: 3ch (count as 1dc), skip first st, *1tr/rf round next st, 1dc into next st; rep from * ending last rep in top of tch, turn.
Rep 2nd row.

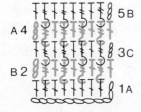

Little Wave Stitch

Multiple of 4 sts + 1.
(add 1 for base chain)

Work 2 rows each in colors A and B alternately.

1st row (right side): 1sc into 2nd ch from hook, *1hdc into next ch, 1dc into next ch, 1hdc into next ch, 1sc into next ch; rep from * to end, turn.
2nd row: 1ch, 1sc into first st, *1hdc into next hdc, 1dc into next dc, 1hdc into next hdc, 1sc into next sc; rep from * to end, skip tch, turn.
3rd row: 3ch (count as 1dc), skip first st, *1hdc into next hdc, 1sc into next dc, 1hdc into next hdc, 1dc into next sc; rep from * to end, skip tch, turn.
4th row: 3ch (count as 1dc), skip first st, *1hdc into next hdc, 1sc into next sc, 1hdc

into next hdc, 1dc into next dc; rep from * ending last rep in top of tch, turn.
5th row: 1ch, 1sc into first st, *1hdc into next hdc, 1dc into next sc, 1hdc into next hdc, 1sc into next dc; rep from * ending last rep in top of tch, turn.
Rep 2nd, 3rd, 4th and 5th rows.

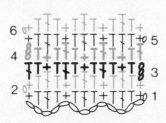

Interlocking Diamond Stitch

Multiple of 6 sts + 1.
(add 1 for base chain)

Work 1st row in color A, then 2 rows each in colors B and A alternately throughout.

1st row (wrong side): Sl st into 2nd ch from hook, *3ch, skip 2ch, 1dc into next ch, 3ch, skip 2ch, sl st into next ch; rep from * to end, turn.
2nd row: 4ch (count as 1dc and 1ch), 1dc into first sl st, *skip 3ch, sl st into next dc**, skip 3ch, work [1dc, 1ch, 1dc, 1ch, 1dc] into next sl st; rep from * ending last rep at ** in last dc, skip 3ch, work [1dc, 1ch, 1dc] into last sl st, turn.
3rd row: 6ch (count as 1dc and 3ch), skip [first st, 1ch and 1dc], *sl st into next sl st**, 3ch, skip 1dc and 1ch, 1dc into next dc, 3ch, skip 1ch and 1dc; rep from * ending last rep at ** in last sl st, 3ch, skip 1dc and 1ch, 1dc into next ch of tch, turn.
4th row: Sl st into first st, *skip 3ch, [1dc, 1ch, 1dc, 1ch, 1dc] all into next sl st, skip 3ch, sl st into next dc; rep from * ending in 3rd ch of tch loop, turn.
5th row: *3ch, skip 1dc and 1ch, 1dc into next dc, 3ch, skip 1ch and 1dc, sl st into next sl st; rep from * to end, turn.
Rep 2nd, 3rd, 4th and 5th rows.

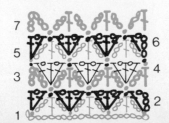

Interlocking Shell Stitch

Multiple of 6 sts + 1.
(add 2 for base chain)

Work 1 row each in colors A and B alternately; fasten off each color at end of each row.

1st row (right side): Skip 2ch (count as 1dc), 2dc into next ch, skip 2ch, 1sc into next ch, *skip 2ch, 5dc into next ch, skip 2ch, 1sc into next ch; rep from * to last 3ch, skip 2ch, 3dc into last ch, turn.
2nd row: 1ch, 1sc into first st, *2ch, dc5tog over next 5 sts, 2ch, 1sc into next st; rep from * ending last rep in top of tch, turn.
3rd row: 3ch (count as 1dc), 2dc into first st, skip 2ch, 1sc into next cluster, *skip 2ch, 5dc into next sc, skip 2ch, 1sc into next cluster; rep from * to last cluster, skip 2ch, 3dc into last sc, skip tch, turn.
Rep 2nd and 3rd rows.

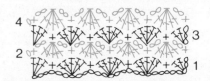

Zig-Zag Pip Stitch

Multiple of 4 sts + 1.
(add 1 for base chain)

Work 1 row each in colors A, B, C, D and E throughout.

1st row (right side): 1sc into 2nd ch from hook, *1ch, skip 1ch, 1sc into next ch; rep from * to end, turn.

Stitch Variations, Abbreviations and Symbols on pages 7 to 15

Patterns for Texture and Color

2nd row: 3ch, 1dc into next ch sp (counts as dc2tog), *1ch, dc2tog inserting hook into same sp as previous st for first leg and into next sp for 2nd leg; rep from * to last sp, ending 1ch, dc2tog over same sp and last sc, skip tch, turn.

3rd row: 1ch, 1sc into first st, *1sc into next sp, 1ch, skip next cluster; rep from * ending 1sc into last sp, 1sc into last st, skip tch, turn.

4th row: 3ch (count as 1dc), dc2tog inserting hook into first st for first leg and into next sp for 2nd leg, *1ch, dc2tog inserting hook into same sp as previous st for first leg and into next sp for 2nd leg; rep from * ending with 2nd leg of last cluster in last sc, 1dc into same place, skip tch, turn.

5th row: 1ch, 1sc into first st, *1ch, skip next cluster, 1sc into next sp; rep from * working last sc into top of tch, turn.

Rep 2nd, 3rd, 4th and 5th rows.

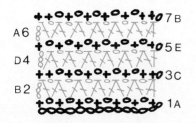

Aligned Railing Stitch

Multiple of 2 sts + 1.
(add 2 for base chain)

On a background of basic double crochets in color M work raised rows — one row each in colors A, B and C throughout.

Work 2 rows basic double crochets in M.

Commence Pattern

1st row (right side): Put working loop temporarily on a stitch holder or safety pin, draw loop of contrast color through top of last background st completed, 1ch, work 1tr/rf round stem of 2nd st in last-but-one row, *1ch, skip 1 st, 1tr/rf round stem of next st in last-but-one row; rep from * ending sl st into top of tch at beg of last background row worked. Fasten off but do not turn work.

2nd row: Replace hook in working loop of M. 3ch, work 1dc inserting hook through top of raised st and background st at the same time, *work 1dc inserting hook under contrast color ch and top of next st in background color at the same time, work 1dc

inserting hook under top of next raised st and background st as before; rep from * to end. Work 1 row in basic double crochets. Rep these 3 rows.

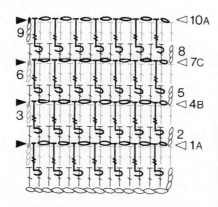

Shadow Tracery Stitch

Multiple of 6 sts + 1.
(add 1 for base chain)

Special Abbreviation

Puff stitch = work hdc5tog all into same place ending with 1ch drawn tightly to close.

Work 1 row each in colors A and B alternately throughout. Do not break yarn when changing color, but fasten off temporarily and begin row at same end as new color.

1st row (right side in A): 1sc into 2nd ch from hook, *3ch, skip 2ch, puff st into next ch, 3ch, skip 2ch, 1sc into next ch; rep from * to end. Do not turn.

2nd row (right side in B): Join yarn into first st, 1ch, 1sc into first st, *3ch, skip 3ch, 1sc into next puff st, 3ch, skip 3ch, 1sc into next sc; rep from * to end, turn.

3rd row (wrong side in A): 6ch (count as 1dc and 3ch), skip first st and 3ch, 1sc into next sc, *3ch, skip 3ch, puff st into next sc, 3ch, skip 3ch, 1sc into next sc; rep from * ending 3ch, skip 3ch, 1dc into last sc. Do not turn.

4th row (wrong side in B): Pick up yarn in 3rd ch of tch, 1ch, 1sc into same place, *3ch, skip 3ch, 1sc into next sc, 3ch, skip 3ch, 1sc into next st; rep from * to end, turn.

5th row (right side in A): 1ch, 1sc into first st, *3ch, skip 3ch, puff st into next sc, 3ch, skip 3ch, 1sc into next sc; rep from * to end. Do not turn.

Rep 2nd, 3rd, 4th and 5th rows.

Fleur de Lys Stitch

Multiple of 6 sts + 1.
(add 2 for base chain)

Special Abbreviations

FC/rf (Fleur Cluster raised at front) = leaving last loop of each st on hook work 1dc/rf round next dc, skip 1ch, 1dc into top of next sc, skip 1ch, 1dc/rf round next dc (4 loops on hook), yo, draw through all loops.

FC/rb (Fleur Cluster raised at back) = as for FC/rf except insert hook at back for first and 3rd legs.

Work 1 row each in colors A and B alternately throughout. Do not break yarn when changing color, but fasten off temporarily and begin row at same end as new color.

1st row (right side in A): Skip 2ch (count as 1dc), 1dc into next ch, *1ch, skip 2ch, 1sc into next ch, 1ch, skip 2ch**, 3dc into next ch; rep from * ending last rep at **, 2dc into last ch. Do not turn.

2nd row (right side in B): Join new yarn into top of tch, 1ch, 1sc into same place, *2ch, FC/rb, 2ch, 1sc into next dc; rep from * to end, turn.

3rd row (wrong side in A): 3ch (count as 1dc), 1dc into first st, *1ch, skip 2ch, 1sc into next cluster, 1ch, skip 2ch**, 3dc into next sc; rep from * ending last rep at **, 2dc into last sc. Do not turn.

4th row (wrong side in B): Rejoin new yarn at top of 3ch, 1ch, 1sc into same place, *2ch, FC/rf, 2ch, 1sc into next dc; rep from * to end, turn.

5th row (right side in A): 3ch (count as 1dc), 1dc into first st, *1ch, skip 2ch, 1sc into next cluster, 1ch, skip 2ch**, 3dc into next sc; rep from * ending last rep at **, 2dc into last sc. Do not turn.

Rep 2nd, 3rd, 4th and 5th rows.

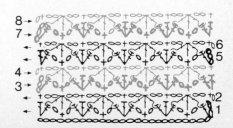

Patterns for Texture and Color

Picot Coronet Stitch

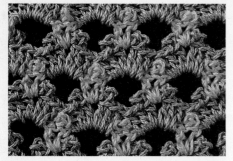

Multiple of 7 sts + 1.
(add 3 for base chain)

Work 1 row each with colors A and B alternately throughout; fasten off each color at end of each row.

1st row (right side): Skip 3ch (count as 1dc), 1dc into next ch, work a picot of [3ch, insert hook down through top of dc just made and work a sl st to close], 2dc into same ch, *skip 6ch, work a Coronet of [3dc, picot, 1ch, 1dc, picot, 2dc] into next ch; rep from * to last 7ch, skip 6ch, [3dc, picot, 1dc] into last ch, turn.

2nd row: 3ch (count as 1dc), 1dc into first st, *3ch, work a picot V st of [1dc, picot, 1dc] into 1ch sp at center of next Coronet; rep from * ending 3ch, 2dc into top of tch, turn.

3rd row: 2ch (count as 1hdc), skip first 2 sts, *Coronet into next 3ch sp, skip next picot V st; rep from * ending Coronet into last sp, 1hdc into top of tch, turn.

4th row: 4ch (count as 1dc and 1ch), *picot V st into sp at center of next Coronet, 3ch; rep from * ending picot V st into last Coronet, 1ch, 1dc into top of tch, turn.

5th row: 3ch (count as 1dc), skip first st, [1dc, picot, 2dc] into next ch sp, *skip next picot V st, Coronet into next sp; rep from * ending skip last picot V st, 3dc into next ch, picot, 1dc into next ch of tch, turn.

Rep 2nd, 3rd, 4th and 5th rows.

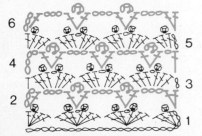

Relief Squares

Multiple of 10 sts + 4.
(add 1 for base chain)

1st base row (right side): Using A, 1sc into 2nd ch from hook, 1sc into next and each ch to end, turn.

2nd base row: 1 ch, 1sc into first and each st to end, skip tch, turn.

Commence Pattern

Change to B and rep the 2nd base row twice.

Change to C and rep the 2nd base row 4 times.

7th row: Using B, 1ch, 1sc into each of first 3 sts, *[1dtr/rf round st corresponding to next st 5 rows below, i.e. last row worked in B] twice, 1sc into each of next 4 sts, [1dtr/rf round st corresponding to next st 5 rows below] twice, 1sc into each of next 2 sts; rep from * ending 1sc into last st, skip tch, turn.

8th row: Using B rep 2nd base row.

9th row: Using A, 1ch, 1sc into first st, *[1quin tr/rf round st corresponding to next st 9 rows below, ie last row worked in A] twice, 1sc into each of next 8 sts; rep from * to last 3 sts, [1quin tr/rf round st corresponding to next st 9 rows below] twice, 1sc into last st, skip tch, turn.

10th row: Using A rep 2nd base row.
Rep these 10 rows.

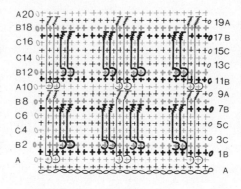

Multi-Colored Parquet Stitch

Multiple of 3 sts + 1.
(add 1 for base chain)

Work 1 row each in colors A, B and C alternately throughout.

1st row (right side): 1sc into 2nd ch from hook, *3ch, 1dc into same place as previous sc, skip 2ch, 1sc into next ch; rep from * to end, turn.

2nd row: 3ch (count as 1dc), 1dc into first st, 1sc into next 3ch arch, *3ch, 1dc into same 3ch arch, 1sc into next 3ch arch; rep

from * ending 2ch, 1dc into last sc, skip tch, turn.

3rd row: 1ch, 1sc into first st, 3ch, 1dc into next 2ch sp, *work [1sc, 3ch, 1dc] into next 3ch arch; rep from * ending 1sc into top of tch, turn.

Rep 2nd and 3rd rows.

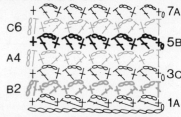

Zig-Zag Lozenge Stitch

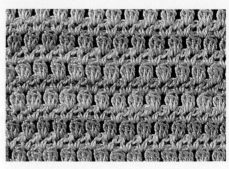

Multiple of 2 sts + 1.
(add 2 for base chain)

Work 1 row each in colors A, B and C alternately throughout.

1st row (wrong side): Skip 2ch (count as 1hdc), 1hdc into next ch, *skip 1ch, [1hdc, 1ch, 1hdc] into next ch; rep from * to last 2 ch, skip 1ch, 2hdc into last ch, turn.

2nd row: 3ch, 1dc into first st (counts as dc2tog), *1ch, work dc3tog into next ch sp; rep from * to last sp, ending 1ch, dc2tog into top of tch, turn.

3rd row: 2ch (count as 1hdc), skip first st, *work [1hdc, 1ch, 1hdc] into next ch sp; rep from * ending 1hdc into top of tch, turn.

4th row: 3ch (count as 1dc), skip first st, *work dc3tog into next sp, 1ch; rep from * ending 1dc into top of tch, turn.

5th row: 2ch (count as 1hdc), 1hdc into first st, *work [1hdc, 1ch, 1hdc] into next ch sp; rep from * ending 2hdc into top of tch, turn.

Rep 2nd, 3rd, 4th and 5th rows.

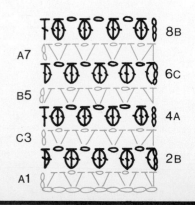

Patterns for Texture and Color

Chevron Stitch I

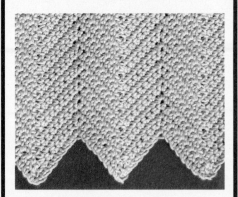

Starting chain: Multiple of 16 sts + 2.

1st row (right side): Work 2sc into 2nd ch from hook, *1sc into each of next 7ch, skip 1ch, 1sc into each of next 7ch, 3sc into next ch; rep from * to end omitting 1sc at end of last rep, turn.

2nd row: 1ch, work 2sc into first sc, *1sc into each of next 7sc, skip 2sc, 1sc into each of next 7sc, 3sc into next sc; rep from * to end omitting 1sc at end of last rep, turn.

Rep 2nd row only.

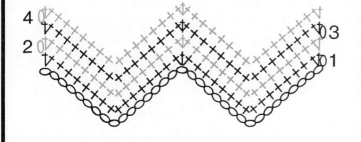

Diagram only: Rep 2nd and 3rd rows.

Chevron Stitch II

Work as given for Chevron Stitch I, working 1 row each in A, B and C throughout.

Curve Fan Stitch

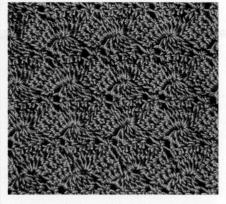

Starting chain: Multiple of 6 sts + 3.

Special Abbreviations

Dc2tog = work 1dc into each of next 2 sts until 1 loop of each remains on hook, yo and through all 3 loops on hook.

Half Cluster = work 1dc into each of next 3 sts until 1 loop of each remains on hook, yo and through all 4 loops on hook.

Cluster = work 1dc into each of next 5 sts until 1 loop of each remains on hook, yo and through all 6 loops on hook.

1st row (right side): Work dc2tog working into 4th and 5th ch from hook, *3ch, 1sc into next ch, turn, 1ch, 1sc into last sc worked, 3sc into last 3ch sp formed, [turn, 1ch, 1sc into each of the 4sc] 3 times, work 1 cluster over next 5ch; rep from * to end but working half cluster at end of last rep, turn.

2nd row: 4ch (count as 1tr), work 2tr into top of first half cluster, skip 3sc, 1sc into next sc, *5tr into top of next cluster, skip 3sc, 1sc into next sc; rep from * to last dc2tog, 3tr into top of 3ch at beg of previous row, turn.

3rd row: 3ch (count as 1dc), skip first tr, work dc2tog over next 2tr, *3ch, 1sc into next sc, turn, 1ch, 1sc into last sc worked, 3sc into last 3ch sp formed, [turn, 1ch, 1sc into each of the 4sc] 3 times, work 1 cluster over next 5tr; rep from * to end but working half cluster at end of last rep placing last dc of half cluster into 4th of 4ch at beg of previous row, turn.

Rep 2nd and 3rd rows ending with a 2nd row.

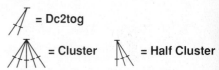

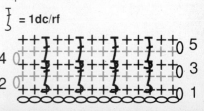

Line shows direction of work for first part of first row.

Bar Stitch

Starting chain: Multiple of 3 sts + 3.

Special Abbreviation

1dc/rf = work 1dc around stem of next st 2 rows below inserting hook round stem from right to left to draw up loops.

1st row (right side): Work 1sc into 2nd ch from hook, 1sc into each ch to end, turn.

2nd row: 1ch, work 1sc into each sc to end, turn.

3rd row: 1ch, work 1sc into each of first 2sc, *1dc/rf round next sc 2 rows below, 1sc into each of next 2sc; rep from * to end, turn.

4th row: 1ch, work 1sc into each st to end, turn.

5th row: 1ch, work 1sc into each of first 2sc, *1dc/rf round stem of next dc/rf 2 rows below, 1sc into each of next 2sc; rep from * to end, turn.

Rep 4th and 5th rows.

= 1dc/rf

Patterns for Texture and Color

Dot and Bar Stitch

Starting chain: Multiple of 12 sts + 8.
Special Abbreviations

Puff st = *yo, insert hook into next st, yo and draw a loop through; rep from * 4 times more inserting hook into same st as before (11 loops on hook), yo and draw through 10 loops, yo and draw through 2 remaining loops.

1dc/rf = work 1dc around stem of next st 2 rows below inserting hook round stem from right to left to draw up loops.

1st row (right side): Work 1sc into 2nd ch from hook, 1sc into each ch to end, turn.

2nd and every alt row: 1ch, work 1sc into each st to end, turn.

3rd row: 1ch, work 1sc into each of first 2sc, 1dc/rf, 1sc into next sc, 1dc/rf, *1sc into each of next 4sc, 1 puff st into next sc, 1sc into each of next 4sc, 1dc/rf, 1sc into next sc, 1dc/rf; rep from * to last 2sc, 1sc into each of last 2sc, turn.

5th row: 1ch, work 1sc into each of first 2sc, 1dc/rf, 1sc into next sc, 1dc/rf, *1sc into each of next 2sc, 1 puff st into next sc, 1sc into each of next 3sc, 1 puff st into next sc, 1sc into each of next 2sc, 1dc/rf, 1sc into next sc, 1dc/rf; rep from * to last 2sc, 1sc into each of last 2sc, turn.

7th row: As 3rd row.

9th row: 1ch, 1sc into each of first 2sc, 1dc/rf, 1sc into next sc, 1dc/rf, *1sc into each of next 9sc, 1dc/rf, 1sc into next sc, 1dc/rf; rep from * to last 2sc, 1sc into each of last 2sc, turn.

Rep 2nd to 9th rows.

Lattice Stitch I

Starting chain: Multiple of 12 sts + 11.

1st row (right side): Using A, work 1sc into 2nd ch from hook, 1sc into each ch to end, turn.

2nd row: Using A, 1ch, work 1sc into each sc to end, turn.

3rd row: Using B, 3ch (count as 1dc), skip first sc, 1dc into next sc, 1hdc into next sc, 1sc into next sc, *2ch, skip 2sc, 1sc into next sc, 1hdc into next sc, 1dc into each of next 2sc, 1tr into each of next 2sc, 1dc into each of next 2sc, 1hdc into next sc, 1sc into next sc; rep from * to last 6sc, 2ch, skip 2sc, 1sc into next sc, 1hdc into next sc, 1dc into each of last 2sc, turn.

4th row: Using B, 3ch, skip first dc, work 1dc into next dc, 1hdc into next hdc, 1sc into next sc, *2ch, 1sc into next sc, 1hdc into next hdc, 1dc into each of next 2dc, 1tr into each of next 2tr, 1dc into each of next 2dc, 1hdc into next hdc, 1sc into next sc; rep from * to last 6 sts, 2ch, 1sc into next sc, 1hdc into next hdc, 1dc into next dc, 1dc into 3rd of 3ch at beg of previous row, turn.

5th row: Using A, 1ch, work 1sc into each of first 4 sts, [inserting hook from front of work, work 1sc into each of 2 free sc in A 3 rows below], *1sc into each of next 10 sts on previous row, work 2sc 3 rows below as before; rep from * to last 4 sts, 1sc into each of next 3 sts, 1sc into 3rd of

3ch at beg of previous row, turn.

6th row: Using A, 1ch, work 1sc into each sc to end, turn.

7th row: Using B, 1ch, *work 1sc into first sc, 1hdc into next sc, 1dc into each of next 2sc, 1tr into each of next 2sc, 1dc into each of next 2sc, 1hdc into next sc, 1sc into next sc, 2ch, skip 2sc; rep from * to end omitting 2ch at end of last rep, turn.

8th row: Using B, 1ch, *work 1sc into next sc, 1hdc into next hdc, 1dc into each of next 2dc, 1tr into each of next 2tr, 1dc into each of next 2dc, 1hdc into next hdc, 1sc into next sc, 2ch; rep from * to end omitting 2ch at end of last rep, turn.

9th row: Using A, 1ch, *1sc into each of next 10 sts, inserting hook from front of work, work 1sc into each of 2 free sc in A 3 rows below; rep from * to end omitting 2sc at end of last rep, turn.

Rep 2nd to 9th rows.

Lattice Stitch II

Work as given for Lattice Stitch I **but** working 2 rows in A, 2 rows in B, 2 rows in A and 2 rows in C throughout.

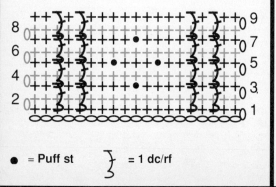

● = Puff st   } = 1 dc/rf

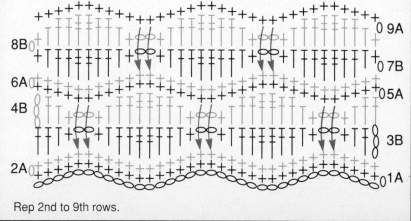

Rep 2nd to 9th rows.

Stitch Variations, Abbreviations and Symbols on pages 7 to 15

Patterns for Texture and Color

Tooth Stitch

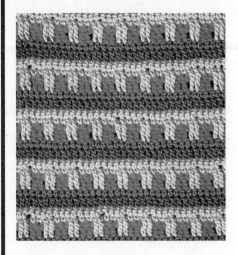

Starting chain: Multiple of 4 sts + 4.

1st row (right side): Using A, work 1dc into 4th ch from hook, 1dc into each ch to end, turn.

2nd row: Using A, 1ch, work 1sc into each dc to end working last sc into top of 3ch, turn.

3rd row: Using B, 3ch (count as 1dc), skip first sc, 1dc into next sc, *2ch, skip 2sc, 1dc into each of next 2sc; rep from * to end, turn.

4th row: Using B, 1ch, work 1sc into each of first 2dc, *2ch, 1sc into each of next 2dc; rep from * to end working last sc into 3rd of 3ch at beg of previous row, turn.

5th row: Using C, 1ch, 1sc into each of first 2sc, *1tr into each of the 2 skipped sc 3 rows below, 1sc into each of next 2sc; rep from * to end, turn.

6th row: Using C, 1ch, 1sc into each sc and each tr to end, turn.

7th row: Using A, 3ch, skip first sc, 1dc into each sc to end, turn.

8th row: Using A, 1ch, 1sc into each dc to end working last sc into 3rd of 3ch at beg of previous row, turn.

Rep 3rd to 8th rows.

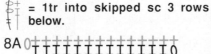

= 1tr into skipped sc 3 rows below.

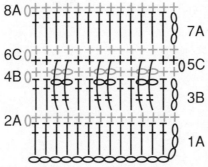

Crown

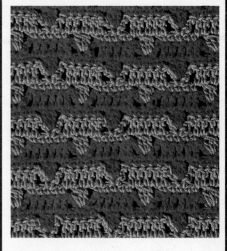

Starting chain: Multiple of 8 sts + 7.

Special Abbreviation

Bobble = work 3dc into next sc until last loop of each dc remains on hook, yo and through all 4 loops.

Note: Count each sc, ch sp and bobble as 1 st throughout.

1st row (wrong side): Using A, work 1dc into 4th ch from hook, 1dc into each of next 3ch, *3ch, skip 1ch, 1sc into next ch, 3ch, skip 1ch, 1dc into each of next 5ch; rep from * to end, turn.

2nd row: Using B, 1ch, work 1sc into each of first 5dc, *1ch, 1 bobble into next sc, 1ch, 1sc into each of next 5dc; rep from * to end placing last sc into top of 3ch, turn.

3rd row: Using B, 6ch (count as 1dc, 3ch), skip first 2sc, 1sc into next sc, 3ch, *skip 1sc, 1dc into each of next 5 sts (see note above), 3ch, skip 1sc, 1sc into next sc, 3ch; rep from * to last 2sc, skip 1sc, 1dc into last sc, turn.

4th row: Using A, 1ch, work 1sc into first dc, 1ch, 1 bobble into next sc, 1ch, *1sc into each of next 5dc, 1ch, 1 bobble into next sc, 1ch; rep from * to last dc, 1sc into 3rd of 6ch at beg of previous row, turn.

5th row: Using A, 3ch (count as 1dc), skip first sc, 1dc into each of next 4 sts, *3ch, skip 1sc, 1sc into next sc, 3ch, skip 1sc, 1dc into each of next 5 sts; rep from * to end, turn.

Rep 2nd to 5th rows.

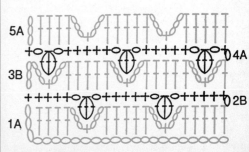

= Bobble

Mirror Stitch

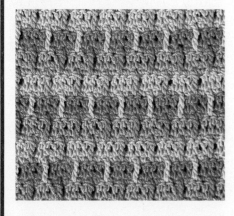

Starting chain: Multiple of 4 sts + 2.

1st row (right side): Using A, work 1sc into 2nd ch from hook, 1sc into next ch, *1ch, skip 1ch, 1sc into each of next 3ch; rep from * to end omitting 1sc at end of last rep, turn.

2nd row: Using A, 3ch (count as 1dc), skip first sc, work 1dc into next sc, *1ch, skip 1ch, 1dc into each of next 3sc; rep from * to end omitting 1dc at end of last rep, turn.

3rd row: Using B, 1ch, work 1sc into each of first 2dc, 1tr into first skipped starting ch, *1sc into next dc, 1ch, skip 1dc, 1sc into next dc, 1tr into next skipped starting ch; rep from * to last 2dc, 1sc into next dc, 1sc into 3rd of 3ch at beg of previous row, turn.

4th row: Using B, 3ch, skip first sc, work 1dc into each of next 3 sts, *1ch, skip 1ch, 1dc into each of next 3 sts; rep from * to last sc, 1dc into last sc, turn.

5th row: Using C, 1ch, work 1sc into each of first 2dc, *1ch, skip 1dc, 1sc into next dc, 1tr into next skipped dc 3 rows below, 1sc into next dc; rep from * to last 3dc, 1ch, skip 1dc, 1sc into next dc, 1sc into 3rd of 3ch at beg of previous row, turn.

6th row: Using C, 3ch, skip first sc, 1dc into next sc, *1ch, skip 1ch, 1dc into each of next 3 sts; rep from * to end omitting 1dc at end of last rep, turn.

7th row: Using A, 1ch, 1sc into each of first 2dc, 1tr into next skipped dc 3 rows below, *1sc into next dc, 1ch, skip 1dc, 1sc into next dc, 1tr into next skipped dc 3 rows below; rep from * to last 2dc, 1sc into each of last 2dc, turn.

8th row: As 4th row **but** using A instead of B.

Rep 5th to 8th rows continuing to work 2 rows each in colors B, C and A as set.

= Work tr into skipped st 3 rows below.

Patterns for Texture and Color

Slot Stitch

On 6th row work dc into ch **not** ch space.
Rep 2nd to 9th rows.

 = 1dtr into skipped sc 3 rows below.

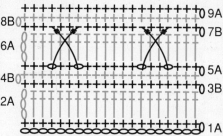

Starting chain: Multiple of 10 sts + 1.
Using A make required number of chain.

1st row (right side): Using A, work 1sc into 2nd ch from hook, 1sc into each ch to end, turn.

2nd row: Using A, 3ch (count as 1dc), skip first sc, work 1dc into each sc to end, turn.

3rd row: Using B, 1ch, work 1sc into each dc to end placing last sc into 3rd of 3ch at beg of previous row, turn.

4th row: Using B, 1ch, work 1sc into each sc to end, turn.

5th row: Using A, 1ch, work 1sc into each of first 3sc, *1ch, skip 1sc, 1sc into each of next 2sc, 1ch, skip 1sc, 1sc into each of next 6sc; rep from * to end omitting 3sc at end of last rep, turn.

6th row: Using A, 3ch (count as 1dc), skip first sc, 1dc into each sc and into each ch to end, turn.

7th row: Using B, 1ch, 1sc into each of first 3dc, *work 1dtr into 2nd skipped sc 3 rows below, skip 1dc, 1sc into each of next 2dc, 1dtr into first skipped sc 3 rows below (thus crossing 2dtr), skip 1dc, 1sc into each of next 6dc; rep from * to end omitting 3sc at end of last rep and placing last sc into 3rd of 3ch at beg of previous row, turn.

8th row: Using B, 1ch, work 1sc into each st to end, turn.

9th row: Using A, 1ch, work 1sc into each sc to end, turn.

Rep 2nd to 9th rows.

Half Moon Stitch

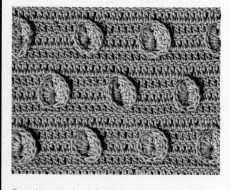

Starting chain: Multiple of 10 sts + 12.

Special Abbreviation

1 Circle = rotating work as required work 6dc **down** and around stem of next dc 1 row below, then work 6dc **up** and around stem of previous dc 1 row below.

1st row (right side): Work 1dc into 4th ch from hook, 1dc into each ch to end, turn.

2nd row: 3ch (count as 1dc), skip first dc, work 1dc into each dc to end working last dc into 3rd of 3ch at beg of previous row, turn.

3rd row: 3ch, skip first dc, work 1dc into each of next 4dc, *work 1 circle, working behind circle work 1dc into each of next 10dc; rep from * to end omitting 5dc at end of last rep and working last dc into 3rd of 3ch at beg of previous row, turn.

4th, 5th and 6th rows: 3ch, skip first dc, work 1dc into each dc to end working last dc into 3rd of 3ch at beg of previous row, turn.

7th row: 3ch, skip first dc, work 1dc into each of next 9dc, *work 1 circle, 1dc into each of next 10dc; rep from * to end working last dc into 3rd of 3ch, turn.

8th and 9th rows: 3ch, skip first dc, work 1dc into each dc to end working last dc into 3rd of 3ch, turn.

Rep 2nd to 9th rows.

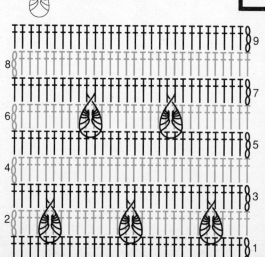 = 1 Circle

Herringbone Box

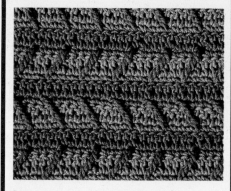

Starting chain: Multiple of 4 sts + 3.
Using A make the required number of chain.

1st row (right side): Using A, work 1sc into 2nd ch from hook, 1sc into each ch to end, turn.

2nd row: Using A, 3ch (count as 1dc), skip first sc, work 1dc into each sc to end, turn.

3rd row: Using B, 1ch, 1sc into each of first 4dc, 1ch, skip 1dc, *1sc into each of next 3dc, 1ch, skip 1dc; rep from * to last dc, 1sc into 3rd of 3ch at beg of previous row, turn.

4th row: Using B, 3ch, skip first sc, work 1dc into each ch and each sc to end, turn.

5th row: Using A, 1ch, 1sc into first dc, *1dtr into next skipped dc 3 rows below, skip 1dc on 4th row, 1sc into each of next 3dc; rep from * to last dc, 1sc into 3rd of 3ch at beg of previous row.

6th row: Using A, 3ch, skip first sc, work 1dc into each sc and each dtr to end, turn.

7th row: Using B, 1ch, work 1sc into first dc, *1ch, skip 1dc, 1sc into each of next 3dc; rep from * to last dc, 1sc into 3rd of 3ch, turn.

8th row: Using B, 3ch, skip first sc, 1dc into each sc and each ch to end, turn.

9th row: Using A, 1ch, 1sc into each of first 4dc, work 1dtr into first skipped dc 3 rows below, skip next dc, *1sc into each of next 3dc, 1dtr into next skipped dc 3 rows below, skip next dc; rep from * to last dc, 1sc into 3rd of 3ch, turn.

10th row: Using A, 3ch, skip first sc, work 1dc into each dtr and each sc to end, turn.

Rep 3rd to 10th rows.

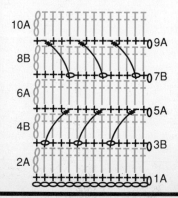

or = 1dtr into skipped dc 3 rows below.

On 4th and 8th rows work dc into ch, **not** ch space.

Stitch Variations, Abbreviations and Symbols on pages 7 to 15

Patterns for Texture and Color

Compass Point

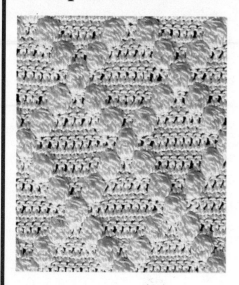

Starting chain: Multiple of 12 sts + 6.

Special Abbreviation

Bobble = working in front of work, work 5tr into ch sp 2 rows below until 1 loop of each tr remains on hook, yo and through all 6 loops.

1st row (right side): Work 1sc into 2nd ch from hook, 1sc into next ch, 1ch, skip 1ch, *1sc into each of next 11ch, 1ch, skip 1ch; rep from * to last 2ch, 1sc into each of last 2ch, turn.

2nd row: 3ch (count as 1dc), skip first sc, work 1dc into next sc, 1ch, skip 1ch sp, *1dc into each of next 11 sts, 1ch, skip 1ch sp; rep from * to last 2sc, 1dc into each of last 2sc, turn.

3rd row: 1ch, work 1sc into each of first 2dc, 1 bobble into ch sp 2 rows below, *1sc into next dc, 1ch, skip 1dc, 1sc into each of next 7dc, 1ch, skip 1dc, 1sc into next dc, 1 bobble into next ch sp 2 rows below; rep from * to last 2dc, 1sc into next dc, 1sc into 3rd of 3ch at beg of previous row, turn.

4th row: 3ch, skip first sc, 1dc into each of next 3 sts, *1ch, skip 1ch sp, 1dc into each of next 7 sts, 1ch, skip 1ch sp, 1dc into each of next 3 sts; rep from * to last sc, 1dc into last sc, turn.

5th row: 1ch, work 1sc into each of first 4dc, *1 bobble into ch sp 2 rows below, 1sc into next dc, 1ch, skip 1dc, 1sc into each of next 3dc, 1ch, skip 1dc, 1sc into next dc, 1 bobble into ch sp 2 rows below, 1sc into each of next 3dc; rep from * to last st, 1sc into 3rd of 3ch at beg of previous row, turn.

6th row: 3ch, skip first sc, work 1dc into each of next 5 sts, *1ch, skip 1ch sp, 1dc into each of next 3 sts, 1ch, skip 1ch sp, 1dc into each of next 7 sts; rep from * to end omitting 1dc at end of last rep, turn.

7th row: 1ch, work 1sc into each of first 6dc, *1 bobble into ch sp 2 rows below, 1sc into next dc, 1ch, skip 1dc, 1sc into next dc, 1 bobble into ch sp 2 rows below, 1sc into each of next 7dc; rep from * to end omitting 1sc at end of last rep, turn.

8th row: 3ch, skip first sc, work 1dc into each of next 7 sts, 1ch, skip 1ch sp, *1dc into each of next 11 sts, 1ch, skip 1ch sp; rep from * to last 8 sts, 1dc into each of last 8 sts, turn.

9th row: 1ch, work 1sc into each of first 6dc, *1ch, skip 1dc, 1sc into next dc, 1 bobble into ch sp 2 rows below, 1sc into next dc, 1ch, skip 1dc, 1sc into each of next 7dc; rep from * to end omitting 1sc at end of last rep, turn.

10th row: As 6th row.

11th row: 1ch, work 1sc into each of first 4dc, *1ch, skip 1dc, 1sc into next dc, 1 bobble into ch sp 2 rows below, 1sc into each of next 3dc, 1 bobble into ch sp 2 rows below, 1sc into next dc, 1ch, skip 1dc, 1sc into each of next 3dc; rep from * to last dc, 1sc into 3rd of 3ch, turn.

12th row: As 4th row.

13th row: 1ch, 1sc into each of first 2dc, 1ch, skip 1dc, 1sc into next dc, *1 bobble into ch sp 2 rows below, 1sc into each of next 7dc, 1 bobble into ch sp 2 rows below, 1sc into next dc, 1ch, skip 1dc, 1sc into next dc; rep from * to last dc, 1sc into 3rd of 3ch, turn.

Rep 2nd to 13th rows.

 = Bobble

Cross Slot Stitch

Starting chain: Multiple of 10 sts + 1.
Using A make required number of chain.

1st row (wrong side): Using A, work 1sc into 2nd ch from hook, 1sc into each ch to end, turn.

2nd row: Using B, 1ch, work 1sc into each of first 8sc, *1ch, skip 1sc, 1sc into each of next 2sc, 1ch, skip 1sc, 1sc into each of next 6sc; rep from * to last 2sc, 1sc into each sc to end, turn.

3rd row: Using B, 3ch (count as 1dc), skip first sc, work 1dc into each sc and into each ch to end, turn.

4th row: Using A, 1ch, work 1sc into each of first 8dc *work 1dtr into 2nd skipped sc 3 rows below, skip 1dc, 1sc into each of next 2dc, 1dtr into first skipped sc 3 rows below (thus crossing 2dtr), skip 1dc, 1sc into each of next 6dc; rep from * to last 2dc, 1sc into next dc, 1sc into 3rd of 3ch at beg of previous row, turn.

5th row: Using A, 1ch, work 1sc into each st to end, turn.

6th row: Using B, 1ch, work 1sc into each of first 3sc, *1ch, skip 1sc, 1sc into each of next 2sc, 1ch, skip 1sc, 1sc into each of next 6sc; rep from * to end omitting 3sc at end of last rep, turn.

7th row: Using B, 3ch, skip first sc, 1dc into each sc and into each ch to end, turn.

8th row: Using A, 1ch, 1sc into each of first 3dc, *work 1dtr into 2nd skipped sc 3 rows below, skip 1dc, 1sc into each of next 2dc, 1dtr into first skipped sc 3 rows below (thus crossing 2dtr), skip 1dc, 1sc into each of next 6dc; rep from * to end omitting 3sc at end of last rep and placing last sc into 3rd of 3ch at beg of previous row, turn.

9th row: Using A, 1ch, work 1sc into each st to end, turn.

Rep 2nd to 9th rows.

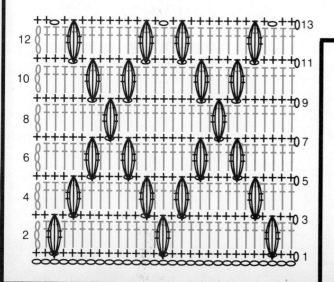

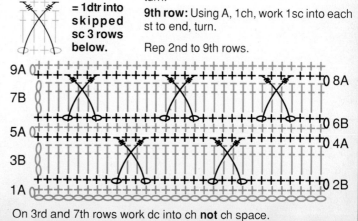

= 1dtr into skipped sc 3 rows below.

On 3rd and 7th rows work dc into ch **not** ch space.

Patterns for Texture and Color

Oval Cluster Stitch

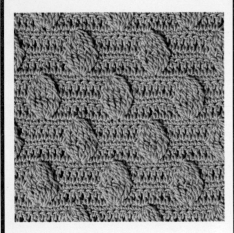

Starting chain: Multiple of 10 sts + 10.

Special Abbreviations

Lower Cluster = work 5tr into next skipped sc 2 rows below.

Upper Cluster = *[yo] twice then insert hook from right to left round stem of next tr 2 rows below, work 1tr in usual way until last loop of tr remains on hook; rep from * 4 times more, yo and through all 6 loops.

Note: Count each ch sp as 1 st throughout.

1st row (right side): Work 1sc into 2nd ch from hook, 1sc into each ch to end, turn.

2nd row: 3ch (count as 1dc), skip first sc, work 1dc into each of next 3sc, *1ch, skip 1sc, 1dc into each of next 9 sts; rep from * to end omitting 5dc at end of last rep, turn.

3rd row: 1ch, work 1sc into each of first 2dc, *work lower cluster, **skip 5 sts of previous row**, 1sc into each of next 5dc; rep from * to end omitting 3sc at end of last rep and placing last sc into 3rd of 3ch at beg of previous row, turn.

4th row: 3ch, skip first sc, work 1dc into each st to end, turn.

5th row: 1ch, work 1sc into each of first 4dc, *work upper cluster over next 5tr 2 rows below, skip next dc on previous row, 1sc into each of next 9dc; rep from * to end omitting 5sc at end of last rep and placing last sc into 3rd of 3ch at beg of previous row, turn.

6th row: 3ch, skip first sc, work 1dc into each of next 8 sts, *1ch, skip 1sc, 1dc into each of next 9 sts; rep from * to end.

7th row: 1ch, work 1sc into each of first 7dc, *work lower cluster, **skip 5 sts of previous row**, 1sc into each of next 5dc; rep from * to last 2dc,1sc into each of last 2dc, working last sc into 3rd of 3ch at beg of previous row, turn.

8th row: 3ch, skip first sc, work 1dc into each st to end, turn.

9th row: 1ch, work 1sc into each of first 9dc, *work upper cluster over next 5tr 2 rows below, skip next dc on previous row, 1sc into each of next 9dc; rep from * to end placing last sc into 3rd of 3ch at beg of previous row, turn.

Rep 2nd to 9th rows.

 = Lower cluster

= Upper cluster

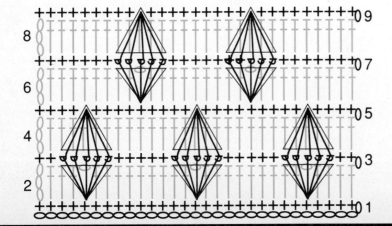

Quiver Stitch I

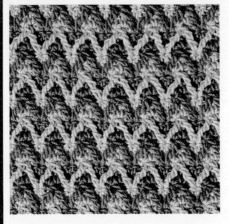

Starting chain: Multiple of 4 sts + 4.

Special Abbreviation

Tr2tog 3 rows below = work 1tr into same st as last tr until last loop of tr remains on hook, skip 3 sts, work 1tr into next skipped st 3 rows below until last loop of tr remains on hook, yo and through all 3 loops. **Note:** Sts either side of tr2tog must be worked behind tr2tog.

Using A make required number of chain.

1st row (right side): Using A, work 1sc into 2nd ch from hook, 1sc into each of next 2ch, *1ch, skip 1ch, 1sc into each of next 3ch; rep from * to end, turn.

2nd row: Using A, 3ch (count as 1dc), skip first sc, work 1dc into each st to end (working into actual st of each ch, not into ch sp), turn.

3rd row: Using B, 1ch, 1sc into first dc, 1tr into first skipped starting ch, skip 1dc on 2nd row, 1sc into next dc, 1ch, skip 1dc, 1sc into next dc, *tr2tog 3 rows below (into skipped starting ch), skip 1dc on 2nd row, 1sc into next dc, 1ch, skip 1dc, 1sc into next dc; rep from * to last 2dc, 1tr into same ch as 2nd leg of last tr2tog, skip 1dc, 1sc into 3rd of 3ch at beg of previous row, turn.

4th row: Using B, 3ch, skip first sc, work 1dc into each st to end, turn.

5th row: Using A, 1ch, 1sc into first dc, 1tr into next skipped dc 3 rows below, skip 1dc on previous row, 1sc into next dc, 1ch, skip 1dc, 1sc into next dc, *tr2tog 3 rows below, skip 1dc on previous row, 1sc into next dc, 1ch, skip 1dc, 1sc into next dc; rep from * to last 2dc, 1tr into same dc as 2nd leg of last tr2tog, skip 1dc, 1sc into 3rd of 3ch at beg of previous row, turn.

6th row: As 4th row **but** using A instead of B.

7th row: As 5th row **but** using B instead of A.

Rep 4th to 7th rows.

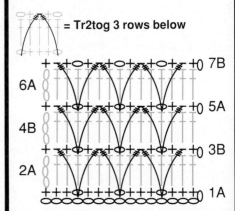

= Tr2tog 3 rows below

Work dc into actual st of ch on wrong side rows, not into ch sp.

Quiver Stitch II

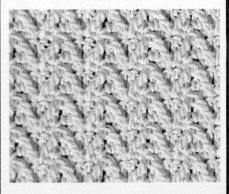

Work as given for Quiver Stitch I **but** using one color throughout.

Stitch Variations, Abbreviations and Symbols on pages 7 to 15

Patterns for Texture and Color

Key Tab Stitch

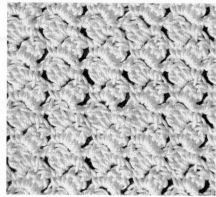

Starting chain: Multiple of 4 sts + 6.

Special Abbreviation
Cluster = work 3dc into next st until 1 loop of each remains on hook, yo and through all 4 loops on hook.

1st row (right side): Work 1 cluster into 5th ch from hook (1dc, 1ch formed at beg of row), 1ch, skip 2ch, 1sc into next ch, *3ch, 1 cluster into next ch, 1ch, skip 2ch, 1sc into next ch; rep from * to last 2ch, 2ch, 1dc into last ch, turn.

2nd row: 4ch (count as 1dc, 1ch), 1 cluster into first 2ch sp, 1ch, *1sc into next 3ch sp, 3ch, 1 cluster into same sp as last sc, 1ch; rep from * to last ch sp, 1sc into last ch sp, 2ch, 1dc into 3rd of 4ch at beg of previous row, turn.

Rep 2nd row.

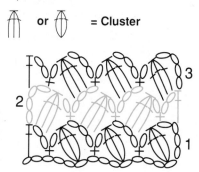

| | or | | = Cluster |

Diagram only: Rep 2nd and 3rd rows.

Connected Spiral

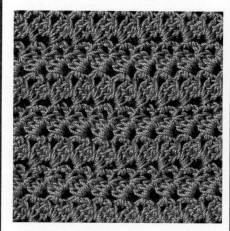

Starting chain: Multiple of 3 sts + 5.

Special Abbreviation
Cluster4 = work 3dc over stem of dc just worked but leaving last loop of each dc on hook, then work 4th dc as indicated leaving last loop as before (5 loops on hook), yo and through all 5 loops.

1st row (right side): Work 1dc into 6th ch from hook, *3ch, skip 2ch, work cluster4 placing 4th dc into next ch; rep from * to last 2ch, 3ch, work cluster4 placing 4th dc in last ch, turn.

2nd row: 3ch (count as 1dc), 1dc into next 3ch sp, *3ch, work cluster4 placing 4th dc into next 3ch sp; rep from * to end placing final dc into top of ch at beg of previous row, turn.

Rep 2nd row.

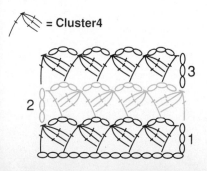

= Cluster4

Diagram only: Rep 2nd and 3rd rows.

Global Connection

Starting chain: Multiple of 8 sts + 2.

Special Abbreviation
Popcorn = work 4dc into next st, drop loop from hook, insert hook from the front into top of first of these dc, pick up dropped loop and draw through dc, 1ch to secure popcorn.

1st row (right side): Work 1sc into 2nd ch from hook, *1ch, skip 3ch, 1dc into next ch, 1ch, into same ch as last dc work [1dc, 1ch, 1dc], 1ch, skip 3ch, 1sc into next ch; rep from * to end, turn.

2nd row: 6ch (count as 1dc, 3ch), skip 1dc, 1sc into next dc, *3ch, 1 popcorn into next sc, 3ch, skip 1dc, 1sc into next dc; rep from * to last sc, 3ch, 1dc into last sc, turn.

Broadway

Starting chain: Multiple of 8 sts + 2.

Special Abbreviations
Cr3R (Cross 3 Right) = skip 2sc, work 1tr into next sc, working behind last tr work 1dc into each of 2 skipped sc.
Cr3L (Cross 3 Left) = skip 1sc, work 1dc into each of next 2sc, working in front of last 2dc work 1tr into skipped sc.

1st row (wrong side): Work 1sc into 2nd ch from hook, 1sc into each ch to end, turn.

2nd row: 3ch (count as 1dc), skip first sc, *Cr3R, 1dc into next sc, Cr3L, 1dc into next sc; rep from * to end, turn.

3rd row: 1ch, work 1sc into each st to end placing last sc into 3rd of 3ch at beg of previous row, turn.

Rep 2nd and 3rd rows.

| | = Cr3R | | = Cr3L |

3rd row: 1ch, 1sc into first dc, *1ch, 1dc into next sc, 1ch, into same st as last dc work [1dc, 1ch, 1dc], 1ch, 1sc into top of next popcorn; rep from * to end, placing last sc into 3rd of 6ch at beg of previous row, turn.

Rep 2nd and 3rd rows.

= Popcorn

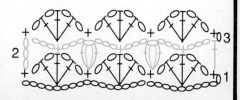

Patterns for Texture and Color

Triangle Stitch

Starting chain: Multiple of 20 sts + 25.

Special Abbreviations

Dc2tog = work 2dc into next st until 1 loop of each remains on hook, yo and through all 3 loops on hook.

Bobble = work 3dc into next st until 1 loop of each remains on hook, yo and through all 4 loops on hook.

1st row (right side): Work 1sc into 7th ch from hook, 5ch, skip 3ch, 1sc into next ch, 1ch, skip 3ch, into next ch work [1 bobble, 1ch] 3 times, *skip 3ch, 1sc into next ch, [5ch, skip 3ch, 1sc into next ch] 3 times, 1ch, skip 3ch, into next ch work [1 bobble, 1ch] 3 times; rep from * to last 10ch, skip 3ch, 1sc into next ch, 5ch, skip 3ch, 1sc into next ch, 2ch, 1dc into last ch, turn.

2nd row: 1ch, 1sc into first dc, 5ch, 1sc into first 5ch arch, 1ch, [1 bobble into next ch sp, 1ch] 4 times, *1sc into next 5ch arch, [5ch, 1sc into next 5ch arch] twice, 1ch, [1 bobble into next ch sp, 1ch] 4 times; rep from * to last 2 arches, 1sc into next 5ch arch, 5ch, skip 2ch, 1sc into next ch, turn.

3rd row: 5ch (count as 1dc, 2ch), 1sc into first 5ch arch, 1ch, [1 bobble into next ch sp, 1ch] 5 times, *1sc into next 5ch arch, 5ch, 1sc into next 5ch arch, 1ch, [1 bobble into next ch sp, 1ch] 5 times; rep from * to last arch, 1sc into last arch, 2ch, 1dc into last sc, turn.

4th row: 1ch, 1sc into first dc, skip 2ch sp, *2ch, [1 bobble into next ch sp, 2ch] 6 times, 1sc into next 5ch arch; rep from * to end placing last sc into 3rd of 5ch at beg of previous row, turn.

5th row: 5ch (count as 1dc, 2ch), skip first 2ch sp, 1sc into next 2ch sp, [5ch, 1sc into next 2ch sp] 4 times, *1ch, into next sc work [1dc, 1ch] twice, skip next 2ch sp, 1sc into next 2ch sp, [5ch, 1sc into next 2ch sp] 4 times; rep from * to last 2ch sp, 2ch, 1dc into last sc, turn.

6th row: 3ch (count as 1dc), into first dc work [1dc, 1ch, 1 bobble], 1ch, 1sc into next 5ch arch, [5ch, 1sc into next 5ch arch] 3 times, *1ch, skip 1ch sp, into next ch sp work [1 bobble, 1ch] 3 times, 1sc into next 5ch arch, [5ch, 1sc into next 5ch arch] 3 times; rep from * to last sp, 1ch, into 3rd of 5ch at beg of previous row work [1 bobble, 1ch, dc2tog], turn.

7th row: 3ch (count as 1dc), [1 bobble into next ch sp, 1ch] twice, 1sc into first 5ch arch, [5ch, 1sc into next 5ch arch] twice, *1ch, [1 bobble into next ch sp, 1ch] 4 times, 1sc into next 5ch arch, [5ch, 1sc into next 5ch arch] twice; rep from * to last bobble, [1ch, 1 bobble into next ch sp] twice, 1dc into 3rd of 3ch at beg of previous row, turn.

8th row: 3ch, 1dc into first dc, 1ch, [1 bobble into next ch sp, 1ch] twice, 1sc into next 5ch arch, 5ch, 1sc into next 5ch arch, *1ch, [1 bobble into next ch sp, 1ch] 5 times, 1sc into next 5ch arch, 5ch, 1sc into next 5ch arch; rep from * to last 2 bobbles, 1ch, [1 bobble into next ch sp, 1ch] twice, dc2tog into 3rd of 3ch at beg of previous row, turn.

9th row: 4ch (count as 1dc, 1ch), [1 bobble into next ch sp, 2ch] 3 times, 1sc into next 5ch arch, *2ch, [1 bobble into next ch sp, 2ch] 6 times, 1sc into next 5ch arch; rep from * to last 2 bobbles, [2ch, 1 bobble into next ch sp] 3 times, 1ch, 1dc into 3rd of 3ch at beg of previous row, turn.

10th row: 1ch, 1sc into first dc, 5ch, skip first ch sp, 1sc into next 2ch sp, 5ch, 1sc into next 2ch sp, 1ch, into next sc work [1dc, 1ch] twice, *skip next 2ch sp, 1sc into next 2ch sp, [5ch, 1sc into next 2ch sp] 4 times, 1ch, into next sc work [1dc, 1ch] twice; rep from * to last 3 bobbles, skip next 2ch sp, [1sc into next 2ch sp, 5ch] twice, 1sc into 3rd of 4ch at beg of previous row, turn.

11th row: 5ch (count as 1dc, 2ch), 1sc into first 5ch arch, 5ch, 1sc into next 5ch arch, 1ch, skip 1ch sp, into next ch sp work [1 bobble, 1ch] 3 times, *1sc into next 5ch arch, [5ch, 1sc into next 5ch arch] 3 times, 1ch, skip 1ch sp, into next ch sp work [1 bobble, 1ch] 3 times; rep from * to last 2 arches, 1sc into next 5ch arch, 5ch, 1sc into next 5ch arch, 2ch, 1dc into last sc, turn.

Rep 2nd to 11th rows.

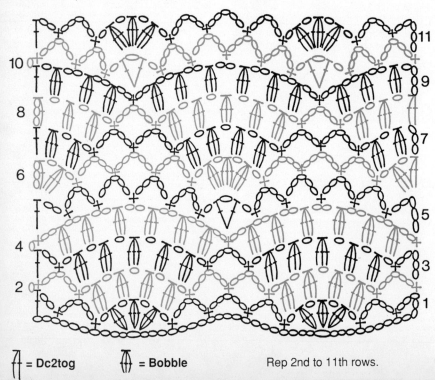

⫙ = Dc2tog   ⫙ = Bobble   Rep 2nd to 11th rows.

Spatter Pattern

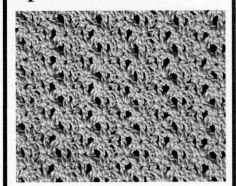

Starting chain: Multiple of 6 sts + 2.

1st row (right side): Work 1sc into 2nd ch from hook, *skip 2ch, 1dc into next ch, 2ch, into same ch as last dc work [1dc, 2ch, 1dc], skip 2ch, 1sc into next ch; rep from * to end, turn.

2nd row: 5ch (count as 1dc, 2ch), 1dc into first sc, skip 1dc, 1sc into next dc, *1dc into next sc, 2ch, into same st as last dc work [1dc, 2ch, 1dc], skip 1dc, 1sc into next dc; rep from * to last sc, into last sc work [1dc, 2ch, 1dc], turn.

3rd row: 1ch, 1sc into first dc, *1dc into next sc, 2ch, into same st as last dc work [1dc, 2ch, 1dc], skip 1dc, 1sc into next dc; rep from * to end placing last sc into 3rd of 5ch at beg of previous row, turn.

Rep 2nd and 3rd rows.

Stitch Variations, Abbreviations and Symbols on pages 7 to 15

Patterns for Texture and Color

Wheatsheaf

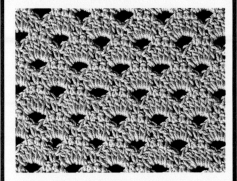

Starting chain: Multiple of 5 sts + 2.

1st row (wrong side): Work 1sc into 2nd ch from hook, 1sc into next ch, *3ch, skip 2ch, 1sc into each of next 3ch; rep from * to end omitting 1sc at end of last rep, turn.

2nd row: 1ch, 1sc into first sc, *5dc into next 3ch arch, skip 1sc, 1sc into next sc; rep from * to end, turn.

3rd row: 3ch (count as 1hdc, 1ch), skip first 2 sts, 1sc into each of next 3dc, *3ch, skip next 3 sts, 1sc into each of next 3dc; rep from * to last 2 sts, 1ch, 1hdc into last sc, turn.

4th row: 3ch (count as 1dc), 2dc into first ch sp, skip 1sc, 1sc into next sc, *5dc into next 3ch arch, skip 1sc, 1sc into next sc; rep from * to last sp, 2dc into last sp, 1dc into 2nd of 3ch at beg of previous row, turn.

5th row: 1ch, 1sc into each of first 2dc, *3ch, skip 3 sts, 1sc into each of next 3dc; rep from * to end omitting 1sc at end of last rep and placing last sc into 3rd of 3ch at beg of previous row, turn.

Rep 2nd to 5th rows.

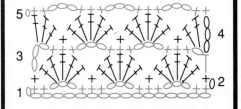

Petal Pattern I

Starting chain: Multiple of 11 sts + 3.

Special Abbreviation

Dc2tog = work 2dc into next st until 1 loop of each remains on hook, yo and through all 3 loops on hook.

1st row (right side): Work 1sc into 2nd ch from hook, 1ch, skip 1ch, 1sc into next ch, [3ch, skip 3ch, 1sc into next ch] twice, *2ch, skip 2ch, 1sc into next ch, [3ch, skip 3ch, 1sc into next ch] twice; rep from * to last 2ch, 1ch, skip 1ch, 1sc into last ch, turn.

2nd row: 3ch (count as 1dc), into first ch sp work [dc2tog, 2ch, dc2tog], 1ch, skip 1sc, 1sc into next sc, *1ch, skip 3ch sp, dc2tog into next 2ch sp, into same sp as last dc2tog work [2ch, dc2tog] 3 times, 1ch, skip 3ch sp, 1sc into next sc; rep from * to last 2 sps, 1ch, skip 3ch sp, into last ch sp work [dc2tog, 2ch, dc2tog], 1dc into last sc, turn.

3rd row: 1ch, 1sc into first dc, *3ch, work 1dc2tog into top of each of next 4dc2tog, 3ch, 1sc into next 2ch sp; rep from * to end placing last sc into 3rd of 3ch at beg of previous row, turn.

4th row: 1ch, 1sc into first sc, *3ch, 1sc into top of next dc2tog, 2ch, skip 2dc2tog, 1sc into top of next dc2tog, 3ch, 1sc into next sc; rep from * to end, turn.

5th row: 1ch, work 1sc into first sc, *1ch, skip 3ch sp, dc2tog into next 2ch sp, into same sp as last dc2tog work [2ch, dc2tog]

3 times, 1ch, skip 3ch sp, 1sc into next sc; rep from * to end, turn.

6th row: 3ch, work 1dc2tog into top of each of next 2dc2tog, 3ch, 1sc into next 2ch sp, 3ch, *dc2tog into top of each 4dc2tog, 3ch, 1sc into next 2ch sp, 3ch; rep from * to last 2dc2tog, work 1dc2tog into each of last 2dc2tog, 1dc into last sc, turn.

7th row: 1ch, 1sc into first dc, 1ch, skip 1dc2tog, 1sc into next dc2tog, 3ch, 1sc into next sc, 3ch, *1sc into top of next dc2tog, 2ch, skip 2dc2tog, 1sc into top of next dc2tog, 3ch, 1sc into next sc, 3ch; rep from * to last 2dc2tog, 1sc into next dc2tog, 1ch, skip 1dc2tog, 1sc into 3rd of 3ch at beg of previous row, turn.

Rep 2nd to 7th rows.

 = Dc2tog

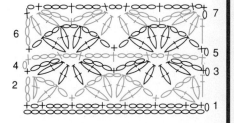

Petal Pattern II

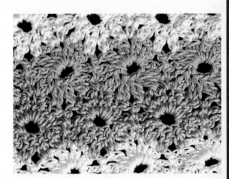

Work as Petal Pattern I **but** working 1st and 2nd rows in A, then work 3 rows each in B, C and A throughout.

Petal Pattern III

Work as Petal Pattern I **but** working 1st and 2nd rows in A then 3 rows each in B and A throughout. **Note:** Cut yarn after each color change.

Cabbage Patch

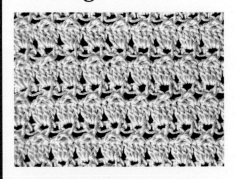

Starting chain: Multiple of 4 sts + 7.

Special Abbreviation

Cross2dc = skip 3dc, work 1dc into next dc, 2ch, working behind last dc work 1dc into the first of the skipped dc.

1st row (right side): Work 4dc into 5th ch from hook, *skip 3ch, 4dc into next ch; rep from * to last 2ch, 1dc into last ch, turn.

2nd row: 3ch (count as 1dc), skip first dc, *cross2dc; rep from * to end, 1dc into top of 3ch at beg of previous row, turn.

3rd row: 3ch, work 4dc into each 2ch sp to end, 1dc into 3rd of 3ch at beg of previous row, turn.

Rep 2nd and 3rd rows.

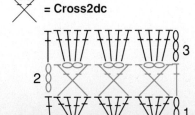 = Cross2dc

51

All-over Patterns

Triple Curve Stitch

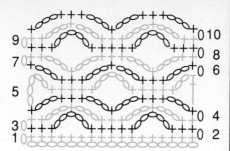

Starting chain: Multiple of 8 sts + 2.

1st row (wrong side): Work 1sc into 2nd ch from hook, 1sc into each ch to end, turn.

2nd row: 1ch, 1sc into each of first 3sc, *5ch, skip 3sc, 1sc into each of next 5sc; rep from * to end omitting 2sc at end of last rep, turn,

3rd row: 1ch, 1sc into each of first 2sc, *3ch, 1sc into next 5ch arch, 3ch, skip 1sc, 1sc into each of next 3sc; rep from * to end omitting 1sc at end of last rep, turn.

4th row: 1ch, 1sc into first sc, *3ch, 1sc into next 3ch arch, 1sc into next sc, 1sc into next 3ch arch, 3ch, skip 1sc, 1sc into next sc; rep from * to end, turn.

5th row: 5ch (count as 1dc, 2ch), 1sc into next 3ch arch, 1sc into each of next 3sc, 1sc into next 3ch arch, *5ch, 1sc into next 3ch arch, 1sc into each of next 3sc, 1sc into next 3ch arch; rep from * to last sc, 2ch, 1dc into last sc, turn.

6th row: 1ch, 1sc into first dc, 3ch, skip 1sc, 1sc into each of next 3sc, *3ch, 1sc into next 5ch arch, 3ch, skip 1sc, 1sc into each of next 3sc; rep from * to last 2ch arch, 3ch, 1sc into 3rd of 5ch at beg of previous row, turn.

7th row: 1ch, 1sc into first sc, 1sc into first 3ch arch, 3ch, skip 1sc, 1sc into next sc, *3ch, 1sc into next 3ch arch, 1sc into next sc, 1sc into next 3ch arch, 3ch, skip 1sc, 1sc into next sc; rep from * to last 3ch arch, 3ch, 1sc into 3ch arch, 1sc into last sc, turn.

8th row: 1ch, 1sc into each of first 2sc, *1sc into next 3ch arch, 5ch, 1sc into next 3ch arch, 1sc into each of next 3sc; rep from * to end omitting 1sc at end of last rep, turn.

Rep 3rd to 8th rows.

Theatre Box

Starting chain: Multiple of 6 sts + 4.

Special Abbreviation

Puff st = [yo, insert hook into next st, yo and draw a loop through] 3 times into same st, yo and draw through 7 loops on hook, work 1 firm ch to close puff st.

1st row (right side): Work 1sc into 2nd ch from hook, 1sc into each ch to end, turn.

2nd row: 3ch (count as 1dc), skip first sc, 1dc into each sc to end, turn.

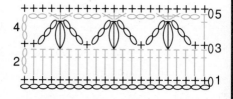

⬮ = Puff st

3rd row: 1ch, 1sc into each of first 2dc, *3ch, skip 2dc, 1 puff st into next dc, 3ch, skip 2dc, 1sc into next dc; rep from * to last dc, 1sc into 3rd of 3ch at beg of previous row, turn.

4th row: 5ch (count as 1dc, 2ch), work 3sc into closing ch of next puff st, *3ch, 3sc into closing ch of next puff st; rep from * to last 2sc, 2ch, 1dc into last sc, turn.

5th row: 1ch, 1sc into first dc, 2sc into first 2ch sp, *1sc into each of next 3sc, 3sc into next 3ch sp; rep from * to end working last sc into 3rd of 5ch at beg of previous row, turn.

Rep 2nd to 5th rows.

Jigsaw Pattern

Starting chain: Multiple of 10 sts + 2.

Special Abbreviations

Bobble = work 4dc into next st until 1 loop of each remains on hook, yo and through all 5 loops on hook.

Dc2tog = work 2dc into next st until 1 loop of each remains on hook, yo and through all 3 loops on hook.

1st row (right side): Work 1sc into 2nd ch from hook, 1sc into each of next 2ch, *3ch, skip 2ch, 1 bobble into next ch, 3ch, skip 2ch, 1sc into each of next 5ch; rep from * to end omitting 2sc at end of last rep, turn.

2nd row: 1ch, 1sc into each of first 2sc, *3ch, 1sc into next 3ch sp, 1sc into top of next bobble, 1sc into next 3ch sp, 3ch, skip 1sc, 1sc into each of next 3sc; rep from * to end omitting 1sc at end of last rep, turn.

3rd row: 3ch (count as 1dc), 1dc into first sc (half bobble made at beg of row), *3ch, 1sc into next 3ch sp, 1sc into each of next 3sc, 1sc into next 3ch sp, 3ch, skip 1sc, 1 bobble into next sc; rep from * to end but working half bobble of dc2tog at end of last rep, turn.

4th row: 1ch, 1sc into top of half bobble, 1sc into first 3ch sp, 3ch, skip 1sc, 1sc into each of next 3sc, *3ch, 1sc into next 3ch sp, 1sc into top of next bobble, 1sc into next 3ch sp, 3ch, skip 1sc, 1sc into each of next 3sc; rep from * to last 3ch sp, 3ch, 1sc into last 3ch sp, 1sc into 3rd of 3ch at beg of previous row, turn.

5th row: 1ch, 1sc into each of first 2sc, *1sc into next 3ch sp, 3ch, skip 1sc, 1 bobble into next sc, 3ch, 1sc into next 3ch sp, 1sc into each of next 3sc; rep from * to end omitting 1sc at end of last rep, turn.

Rep 2nd to 5th rows.

⬮ = Bobble ⬮ = Dc2tog

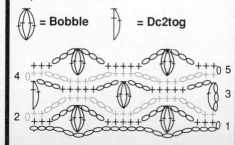

Angel Stitch

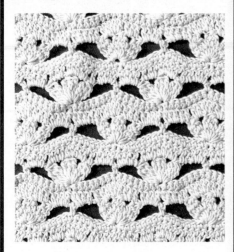

Starting chain: Multiple of 16 sts + 3.

Special Abbreviations

Cluster = work 1dc into same arch as last 3dc until 2 loops remain on hook, skip 1sc, work 1dc into next arch until 3 loops remain on hook, yo and through all 3 loops on hook.

Bobble = work 3tr into next sc until 1 loop of each remains on hook, yo and through all 4 loops on hook.

1st row (right side): Work 1dc into 4th ch from hook, 1dc into each of 6ch, work 3dc into next ch, 1dc into each of next 6ch, *work 1dc into next ch until 2 loops remain on hook, skip 1ch, 1dc into next ch until 3 loops remain on hook, yo and through all 3 loops on hook, work 1dc into each of next 6ch, 3dc into next ch, 1dc into each of next 6ch; rep from * to last 2 ch, work 1dc into next ch until 2 loops remain on hook, 1dc into last ch until 3 loops remain on hook, yo and through all 3 loops (cluster made at end of row), turn.

2nd row: 1ch, work 1sc into each st to last dc, skip last dc, 1sc into top of 3ch, turn.

3rd row: 4ch, work 1tr into first sc (half bobble made at beg of row), 2ch, 1 bobble into same sc as half bobble, 4ch, skip 7sc, 1sc into next sc, *4ch, skip 7sc, work 1 bobble into next sc, into same sc as last bobble work [2ch, 1 bobble] twice, 4ch, skip 7sc, 1sc into next sc; rep from * to last 8sc, 4ch, work 1 bobble into last sc, 2ch, work 2tr into same sc as last bobble until 1 loop of each remains on hook, yo and through all 3 loops on hook (half bobble made at end of row), turn.

Mosaic

4th row: 3ch (count as 1dc), 1dc into top of first half bobble, work 2dc into 2ch sp, 1dc into next bobble, 3dc into next 4ch arch, 1 cluster, 3dc into same arch as 2nd leg of last cluster, *1dc into top of next bobble, 2dc into 2ch sp, 3dc into top of next bobble, 2dc into next 2ch sp, 1dc into top of next bobble, 3dc into next 4ch arch, 1 cluster, 3dc into same arch as 2nd leg of last cluster; rep from * to last bobble, 1dc into last bobble, 2dc into next 2ch sp, 2dc into top of half bobble, turn.

5th row: 1ch, 1sc into each st to end, placing last sc into 3rd of 3ch at beg of previous row, turn.

6th row: 1ch, 1sc into first sc, *4ch, skip 7sc, 1 bobble into next sc, into same sc as last bobble work [2ch, 1 bobble] twice, 4ch, skip 7 sc, 1sc into next sc; rep from * to end, turn.

7th row: 3ch, 4dc into first 4ch arch, 1dc into next bobble, 2dc into next 2ch sp, 3dc into next bobble, 2dc into next 2ch sp, 1dc into next bobble, *3dc into next 4ch arch, 1 cluster, 3dc into same arch as 2nd leg of last cluster, 1dc into next bobble, 2dc into next 2ch sp, 3dc into next bobble, 2dc into next 2ch sp, 1dc into next bobble; rep from * to last 4ch arch, 3dc into last arch, 1 cluster working into last arch and last sc, turn.

Rep 2nd to 7th rows.

Starting chain: Multiple of 8 sts + 2.

Special Abbreviation

Bobble = work 4dc into next st until 1 loop of each remains on hook, yo and through all 5 loops on hook.

1st row (wrong side): Work 1sc into 2nd ch from hook, 1sc into each ch to end, turn.

2nd row: 4ch (count as 1dc, 1ch), skip first 2sc, 1 bobble into next sc, 1ch, skip 1sc, 1dc into next sc, *1ch, skip 1sc, 1 bobble into next sc, 1ch, skip 1sc, 1dc into next sc; rep from * to end, turn.

3rd row: 1ch, work 1sc into each dc, ch sp and bobble to end, working last 2sc into 4th and 3rd of 4ch at beg of previous row, turn.

4th row: 1ch, 1sc into each of first 3sc, *5ch, skip 3sc, 1sc into each of next 5sc; rep from * to end omitting 2sc at end of last rep, turn.

5th row: 1ch, 1sc into each of first 2sc, *3ch, 1sc into 5ch arch, 3ch, skip 1sc, 1sc into each of next 3sc; rep from * to end omitting 1sc at end of last rep, turn.

6th row: 1ch, 1sc into first sc, *3ch, 1sc into next 3ch arch, 1sc into next sc, 1sc into next 3ch arch, 3ch, skip 1sc, 1sc into next sc; rep from * to end, turn.

7th row: 5ch (count as 1dc, 2ch), 1sc into next 3ch arch, 1sc into each of next 3sc, 1sc into next 3ch arch, *5ch, 1sc into next 3ch arch, 1sc into each of next 3sc, 1sc into next 3ch arch; rep from * to last sc, 2ch, 1dc into last sc, turn.

8th row: 1ch, 1sc into first dc, *3ch, skip 1sc, 1sc into each of next 3sc, 3ch, 1sc into next 5ch arch; rep from * to end placing last sc into 3rd of 5ch at beg of previous row, turn.

9th row: 1ch, 1sc into first sc, *1sc into next 3ch arch, 3ch, skip 1sc, 1sc into next sc, 3ch, 1sc into next 3ch arch, 1sc into next sc; rep from * to end, turn.

10th row: 1ch, 1sc into each of first 2sc, *1sc into next 3ch arch, 3ch, 1sc into next 3ch arch, 1sc into each of next 3sc; rep from * to end omitting 1sc at end of last rep, turn.

11th row: 1ch, 1sc into each of first 3sc, *3sc into next 3ch arch, 1sc into each of next 5sc; rep from * to end omitting 2sc at end of last rep, turn.

Rep 2nd to 11th rows.

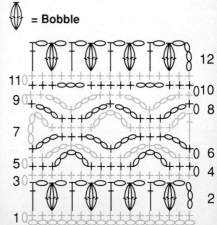

= Bobble

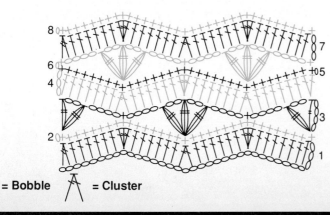

= Bobble   = Cluster

All-over Patterns

Roller Coaster

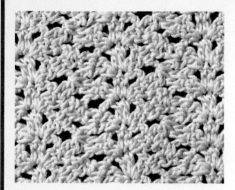

Diagram only: Rep 2nd and 3rd row.

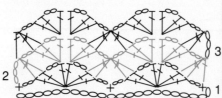

⤬ ⤬ = 2dc Cluster

⤬ = 4dc Cluster

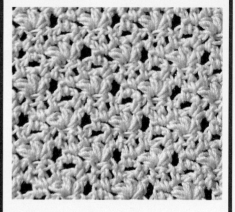

Starting chain: Multiple of 10 sts + 2.

Special Abbreviations

2dc Cluster = work 1dc into each of next 2dc until 1 loop of each remains on hook, yo and through all 3 loops on hook.

4dc Cluster = work 1dc into each of next 4dc until 1 loop of each remains on hook, yo and through all 5 loops on hook.

1st row (right side): Work 1sc into 2nd ch from hook, *2ch, skip 4ch, 2dc into next ch, into same ch as last 2dc work [2ch, 2dc] twice, 2ch, skip 4ch, 1sc into next ch; rep from * to end, turn.

2nd row: 3ch (count as 1dc), work a 2dc cluster over next 2dc, 2ch, into next dc work [2dc, 2ch, 1dc], into next dc work [1dc, 2ch, 2dc], 2ch, *work a 4dc cluster over next 4dc, 2ch, into next dc work [2dc, 2ch, 1dc], into next dc work [1dc, 2ch, 2dc], 2ch; rep from * to last 2dc, work a 2dc cluster over last 2dc, 1dc into last sc, turn.

3rd row: 3ch (count as 1dc), skip first dc and cluster, work a 2dc cluster over next 2dc, 2ch, into next dc work [2dc, 2ch, 1dc], into next dc work [1dc, 2ch, 2dc], 2ch, *work a 4dc cluster over next 4dc (excluding 4dc cluster of previous row), 2ch, into next dc work [2dc, 2ch, 1dc], into next dc work [1dc, 2ch, 2dc], 2ch; rep from * to last 4 sts (excluding 2ch sp), work a 2dc cluster over next 2dc, 1dc into 3rd of 3ch at beg of previous row, turn.

Rep 3rd row only.

Flame Stitch

Starting chain: Multiple of 10 sts + 2.

Special Abbreviation

Dc2tog = work 2dc into next 3ch arch until 1 loop of each remains on hook, yo and through all 3 loops on hook.

1st row (wrong side): Work 1sc into 2nd ch from hook, *3ch, skip 3ch, 1sc into next ch, 3ch, skip 1ch, 1sc into next ch, 3ch, skip 3ch, 1sc into next ch; rep from * to end, turn.

2nd row: 1ch, 1sc into first sc, *1ch, skip next 3ch sp, dc2tog into next 3ch arch, into same arch as last dc2tog work [3ch, dc2tog] 4 times, 1ch, skip next 3ch sp, 1sc into next sc; rep from * to end, turn.

3rd row: 7ch (count as 1tr, 3ch), skip next 3ch arch, 1sc into next 3ch arch, 3ch, 1sc into next 3ch arch, 3ch, 1tr into next sc, *3ch, skip next 3ch arch, 1sc into next 3ch arch, 3ch, 1sc into next 3ch arch, 3ch, 1tr into next sc; rep from * to end, turn.

4th row: 1ch, 1sc into first tr, *1ch, skip next 3ch sp, dc2tog into next 3ch arch, into same arch as last dc2tog work [3ch, dc2tog] 4 times, 1ch, 1sc into next tr; rep from * to end, working last sc into 4th of 7ch at beg of previous row, turn.

Rep 3rd and 4th rows.

⬍ = Dc2tog

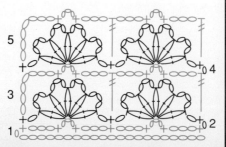

Country Style

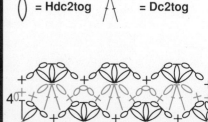

Starting chain: Multiple of 6 sts + 2.

Special Abbreviations

Hdc2tog = *yo, insert hook into st, yo and draw a loop through (3 loops on hook); rep from * once more into same st, yo and through all 5 loops on hook.

Dc2tog = work 1dc into next ch sp until 2 loops remain on hook, work a 2nd dc into next ch sp until 3 loops remain on hook, yo and through all 3 loops on hook.

1st row (right side): Work 1sc into 2nd ch from hook, *1ch, skip 2ch, into next ch work [hdc2tog, 1ch] 3 times, skip 2ch, 1sc into next ch; rep from * to end, turn.

2nd row: 4ch (count as 1dc, 1ch), skip first ch sp, 1sc into next ch sp, 3ch, 1sc into next ch sp, *1ch, dc2tog over next 2 ch sps, 1ch, 1sc into next ch sp, 3ch, 1sc into next ch sp; rep from * to last sc, 1ch, 1dc into last sc, turn.

3rd row: 3ch (count as 1hdc, 1ch), hdc2tog into first dc, 1ch, 1sc into next 3ch sp, 1ch, *into top of next dc2tog work [hdc2tog, 1ch] 3 times, 1sc into next 3ch sp, 1ch; rep from * to last ch sp, into 3rd of 4ch at beg of previous row work [hdc2tog, 1ch, 1hdc], turn.

4th row: 1ch, 1sc into first hdc, 1sc into first ch sp, 1ch, dc2tog over next 2 ch sps, 1ch, *1sc into next ch sp, 3ch, 1sc into next ch sp, 1ch, dc2tog over next 2 ch sps, 1ch; rep from * to last ch sp, 1sc into last ch sp, 1sc into 2nd of 3ch at beg of previous row, turn.

5th row: 1ch, 1sc into first sc, *1ch, into top of next dc2tog work [hdc2tog, 1ch] 3 times, 1sc into next 3ch sp; rep from * to end placing last sc into last sc, turn.

Rep 2nd to 5th rows.

⬍ = Hdc2tog   ⋀ = Dc2tog

Shallow Curve

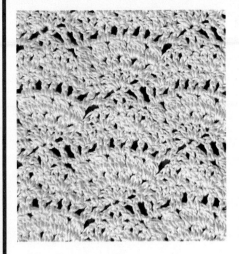

Starting chain: Multiple of 24 sts + 5.

Special Abbreviations

Dc2tog = work 2dc into next st until 1 loop of each remains on hook, yo and through all 3 loops on hook.

Bobble = work 4dc into next st until 1 loop of each remains on hook, yo and through all 5 loops on hook.

Group = work 1dc into next st, into same st as last dc work [1ch, 1dc] twice.

1st row (right side): Work 1dc into 5th ch from hook, skip 2ch, 1sc into next ch, skip 2ch, 1 group into next ch, skip 2ch, 1sc into next ch, skip 2ch, 5dc into next ch, *skip 2ch, 1sc into next ch, [skip 2ch, 1 group into next ch, skip 2ch, 1sc into next ch] 3 times, skip 2ch, 5dc into next ch; rep from * to last 12ch, skip 2ch, 1sc into next ch, skip 2ch, 1 group into next ch, skip 2ch, 1sc into next ch, skip 2ch, into last ch work [1dc, 1ch, 1dc], turn.

2nd row: 1ch, 1sc into first dc, 1 group into next sc, 1sc into center dc of next group, skip 1dc, 2dc into each of next 5dc, *1sc into center dc of next group, [1 group into next sc, 1sc into center dc of next group] twice, skip 1dc, 2dc into each of next 5dc; rep from * to last group, 1sc into center dc of next group, 1 group into next sc, 1 sc into next ch, turn.

3rd row: 4ch (count as 1dc, 1ch), 1dc into first sc, 1sc into center dc of first group, 2ch, [1 bobble between next pair of dc, 2ch] 5 times, *1sc into center dc of next group, 1 group into next sc, 1sc into center dc of next group, 2ch, [1 bobble between next pair of dc, 2ch] 5 times; rep from * to last group, 1sc into center dc of last group, into last sc work [1dc, 1ch, 1dc], turn.

4th row: 1ch, 1sc into first dc, *1ch, 1dc into next 2ch sp, [1ch, 1dc into top of next bobble, 1ch, 1dc into next 2ch sp] 5 times, 1ch, 1sc into center dc of next group; rep from * to end placing last sc into 3rd of 4ch at beg of previous row, turn.

5th row: 3ch (count as 1dc), 2dc into first sc, *skip 1ch sp, 1sc into next ch sp, [skip 1ch sp, 1 group into next dc, skip 1ch sp, 1sc into next ch sp] 3 times, 5dc into next sc; rep from * to end omitting 2dc at end of last rep, turn.

6th row: 3ch (count as 1dc), 1dc into first dc, 2dc into each of next 2dc, 1sc into center dc of next group, [1 group into next sc, 1sc into center dc of next group] twice, *skip 1dc, 2dc into each of next 5dc, 1sc into center dc of next group, [1 group into next sc, 1sc into center dc of next group] twice; rep from * to last 5 sts, skip next dc and sc, 2dc into each of next 2dc, 2dc into 3rd of 3ch at beg of previous row, turn.

7th row: 3ch (count as 1dc), dc2tog between first pair of dc, 2ch, [1 bobble between next pair of dc, 2ch] twice, 1sc into center dc of next group, 1 group into next sc, 1sc into center dc of next group, *2ch, skip [1dc, 1sc], [1 bobble between next pair of dc, 2ch] 5 times, 1sc into center dc of next group, 1 group into next sc, 1sc into center dc of next group; rep from * to last 3 pairs of dc, [2ch, 1 bobble between next pair of dc] twice, 2ch, dc2tog between last pair of dc, 1dc into 3rd of 3ch at beg of previous row, turn.

8th row: 4ch (count as 1dc, 1ch), 1dc into first 2ch sp, 1ch, [1dc into top of next bobble, 1ch, 1dc into next 2ch sp, 1ch] twice, 1sc into center dc of next group, *1ch, 1dc into next 2ch sp, 1ch, [1dc into top of next bobble, 1ch, 1dc into next 2ch sp, 1ch] 5 times, 1sc into center dc of next group; rep from * to last 3 2ch sps, 1ch, 1dc into next 2ch sp, [1ch, 1dc into top of next bobble, 1ch, 1dc into next 2ch sp] twice, 1ch, 1dc into 3rd of 3ch at beg of previous row, turn.

9th row: 4ch (count as 1dc, 1ch), 1dc into first dc, skip 1ch sp, 1sc into next ch sp, skip 1ch sp, 1 group into next dc, skip 1ch sp, 1sc into next ch sp, 5dc into next sc, *skip 1ch sp, 1sc into next ch sp, [skip 1ch sp, 1 group into next dc, skip 1ch sp, 1sc into next ch sp] 3 times, 5dc into next sc; rep from * to last 6 ch sps, skip 1ch sp, 1sc into next ch sp, skip 1ch sp, 1 group into next dc, skip 1ch sp, 1sc into next ch sp, into 3rd of 4ch at beg of previous row work [1dc, 1ch, 1dc], turn.

Rep 2nd to 9th rows.

Mat Stitch

Starting chain: Multiple of 6 sts + 2.

1st row (right side): Work 1sc into 2nd ch from hook, *skip 2ch, 1dc into next ch, 1ch, into same ch as last dc work [1dc, 1ch, 1dc], skip 2ch, 1sc into next ch; rep from * to end, turn.

2nd row: 4ch (count as 1dc, 1ch), 1dc into first sc, skip 1dc, 1sc into next dc, *1dc into next sc, 1ch, into same st as last dc work [1dc, 1ch, 1dc], skip 1dc, 1sc into next dc; rep from * to last sc, into last sc work [1dc, 1ch, 1dc], turn.

3rd row: 1ch, 1sc into first dc, *1dc into next sc, 1ch, into same st as last dc work [1dc, 1ch, 1dc], skip 1dc, 1sc into next dc; rep from * to end placing last sc into 3rd of 4ch at beg of previous row, turn.

Rep 2nd and 3rd rows.

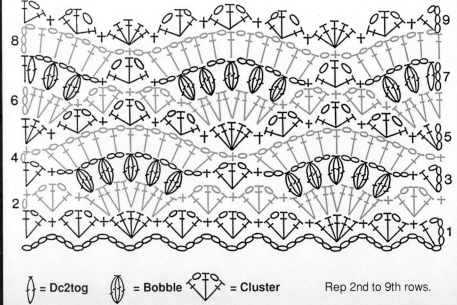

◊ = Dc2tog   ◊ = Bobble   ⋀ = Cluster   Rep 2nd to 9th rows.

All-over Patterns

Rack Stitch

Diagram only: Rep 2nd to 7th rows.

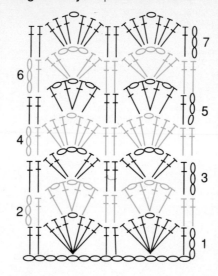

Starting chain: Multiple of 7 sts + 4.

1st row (right side): Work 1dc into 4th ch from hook, *skip 2ch, into next ch work [3dc, 1ch, 3dc], skip 2ch, 1dc into each of next 2ch; rep from * to end, turn.

2nd row: 3ch (count as 1dc), skip first dc, 1dc into next dc, *skip 2ch, 1dc into next dc, 1ch, into next ch sp work [1dc, 1ch, 1dc], 1ch, 1dc into next dc, skip 2ch, 1dc into each of next 2dc; rep from * to end placing last dc into 3rd of 3ch at beg of previous row, turn.

3rd row: 3ch, skip first dc, 1dc into next dc, *skip next ch sp, into next ch sp work [2dc, 3ch, 2dc], skip 2dc, 1dc into each of next 2dc; rep from * to end placing last dc into 3rd of 3ch at beg of previous row, turn.

4th row: 3ch, skip first dc, 1dc into next dc, *into next 3ch sp work [3dc, 1ch, 3dc], skip 2dc, 1dc into each of next 2dc; rep from * to end placing last dc into 3rd of 3ch at beg of previous row, turn.

Rep 2nd to 4th rows.

Arch Gallery

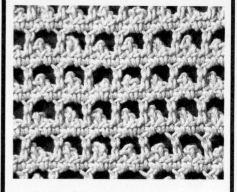

Starting chain: Multiple of 3 sts + 2.

1st row (right side): Work 1sc into 2nd ch from hook, 1sc into next ch, *4ch, sl st into 4th ch from hook (1 picot made), 1sc into each of next 3sc; rep from * to end omitting 1sc at end of last rep, turn.

2nd row: 5ch (count as 1dc, 2ch), skip 2sc, 1dc into next sc, *2ch, skip 2sc, 1dc into next sc; rep from * to end, turn.

3rd row: 1ch, 1sc into first dc, *into next 2ch sp work [1sc, 1 picot, 1sc], 1sc into next dc; rep from * to end placing last sc into 3rd of 5ch at beg of previous row, turn.

Rep 2nd and 3rd rows.

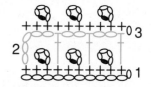

Cool Design

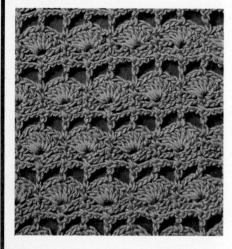

Starting chain: Multiple of 8 sts + 4.

1st row (right side): Work 3dc into 4th ch from hook, skip 3ch, 1sc into next ch, *skip 3ch, 7dc into next ch, skip 3ch, 1sc into next ch; rep from * to last 4ch, skip 3ch, 4dc into last ch, turn.

2nd row: 6ch (count as 1dc, 3ch), 1dc into next sc, *3ch, skip 3dc, 1dc into next dc, 3ch, 1dc into next sc; rep from * to last 4 sts, 3ch, 1dc into top of 3ch at beg of previous row, turn.

3rd row: 1ch, *1sc into next dc, 3ch; rep from * to last st, 1sc into 3rd of 6ch at beg of previous row, turn.

4th row: 1ch, 1sc into first sc, *3ch, 1sc into next sc; rep from * to end, turn.

5th row: 1ch, 1sc into first sc, *7dc into next sc, 1sc into next sc; rep from * to end, turn.

6th row: 6ch, skip 3dc, 1dc into next dc, 3ch, 1dc into next sc, *3ch, skip 3dc, 1dc into next dc, 3ch, 1dc into next sc; rep from * to end, turn.

7th and 8th rows: As 3rd and 4th rows.

9th row: 3ch (count as 1dc), 3dc into first sc, 1sc into next sc, *7dc into next sc, 1sc into next sc; rep from * to last sc, 4dc into last sc, turn.

Rep 2nd to 9th rows.

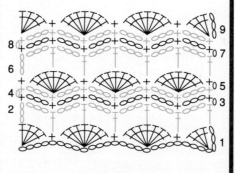

Tortoise Shell

Starting chain: Multiple of 5 sts + 2.

1st row (wrong side): Work 1sc into 2nd ch from hook, *5ch, skip 4ch, 1sc into next ch; rep from * to end, turn.

2nd row: 5ch (count as 1tr, 1ch), *into next 5ch arch work [1tr, 1dc, 4ch, sl st into 4th ch from hook, 1dc, 1tr], 2ch; rep from * to end omitting 1ch at end of last rep, 1tr into last sc, turn.

3rd row: 1ch, 1sc into first tr, *5ch, 1sc into next 2ch sp; rep from * to end placing last sc into 4th of 5ch at beg of previous row, turn.

Rep 2nd and 3rd rows.

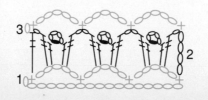

Stitch Variations, Abbreviations and Symbols on pages 7 to 15

Fossil Stitch

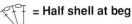

Starting chain: Multiple of 9 sts + 4.

Special Abbreviations

Shell = work 1dc into next dc, 1ch, between last dc and next dc work [1dc, 1ch, 1dc], 1ch, 1dc into next dc.

Half shell at beg of row = 4ch (count as 1dc, 1ch), 1dc between first 2dc, 1ch, 1dc into next dc.

Half shell at end of row = 1dc into next dc, 1ch, 1dc between last dc worked into and last dc (the 3ch at beg of previous row), 1ch, 1dc into 3rd of 3ch at beg of previous row.

1st row (right side): Work 1dc into 4th ch from hook, *skip 3ch, into next ch work [3dc, 1ch, 3dc], skip 3ch, 1dc into each of next 2ch; rep from * to end, turn.

2nd row: Work half shell over first 2dc, 1sc into next ch sp, *skip 3dc, 1 shell over next 2dc, 1sc into next ch sp; rep from * to last 5 sts, skip 3dc, half shell over last 2dc, turn.

3rd row: 4ch (count as 1dc, 1ch), 2dc into first ch sp, skip 1dc, 1dc into each of next 2dc, *skip 1ch sp, into next ch sp work [2dc, 3ch, 2dc], skip 1dc, 1dc into each of next 2dc; rep from * to last 2dc, 2dc into last ch sp, 1ch, 1dc into 3rd of 4ch at beg of previous row, turn.

Rep 2nd to 7th rows.

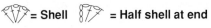

⟨shell symbol⟩ = **Shell**   ⟨half shell symbol⟩ = **Half shell at end**

⟨half shell symbol⟩ = **Half shell at beg**

4th row: 4ch (count as 1dc, 1ch), 3dc into first ch sp, skip 2dc, 1dc into each of next 2dc, *into next 3ch sp work [3dc, 1ch, 3dc], skip 2dc, 1dc into each of next 2dc; rep from * to last 3dc, work 3dc into last ch sp, 1ch, 1dc into 3rd of 4ch at beg of previous row, turn.

5th row: 1ch, 1sc into first dc, 1sc into first ch sp, *skip 3dc, 1 shell over next 2dc, 1sc into next ch sp; rep from * to end, 1sc into 3rd of 4ch at beg of previous row, turn.

6th row: 3ch (count as 1dc), skip first sc, 1dc into next sc, skip 1ch sp, into next ch sp work [2dc, 3ch, 2dc], *skip 1dc, work 1dc into each of next 2dc, skip 1ch sp, into next ch sp work [2dc, 3ch, 2dc]; rep from * to last 2dc, 1dc into each of last 2sc, turn.

7th row: 3ch (count as 1dc), skip first dc, 1dc into next dc, *into next 3ch sp work [3dc, 1ch, 3dc], skip 2dc, 1dc into each of next 2dc; rep from * to end placing last dc into 3rd of 3ch at beg of previous row, turn.

Rep 2nd to 7th rows.

Rose Buds

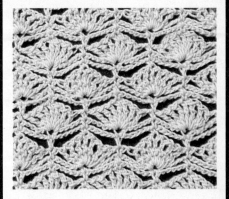

Starting chain: Multiple of 12 sts + 6.

1st row (right side): Work [1tr, 1ch] 3 times into 6th ch from hook, skip 5ch, 1sc into next ch, *1ch, skip 5ch, into next ch work [1tr, 1ch] 7 times, skip 5ch, 1sc into next ch; rep from * to last 6ch, 1ch, into last ch work [1tr, 1ch] 3 times, 1tr into same ch as last 3tr, turn.

2nd row: 1ch, 1sc into first tr, *6ch, 1sc into next sc, 6ch, skip 3tr, 1sc into next tr; rep from * to end placing last tr into 4th of 5ch at beg of previous row, turn.

3rd row: 1ch, 1sc into first sc, *6ch, 1sc into next sc; rep from * to end, turn.

4th row: 1ch, 1sc into first sc, *1ch, into next sc work [1tr, 1ch] 7 times, 1sc into next sc; rep from * to end, turn.

5th row: 1ch, 1sc into first sc, *6ch, skip 3tr, 1sc into next tr, 6ch, 1sc into next sc; rep from * to end, turn.

6th row: 1ch, 1sc into first sc, *6ch, 1sc into next sc; rep from * to end, turn.

7th row: 5ch (count as 1tr, 1ch), into first sc work [1tr, 1ch] 3 times, 1sc into next sc, *1ch, into next sc work [1tr, 1ch] 7 times, 1sc into next sc; rep from * to last sc, into last sc work [1ch, 1tr] 4 times, turn.

Rep 2nd to 7th rows.

Garland Pattern

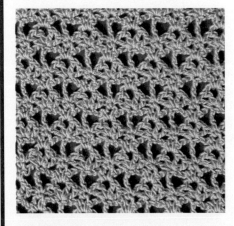

Starting chain: Multiple of 8 sts + 2.

1st row (right side): Work 1sc into 2nd ch from hook, *skip 3ch, into next ch work [1dc, 1ch, 1dc, 3ch, 1dc, 1ch, 1dc], skip 3ch, 1sc into next ch; rep from * to end, turn.

2nd row: 7ch (count as 1tr, 3ch), *skip 1ch sp, into next 3ch sp work [1sc, 3ch, 1sc], 3ch, 1tr into next sc, 3ch; rep from * to end omitting 3ch at end of last rep, turn.

3rd row: 4ch (count as 1dc, 1ch), into first tr work [1dc, 1ch, 1dc], skip 3ch sp, 1sc into next 3ch sp, *into next tr work [1dc, 1ch, 1dc, 3ch, 1dc, 1ch, 1dc], skip 3ch sp, 1sc into next 3ch sp; rep from * to last sp, skip 3ch, 1dc into next ch, work [1ch, 1dc] twice into same ch as last dc, turn.

4th row: 1ch, 1sc into first dc, 1sc into first ch sp, 3ch, 1tr into next sc, *3ch, skip 1ch sp, into next 3ch sp work [1sc, 3ch, 1sc], 3ch, 1tr into next sc; rep from * to last 3dc, 3ch, skip 1ch sp, 1sc into each of next 2ch, turn.

5th row: 1ch, 1sc into first sc, *into next tr work [1dc, 1ch, 1dc, 3ch, 1dc, 1ch, 1dc], skip 3ch sp, 1sc into next 3ch sp; rep from * to end placing last sc into last sc, turn.

Rep 2nd to 5th rows.

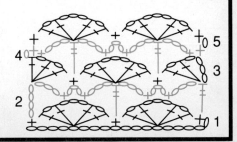

All-over Patterns

Flying Stitch

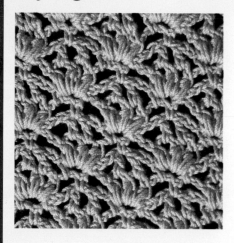

Starting chain: Multiple of 10 sts + 14.

Special Abbreviation

Puff st = [yo, insert hook into sp, yo and draw a loop through] 3 times into same space, yo and through all 7 loops on hook, work 1 firm ch to close puff st.

1st row (wrong side): Work 1sc into 9th ch from hook, (first 3ch sp made), 1ch, skip 1ch, 1sc into next ch, *3ch, skip 2ch, 1dc into next ch, 1ch, skip 1ch, 1dc into next ch, 3ch, skip 2ch, 1sc into next ch, 1ch, skip 1ch, 1sc into next ch; rep from * to last 3ch, 3ch, skip 2ch, 1dc into last ch, turn.

2nd row: 1ch, 1sc into first dc, *3ch, skip 3ch sp, 1 puff st into next ch sp, 2ch, into same ch sp as last puff st work [1 puff st, 2ch, 1 puff st], 3ch, skip 3ch sp, 1sc into next ch sp; rep from * to end working last sc into 4th ch, turn.

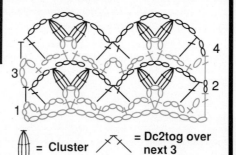

= Puff st

3rd row: 1ch, 1sc into first sc, 3ch, skip first 3ch arch, 1dc into next 2ch arch, 1ch, 1dc into next 2ch arch, 3ch, 1sc into next 3ch arch, *1ch, 1sc into next 3ch arch, 3ch, 1dc into next 2ch arch, 1ch, 1dc into next 2ch arch, 3ch, 1sc into next 3ch arch; rep from * to end placing last sc into last sc, turn.

4th row: 6ch (count as 1dc, 3ch), skip 3ch arch, 1sc into next ch sp, *3ch, skip 3ch arch, 1 puff st into next ch sp, 2ch, into same ch sp as last puff st work [1 puff st, 2ch, 1 puff st], 3ch, skip 3ch arch, 1sc into next ch sp; rep from * to last 3ch arch, 3ch, 1dc into last sc, turn.

5th row: 6ch (count as 1dc, 3ch), 1sc into first 3ch arch, 1ch, 1sc into next 3ch arch, *3ch, 1dc into next 2ch arch, 1ch, 1dc into next 2ch arch, 3ch, 1sc into next 3ch arch, 1ch, 1sc into next 3ch arch; rep from * to end, 3ch, 1dc into 3rd of 6ch at beg of previous row, turn.

Rep 2nd to 5th rows.

Crown Stitch

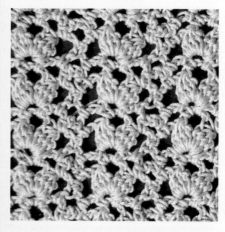

Starting chain: Multiple of 9 sts + 14.

Special Abbreviations

Cluster = work 4dc into next 3ch arch until 1 loop of each remains on hook, yo and through all 5 loops on hook.

Dc2tog over next 3 3ch arches = work 1dc into next 3ch arch until 2 loops remain on hook, skip next 3ch arch, 1dc into next 3ch arch until 3 loops remain on hook, yo and through all 3 loops on hook.

= Cluster

= Dc2tog over next 3 3ch arches

1st row (wrong side): Work 1sc into 6th ch from hook, 3ch, skip 2ch, into next ch work [1sc, 3ch, 1sc], *[3ch, skip 2ch, 1sc into next ch] twice, 3ch, skip 2ch, into next ch work [1sc, 3ch, 1sc]; rep from * to last 5ch, 3ch, skip 2ch, 1sc into next sc, 1ch, skip 1ch, 1dc into last ch, turn.

2nd row: 2ch (count as 1hdc), 1dc into first 3ch arch, 3ch, into next 3ch arch work [1 cluster, 4ch, 1 cluster], 3ch, *dc2tog over next 3 3ch arches, 3ch, into next 3ch arch work [1 cluster, 4ch, 1 cluster], 3ch; rep from * to last 2 arches, work 1dc into next 3ch arch, skip 1ch, 1hdc into next ch, turn.

3rd row: 4ch (count as 1dc, 1ch), 1sc into next 3ch arch, 3ch, into next 4ch arch work [1sc, 3ch, 1sc], *3ch, [1sc into next 3ch arch, 3ch] twice, into next 4ch arch work [1sc, 3ch, 1sc]; rep from * to last 3ch arch, 3ch, 1sc into last 3ch arch, 1ch, 1dc into 2nd of 2ch at beg of previous row, turn.

Rep 2nd and 3rd rows.

Sprig Pattern

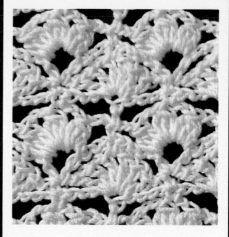

Starting chain: Multiple of 10 sts + 5.

Special Abbreviation

Cluster = work 3dc into next space until 1 loop of each remains on hook, yo and through all 4 loops on hook.

1st row (right side): Work [1dc, 1ch, 1dc] into 5th ch from hook (1dc and 1ch sp formed at beg of row), 1ch, skip 4ch, 1sc into next ch, *1ch, skip 4ch, into next ch work [1dc, 1ch] 6 times, skip 4ch, 1sc into next ch; rep from * to last 5ch, 1ch, 1dc into last ch, [1ch, 1dc] twice into same ch as last dc, turn.

2nd row: 1ch, 1sc into first dc, 3ch, into next sc work [1dc, 3ch, 1dc], *3ch, skip 3dc, 1sc into next ch sp, 3ch, into next sc work [1dc, 3ch, 1dc]; rep from * to last 3dc, 3ch, 1sc into 3rd of 4ch at beg of previous row, turn.

3rd row: 1ch, 1sc into first sc, *2ch, skip 3ch sp, 1 cluster into next 3ch sp, 2ch, into same sp as last cluster work [1 cluster, 2ch] twice, 1sc into next sc; rep from * to end, turn.

4th row: 7ch (count as 1dc, 4ch), *skip 1 cluster, 1sc into next cluster, 4ch, 1dc into next sc, 4ch; rep from * to end omitting 4ch at end of last rep, turn.

5th row: 4ch (count as 1dc, 1ch), into first dc work [1dc, 1ch] twice, 1sc into next sc, *1ch, into next dc work [1dc, 1ch] 6 times, 1sc into next sc; rep from * to last dc, 1ch, work 1dc into 3rd of 7ch at beg of previous row, [1ch, 1dc] twice into same ch as last dc, turn.

Rep 2nd to 5th rows.

= Cluster

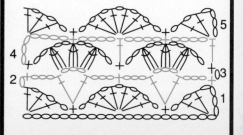

Stitch Variations, Abbreviations and Symbols on pages 7 to 15

Open Fan

Starting chain: Multiple of 30 sts + 32.

1st row (right side): Work 1sc into 2nd ch from hook, [skip 2ch, 5dc into next ch, skip 2ch, 1sc into next ch] twice, skip 2ch, 1dc into next ch, 1ch, into same ch as last dc work [1dc, 1ch, 1dc], *skip 2ch, 1sc into next ch, [skip 2ch, 5dc into next ch, skip 2ch, 1sc into next ch] 4 times, skip 2ch, 1dc into next ch, 1ch, into same ch as last dc work [1dc, 1ch, 1dc]; rep from * to last 15ch, skip 2ch, 1sc into next ch, [skip 2ch, 5dc into next ch, skip 2ch, 1sc into next ch] twice, turn.

2nd row: 3ch (count as 1dc), 2dc into first sc, skip 2dc, 1sc into next dc, 5dc into next sc, skip 2dc, 1sc into next dc, 1ch, skip 2dc, 1dc into next dc, 1ch, [1dc into next ch sp, 1ch, 1dc into next dc, 1ch] twice, *skip 2dc, 1sc into next dc, [5dc into next sc, skip 2dc, 1sc into next dc] 3 times, 1ch, skip 2dc, 1dc into next dc, 1ch, [1dc into next ch sp, 1ch, 1dc into next dc, 1ch] twice; rep from * to last 2 groups of 5dc, skip 2dc, 1sc into next dc, 5dc into next sc, skip 2dc, 1sc into next dc, 3dc into last sc, turn.

3rd row: 1ch, 1sc into first dc, 5dc into first sc, skip 2dc, 1sc into next dc, 2ch, skip 2dc, [1dc into next dc, 2ch] 5 times, *skip 2dc, 1sc into next dc, [5dc into next sc, skip 2dc, 1sc into next dc] twice, skip 2dc, [1dc into next dc, 2ch] 5 times; rep from * to last group of 5dc, skip 2dc, 1sc into next dc, 5dc into next sc, 1sc into 3rd of 3ch at beg of previous row, turn.

4th row: 3ch (count as 1dc), 2dc into first sc, skip 2dc, 1sc into next dc, 1ch, 1dc into next 2ch sp, [1ch, 1dc into next dc, 1ch, 1dc into next 2ch sp] 5 times, *1ch, skip 2dc, 1sc into next dc, 5dc into next sc, skip 2dc, 1sc into next dc, 1ch, 1dc into next 2ch sp, [1ch, 1dc into next dc, 1ch, 1dc into next 2ch sp] 5 times; rep from * to last group of 5dc, 1ch, skip 2dc, 1sc into next dc, 3dc into last sc, turn.

5th row: 1ch, 1sc into first dc, *5dc into next sc, skip 1ch sp, 1sc into next ch sp, [skip 1ch sp, 5dc into next dc, skip 1ch sp, 1sc into next ch sp] 3 times, 5dc into next sc, 1sc into center dc of next group of 5; rep from * to end placing last sc into 3rd of 3ch at beg of previous row, turn.

6th row: 4ch (count as 1dc), 1dc into first sc, 1sc into center dc of first group of 5, [5dc into next sc, 1sc into center dc of next group of 5] 4 times, *1dc into next sc, 1ch, into same st as last dc work [1dc, 1ch, 1dc], 1sc into center dc of next group of 5, [5dc into next sc, 1sc into center dc of next group of 5] 4 times; rep from * to last sc, into last sc work [1dc, 1ch, 1dc], turn.

7th row: 4ch (count as 1dc), 1dc into first ch sp, 1ch, 1dc into next dc, 1ch, 1sc into center dc of first group of 5, [5dc into next sc, 1sc into center dc of next group of 5] 3 times, *1ch, skip 2dc, 1dc into next dc, 1ch, [1dc into next ch sp, 1ch, 1dc into next dc, 1ch] twice, 1sc into center dc of next group of 5, [5dc into next sc, 1sc into center dc of next group of 5] 3 times; rep from * to last 4dc, 1ch, skip 2dc, 1dc into next dc, 1ch, 1dc into last ch sp, 1ch, 1dc into 3rd of 4ch at beg of previous row, turn.

8th row: 5ch (count as 1dc, 2ch), skip first dc, [1dc into next dc, 2ch] twice, 1sc into center dc of group of 5, [5dc into next sc, 1sc into center dc of next group of 5] twice, *2ch, skip 2dc, [1dc into next dc, 2ch] 5 times, 1sc into center dc of next group of 5, [5dc into next sc, 1sc into center dc of next group of 5] twice; rep from * to last 5dc, 2ch, skip 2dc, [1dc into next dc, 2ch] twice, 1dc into 3rd of 4ch at beg of previous row, turn.

9th row: 4ch (count as 1dc, 1ch), 1dc into first 2ch sp, 1ch, [1dc into next dc, 1ch, 1dc into next 2ch sp, 1ch] twice, 1sc into center dc of first group of 5, 5dc into next sc, 1sc into center dc of next group of 5, *1ch, 1dc into next 2ch sp, 1ch, [1dc into next dc, 1ch, 1dc into next 2ch sp, 1ch] 5 times, 1sc into center dc of next group of 5, 5dc into next sc, 1sc into center dc of next group of 5; rep from * to last 5dc, 1ch, 1dc into next 2ch sp, 1ch, [1dc into next dc, 1ch, 1dc into next 2ch sp, 1ch] twice, 1dc into 3rd of 5ch at beg of previous row, turn.

10th row: 3ch (count as 1dc), 2dc into first dc, skip 1ch sp, 1sc into next ch sp, skip 1ch sp, 5dc into next dc, skip 1ch sp, 1sc into next ch sp, 5dc into next sc, 1sc into center dc of next group of 5, 5dc into next sc, *skip 1ch sp, 1sc into next ch sp, [skip 1ch sp, 5dc into next dc, skip 1ch sp, 1sc into next ch sp] 3 times, 5dc into next sc, 1sc into center dc of next group of 5, 5dc into next sc; rep from * to last 6dc, skip 1ch sp, 1sc into next ch sp, skip 1ch sp, 5dc into next dc, skip 1ch sp, 1sc into next ch sp, 3dc into 3rd of 4ch at beg of previous row, turn.

11th row: 1ch, 1sc into first dc, [5dc into next sc, 1sc into center dc of next group of 5] twice, 1dc into next sc, 1ch, into same st as last dc work [1dc, 1ch, 1dc], *1sc into center dc of next group of 5, [5dc into next sc, 1sc into center dc of next group of 5] 4 times, 1dc into next sc, 1ch, into same st as last dc work [1dc, 1ch, 1dc]; rep from * to last 2 groups of 5dc, [1sc into center dc of next group of 5, 5dc into next sc] twice, 1sc into 3rd of 3ch at beg of previous row, turn.

Rep 2nd to 11th rows.

All-over Patterns

Column and Bowl

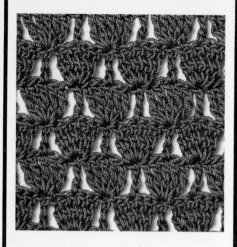

Starting chain: Multiple of 8 sts + 12.

1st row (right side): Work 5tr into 8th ch from hook, skip 3ch, 1tr into next ch, *skip 3ch, 5tr into next ch, skip 3ch, 1tr into next ch; rep from * to end, turn.

2nd row: 4ch (count as 1tr), 2tr into first tr, skip 2tr, 1tr into next tr, *skip 2tr, 5tr into next tr, skip 2tr, 1tr into next tr; rep from * to last 3 sts, skip 2tr, 3tr into next ch, turn.

3rd row: 4ch, *skip 2tr, 5tr into next tr, skip 2tr, 1tr into next tr; rep from * to end placing last tr into 4th of 4ch at beg of previous row, turn.

Rep 2nd and 3rd rows.

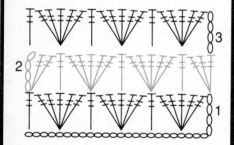

Column Stitch

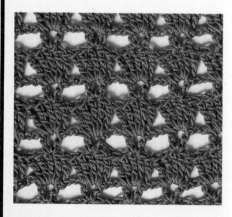

Starting chain: Multiple of 5 sts + 6.

1st row (wrong side): Work [1dc, 2ch, 1dc] into 8th ch from hook, *3ch, skip 4ch, work [1dc, 2ch, 1dc] into next ch; rep from * to last 3ch, 2ch, 1dc into last ch, turn.

Cone Stitch

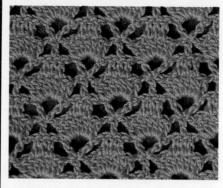

Starting chain: Multiple of 8 sts + 3.

1st row (wrong side): Work 1dc into 4th ch from hook, *1ch, skip 2ch, into next ch work [1dc, 3ch, 1dc], 1ch, skip 2ch, 1dc into each of next 3ch; rep from * to end omitting 1dc at end of last rep, turn.

2nd row: 4ch (count as 1dc, 1ch), work 7dc into next 3ch arch, *1ch, skip 2dc, 1dc into next dc, 1ch, 7dc into next 3ch arch; rep from * to last 3dc, 1ch, skip 2dc, 1dc into top of 3ch, turn.

3rd row: 4ch, 1dc into first dc, 1ch, skip 2dc, 1dc into each of next 3dc, *1ch, skip 2dc, into next dc work [1dc, 3ch, 1dc], 1ch, skip 2dc, 1dc into each of next 3dc; rep from * to last 3dc, skip 2dc, into 3rd of 4ch at beg of previous row work [1dc, 1ch, 1dc], turn.

4th row: 3ch (count as 1dc), 3dc into first ch sp, 1ch, skip 2dc, 1dc into next dc, *1ch, 7dc into next 3ch arch, 1ch, skip 2dc, 1dc into next dc; rep from * to last 3dc, 1ch, skip 2dc, 3dc into last ch sp, 1dc into 3rd of 4ch at beg of previous row, turn.

5th row: 3ch, skip first dc, 1dc into next dc, *1ch, skip 2dc, into next dc work [1dc, 3ch, 1dc], 1ch, skip 2dc, 1dc into each of next 3dc; rep from * to end omitting 1dc at end of last rep and placing last dc into 3rd of 3ch at beg of previous row, turn.

Rep 2nd to 5th rows.

2nd row: 4ch (count as 1tr), skip first 2ch sp, work 5tr into next 2ch sp, *skip 3ch sp, work 5tr into next 2ch sp; rep from * to last sp, skip 2ch, 1tr into next ch, turn.

3rd row: 5ch (count as 1dc, 2ch), skip first 3tr, into next tr work [1dc, 2ch, 1dc], *3ch, skip 4tr, into next tr work [1dc, 2ch, 1dc]; rep from * to last 3tr, 2ch, 1dc into 4th of 4ch at beg of previous row, turn.

Rep 2nd and 3rd rows.

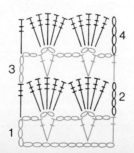

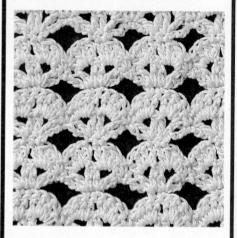

Rep 2nd to 5th rows.

Umbrella Stitch

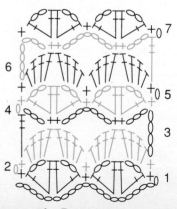

Starting chain: Multiple of 9 sts + 2.

1st row (right side): Work 1sc into 2nd ch from hook, *skip 3ch, into each of next 2ch work [1dc, 2ch, 1dc], skip 3ch, 1sc into next ch; rep from * to end, turn.

2nd row: 1ch, 1sc into first sc, *into next 2ch sp work [1hdc, 3dc], into next 2ch sp work [3dc, 1hdc], 1sc into next sc; rep from * to end, turn.

3rd row: 7ch (count as 1tr, 3ch), skip first 4 sts, 1sc into each of next 2dc, *7ch, skip 7 sts, 1sc into each of next 2dc; rep from * to last 4 sts, 3ch, 1tr into last sc, turn.

4th row: 1ch, 1sc into first tr, *into each of next 2sc work [1dc, 2ch, 1dc], 1sc into 7ch arch; rep from * to end placing last sc into 4th of 7ch at beg of previous row, turn.

Rep 2nd to 4th rows.

Diagram only: Rep 2nd to 7th rows.

Stitch Variations, Abbreviations and Symbols on pages 7 to 15

Medallion Pattern

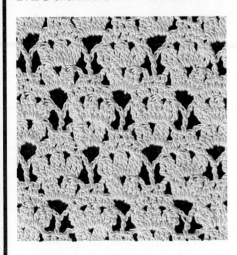

Starting chain: Multiple of 10 sts + 2.

Special Abbreviation

Bobble = work 3tr into next st until 1 loop of each remains on hook, yo and through all 4 loops on hook.

1st row (right side): Work 1hdc into 3rd ch from hook, 1hdc into each of next 2ch, *3ch, skip 3ch, 1hdc into each of next 7ch; rep from * to end omitting 3hdc at end of last rep, turn.

2nd row: 2ch (count as 1hdc), working between sts work 1hdc between first and 2nd hdc then between 2nd and 3rd hdc, 2ch, into next 3ch sp work [1 bobble, 2ch] twice, *skip 1hdc, [1hdc between next 2hdc] 4 times, 2ch, into next 3ch sp work [1 bobble, 2ch] twice; rep from * to last 4 sts, skip 1hdc, 1hdc between next 2hdc, 1hdc between last hdc and 2ch, 1hdc into top of 2ch, turn.

3rd row: 5ch (count as 1dc, 2ch), *1 bobble into next bobble, 2ch, 1 bobble into next 2ch sp, 2ch, 1 bobble into next bobble, 2ch, 1dc between 2nd and 3rd hdc, 2ch; rep from * to end omitting 2ch at end of last rep and placing last dc into 2nd of 2ch at beg of previous row, turn.

4th row: 5ch, *1hdc into next bobble, [2hdc into next 2ch sp, 1hdc into next bobble] twice, 3ch; rep from * to end omitting 1ch at end of last rep, work 1dc into 3rd of 5ch at beg of previous row, turn.

5th row: 4ch (count as 1dc, 1ch), 1 bobble into first 2ch sp, 2ch, skip 1hdc, [1hdc between next 2hdc] 4 times, *2ch, into next 3ch sp work [1 bobble, 2ch] twice, skip 1hdc, [1hdc between next 2hdc] 4 times; rep from * to last 2ch sp, 2ch, work 1 bobble into last 2ch sp, 1ch, 1dc into 3rd of 5ch at beg of previous row, turn.

6th row: 4ch (count as 1tr), 1tr into first ch sp, 2ch, 1 bobble into next bobble, 2ch, skip 1hdc, 1dc between next 2hdc, 2ch, *1 bobble into next bobble, 2ch, 1 bobble into next 2ch sp, 2ch, 1 bobble into next bobble, 2ch, skip 1hdc, 1dc between next 2hdc; rep from * to last bobble, 2ch, 1 bobble into next bobble, 2ch, work 1tr into last ch sp until last loop of tr remains on hook, 1tr into 3rd of 4ch until 3 loops remain on hook, yo and through all 3 loops on hook, turn.

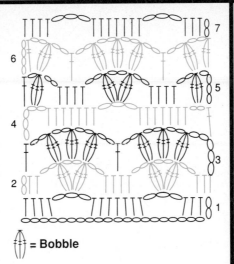

7th row: 2ch, 2hdc into first 2ch sp, 1hdc into next bobble, 3ch, *1hdc into next bobble, [2hdc into next 2ch sp, 1hdc into next bobble] twice, 3ch; rep from * to last bobble, 1hdc into last bobble, 2hdc into next 2ch sp, 1hdc into 4th of 4ch at beg of previous row, turn.

Rep 2nd to 7th rows.

⬥ **= Bobble**

Candelabra

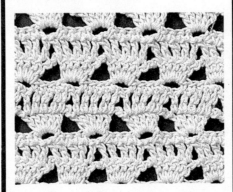

Starting chain: Multiple of 7 sts + 3.

1st row (right side): Work 1sc into 2nd ch from hook, 1sc into each of next 2ch, *3ch, skip 3ch, 1sc into each of next 4ch; rep from * to end omitting 1sc at end of last rep, turn.

2nd row: 4ch (count as 1dc, 1ch), work 5dc into first 3ch sp, *3ch, 5dc into next 3ch sp; rep from * to last 3sc, 1ch, 1dc into last sc, turn.

3rd row: 3ch (count as 1dc), skip first dc, *1dc into next dc, [1ch, 1dc into next dc] 4 times; rep from * to last dc, 1dc into 3rd of 4ch at beg of previous row, turn.

4th row: 1ch, 1sc into first dc, 1ch, [1sc

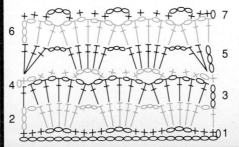

Paradise Stitch

Starting chain: Multiple of 4 sts + 3.

Special Abbreviation

Bobble = work 3dc into next st until 1 loop of each remains on hook, yo and through all 4 loops on hook.

1st row (wrong side): Work 1dc into 4th ch from hook, 1dc into each of next 2ch, *2ch, skip 1ch, 1dc into each of next 3ch; rep from * to last ch, 1dc into last ch, turn.

2nd row: 3ch (count as 1dc), skip first 2dc, into next dc work [1 bobble, 3ch, 1 bobble], *skip 2dc, into next dc work [1 bobble, 3ch, 1 bobble]; rep from * to last 2dc, 1dc into 3rd of 3ch at beg of previous row, turn.

3rd row: 3ch, work 3dc into first 3ch arch, *2ch, 3dc into next 3ch arch; rep from * to last 2 sts, 1dc into 3rd of 3ch at beg of previous row, turn.

Rep 2nd and 3rd rows.

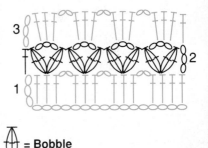

⬥ **= Bobble**

into next ch sp, skip 1dc] 4 times, *3ch, [1sc into next ch sp, skip 1dc] 4 times; rep from * to last 2dc, 1ch, 1sc into 3rd of 3ch at beg of previous row, turn.

5th row: 3ch, 2dc into first sc, 3ch, *5dc into next 3ch sp, 3ch; rep from * to last sc, 3dc into last sc, turn.

6th row: 4ch, skip first dc, 1dc into next dc, 1ch, 1dc into next dc, *1dc into next dc, [1ch, 1dc into next dc] 4 times; rep from * to last 3dc, [1dc into next dc, 1ch] twice, 1dc into 3rd of 3ch at beg of previous row, turn.

7th row: 1ch, 1sc into first dc, [1sc into next ch sp, skip 1dc] twice, 3ch, *[1sc into next ch sp, skip 1dc] 4 times, 3ch; rep from * to last 3dc, 1sc into next ch sp, skip 1dc, 1sc into next ch sp, 1sc into 3rd of 4ch at beg of previous row, turn.

Rep 2nd to 7th rows.

All-over Patterns

Acorn Stitch

Starting chain: Multiple of 6 sts + 5.

Special Abbreviations

Dc2tog = work 2dc into next st until 1 loop of each remains on hook, yo and through all 3 loops on hook.

Shell = work [dc2tog, 1dc, dc2tog] all into next st.

Group = into first dc2tog of shell work 2dc until 1 loop of each remains on hook, 1dc into dc of same shell until 4 loops remain on hook, into 2nd dc2tog of shell work 2dc until 1 loop of each remains on hook, yo and through all 6 loops.

1st row (right side): Work 1dc into 8th ch from hook (1dc and 2ch sp at beg of row), *1ch, skip 2ch, work 1 shell into next ch, 1ch, skip 2ch, 1dc into next ch; rep from * to last 3ch, 2ch, skip 2ch, 1dc into last ch, turn.

2nd row: 5ch (count as 1dc, 2ch), skip first dc, 1dc into next dc, 2ch, *work 1 group over next shell, 2ch, 1dc into next dc, 2ch; rep from * to last dc, skip 2ch, 1dc into next ch, turn.

3rd row: 4ch (count as 1dc, 1ch), skip first dc, *work 1 shell into next dc, 1ch, 1dc into top of next group, 1ch; rep from * to end omitting 1ch at end of last rep and placing last dc into 3rd of 5ch at beg of previous row, turn.

4th row: 5ch, *work 1 group over next shell, 2ch, 1dc into next dc, 2ch; rep from * to end omitting 2ch at end of last rep and placing last dc into 3rd of 4ch at beg of previous row, turn.

5th row: 5ch, 1dc into top of next group, *1ch, work 1 shell into next dc, 1ch, 1dc into top of next group; rep from * to last dc, 2ch, 1dc into 3rd of 5ch at beg of previous row, turn.

Rep 2nd to 5th rows.

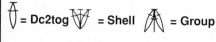

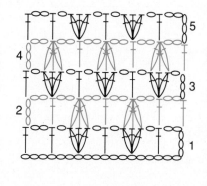

Carpet Bag Stitch

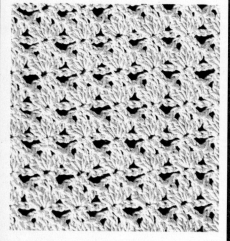

Starting chain: Multiple 5 sts + 6.

Special Abbreviation

Dc2tog = work 2dc into next st until 1 loop of each remains on hook, yo and through all 3 loops on hook.

1st row (right side): Work dc2tog into 6th ch from hook, (1dc and 2ch sp at beg of row), *skip 4ch, dc2tog into next ch, 2ch, into same ch as last dc2tog work [dc2tog, 2ch, dc2tog]; rep from * to last 5ch, skip 4ch, into last ch work [dc2tog, 2ch, 1dc], turn.

2nd row: 1ch, 1sc into first dc, *4ch, skip 2 dc2tog, 1sc into top of next dc2tog; rep from * to end placing last sc into 3rd ch, turn.

3rd row: 5ch (count as 1dc, 2ch), work dc2tog into first sc, *work dc2tog into next sc, 2ch, into same st as last dc2tog work [dc2tog, 2ch, dc2tog]; rep from * to last sc, into last sc work [dc2tog, 2ch, 1dc], turn.

Rep 2nd and 3rd rows.

 = Dc2tog

Metric Stitch

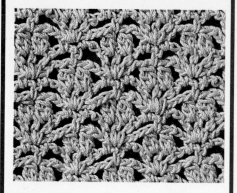

Starting chain: Multiple of 10 sts + 2.

Special Abbreviation

Dc2tog = work 2dc into next st until 1 loop of each remains on hook, yo and through all 3 loops on hook.

1st row (right side): Work 1sc into 2nd ch from hook, 1sc into next ch, 3ch, skip 2ch, dc2tog into next ch, 1ch, skip 1ch, dc2tog into next ch, *3ch, skip 2ch, 1sc into next ch, 1ch, skip 1ch, 1sc into next ch, 3ch, skip 2ch, dc2tog into next ch, 1ch, skip 1ch, dc2tog into next ch; rep from * to last 4ch, 3ch, skip 2ch, 1sc into each of last 2ch, turn.

2nd row: 4ch (count as 1dc, 1ch), 1dc into first sc, 3ch, skip next 3ch sp, 1sc into next ch sp, *3ch, skip next 3ch sp, 1dc into next ch sp, 1ch, into same ch sp as last dc work [1dc, 1ch, 1dc], 3ch, skip next 3ch sp, 1sc into next ch sp; rep from * to last 3ch sp, 3ch, into last sc work [1dc, 1ch, 1dc], turn.

3rd row: 3ch (count as 1dc), dc2tog into first ch sp, 3ch, 1sc into next 3ch sp, 1ch, 1sc into next 3ch sp, *3ch, dc2tog into next ch sp, 1ch, dc2tog into next ch sp, 3ch, 1sc into next 3ch sp, 1ch, 1sc into next 3ch sp; rep from * to last ch sp, 3ch, dc2tog into last ch sp, 1dc into 3rd of 4ch at beg of previous row, turn.

4th row: 1ch, 1sc into first dc, *skip next 3ch sp, 3ch, 1dc into next ch sp, 1ch, into same ch sp as last dc work [1dc, 1ch, 1dc], 3ch, skip next 3ch sp, 1sc into next ch sp; rep from * to end placing last sc into 3rd of 3ch at beg of previous row, turn.

5th row: 1ch, 1sc into first sc, 1sc into first 3ch sp, 3ch, dc2tog into next ch sp, 1ch, dc2tog into next ch sp, *3ch, 1sc into next 3ch sp, 1ch, 1sc into next 3ch sp, 3ch, dc2tog into next ch sp, 1ch, dc2tog into next ch sp; rep from * to last 3ch sp, 3ch, 1sc into last 3ch sp, 1sc into last sc, turn.

Rep 2nd to 5th rows.

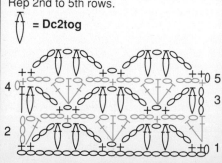 = Dc2tog

Rover Stitch

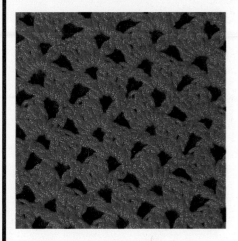

Starting chain: Multiple of 6 sts + 5.

1st row (right side): Work 1dc into 6th ch from hook, 1dc into each of next 2ch, 3ch, 1dc into next ch, *skip 2ch, 1dc into each of next 3ch, 3ch, 1dc into next ch; rep from * to last 2ch, skip 1ch, 1dc into last ch, turn.

Candy Cover

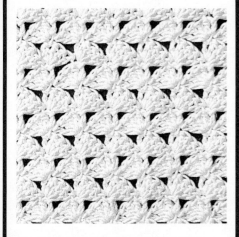

Starting chain: Multiple of 4 sts + 4.

1st row (right side): Work 4dc into 4th ch from hook, skip 3ch, 1sc into next ch, *2ch, 4dc into same ch as last sc, skip 3ch, 1sc into next ch; rep from * to end, turn.

2nd row: 5ch, work 4dc into 4th ch from hook, *skip 4dc, 1sc between last dc skipped and next 2ch, 2ch, 4dc into side of last sc worked; rep from * to last 4dc, skip 4dc, 1sc into next ch, turn.

Rep 2nd row.

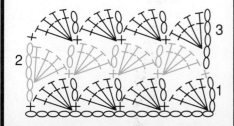

Diagram only: Rep 2nd and 3rd rows.

Diagram only: Rep 2nd and 3rd rows.

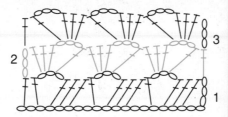

2nd row: 3ch (count as 1dc), *into next 3ch arch work [3dc, 3ch, 1dc]; rep from * to last 3dc, skip 3dc, 1dc into next ch, turn.
3rd row: 3ch, *into next 3ch arch work [3dc, 3ch, 1dc]; rep from * to last 4dc, skip 3dc, 1dc into 3rd of 3ch at beg of previous row, turn.
Rep 3rd row.

Warm Glow

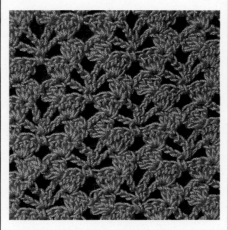

Starting chain: Multiple of 13 sts + 9.

1st row (right side): Work 3dc into 4th ch from hook, skip 4ch, 4dc into next ch, *3ch, skip 3ch, 1sc into next ch, 3ch, skip 3ch, 4dc into next ch, skip 4ch, 4dc into next ch; rep from * to end, turn.

2nd row: 3ch (count as 1dc), 3dc into first dc, skip 6dc, work 4dc into next dc, *3ch, 1sc into next sc, 3ch, 4dc into next dc, skip 6dc, 4dc into next dc; rep from * to end placing last group of 4dc into top of 3ch, turn.

3rd row: 6ch (count as 1dc, 3ch), work 1sc between next 2 groups of 4dc, *3ch, skip 3dc, 4dc into each of next 2dc, 3ch, 1sc between next 2 groups of 4dc; rep from * to last group, 3ch, 1dc into 3rd of 3ch at beg of previous row, turn.

4th row: 6ch, work 1sc into first sc, 3ch, *4dc into next dc, skip 6dc, 4dc into next dc, 3ch, 1sc into next sc, 3ch; rep from * to last arch, 1dc into 3rd of 6ch at beg of previous row, turn.

5th row: 3ch, 3dc into first dc, work 4dc into next dc, *3ch, 1sc between next 2 groups of 4dc, 3ch, skip 3dc, 4dc into each of next 2dc; rep from * to end placing last group of 4dc into 3rd of 6ch at beg of previous row, turn.

Rep 2nd to 5th rows.

Vine Leaf

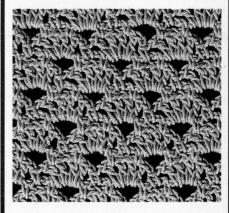

Starting chain: Multiple of 7 sts + 4.

1st row (wrong side): Work 1sc into 5th ch from hook, 3ch, skip 3ch, 1sc into next ch, *3ch, skip 2ch, 1sc into next ch, 3ch, skip 3ch, 1sc into next ch; rep from * to last 2ch, 1ch, 1hdc into last ch, turn.

2nd row: 1ch, 1sc into first hdc, *1ch, into next 3ch arch work [1dc, 1ch] 4 times, 1sc into next 3ch arch; rep from * to end placing last sc into 2nd ch, turn.

3rd row: 4ch (count as 1dc, 1ch), skip first ch sp, 1sc into next ch sp, 3ch, skip 1ch sp, 1sc into next ch sp, *3ch, skip 2ch sps, 1sc into next ch sp, 3ch, skip 1ch sp, 1sc into next ch sp; rep from * to last ch sp, 1ch, 1dc into last sc, turn.

4th row: 3ch (count as 1dc), work [1dc, 1ch] twice into first ch sp, 1sc into next 3ch arch, *1ch, work [1dc, 1ch] 4 times into next 3ch arch, 1sc into next 3ch arch; rep from * to last sp, 1ch, work [1dc, 1ch, 1dc] into last ch sp, 1dc into 3rd of 4ch at beg of previous row, turn.

5th row: 3ch (count as 1hdc, 1ch), 1sc into first ch sp, 3ch, skip 2ch sps, 1sc into next ch sp, *3ch, skip 1ch sp, 1sc into next ch sp, 3ch, skip 2ch sps, 1sc into next ch sp; rep from * to last 2dc, 1ch, 1hdc into 3rd of 3ch at beg of previous row, turn.

Rep 2nd to 5th rows.

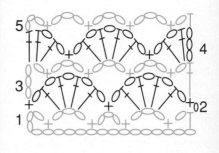

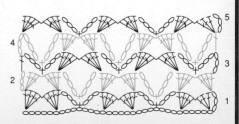

Openwork and Lace Patterns

Starburst

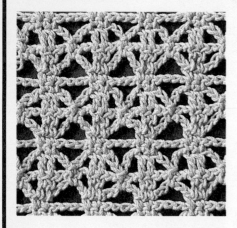

Starting chain: Multiple of 6 sts + 3.

1st row (right side): Work 1sc into 2nd ch from hook, 1sc into next ch, *6ch, skip 4ch, 1sc into each of next 2ch; rep from * to end, turn.

2nd row: 3ch (count as 1dc), skip first sc, 1dc into next sc, *2ch, 1sc into 6ch arch, 2ch, 1dc into each of next 2sc; rep from * to end, turn.

3rd row: 3ch, skip first dc, 1dc into next dc, *3ch, 1 sl st into next sc, 3ch, 1dc into each of next 2dc; rep from * to end placing last dc into 3rd of 3ch at beg of previous row, turn.

4th row: 1ch, 1sc into each of first 2dc, *4ch, 1sc into each of next 2dc; rep from * to end placing last sc into 3rd of 3ch at beg of previous row, turn.

5th row: 1ch, 1sc into each of first 2sc, *6ch, 1sc into each of next 2sc; rep from * to end, turn.

Rep 2nd to 5th rows.

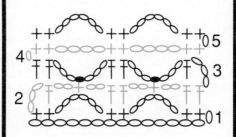

Bridge Stitch

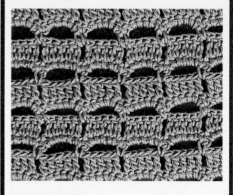

Starting chain: Multiple of 5 sts + 2.

1st row (right side): Work 1sc into 2nd ch from hook, *5ch, skip 4ch, 1sc into next ch; rep from * to end, turn.

2nd row: 1ch, work 1sc into first sc, *5sc into 5ch sp, 1sc into next sc; rep from * to end, turn.

3rd row: 3ch (count as 1dc), skip first sc, work 1dc into each of next 5sc, *1ch, skip 1sc, 1dc into each of next 5sc; rep from * to last sc, 1dc into last sc, turn.

4th row: 1ch, 1sc into first dc, *5ch, 1sc into next ch sp; rep from * to end placing last sc into 3rd of 3ch at beg of previous row, turn.

Rep 2nd to 4th rows.

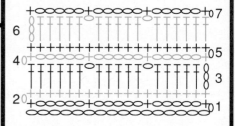

Diagram only: Rep 2nd to 7th rows.

Inverted Triangle

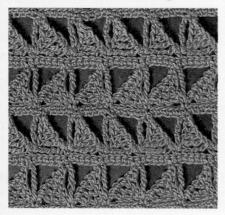

Starting chain: Multiple of 6 sts + 2.

1st row (right side): Work 1sc into 2nd ch from hook, 1sc into each ch to end, turn.

2nd row: 1ch, 1sc into first sc, *6ch, work 1sc into 2nd ch from hook, then working 1 st into each of next 4ch work 1hdc, 1dc, 1tr and 1dtr, skip 5sc on previous row, 1sc into next sc; rep from * to end, turn.

3rd row: 5ch (count as 1dtr), *1sc into ch at top of next triangle, 4ch, 1dtr into next sc; rep from * to end, turn.

4th row: 1ch, work 1sc into each [dtr, ch and sc] to end, placing last sc into top of 5ch at beg of previous row, turn.

Rep 2nd to 4th rows.

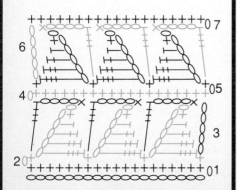

Diagram only: Rep 2nd to 7th rows.

Square Coin

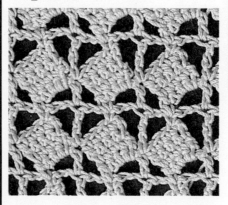

Starting chain: Multiple of 6 sts + 6.

1st row (right side): Work 1sc into 9th ch from hook (1dc and 3ch sp formed at beg of row), turn, 1ch, 1sc into sc, 3sc into 3ch sp, [turn, 1ch, 1sc into each of the 4sc] 3 times, skip next 2ch on starting chain, 1dc into next ch, *3ch, skip next 2ch on starting ch, 1sc into next ch, turn, 1ch, 1sc into sc, 3sc into 3ch sp, [turn, 1ch, 1sc into each of the 4sc] 3 times, skip next 2ch on starting ch, 1dc into next ch; rep from * to end, turn.

2nd row: 6ch (count as 1tr, 2ch), skip 1dc and 3sc, 1sc into next sc, 2ch, 1tr into next dc, *2ch, skip 3sc, 1sc into next sc, 2ch, 1tr into next dc; rep from * to end placing last tr into top of ch at beg of previous row, turn.

3rd row: 6ch (count as 1dc, 3ch), 1sc into first sc, turn, 1ch, 1sc into sc, 3sc into 3ch sp, [turn, 1ch, 1sc into each of the 4sc] 3 times, 1dc into next tr, *3ch, 1sc into next sc, turn, 1ch, 1sc into sc, 3sc into 3ch sp, [turn, 1ch, 1sc into each of the 4sc] 3 times, 1dc into next tr; rep from * to end placing last dc into 4th of 6ch at beg of previous row, turn.

Rep 2nd and 3rd rows ending with a 2nd row.

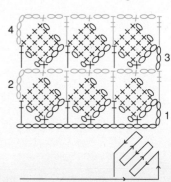

Line shows direction of work for first part of first row.

Stitch Variations, Abbreviations and Symbols on pages 7 to 15

Openwork and Lace Patterns

Two Leaf Bar

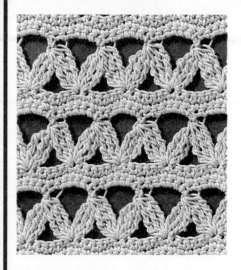

1st row (right side): Work 1sc into 2nd ch from hook, 1sc into each ch to end, turn.

2nd row: 1ch, work 1sc into each sc to end, turn.

3rd row: 5ch (count as 1dtr), skip first 3sc, work 1dtr group into next sc, 5ch, *1 double dtr group, 5ch; rep from * to last 3sc, into same sc as last group work 3dtr until 1 loop of each remains on hook (4 loops on hook), 1dtr into last sc until 5 loops remain on hook, yo and through all 5 loops, turn.

4th row: 1ch, 1sc into top of first group, 5sc into 5ch arch, *1sc into top of next group, 5sc into next 5ch arch; rep from * to last group, 1sc into 5th of 5ch at beg of previous row, turn.

5th row: 1ch, work 1sc into each sc to end, turn.

Rep 2nd to 5th rows.

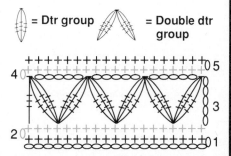

= Dtr group   = Double dtr group

Starting chain: Multiple of 6 sts + 2.

Special Abbreviations

Dtr group = work 3dtr into next sc until 1 loop of each remains on hook, yo and through all 4 loops on hook.

Double dtr group = work 3dtr into same sc as last group until 1 loop of each remains on hook (4 loops on hook), skip 5sc, into next sc work 3dtr until 1 loop of each remains on hook, yo and through all 7 loops on hook.

Braided Pattern

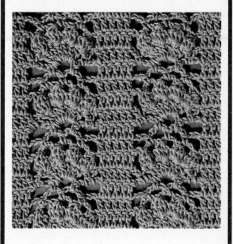

Starting chain: Multiple of 16 sts + 7.

Special Abbreviation

Bobble = work 4dc into next st until 1 loop of each remains on hook, yo and through all 5 loops on hook.

1st row (right side): Work 1dc into 4th ch from hook, 1dc into each of next 3ch, *4ch, skip 4ch, 1sc into next ch, 3ch, skip 1ch, 1sc into next ch, 4ch, skip 4ch, 1dc into each of next 5ch; rep from * to end, turn.

2nd row: 3ch (count as 1dc), skip first dc, 1dc into each of next 4dc, *2ch, 1sc into next 4ch arch, 1ch, work 7dc into next 3ch arch, 1ch, 1sc into next 4ch arch, 2ch, 1dc into each of next 5dc; rep from * to end placing last dc into top of 3ch at beg of previous row, turn.

3rd row: 3ch, skip first dc, 1dc into each of next 4dc, *1ch, 1 bobble into next dc, [3ch, skip 1dc, 1 bobble into next dc] 3 times, 1ch, 1dc into each of next 5dc; rep from * to end placing last dc into 3rd of 3ch at beg of previous row, turn.

4th row: 3ch, skip first dc, 1dc into each of next 4dc, *2ch, 1sc into next 3ch arch, [3ch, 1sc into next 3ch arch] twice, 2ch, 1dc into each of next 5dc; rep from * to end placing last dc into 3rd of 3ch at beg of previous row, turn.

5th row: 3ch, skip first dc, 1dc into each of next 4dc, *4ch, skip 2ch sp, 1sc into next 3ch arch, 3ch, 1sc into next 3ch arch, 4ch, 1dc into each of next 5dc; rep from * to end placing last dc into 3rd of 3ch at beg of previous row.

Rep 2nd to 5th rows.

Clover Leaf

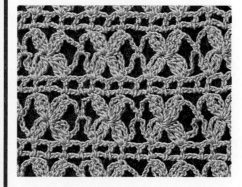

1st row (right side): Work 1dc into 8th ch from hook, *2ch, skip 2ch, 1dc into next ch; rep from * to end, turn.

2nd row: 1ch, 1sc into first dc, *9ch, skip 1dc, into next dc work [1sc, 4ch, tr2tog], skip 1dc, into next dc work [tr2tog, 4ch, 1sc]; rep from * to last 2 sps, 9ch, skip 1dc, 1sc into 3rd ch, turn.

3rd row: 10ch (count as ttr, 4ch), 1sc into first 9ch arch, *4ch, into top of next tr2tog work [tr2tog, 4ch, 1 sl st, 4ch, tr2tog], 4ch, 1sc into next 9ch arch; rep from * to end, 4ch, 1ttr into last sc, turn.

4th row: 1ch, 1sc into first ttr, *5ch, 1sc into top of next tr2tog; rep from * to end placing last sc into 6th of 10ch at beg of previous row, turn.

5th row: 5ch (count as 1dc, 2ch), 1dc into next 5ch arch, 2ch, 1dc into next sc, *2ch, 1dc into next 5ch arch, 2ch, 1dc into next sc; rep from * to end, turn.

Rep 2nd to 5th rows.

Starting chain: Multiple of 12 sts + 11.

Special Abbreviation

Tr2tog = work 2tr into next st until 1 loop of each remains on hook, yo and through all 3 loops on hook.

= Tr2tog

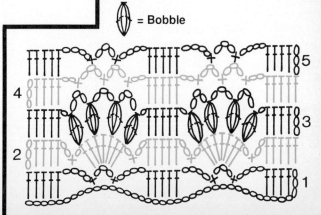

= Bobble

Openwork and Lace Patterns

Plaid Diagonal

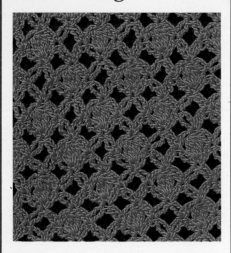

Starting chain: Multiple of 12 sts + 8.

Special Abbreviations

Cluster = 3ch, 1tr worked until 2 loops remain on hook (first leg), 1tr worked until 3 loops remain, yo and through all 3 loops, 3ch, 1sc into same st as last tr (2nd leg).

Bobble on cluster = work first leg of cluster then work 4tr into next sc until 1 loop of each remains on hook (6 loops on hook), work 2nd leg of cluster but bringing yarn through all 7 loops on hook to finish tr, complete 2nd leg as for cluster.

1st row (right side): Work 1sc into 2nd ch from hook, *work first leg of cluster into same ch as last sc, skip 5ch, work 2nd leg of cluster into next ch; rep from * to end, turn.

2nd row: 4ch (count as 1tr), into top of first cluster work [1tr, 3ch, 1sc], *work next cluster placing 2nd leg into top of next cluster; rep from * finishing with 2nd leg worked into top of last cluster, work first leg of cluster, 1tr into last sc until 3 loops remain, yo and through all 3 loops, turn.

3rd row: 1ch, 1sc into first st, *work cluster placing 2nd leg into top of next cluster; rep from * to end **but** working bobble on next and every alt cluster, turn.

4th row: As 2nd row.

5th row: As 3rd row **but** working bobble on first then every alt cluster, turn.

Rep 2nd to 5th rows.

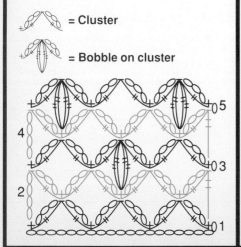

= Cluster

= Bobble on cluster

Wider View

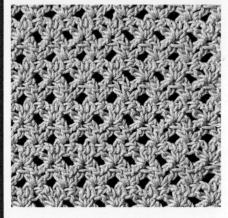

Starting chain: Multiple of 4 sts + 2.

1st row (right side): Work 1sc into 2nd ch from hook, *2ch, into same ch as last sc work 1dc until 2 loops remain on hook, skip 3ch, work 1dc into next ch until 3 loops remain on hook, yo and through all 3 loops, 2ch, 1sc into same ch as last dc, (1 cluster made); rep from * to end, turn.

2nd row: 3ch (count as 1dc), work 1dc into top of first cluster, *2ch, into same cluster as last dc work [1sc, 2ch, 1dc until 2 loops remain on hook], 1dc into top of next cluster until 3 loops remain on hook, yo and through all 3 loops; rep from * to end placing last dc into last sc, turn.

3rd row: 1ch, into first cluster work [1sc, 2ch, 1dc until 2 loops remain on hook], 1dc into top of next cluster until 3 loops remain on hook, yo and through all 3 loops, *2ch, into same cluster as last dc work [1sc, 2ch, 1dc until 2 loops remain on hook], 1dc into next cluster until 3 loops remain on hook, yo and through all 3 loops; rep from * to end, 2ch, 1sc into 3rd of 3ch at beg of previous row, turn.

Rep 2nd and 3rd rows.

Crossbar Diamond

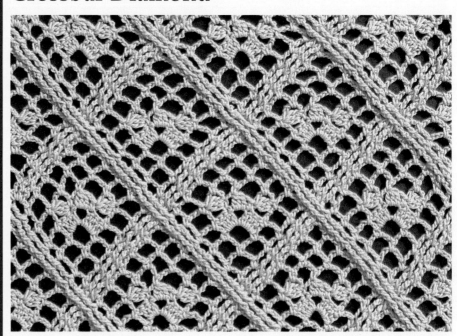

Starting chain: Multiple of 24 sts + 6.

Special Abbreviations

Bobble = work 3dc into next st until 1 loop of each dc remains on hook, yo and through all 4 loops on hook.

Tr/rf (Treble round front) = on a right side row: **working from front of work**, work 1tr inserting hook from right to left under stem of next dc or tr in previous row.

Tr/rb (Treble round back) = on a wrong side row: **working at back** (right side of work), work 1tr inserting hook from right to left under stem of next dc or tr in previous row. (See page 10).

Cross 4tr/rf (Cross 4 treble round front) = skip next 2tr, work 1tr/rf round each of next 2tr, 1ch, work 1tr/rf around each of the 2 skipped tr.

1st row (right side): Work 1sc into 2nd ch from hook, 3ch, skip 1ch, 2dc into next ch, skip 1ch, 1sc into next ch, 5ch, skip 3ch, 1sc into next ch, 4ch, 1 bobble into side of last sc worked, skip 3ch, 1sc into next ch, 2ch, skip 1ch, 1 bobble into next ch, 2ch, skip 1ch, 1sc into next ch, 4ch, 1 bobble into side of last sc worked, skip 3ch, 1sc into next ch, 5ch, skip 3ch, 1sc into next ch, skip 1ch, *into next ch work [2dc, 1ch, 2dc], skip 1ch, 1sc into next ch, 5ch, skip 3ch, 1sc into next ch, 4ch, 1 bobble into

Stitch Variations, Abbreviations and Symbols on pages 7 to 15

Openwork and Lace Patterns

side of last sc worked, skip 3ch, 1sc into next ch, 2ch, skip 1ch, 1 bobble into next ch, 2ch, skip 1ch, 1sc into next ch, 4ch, 1 bobble into side of last sc worked, skip 3ch, 1sc into next ch, 5ch, skip 3ch, 1sc into next ch, skip 1ch; rep from * to last 3ch, 2dc into next ch, 3ch, skip 1ch, 1sc into last ch, turn.

2nd row: 6ch (count as 1tr, 2ch), 1sc into next 3ch arch, *3ch, 1tr/rb around each of next 2dc, 1sc into next 5ch arch, 5ch, 1sc into next 4ch arch, 5ch, 1sc into top of next bobble, 5ch, 1sc into next 4ch arch, 5ch, 1sc into next 5ch arch, 1tr/rb around each of next 2dc, 3ch, 1sc into next ch sp; rep from * to last sc placing last sc into last 3ch arch, 2ch, 1tr into last sc, turn.

3rd row: 1ch, 1sc into first tr, 5ch, skip 2ch arch, *1sc into next 3ch arch, 3ch, 1tr/rf around each of next 2tr, 1sc into next 5ch arch, [5ch, 1sc into next 5ch arch] 3 times, 1tr/rf around each of next 2tr, 3ch, 1sc into next 3ch arch, 5ch; rep from * to last 2ch sp, 1sc into 4th of 6ch at beg of previous row, turn.

4th row: 6ch, 1sc into next 5ch arch, *5ch, 1sc into next 3ch arch, 3ch, 1tr/rb around each of next 2tr, 1sc into next 5ch arch, [5ch, 1sc into next 5ch arch] twice, 1tr/rb around each of next 2tr, 3ch, 1sc into next 3ch arch, 5ch, 1sc into next 5ch arch; rep from * to last sc, 2ch, 1tr into last sc, turn.

5th row: 1ch, 1sc into first tr, 5ch, 1sc into next 5ch arch, 5ch, 1sc into next 3ch arch, 3ch, 1tr/rf around each of next 2tr, 1sc into next 5ch arch, 5ch, 1sc into next 5ch arch, 1tr/rf around each of next 2tr, *3ch, 1sc into next 3ch arch, 5ch, [1sc into next 5ch arch, 5ch] twice, 1sc into next 3ch arch, 3ch, 1tr/rf around each of next 2tr, 1sc into next 5ch arch, 5ch, 1sc into next 5ch arch, 1tr/rf around each of next 2tr; rep from * to last 3 arches, 3ch, 1sc into next 3ch arch, 5ch, 1sc into next 5ch arch, 5ch, 1sc into 4th of 6ch at beg of previous row, turn.

6th row: 4ch (count as 1tr), work [1dc, 2ch, 3dc] into first 5ch arch, 1sc into next 5ch arch, 5ch, 1sc into next 3ch arch, 3ch, 1tr/rb around each of next 2tr, 1sc into next 5ch arch, 1tr/rb around each of next 2tr, *3ch, 1sc into next 3ch arch, 5ch, 1sc into next 5ch arch, into next 5ch arch work [3dc, 3ch, 3dc], 1sc into next 5ch arch, 5ch, 1sc into next 3ch arch, 3ch, 1tr/rb around each of next 2tr, 1sc into next 5ch arch, 1tr/rb around each of next 2tr; rep from * to last 3 arches, 3ch, 1sc into next 3ch arch, 5ch, 1sc into next 5ch arch, work [3dc, 2ch, 1dc] into last 5ch arch, 1tr into last sc, turn.

7th row: 1ch, 1sc into first tr, 2ch, 1 bobble into first 2ch sp, 2ch, 1sc into next dc, *4ch, 1 bobble into side of last sc worked, 1sc into next 5ch arch, 5ch, 1sc into next 3ch arch, cross 4tr/rf, 1sc into next 3ch arch, 5ch, 1sc into next 5ch arch, 4ch, 1 bobble into side of last sc worked, skip 2dc, 1sc into next dc, 2ch, 1 bobble into next 3ch arch, 2ch, 1sc into next dc; rep from * to end placing last bobble into last 2ch sp and last sc into 4th of 4ch at

beg of previous row, turn.

8th row: 6ch, work 1sc into top of first bobble, *5ch, 1sc into next 4ch arch, 5ch, 1sc into next 5ch arch, 1tr/rb around each of next 2tr, 3ch, 1sc into ch sp, 3ch, 1tr/rb around each of next 2tr, 1sc into next 5ch arch, 5ch, 1sc into next 4ch arch, 5ch, 1sc into top of next bobble; rep from * to last sc, 2ch, 1tr into last sc, turn.

9th row: 1ch, 1sc into first tr, [5ch, 1sc into next 5ch arch] twice, 1tr/rf around each of next 2tr, 3ch, 1sc into next 3ch arch, 5ch, 1sc into next 3ch arch, 3ch, 1tr/rf around each of next 2tr, *1sc into next 5ch arch, [5ch, 1sc into next 5ch arch] 3 times, 1tr/rf around each of next 2tr, 3ch, 1sc into next 3ch arch, 5ch, 1sc into next 3ch arch, 3ch, 1tr/rf around each of next 2tr; rep from * to last 3 arches, [1sc into next 5ch arch, 5ch] twice, 1sc into 4th of 6ch, turn.

10th row: 6ch, 1sc into first 5ch arch, 5ch, 1sc into next 5ch arch, 1tr/rb around each of next 2tr, 3ch, 1sc into next 3ch arch, 5ch, 1sc into next 5ch arch, 5ch, 1sc into next 3ch arch, 3ch, 1tr/rb around each of next 2tr, *1sc into next 5ch arch, [5ch, 1sc into next 5ch arch] twice, 1tr/rb around each of next 2tr, 3ch, 1sc into next 3ch arch, 5ch, 1sc into next 5ch arch, 5ch, 1sc into next 3ch arch, 3ch, 1tr/rb around each of next 2tr; rep from * to last 2 arches, 1sc into next 5ch arch, 5ch, 1sc into last 5ch arch, 2ch, 1tr into last sc, turn.

11th row: 1ch, 1sc into first tr, 5ch, 1sc into next 5ch arch, *1tr/rf around each of next 2tr, 3ch, 1sc into next 3ch arch, 5ch, [1sc into next 5ch arch, 5ch] twice, 1sc into next 3ch arch, 3ch, 1tr/rf around each of next 2tr, 1sc into next 5ch arch, 5ch, 1sc into next 5ch arch; rep from * to end placing last sc into 4th of 6ch, turn.

12th row: 6ch, 1sc into first 5ch arch, *1tr/rb around each of next 2tr, 3ch, 1sc into next 3ch arch, 5ch, 1sc into next 5ch arch, into next 5ch arch work [3dc, 3ch, 3dc], 1sc into next 5ch arch, 5ch, 1sc into next 3ch arch, 3ch, 1tr/rb around each of next 2tr, 1sc into next 5ch arch; rep from * to last sc, 2ch, 1tr into last sc, turn.

13th row: 1ch, 1sc into first tr, 1tr/rf around each of next 2tr, 3ch, 1sc into next 3ch arch, 5ch, 1sc into next 5ch arch, 4ch, 1 bobble into side of last sc worked, skip 2dc, 1sc into next dc, 2ch, 1 bobble into next 3ch arch, 2ch, 1sc into next dc, 4ch, 1 bobble into side of last sc worked, 1sc into next 5ch arch, 5ch, 1sc into next 3ch arch, *cross 4tr/rf, 1sc into next 3ch arch, 5ch, 1sc into next 5ch arch, 4ch, 1 bobble into side of last sc worked, skip 2dc, 1sc into next dc, 2ch, 1 bobble into next 3ch arch, 2ch, 1sc into next dc, 4ch, 1 bobble into side of last sc worked, 1sc into next 5ch arch, 5ch, 1sc into next 3ch arch; rep from * to last 2tr, 3ch, 1tr/rf around each of next 2tr, 1sc into 4th of 6ch, turn.

14th row: 6ch, 1sc into first 3ch arch, 3ch, 2tr into same 3ch arch as last sc, 1sc into next 5ch arch, 5ch, 1sc into next 4ch arch, 5ch, 1sc into top of next bobble, 5ch, 1sc into next 4ch arch, 5ch, 1sc into next 5ch arch, *1tr/rb around each of next 2tr, 3ch, 1sc into next ch sp, 3ch, 1tr/rb around each of next 2tr, 1sc into next 5ch arch, 5ch, 1sc into next 4ch arch, 5ch, 1sc into top of next bobble, 5ch, 1sc into next 4ch arch, 5ch, 1sc into next 5ch arch; rep from * to last 3ch arch, into last 3ch arch work [2tr, 3ch, 1sc], 2ch, 1tr into last sc, turn.

Rep 3rd to 14th rows.

= Tr/rf	= Tr/rb	= Bobble	=Cross 4 tr/rf

= 1sc, 4ch, work 1 bobble into side of sc just worked

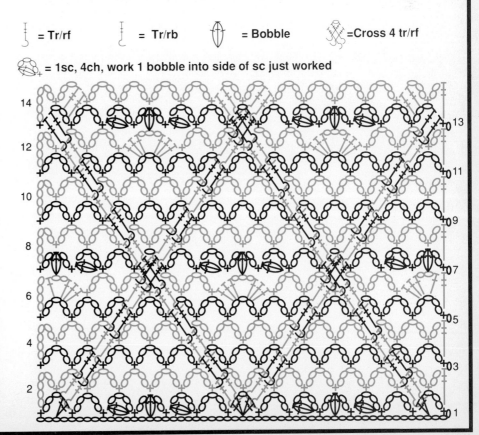

Openwork and Lace Patterns

Eight Bar Stitch

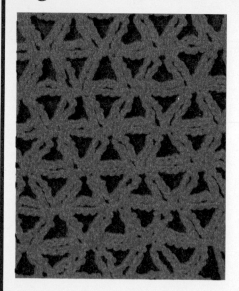

Starting chain: Multiple of 8 sts + 4.

1st row (right side): Work 1sc into 2nd ch from hook, 1sc into next ch, 9ch, 1sc into next ch, 5ch, skip 5ch, 1sc into next ch, *[9ch, 1sc into next ch] twice, 5ch, skip 5ch, 1sc into next ch; rep from * to last 2ch, 9ch, 1sc into each of last 2ch, turn.

2nd row: 7ch (count as 1tr, 3ch), *1sc into next 9ch loop, 1ch, 1sc into next 9ch loop, 5ch; rep from * to end omitting 2ch at end of last rep, 1tr into last sc, turn.

3rd row: 1ch, 1sc into first tr, 3ch, *1sc into next sc, 9ch, 1sc into next ch sp, 9ch, 1sc into next sc, 5ch; rep from * to end omitting 2ch at end of last rep, 1sc into 4th of 7ch at beg of previous row, turn.

4th row: 5ch (count as 1tr, 1ch), *1sc into next 9ch loop, 5ch, 1sc into next 9ch loop, 1ch; rep from * to end, 1tr into last sc, turn.

5th row: 1ch, 1sc into first tr, 1sc into next ch sp, 9ch, 1sc into next sc, 5ch, *1sc into next sc, 9ch, 1sc into next ch sp, 9ch, 1sc

into next sc, 5ch; rep from * to last sc, 1sc into last sc, 9ch, 1sc into ch sp, 1sc into 4th of 5ch at beg of previous row, turn.

Rep 2nd to 5th rows ending with a 2nd or 4th row.

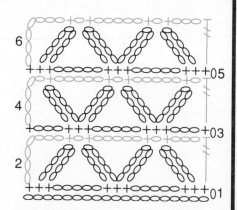

Open Link

Starting chain: Multiple of 18 sts + 8.

1st row (right side): Work 1dc into 8th ch from hook, *2ch, skip 2ch, 1dc into next ch; rep from * to end, turn.

2nd row: 5ch (count as 1dc, 2ch), skip first dc, 1dc into next dc, *4ch, 1tr into each of next 4dc, 4ch, 1dc into next dc, 2ch, 1dc into next dc; rep from * to end placing last dc into 3rd turning ch at beg of previous row, turn.

3rd row: 5ch, skip first dc, 1dc into next dc, *4ch, 1sc into each of next 4tr, 4ch, 1dc into next dc, 2ch, 1dc into next dc; rep from * to end placing last dc into 3rd of 5ch at beg of previous row, turn.

4th row: 5ch, skip first dc, 1dc into next dc, *4ch, 1sc into each of next 4sc, 4ch, 1dc into next dc, 2ch, 1dc into next dc; rep from * to end placing last dc into 3rd of 5ch at beg of previous row, turn.

5th row: As 4th row.

6th row: 5ch, skip first dc, 1dc into next dc, *2ch, [1tr into next sc, 2ch] 4 times, 1dc into next dc, 2ch, 1dc into next dc; rep from * to end placing last dc into 3rd of 5ch at beg of previous row, turn.

7th row: 5ch, skip first dc, 1dc into next dc, *2ch, [1dc into next tr, 2ch] 4 times, 1dc into next dc, 2ch, 1dc into next dc; rep from * to end placing last dc into 3rd of 5ch at beg of previous row, turn.

Rep 2nd to 7th rows.

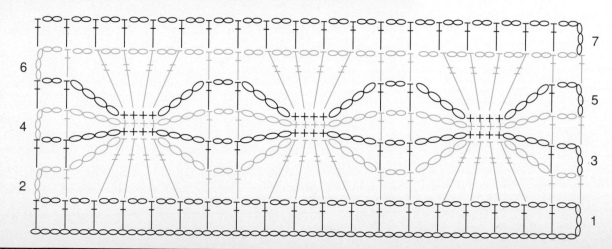

Stitch Variations, Abbreviations and Symbols on pages 7 to 15

Openwork and Lace Patterns

Block Trellis Stitch

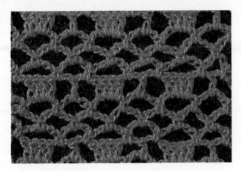

Multiple of 8 sts + 5.
(add 1 for base chain)

1st row (right side): 1sc into 2nd ch from hook, *5ch, skip 3ch, 1sc into next ch; rep from * to end, turn.

2nd row: *5ch, 1sc into next 5ch arch; rep from * ending 2ch, 1dc into last sc, skip tch, turn.

3rd row: 3ch (count as 1dc), 1dc into first st, 2ch, 1dc into next 5ch arch, *2ch, 4dc into next arch, 2ch, 1dc into next arch; rep from * to end, turn.

4th row: *5ch, 1sc into next 2ch sp; rep from * ending 2ch, 1dc into top of tch, turn.

5th row: 1ch, 1sc into first st, *5ch, 1sc into next 5ch arch; rep from * to end, turn.

Rep 2nd, 3rd, 4th and 5th rows.

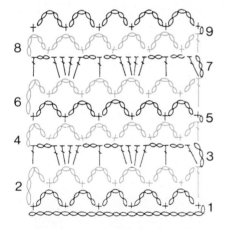

Bullion Trellis Stitch

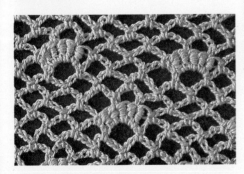

Multiple of 16 sts + 5.
(add 1 for base chain)

Base row (right side): 1sc into 2nd ch from hook, *[5ch, skip 3ch, 1sc into next ch] twice, skip 3ch, work 5 Bullion sts into next ch, skip 3ch, 1sc into next ch; rep from * to last 4ch, 5ch, skip 3ch, 1sc into last ch, turn.

Commence Pattern

1st row: 5ch, 1sc into next 5ch arch, *5ch, 1sc into 2nd of next 5 Bullion sts, 5ch, 1sc into 4th Bullion st of same group, [5ch, 1sc into next arch] twice; rep from * ending 2ch, 1dc into last sc, skip tch, turn.

2nd row: 1ch, 1sc into first st, *5ch, 1sc into next arch; rep from * to end, turn.

3rd row: *5ch, 1sc into next arch; rep from * ending 2ch, 1dc into last sc, skip tch, turn.

4th row: 1ch, 1sc into first st, skip 2ch sp, *5 Bullion sts into next 5ch arch, 1sc into next arch, [5ch, 1sc into next arch] twice; rep from * ending 5ch, 1sc into tch arch, turn.

5th row: 5ch, 1sc into next 5ch arch, *[5ch, 1sc into next arch] twice, 5ch, 1sc into 2nd of next 5 Bullion sts, 5ch, 1sc into 4th Bullion st of same group; rep from * ending 2ch, 1dc into last sc, skip tch, turn.

6th row: As 2nd row.

7th row: As 3rd row.

8th row: 1ch, 1sc into first st, *[5ch, 1sc into next 5ch arch] twice, 5 Bullion sts into next arch, 1sc into next arch; rep from * ending 5ch, 1sc into tch arch, turn.

Rep these 8 rows.

Ŧ = Bullion st with [yo] 7 times.

Shell Trellis Stitch

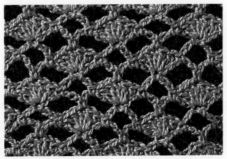

Multiple of 12 sts + 1.
(add 2 for base chain)

1st row (right side): 2dc into 3rd ch from hook, *skip 2ch, 1sc into next ch, 5ch, skip 5ch, 1sc into next ch, skip 2ch, 5dc into next ch; rep from * ending last rep with only 3dc into last ch, turn.

2nd row: 1ch, 1sc into first st, *5ch, 1sc into next 5ch arch, 5ch, 1sc into 3rd dc of next 5dc; rep from * ending last rep with 1sc into top of tch, turn.

3rd row: *5ch, 1sc into next 5ch arch, 5dc into next sc, 1sc into next arch; rep from * ending 2ch, 1dc into last sc, skip tch, turn.

4th row: 1ch, 1sc into first st, *5ch, 1sc into 3rd dc of next 5dc, 5ch, 1sc into next 5ch arch; rep from * to end, turn.

5th row: 3ch (count as 1dc), 2dc into first st, *1sc into next arch, 5ch, 1sc into next arch, 5dc into next sc; rep from * ending last rep with only 3dc into last sc, skip tch, turn.

Rep 2nd, 3rd, 4th and 5th rows.

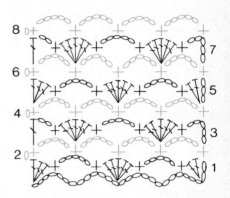

Puff Cluster Trellis Stitch

Multiple of 6 sts + 2.
(add 3 for base chain)

1st row (right side): 1sc into 5th ch from hook, *3ch, skip 2ch, 1sc into next ch; rep from * to end, turn.

2nd row: 3ch, 1sc into next 3ch arch, *3ch, hdc3tog into next arch, 3ch, 1sc into next arch; rep from * to end, turn.

3rd row: *3ch, 1sc into next 3ch arch; rep from * to end, turn.

4th row: *3ch, hdc3tog into next 3ch arch, 3ch, 1sc into next arch; rep from * ending 3ch, hdc3tog into tch arch, turn.

5th row: As 3rd row.

Rep 2nd, 3rd, 4th and 5th rows.

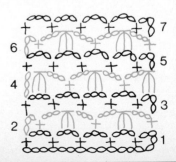

Openwork and Lace Patterns

Fan Trellis Stitch

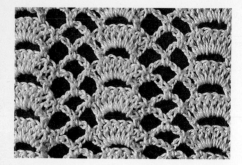

Multiple of 12 sts + 11.
(add 1 for base chain)

1st row (wrong side): 1sc into 2nd ch from hook, *5ch, skip 3ch, 1sc into next ch; rep from * to last 2ch, 2ch, skip 1ch, 1dc into last ch, turn.

2nd row: 1ch, 1sc into first st, skip 2ch sp, *7dc into next 5ch arch, 1sc into next arch**, 5ch, 1sc into next arch; rep from * ending last rep at **, 2ch, 1tr into last sc, skip tch, turn.

3rd row: 1ch, 1sc into first st, *5ch, 1sc into 2nd of next 7dc, 5ch, 1sc into 6th dc of same group**, 5ch, 1sc into next 5ch arch; rep from * ending last rep at **, 2ch, 1tr into last sc, skip tch, turn.

Rep 2nd and 3rd rows.

Floral Trellis Stitch

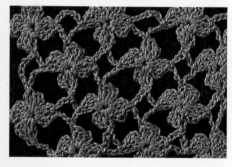

Any number of Flower Units.

1st row (right side): 7ch, *sl st into 4th ch from hook, 3ch, into ring just formed work a Base Flower Unit of [2dc, 3ch, sl st, 3ch, 2dc]**, 10ch; rep from * ending last rep at ** when fabric is required width, then keep same side facing and turn so as to be able to work along underside of Base Flower Units.

2nd row (right side): *3ch, sl st into ch ring at center of Flower, 3ch, [2dc, 3ch, sl st — center Petal completed, 3ch, 2dc] all into same ring, skip 2ch of base chain which connects Units, sl st into next ch, 7ch, skip 2ch,

---

sl st into next ch; rep from * into next and each Base Flower Unit to end, turn. **Note:** Check that each Base Flower Unit is not twisted before you work into it.

3rd row: 11ch, sl st into 4th ch from hook, 3ch, 2dc into ring just formed, 3ch, sl st into top of 3ch of center Petal of last Flower made in previous row (see diagram), *10ch, sl st into 4th ch from hook, 3ch, 2dc into ring just formed, sl st into 4th of next 7ch arch of previous row, 3ch, [sl st, 3ch, 2dc] into same ch ring as last 2dc, 3ch, sl st into top of 3ch of center Petal of next Flower in previous row; rep from * to end, turn.

4th row: 9ch, skip 2ch, sl st into next ch, *3ch, sl st into ch ring at center of Flower, 3ch, work [2dc, 3ch, sl st, 3ch, 2dc] into same ring, skip 2ch, sl st into next ch, 7ch, skip [3ch, sl st and next 2ch], sl st into next ch; rep from * ending 3ch, sl st into ch ring at center of last Flower, 3ch, 2dc into same ring, turn.

5th row: *10ch, sl st into 4th ch from hook, 3ch, 2dc into ring just formed, sl st into 4th ch of next arch of previous row, 3ch, [sl st, 3ch, 2dc] into same ch ring as last 2dc**, 3ch, sl st into top of 3ch of center Petal of next Flower in previous row; rep from * ending last rep at **, turn.

Rep 2nd, 3rd, 4th and 5th rows.

When fabric is required length, finishing after a 4th (right side) row (see asterisk on diagram), continue down left side to complete edge Flowers as follows: *3ch, [sl st, 3ch, 2dc, 3ch, sl st, 3ch, 2dc] all into ch ring at center of edge Flower, skip 3ch, sl st into next ch**, 6ch, sl st into last ch before center Petal of next edge Flower (see diagram); rep from * ending last rep at ** after last edge Flower.

Fasten off.

Double Trellis Stitch

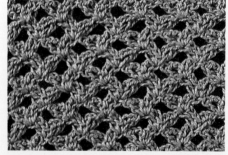

Multiple of 4 sts + 1.
(add 1 for base chain)

1st row (right side): 1sc into 2nd ch from hook, *3ch, dc2tog inserting hook into same place as sc just made for first leg and then into following 4th ch for 2nd leg, (skipping 3ch between), 3ch, 1sc into same place as 2nd leg of cluster just made; rep from * to end, turn.

2nd row: 4ch, 1dc into top of next cluster (counts as edge cluster), 3ch, 1sc into same place as dc just made, *3ch, dc2tog inserting hook into same place as sc just made for first leg and then into next cluster for 2nd leg, 3ch, 1sc into same place as 2nd leg of cluster just made; rep from * ending 3ch, yo, insert hook into same place as sc just made, yo, draw loop through, yo, draw through 2 loops, [yo] twice, insert hook into last sc, yo, draw loop through, [yo, draw through 2 loops] twice, yo, draw through all 3 loops on hook, skip tch, turn.

3rd row: 1ch, 1sc into first st, *3ch, dc2tog inserting hook into same place as sc just made for first leg and then into next cluster for 2nd leg, 3ch, 1sc into same place as 2nd leg of cluster just made; rep from * to end, turn.

Rep 2nd and 3rd rows.

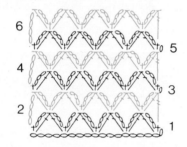

Diamond Shell Trellis Stitch

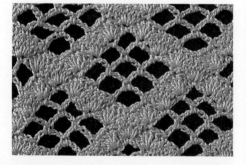

Multiple of 16 sts + 5.
(add 1 for base chain)

Base row (right side): 1sc into 2nd ch from hook, [5ch, skip 3ch, 1sc into next ch] twice, *skip 1ch, 5dc into next ch, skip 1ch, 1sc into next ch**, [5ch, skip 3ch, 1sc into next ch] 3 times; rep from * ending last rep at ** when 8ch remain, [5ch, skip 3ch, 1sc into next ch] twice, turn.

Commence Pattern

1st row: *[5ch, 1sc into next 5ch arch] twice, 5dc into next sc, 1sc into 3rd of next 5dc, 5dc into next sc, 1sc into next arch; rep from * ending 5ch, 1sc into next arch, 2ch, 1dc into last sc, skip tch, turn.

Stitch Variations, Abbreviations and Symbols on pages 7 to 15

Openwork and Lace Patterns

2nd row: 1ch, 1sc into first st, skip 2ch, *5ch, 1sc into next 5ch arch, 5dc into next sc, 1sc into 3rd of next 5dc, 5ch, 1sc into 3rd of next 5dc, 5dc into next sc, 1sc into next arch; rep from * ending 5ch, 1sc into tch arch, turn.

3rd row: 3ch (count as 1dc), 2dc into first st, *1sc into next 5ch arch, 5dc into next sc, 1sc into 3rd of next 5dc, 5ch, 1sc into next arch, 5ch, 1sc into 3rd of next 5dc, 5dc into next sc; rep from * ending 1sc into next arch, 3dc into last sc, skip tch, turn.

4th row: 1ch, 1sc into first st, *5dc into next sc, 1sc into 3rd of next 5dc, [5ch, 1sc into next arch] twice, 5ch, 1sc into 3rd of next 5dc; rep from * ending 5dc into next sc, 1sc into top of tch, turn.

5th row: 3ch (count as 1dc), 2dc into first st, *1sc into 3rd of next 5dc, 5dc into next sc, 1sc into next arch, [5ch, 1sc into next arch] twice, 5dc into next sc; rep from * ending 1sc into 3rd of next 5dc, 3dc into last sc, skip tch, turn.

6th row: 1ch, 1sc into first st, *5ch, 1sc into 3rd of next 5dc, 5dc into next sc, 1sc into next arch, 5ch, 1sc into next arch, 5dc into next sc, 1sc into 3rd of next 5dc; rep from * ending 5ch, 1sc into top of tch, turn.

7th row: *5ch, 1sc into next 5ch arch, 5ch, 1sc into 3rd of next 5dc, 5dc into next sc, 1sc into next arch, 5dc into next sc, 1sc into 3rd of next 5dc; rep from * ending 5ch, 1sc into next arch, 2ch, 1dc into last sc, skip tch, turn.

8th row: 1ch, 1sc into first st, skip 2ch, 5ch, 1sc into next 5ch arch, 5ch, 1sc into 3rd of next 5dc, *5dc into next sc, 1sc into 3rd of next 5dc, [5ch, 1sc into next arch] twice**, 5ch, 1sc into 3rd of next 5dc; rep from * ending last rep at ** in tch arch, turn.

Rep these 8 rows.

Ruled Lattice

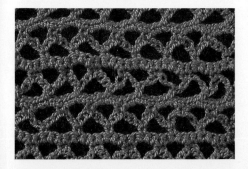

Multiple of 4 sts + 1.
(add 1 for base chain)

1st row (right side): 1sc into 2nd ch from hook, 1sc into each ch to end, turn.

2nd row: 7ch, skip first 2 sts, 1sc into next st, *7ch, skip 3 sts, 1sc into next st; rep from * to last 2 sts, 3ch, skip 1 st, 1dc into last st, skip tch, turn.

3rd row: 1ch, 1sc into first st, *3ch, 1sc into next 7ch arch; rep from * to end, turn.

4th row: 1ch, 1sc into first st, *3sc into next 3ch arch, 1sc into next sc; rep from * to end, skip tch, turn.

Rep 2nd, 3rd and 4th rows.

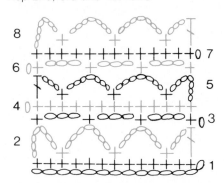

Doubled Lattice Stitch

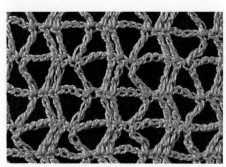

Multiple of 6 sts + 2.
(add 3 for base chain)

1st row (right side): Skip 6ch, 1tr into next ch (counts as edge cluster), 4ch, 1tr into same ch as tr just made, *tr2tog inserting hook into next ch for first leg and then into following 5th ch for 2nd leg (skipping 4ch between), 4ch, 1tr into same ch as 2nd leg of cluster just made; rep from * to last 4ch, tr2tog inserting hook into next ch for first leg and into last ch for 2nd leg, (skipping 2ch between), turn.

2nd row: 6ch (count as 1tr and 2ch), 1tr into first st, *tr2tog inserting hook into next tr for first leg and then into next cluster for 2nd leg**, 4ch, 1tr into same place as 2nd leg of cluster just made; rep from * ending last rep at ** when 2nd leg is in edge cluster, 2ch, 1tr into same place, turn.

3rd row: 4ch, skip 2ch, 1tr into next cluster (counts as edge cluster), *4ch, 1tr into same place as tr just made**, tr2tog inserting hook into next tr for first leg and then into next cluster for 2nd leg; rep from * ending last rep at **, tr2tog inserting hook into next tr for first leg and then into following 3rd ch for 2nd leg, turn.

Rep 2nd and 3rd rows.

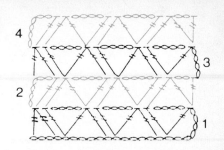

Crown Puff Lattice

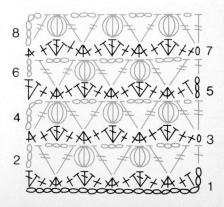

Multiple of 6 sts + 1.
(add 2 for base chain)

1st row (right side): 1hdc into 3rd ch from hook, *1sc into next ch, sc3tog over next 3ch, 1sc into next ch, [1hdc, 1dc, 1hdc] into next ch; rep from * omitting 1hdc at end of last rep, turn.

2nd row: 3ch (count as 1dc), skip first 3 sts, *[1tr, 3ch, 1tr] into next sc cluster, skip 2 sts**, work hdc5tog into next dc; rep from * ending last rep at **, 1dc into top of tch, turn.

3rd row: 1ch, skip 1 st, 1sc into next tr (all counts as sc cluster), *[1sc, 1hdc, 1dc, 1hdc, 1sc] into next 3ch arch**, sc3tog over next 3 sts; rep from * ending last rep at **, sc2tog over last st and top of tch, turn.

4th row: 5ch (count as 1tr and 1ch), 1tr into first st, *skip 2 sts, hdc5tog into next dc, skip 2 sts**, [1tr, 3ch, 1tr] into next sc cluster; rep from * ending last rep at **, [1tr, 1ch, 1tr] into top of tch, turn.

5th row: 3ch (count as 1dc), 1hdc into first st, 1sc into next ch sp, *sc3tog over next 3 sts**, [1sc, 1hdc, 1dc, 1hdc, 1sc] into next 3ch arch; rep from * ending last rep at **, 1sc into next ch of tch, [1hdc, 1dc] into next ch, turn.

Rep 2nd, 3rd, 4th and 5th rows.

Openwork and Lace Patterns

Crow's Foot Lattice

Multiple of 6 sts + 1.
(add 4 for base chain)

1st row (wrong side): Skip 4ch (count as 1tr and 1ch), 1dc into next ch, 1ch, skip 2ch, 1sc into next ch, *1ch, skip 2ch, work [1dc, 1ch, 1tr, 1ch, 1dc] into next ch, 1ch, skip 2ch, 1sc into next ch; rep from * to last 3ch, 1ch, skip 2ch, [1dc, 1ch, 1tr] into last ch, turn.

2nd row: 1ch, 1sc into first st, *1ch, skip 2 sps, 1tr into next sc, 1ch, 1dc into base of tr just made, 1ch, skip 2 sps, 1sc into next tr; rep from * ending last rep in tch, turn.

3rd row: 1ch, 1sc into first st, *1ch, skip sp, work [1dc, 1ch, 1tr, 1ch, 1dc] into next sp, 1ch, skip sp, 1sc into next sc; rep from * to end, turn.

4th row: 4ch (count as 1tr), 1dc into 4th ch from hook, *1ch, skip 2 sps, 1sc into next tr, 1ch, 1tr into next sc**, 1ch, 1dc into base of tr just made; rep from * ending last rep at **, 1dc into base of tr just made, turn.

5th row: 5ch (count as 1tr and 1ch), 1dc into first st, 1ch, skip sp, 1sc into next sc, *1ch, skip sp, work [1dc, 1ch, 1tr, 1ch, 1dc] into next sp, 1ch, skip sp, 1sc into next sc; rep from * ending 1ch, skip sp, [1dc, 1ch, 1tr] into top of tch, turn.

Rep 2nd, 3rd, 4th and 5th rows.

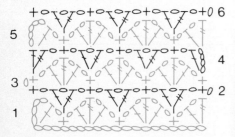

Open Fan Stitch

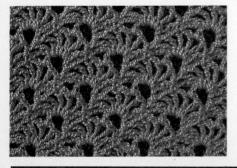

Multiple of 10 sts + 6.
(add 1 for base chain)

1st row (right side): 1sc into 2nd ch from hook, *1ch, skip 4ch, into next ch work a Fan of 1tr, [2ch, 1tr] 4 times, then 1ch, skip 4ch, 1sc into next ch; rep from * to last 5ch, 1ch, skip 4ch, into last ch work [1tr, 2ch] twice and 1tr, turn.

2nd row: 1ch, 1sc into first st, *3ch, skip next 2ch sp, 1dc into next sp**, 2ch, skip next tr, sc and tr and work 1dc into first 2ch sp of next Fan, 3ch, work 1sc into center tr of Fan; rep from * ending last rep at **, 1ch, 1tr into last sc, skip tch, turn.

3rd row: 7ch (count as 1tr and 2ch), skip first tr, work [1tr, 2ch, 1tr] into next 1ch sp, 1ch, skip 3ch sp, 1sc into next sc, *1ch, skip next 3ch sp, work a Fan into next 2ch sp, 1ch, skip next 3ch sp, 1sc into next sc; rep from * to end, skip tch, turn.

4th row: 6ch (count as 1tr and 1ch), skip first tr, work 1dc into next 2ch sp, 3ch, 1sc into center tr of Fan, *3ch, skip next 2ch sp, 1dc into next 2ch sp, 2ch, skip next tr, sc and tr, work 1dc into next 2ch sp, 3ch, 1sc into center tr of Fan; rep from * ending last rep in 3rd of tch, turn.

5th row: 1ch, *1sc into sc, 1ch, skip next 3ch sp, Fan into next 2ch sp, 1ch, skip next 3ch sp; rep from * to last sc, 1sc into sc, 1ch, skip next 3ch sp, work [1tr, 2ch] twice and 1tr all into top of tch, turn.

Rep 2nd, 3rd, 4th and 5th rows.

Open Shell and Picot Stitch

Multiple of 7 sts.
(add 1 for base chain)

1st row (right side): 1sc into 2nd ch from hook, *skip 2ch, work a Shell of [1dc, 1ch, 1dc, 1ch, 1dc] into next ch, skip 2ch, 1sc into next ch**, 3ch, 1sc into next ch; rep from * ending last rep at ** in last ch, turn.

2nd row: 7ch (count as 1tr and 3ch), *work a Picot of [1sc, 3ch, 1sc] into center dc of next Shell, 3ch**, 1dc into next 3ch arch; rep from * ending last rep at **, 1tr into last

sc, skip tch, turn.

3rd row: 1ch, 1sc into first st, *skip next 3ch sp, Shell into center of next Picot, skip next 3ch sp**, Picot into next dc; rep from * ending last rep at **, 1sc into next ch of tch, turn.

Rep 2nd and 3rd rows.

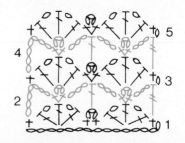

Ridged String Network

Multiple of 4 sts + 1.
(add 1 for base chain)

1st row (right side): 1sc into 2nd ch from hook, *3ch, skip 3ch, 1sc into next ch; rep from * to end, turn.

2nd row: 1ch, working into back loop only of each st work 1sc into first st, *3ch, skip 3ch, 1sc into next sc; rep from * to end, skip tch, turn.

Rep 2nd row.

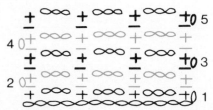

Double Picot String Network

Stitch Variations, Abbreviations and Symbols on pages 7 to 15

Openwork and Lace Patterns

Multiple of 6 sts + 5.
(add 1 for base chain)

1st row (wrong side): 1sc into 2nd ch from hook, *3ch, skip 4ch, work a picot of [1sc, 3ch, 1sc] into next ch; rep from * to last 5ch, 3ch, skip 4ch, 1sc into last ch, turn.

2nd row: 1ch, 1sc into first st, *3ch, skip 3ch, 2 picots into next 3ch arch; rep from * ending 3ch, skip 3ch, 1sc into last sc, turn.

3rd row: 6ch (count as 1dc and 3ch), skip 3ch, *1sc into next picot arch, 3ch, 1sc into next picot arch, 3ch, skip 3ch; rep from * ending 1dc into last sc, skip tch, turn.

Rep 2nd and 3rd rows.

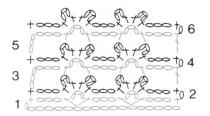

Zig-Zag Double String Network

Multiple of 6 sts + 1.
(add 1 for base chain)

Base row (right side): 1sc into 2nd ch from hook, *5ch, skip 5ch, 1sc into next ch; rep from * to end, turn.

Commence Pattern

1st row: 1ch, 1sc into first st, *5ch, skip 5ch, 1sc into next sc; rep from * to end, skip tch, turn.

2nd row: 1ch, 1sc into first st, *7ch, skip 5ch, 1sc into next sc; rep from * to end, skip tch, turn.

3rd row: 1ch, 1sc into first st, *7ch, skip 7ch, 1sc into next sc; rep from * to end, skip tch, turn.

4th row: 5ch (count as 1dc and 2ch), inserting hook under the 7ch arch made in the 2nd row, work 1sc thus binding the arches of the 2nd and 3rd rows together, *5ch, 1sc under next pair of arches as before; rep from * ending 2ch, 1dc into last sc, skip tch, turn.

5th row: 1ch, 1sc into first st, 2ch, skip 2ch, 1sc into next sc, *5ch, skip 5ch, 1sc into next sc; rep from * ending 2ch, skip next 2ch of tch, 1sc into next ch, turn.

6th row: 6ch (count as 1dc and 3ch), skip 2ch, 1sc into next sc, *7ch, skip 5ch, 1sc into next sc; rep from * ending 3ch, skip 2ch, 1dc into last sc, skip tch, turn.

7th row: 1ch, 1sc into first st, 3ch, skip 3ch,

1sc into next sc, *7ch, skip 7ch, 1sc into next sc; rep from * ending 3ch, skip next 3ch of tch, 1sc into next ch, turn.

8th row: 1ch, 1sc into first st, *5ch, 1sc under next pair of arches together; rep from * ending last rep with 1sc into last sc, skip tch, turn.

Rep these 8 rows.

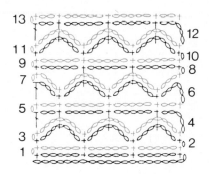

Zig-Zag Popcorn Network

Multiple of 10 sts + 1.
(add 5 for base chain)

1st row (right side): 1sc into 9th ch from hook, 1sc into each of next 2ch, *3ch, skip 3ch, 5dc popcorn into next ch, 3ch, skip 3ch, 1sc into each of next 3ch; rep from * to last 4ch, 3ch, skip 3ch, 1dc into last ch, turn.

2nd row: 1ch, 1sc into first st, *1sc into next arch, 3ch, 5dc popcorn into 2nd of next 3sc, 3ch**, 1sc into next arch, 1sc into next popcorn; rep from * ending last rep at **, skip 2ch of tch arch, 1sc into each of next 2ch, turn.

3rd row: 6ch (count as 1dc and 3ch), *1sc into next arch, 1sc into next popcorn, 1sc into next arch, 3ch**, 5dc popcorn into 2nd of next 3sc, 3ch; rep from * ending last rep at **, 1dc into last sc, skip tch, turn.

Rep 2nd and 3rd rows.

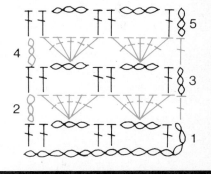

Boxed Shell Stitch

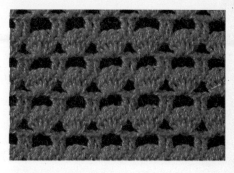

Multiple of 5 sts + 2.
(add 2 for base chain)

1st row (right side): Skip 3ch (count as 1dc), 1dc into next ch, *3ch, skip 3ch, 1dc into each of next 2ch; rep from * to end, turn.

2nd row: 3ch (count as 1dc), skip first st, *5dc into 2nd ch of next 3ch arch; rep from * ending 1dc into top of tch, turn.

3rd row: 3ch (count as 1dc), skip first st, 1dc into next dc, *3ch, skip 3dc, 1dc into each of next 2dc; rep from * to end, turn.

Rep 2nd and 3rd rows.

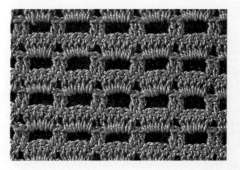

Boxed Block Stitch

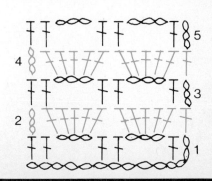

Worked as Boxed Shell Stitch, except that on 2nd and every alternate row 5dc are worked under 3ch arch instead of into actual st, thus making a block rather than a shell.

Openwork and Lace Patterns

Norman Arch Stitch

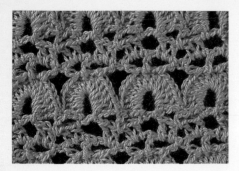

Multiple of 9 sts + 1.
(add 1 for base chain)

1st row (wrong side): 1sc into 2nd ch from hook, *3ch, skip 3ch, 1sc into next ch, 7ch, 1sc into next ch, 3ch, skip 3ch, 1sc into next ch; rep from * to end, turn.

2nd row: 1ch, 1sc into first sc, *skip 3ch, work 13dc into next 7ch arch, skip 3ch, 1sc into next sc; rep from * to end, skip tch, turn.

3rd row: 5ch (count as 1dtr), skip first sc and next 5dc, *[1dc into next dc, 3ch] twice, 1dc into next dc**, skip [next 5dc, 1sc and 5dc]; rep from * ending last rep at **, skip next 5dc, 1dtr into last sc, skip tch, turn.

4th row: 3ch (count as 1dc), skip first st and next dc, *1dc into next ch, 1ch, skip 1ch, 1dc into next ch, 3ch, skip 1ch, 1dc into next ch, 1ch, skip 1ch, 1dc into next ch**, skip next 2dc; rep from * ending last rep at **, skip next dc, 1dc into top of tch, turn.

5th row: 6ch (count as 1dc and 3ch), *skip next 1ch sp, work [1sc, 7ch, 1sc] into next 3ch sp, skip next 1ch sp**, 1dc between next 2dc; rep from * ending last rep at **, 1dc into top of tch, turn.
Rep 2nd, 3rd, 4th and 5th rows.

Multiple of 10 sts + 1.
(add 8 for base chain)

1st row (wrong side): 1sc into 14th ch from hook, *5ch, skip 4ch, 1dc into next ch**, 5ch, skip 4ch, 1sc into next ch; rep from * ending last rep at **, turn.

2nd row: 1ch, 1sc into first dc, *6sc into next 5ch arch, 1sc into next sc, 3sc into beginning of next 5ch arch, work a 'back double' of [4ch, then without turning work, skip 6 previous sc and work a sl st back into previous sc, now work 5sc in the normal direction into 4ch arch just worked], 3sc into remaining part of 5ch arch**, 1sc into next dc; rep from * ending last rep at **, 1sc into next ch, turn.

3rd row: 1ch, 1sc into first st, *5ch, 1dc into 3rd of 5sc of next 'back double', 5ch, 1sc into sc over dc of previous row; rep from * ending last rep in last sc, turn.

4th row: 1ch, 1sc into first st, 3sc into beginning of next 5ch arch, turn, 2ch, skip 3 previous sc, work 1dc into first sc, 1ch, turn, 1sc into dc, 2sc into 2ch arch, 3sc into remaining part of 5ch arch, *1sc into next dc, 6sc into next 5ch arch, 1sc into next sc**, 3sc into beginning of 5ch arch, 1 'back double' as before, 3sc into remaining part of 5ch arch; rep from * ending last rep at ** in last sc, 5ch, skip 3 previous sc, sl st back into next sc, 3sc in normal direction into beginning of 5ch arch, turn.

5th row: 8ch, *1sc into sc over dc of previous row, 5ch**, 1dc into 3rd of 5sc of next 'back double', 5ch; rep from * ending last rep at ** 1dc into last sc, skip tch, turn.
Rep 2nd, 3rd, 4th and 5th rows.

ch from hook, 7ch, sl st into 7th ch from hook, 5ch, sl st into 5th ch from hook], work 7sc into arch; rep from * ending sl st into last sc, turn.

2nd row: 11ch (count as 1ttr and 4ch), *1sc into 7ch arch at center of next Coronet, 7ch; rep from * ending 1sc into 7ch arch at center of last Coronet, 2ch, 1ttr into last sc, skip tch, turn.

3rd row: 1ch, 1sc into first st, 1sc into each of next 2ch and next sc, turn, 4ch, skip 3ch, 1tr into last sc, turn, 8ch, sl st into 7th ch from hook, 5ch, sl st into 5th ch from hook (½ Coronet worked), 7sc into next 4ch arch, *1sc into each of next 4ch, 3ch Picot, 1sc into each of next 3ch, 1sc into next sc, work 9ch, skip 7 previous sc, sl st back into previous sc, work 7sc into 9ch arch, work a Coronet as before, then 7sc into 9ch loop; rep from * ending 1sc into each of next 4ch of tch arch, 9ch, skip previous 3sc, sl st into previous sc, work 7sc into 9ch arch, work a ½ Coronet of 5ch, sl st into 5th ch from hook, 1sc into 9ch arch, 3ch, 1tr into last sc, turn.

4th row: 1 ch, 1sc into top of 3ch, *7ch, 1sc into 7ch arch at center of next Coronet; rep from * ending last rep in 8ch arch of ½ Coronet, turn.

5th row: 1ch, 1sc into first st, 1sc into each of next 3ch, *3ch Picot, 1sc into each of next 3ch, 1sc into next sc, 9ch, skip 7 previous sc, sl st back into previous sc, work 7sc, Coronet and 7sc into arch**, 1sc into each of next 4ch; rep from * ending last rep at **, sl st into last sc, turn.
Rep 2nd, 3rd, 4th and 5th rows.

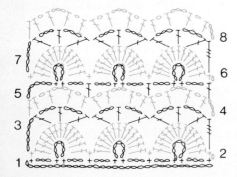

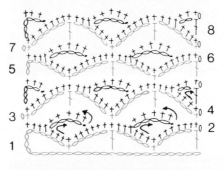

Coronet Ground

Multiple of 8 sts.
(add 1 for base chain)

1st row (right side): Skip 1ch, *1sc into each of next 4ch, work a picot of [3ch, insert hook down through top of last sc made and work sl st to close], 1sc into each of next 4ch, work 9ch then without turning skip 7 previous sc, work a sl st back into previous sc, then working in the normal direction work 7sc into 9ch arch, work a Coronet of [5ch, sl st into 5th

Double Arch Ground

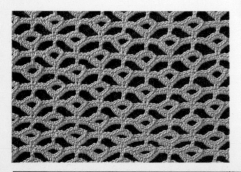

Shell and V Stitch

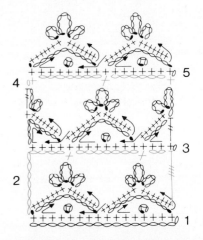

Multiple of 8 sts + 1.
(add 2 for base chain)

1st row (right side): Skip 2ch (count as 1dc), 2dc into next ch, *skip 3ch, work a V st of

Stitch Variations, Abbreviations and Symbols on pages 7 to 15

Openwork and Lace Patterns

[1dc, 1ch, 1dc] into next ch, skip 3ch**, 5dc into next ch; rep from * ending last rep at **, 3dc into last ch, turn.

2nd row: 3ch (count as 1dc), 1dc into first st, *5dc into sp at center of next V st**, V st into 3rd of next 5dc; rep from * ending last rep at **, 2dc into top of tch, turn.

Rep 2nd row.

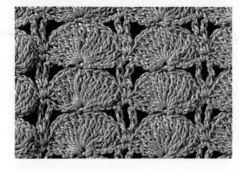

Fan and V Stitch

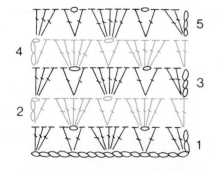

Multiple of 8 sts + 1.
(add 1 for base chain)

1st row (right side): 1sc into 2nd ch from hook, *skip 3ch, 9dc into next ch, skip 3ch, 1sc into next ch; rep from * to end, turn.

2nd row: 3ch (count as 1dc), 1dc into first st, *5ch, skip 9dc group, work a V st of [1dc, 1ch, 1dc] into next sc; rep from * ending 5ch, skip last 9dc group, 2dc into last sc, skip tch, turn.

3rd row: 3ch (count as 1dc), 4dc into first st, *working over next 5ch so as to enclose it, work 1sc into 5th dc of group in row below**, 9dc into sp at center of next V st; rep from * ending last rep at **, 5dc into top of tch, turn.

4th row: 3ch, skip 5dc, V st into next sc, *5ch, skip 9dc group, V st into next sc; rep from * ending 2ch, sl st to top of tch, turn.

5th row: 1ch, 1sc over sl st into first st of row below, *9dc into sp at center of next V st, working over next 5ch so as to enclose it work 1sc into 5th dc of group in row below; rep from * to end, turn.

Rep 2nd, 3rd, 4th and 5th rows.
End with a wrong side row working [2ch, sl st to 5th dc of group, 2ch] in place of 5ch between the V sts.

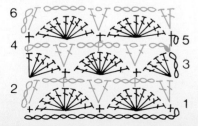

Peacock Fan Stitch

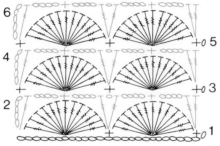

Multiple of 12 sts + 1.
(add 1 for base chain)

1st row (right side): 1sc into 2nd ch from hook, *skip 5ch, 13dtr into next ch, skip 5ch, 1sc into next ch; rep from * to end, turn.

2nd row: 5ch (count as 1dtr), 1dtr into first st, *4ch, skip 6dtr, 1sc into next dtr, 4ch, skip 6dtr**, work [1dtr, 1ch, 1dtr] into next sc; rep from * ending last rep at **, 2dtr into last sc, skip tch, turn.

3rd row: 1ch, 1sc into first st, *skip [1dtr and 4ch], 13dtr into next sc, skip [4ch and 1dtr], 1sc into next ch; rep from * to end, turn.

Rep 2nd and 3rd rows.

Block and Offset Shell Stitch

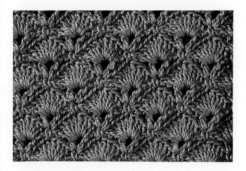

Multiple of 11 sts + 4.
(add 2 for base chain)

1st row (right side): Skip 3ch (count as 1dc), 1dc into each of next 4ch, *skip 2ch, 5dc into next ch, 2ch, skip 3ch, 1dc into each of next 5ch; rep from * to end, turn.

2nd row: 3ch (count as 1dc), skip first st, 1dc into each of next 4 sts, *skip 2ch, 5dc into next dc, 2ch, skip 4dc, 1dc into each of next 5 sts; rep from * to end, turn.

Rep 2nd row.

Soft Fan Stitch

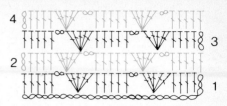

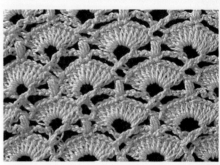

Multiple of 10 sts + 1.
(add 1 for base chain)

1st row (wrong side): 1sc into 2nd ch from hook, *3ch, work 2 crossed dcs as follows: skip 5ch, 1dc into next ch, 5ch, inserting hook behind dc just made work 1dc into 4th of 5ch just skipped, then 3ch, skip 3ch, 1sc into next ch; rep from * to end, turn.

2nd row: 3ch (count as 1dc), skip first st, *skip next 3ch sp, work a group of 11dc into next 5ch arch, skip next 3ch sp, work hdc3tog into next sc, 1ch; rep from * omitting hdc3tog and 1ch at end of last rep and working 1dc into last sc, skip tch, turn.

3rd row: 2ch, skip first 2 dc, 1hdc into next dc, 4ch, 1hdc into top of hdc just made, *3ch, skip 3dc, 1sc into next dc, 3ch**, work 2 crossed dcs as follows: 1dc into 2nd dc of next 11dc group, 5ch, going behind dc just made work 1dc into 10th dc of previous 11dc group; rep from * ending last rep at **, 1dc into top of tch, 2ch, going behind dc just made work 1dc into 10th dc of previous 11dc group, turn.

4th row: 3ch (count as 1dc), skip first st, 5dc into next 2ch sp, *skip next 3ch sp, work hdc3tog into next sc, 1ch, skip next 3ch sp**, 11dc into next 5ch arch; rep from * ending last rep at **, 6dc into top of tch, turn.

5th row: 1ch, 1sc into first st, 3ch, 1dc into 2nd dc of next 11dc group, 5ch, going behind dc just made work 1dc into 5th dc of previous 6dc group, *3ch, skip 3dc, 1sc into next dc**, 3ch, 1dc into 2nd dc of next dc group, 5ch, going behind dc just made work 1dc into 10th dc of previous dc group; rep from * ending last rep at ** in top of tch, turn.

Rep 2nd, 3rd, 4th and 5th rows.

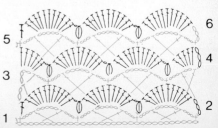

Openwork and Lace Patterns

Hotcross Bun Stitch

Multiple of 3 sts + 2.
(add 1 for base chain)

Special Abbreviation

TrX (treble 'X' shape — worked over 3 sts) = [yo] twice, insert hook into next st, yo, draw loop through, yo, draw through 2 loops, skip next st, yo, insert hook into next st, yo, draw loop through, [yo, draw through 2 loops] 4 times, 1ch, yo, insert hook half way down st just made where lower 'legs' join, yo, draw loop through, [yo, draw through 2 loops] twice

1st row (wrong side): 1sc into 2nd ch from hook, 1sc into next and each ch to end, turn.

2nd row: 4ch (count as 1tr), skip first st, *TrX over next 3 sts; rep from * ending 1tr into last st, skip tch, turn.

3rd row: 4ch (count as 1dc and 1ch), *work dc3tog into next 1ch sp**, 2ch; rep from * ending last rep at **, 1ch, 1dc into top of tch, turn.

4th row: 1ch, 1sc into first st, 1sc into next ch, *1sc into next cluster, 1sc into each of next 2ch; rep from * to end, turn.

Rep 2nd, 3rd and 4th rows.

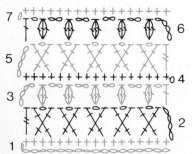

Hearts and Diamonds Stitch

Multiple of 10 sts + 7.
(add 5 for base chain)

Special Abbreviation

Diamond = 4 rows inside a main row worked as follows: Turn, **1st row:** 1ch, 1sc into first sc, 1sc into each of next 3ch, turn. **Next row:** 1ch, 1sc into each of next 4sc, skip tch, turn. Rep the last row twice more.

1st row (wrong side): 1sc into 9th ch from hook, *2ch, skip 4ch, work a Heart of [3dc, 1ch, 3dc] into next ch, 2ch, skip 4ch, 1sc into next ch; rep from * to last 3ch, 2ch, skip 2ch, 1dc into last ch, turn.

2nd row: 6ch, skip first st and next 2ch, 1sc into next sc, work a Diamond, *skip 2ch, 1 Heart into ch sp at center of next Heart, 3ch, skip 2ch, 1sc into next sc, work Diamond; rep from * ending skip 2ch, 1dc into next ch of tch, turn.

3rd row: 5ch (count as 1dc and 2ch), *1sc into top corner of next Diamond, 2ch**, 1 Heart into sp at center of next Heart, 2ch; rep from * ending last rep at **, 1dc into 3rd ch of tch, turn.

Rep 2nd and 3rd rows.

Tread Pattern Stitch

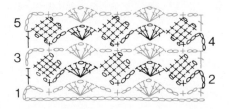

Multiple of 8 sts + 3.
(add 2 for base chain)

1st row (right side): Skip 3ch (count as 1dc), 1dc into each of next 2ch, *skip 2ch, 1dc into next ch, 3ch, work a block of 3dc evenly spaced into side of dc just made, skip 2ch, 1dc into each of next 3ch; rep from * to end, turn.

2nd row: 3ch (count as 1dc), skip first st, 1dc into each of next 2dc, *2ch, 1sc into top of 3ch at corner of next block, 2ch, skip dc which forms base of same block, 1dc into each of next 3dc; rep from * ending last rep in top of tch, turn.

3rd row: 3ch (count as 1dc), skip first st, 1dc into each of next 2dc, *skip 2ch, 1dc into next sc, 3ch, 3dc evenly spaced into side of dc just made, skip 2ch, 1dc into each of next 3dc; rep from * ending last rep in top of tch, turn.

Rep 2nd and 3rd rows.

Butterfly Lace

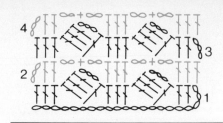

Multiple of 12 sts + 3.
(add 1 for base chain)

1st row (right side): 1sc into 2nd ch from hook, 2ch, skip 1ch, 1sc into next ch, *skip 3ch, work [3tr, 4ch, 1sc] into next ch, 2ch, skip 1ch, work [1sc, 4ch, 3tr] into next ch, skip 3ch, 1sc into next ch, 2ch, skip 1ch, 1sc into next ch; rep from * to end, turn.

2nd row: 4ch (count as 1dc and 1ch), skip first sc, 1dc into next 2ch sp, *1ch, skip 3tr, 1sc into top of 4ch, 2ch, work dc2tog into next 2ch sp, 2ch, skip 3ch, 1sc into next ch, 1ch**, work [1dc, 1ch, 1dc] into next sp; rep from * ending last rep at **, 1dc into last sp, 1ch, 1dc into last sc, skip tch, turn.

3rd row: 1ch, 1sc into first st, 2ch, skip [1ch and 1dc], 1sc into next ch, *work [3tr, 4ch, 1sc] into next 2ch sp, 2ch, skip next cluster, work [1sc, 4ch, 3tr] into next 2ch sp, 1sc into next 1ch sp, 2ch, skip 1ch, 1sc into next 1ch sp; rep from * ending last rep in 3rd ch of tch, turn.

Rep 2nd and 3rd rows.

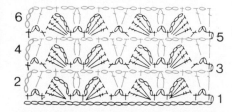

Cluster Lace Stitch

Openwork and Lace Patterns

Multiple of 8 sts + 1.
(add 1 for base chain)

1st row (right side): 1sc into 2nd ch from hook, 1sc into next ch, *4ch, work dc4tog over next 5ch as follows: leaving last loop of each st on hook work 1dc into each of next 2ch, skip 1ch, 1dc into each of next 2ch, yo and draw through all 5 loops on hook, 4ch, 1sc into next ch**, 1ch, skip 1ch, 1sc into next ch; rep from * ending last rep at **, 1sc into last ch, turn.

2nd row: 3ch (count as 1dc), 1dc into first st, *3ch, 1sc into top of next 4ch, 1ch, skip cluster, 1sc into top of next 4ch, 3ch, skip 1sc**, dc3tog into next 1ch sp; rep from * ending last rep at **, dc2tog into last sc, skip tch, turn.

3rd row: 1ch, 1sc into first st, *1sc into next ch, 4ch, dc4tog as follows: leaving last loop of each st on hook work 1dc into each of next 2ch, skip [1sc, 1ch and 1sc], 1dc into each of next 2ch, yo and draw through all 5 loops on hook, 4ch, 1sc into next ch**, 1ch, skip cluster; rep from * ending last rep at **, 1sc into top of tch, turn.

Rep 2nd and 3rd rows.

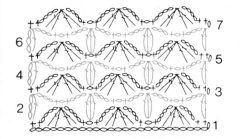

Triple Picot V Stitch

Multiple of 11 sts + 7.
(add 3 for base chain)

1st row (right side): 1dc into 4th ch from hook, *3ch, skip 3ch, 1sc into next ch**, work a picot of [3ch, 1sc into next ch] 3 times, 3ch, skip 3ch, [1dc, 2ch, 1dc] into next ch; rep from * ending last rep at ** when 2ch remain, 3ch, 1sc into next ch, 1ch, 1hdc into last ch, turn.

2nd row: 4ch (count as 1dc and 1ch), 1dc into first st, *3ch, skip 1 Picot and 3ch**, into next 2ch sp work 1sc, [3ch, 1sc] 3 times, then 3ch, skip 3ch and 1 Picot, [1dc, 2ch, 1dc] into next Picot; rep from * ending last rep at **, work [1sc, 3ch, 1sc] into top of tch, 1ch, 1hdc into next ch, turn.

Rep 2nd row.

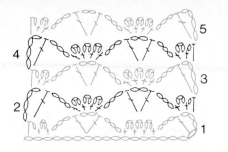

Lacy Wave Stitch

Multiple of 11 sts + 1.
(add 1 for base chain)

1st row (right side): 1sc into 2nd ch from hook, *2ch, skip 2ch, 1dc into each of next 2ch, 2ch, skip 2ch, 1sc into each of next 5ch; rep from * to end, turn.

2nd row: 5ch (count as 1dc and 2ch), 1dc into first st, *[1ch, skip 1 st, 1dc into next st] twice, 1ch, 1dc into next 2ch sp, skip 2dc**, 5dc into next 2ch sp, 2ch, 1dc into next st; rep from * ending last rep at **, 4dc into last 2ch sp, 1dc into last sc, skip tch, turn.

3rd row: 5ch (count as 1dc and 2ch), 1dc into first st, *[1ch, skip 1 st, 1dc into next st] twice, 1ch, skip 1 st, 1dc into next ch, skip [1dc, 1ch, 1dc, 1ch and 1dc], 5dc into next 2ch sp**, 2ch, 1dc into next st; rep from * ending last rep at ** in tch, turn.

Rep 3rd row.

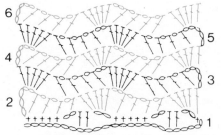

Alternative V Stitch

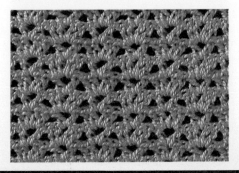

Multiple of 9 sts + 1.
(add 2 for base chain)

1st row: 2dc into 5th ch from hook, *1ch, 2dc into next ch, skip 3ch, work [1dc, 2ch, 1dc] into next ch**; skip 3ch, 2dc into next ch; rep from * ending last rep at ** when 2ch remain, skip 1ch, 1dc into last ch, turn.

2nd row: 3ch (count as 1dc), skip first st, *work [2dc, 1ch, 2dc] into next 2ch sp, work [1dc, 2ch, 1dc] into next 1ch sp; rep from * ending 1dc into top of tch, turn.

Rep 2nd row.

Shell Filigree Stitch

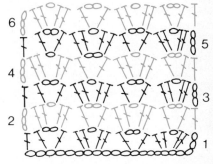

Multiple of 5 sts + 1.
(add 2 for base chain)

1st row (wrong side): 2dc into 3rd ch from hook, *1ch, skip 4ch, 5dc into next ch; rep from * working only 3dc at end of last rep, turn.

2nd row: 1ch, 1sc into first st, *2ch, skip 2dc, work a Picot V st of [1dc, 3ch, insert hook down through top of dc just made and work a sl st to close, 1dc] into next 1ch sp, 2ch, skip 2dc, 1sc into next dc; rep from * ending last rep in top of tch, turn.

3rd row: 3ch (count as 1dc), 2dc into first sc, *1ch, skip 2ch, Picot V st and 2ch, work 5dc into next sc; rep from * finishing with only 3dc at end of last rep, skip tch, turn.

Rep 2nd and 3rd rows.

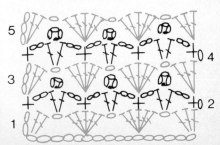

Openwork and Lace Patterns

Arched Lace Stitch

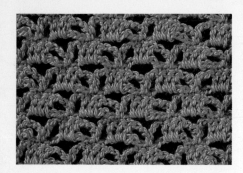

Multiple of 8 sts + 1.
(add 1 for base chain)

1st row (right side): 1sc into 2nd ch from hook, 1sc into next ch, *5ch, skip 5ch, 1sc into each of next 3ch; rep from * omitting 1sc at end of last rep, turn.

2nd row: 1ch, 1sc into first st, *3ch, skip next sc, 3dc into next 5ch arch, 3ch, skip 1sc, 1sc into next sc; rep from * to end, skip tch, turn.

3rd row: 6ch (count as 1tr and 2ch), skip 3ch, *1sc into each of next 3dc**, 5ch, skip [3ch, 1sc and 3ch]; rep from * ending last rep at **, 2ch, skip 3ch, 1tr into last sc, skip tch, turn.

4th row: 3ch (count as 1dc), skip first st, 1dc into 2ch sp, *3ch, skip next sc, 1sc into next sc, 3ch, skip 1sc**, 3dc into next 5ch arch; rep from * ending last rep at **, skip 1ch, 1dc into each of next 2ch of tch, turn.

5th row: 1ch, 1sc into first st, 1sc into next st, *5ch, skip [3ch, 1sc and 3ch], 1sc into each of next 3dc; rep from * to end, omitting 1sc at end of last rep, turn.

Rep 2nd, 3rd, 4th and 5th rows.

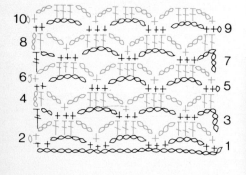

Chain Lace Stitch

Multiple of 10 sts + 1.
(add 7 for base chain)

Special Abbreviation
TP (Triple Picot) = work 1sc, [7ch, 1sc] 3 times all into same place.

1st row (right side): TP into 12th ch from hook, *4ch, skip 4ch, 1dc into next ch**, 4ch, skip 4ch, TP into next ch; rep from * ending last rep at ** in last ch, turn.

2nd row: 1ch, 1sc into first st, *1ch, 1sc into first arch of next TP, [3ch, 1sc into next arch of same TP] twice, 1ch, skip 4ch, 1sc into next dc; rep from * to end placing last sc into arch of tch, turn.

3rd row: 8ch, work [1sc, 7ch, 1sc] into first sc, *4ch, skip [1ch, 1sc and 3ch], 1dc into next sc, 4ch, skip [3ch, 1sc and 1ch]**, TP into next sc; rep from * ending last rep at **, work [1sc, 7ch, 1sc, 3ch and 1tr] into last sc, skip tch, turn.

4th row: 1ch, 1sc into first st, 3ch, 1sc into next 7ch arch, *1ch, skip 4ch, 1sc into next dc, 1ch, 1sc into first arch of next TP**, [3ch, 1sc into next arch of same TP] twice; rep from * ending last rep at **, 3ch, 1sc into tch arch, turn.

5th row: 7ch, skip [3ch, 1sc and 1ch], *TP into next sc, 4ch, skip [1ch, 1sc and 3ch], 1dc into next sc**, 4ch, skip [3ch, 1sc and 1ch]; rep from * ending last rep at **, turn.

Rep 2nd, 3rd, 4th and 5th rows.

Wavy Lace Stitch

Multiple of 12 sts + 1.
(add 4 for base chain)

Base row (right side): 1sc into 7th ch from hook, *3ch, skip 3ch, 1dc into next ch**, [3ch, skip 3ch, 1sc into next ch] twice; rep from * ending last rep at **, 3ch, skip 3ch, 1sc into next ch, 1ch, skip 1ch, 1dc into last ch, turn.

Commence Pattern
1st row: 4ch (count as 1tr), [1tr, 1ch, 1tr] all into next 1ch sp, *3ch, skip 3ch, 1sc into next dc, 3ch, skip 3ch**, work 1tr, [1ch, 1tr] 3 times all into next 3ch arch; rep from * ending last rep at **, 1tr into next ch, 1ch, 2tr into next ch of tch, turn.

2nd row: 4ch (count as 1dc and 1ch), skip first 2tr, 1sc into 1ch sp, *3ch, skip [1tr and 3ch], 1sc into next sc, 3ch, skip [3ch and

1tr], 1sc into next ch sp**, 4ch, skip next sp, 1sc into next sp; rep from * ending last rep at **, 1ch, skip 1tr, 1dc into top of tch, turn.

3rd row: 1ch, 1sc into first st, skip 1ch, *[3ch, 1sc into next 3ch arch] twice, 3ch, 1sc into next 4ch arch; rep from * to end, turn.

4th row: 1ch, 1sc into first st, *3ch, skip 3ch, work 1tr, [1ch, 1tr] 3 times into next 3ch arch, 3ch, skip 3ch, 1sc into next sc; rep from * to end, skip tch, turn.

5th row: 1ch, 1sc into first st, *3ch, skip [3ch and 1tr], 1sc into next ch sp, 4ch, skip next sp, 1sc into next sp, 3ch, skip [1tr and 3ch], 1sc into next sc; rep from * to end, skip tch, turn.

6th row: 5ch (count as 1tr and 1ch), *1sc into next 3ch arch, 3ch, 1sc into next 4ch arch, 3ch, 1sc into next arch**, 3ch; rep from * ending last rep at **, 1ch, 1tr into last sc, skip tch, turn.

Rep these 6 rows.

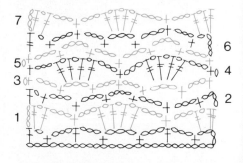

Petal Stitch

Multiple of 8 sts + 1.
(add 1 for base chain)

1st row (wrong side): 1sc into 2nd ch from hook, *2ch, skip 3ch, 4tr into next ch, 2ch, skip 3ch, 1sc into next ch; rep from * to end, turn.

2nd row: 1ch, 1sc into first st, *3ch, skip 2ch and 1tr, 1sc into next tr, 3ch, skip 2tr and 2ch, 1sc into next sc; rep from * to end, skip tch, turn.

3rd row: 4ch (count as 1tr), 1tr into first st, *2ch, skip 3ch, 1sc into next sc, 2ch, skip 3ch, 4tr into next sc; rep from * to end omitting 1tr at end of last rep, skip tch, turn.

4th row: 1ch, 1sc into first st, *3ch, skip 2tr and 2ch, 1sc into next sc, 3ch, skip 2ch and 1tr, 1sc into next tr; rep from * ending last rep in top of tch, turn.

5th row: 1ch, 1sc into first st, *2ch, skip 3ch, 4tr into next sc, 2ch, skip 3ch, 1sc into next sc; rep from * to end, skip tch, turn.

Rep 2nd, 3rd, 4th and 5th rows.

Stitch Variations, Abbreviations and Symbols on pages 7 to 15

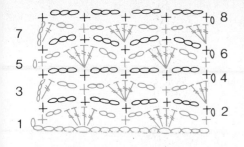

Webbed Lace Stitch

Multiple of 7 sts.
(add 4 for base chain)

1st row: 1dc into 5th ch from hook, *2ch, skip 5ch, 4dc into next ch**, 2ch, 1dc into next ch; rep from * ending last rep at ** in last ch, turn.

2nd row: 4ch, 1dc into first st, *2ch, skip [3dc, 2ch and 1dc]**, work [4dc, 2ch, 1dc] into next 2ch sp; rep from * ending last rep at **, 4dc into tch, turn.

Rep 2nd row.

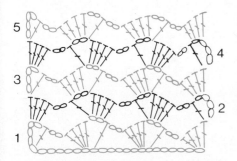

Acrobatic Stitch

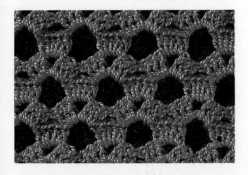

Multiple of 6 sts + 1.
(add 2 for base chain)

1st row (right side): 2dc into 3rd ch from

hook, *4ch, skip 5ch, 5dc into next ch; rep from * working only 3dc at end of last rep, turn.

2nd row: 2ch (count as 1dc), skip first 3 sts, *work [3dc, 3ch, 3dc] into next 4ch arch**, skip next 5dc; rep from * ending last rep at **, skip 2dc, 1dc into top of tch, turn.

3rd row: 6ch (count as 1dtr and 1ch), *5dc into next 3ch arch**, 4ch; rep from * ending last rep at **, 1ch, 1dtr into top of tch, turn.

4th row: 5ch (count as 1tr and 1ch), 3dc into next 1ch sp, *skip 5dc, work [3dc, 3ch, 3dc] into next 4ch arch; rep from * ending skip 5dc, work [3dc, 1ch, 1tr] into tch, turn.

5th row: 3ch (count as 1dc), 2dc into next 1ch sp, *4ch, 5dc into next 3ch arch; rep from * ending 4ch, 3dc into tch, turn.

Rep 2nd, 3rd, 4th and 5th rows.

Diamond Lace Stitch

Multiple of 8 sts + 1.
(add 1 for base chain)

Base row (right side): 1sc into 2nd ch from hook, 1sc into each of next 2ch, *5ch, skip 3ch**, 1sc into each of next 5ch; rep from * ending last rep at **, 1sc into each of last 3ch, turn.

Commence Pattern

1st row: 1ch, 1sc into each of first 2 sts, *3ch, skip 1sc, 1sc into next 5ch arch, skip 1sc**, 1sc into each of next 3sc; rep from * ending last rep at **, 1sc into each of last 2sc, skip tch, turn.

2nd row: 1ch, 1sc into first st, *3ch, skip 1sc, 1sc into next 3ch sp, 1sc into next sc, 1sc into next 3ch sp, 3ch, skip 1sc, 1sc into next sc; rep from * to end, skip tch, turn.

3rd row: 5ch (count as 1dc and 2ch), *1sc into next 3ch sp, 1sc into each of next 3sc, 1sc into next 3ch sp**, 5ch; rep from * ending last rep at **, 2ch, 1dc into last sc, skip tch, turn.

4th row: 1ch, 1sc into first st, *3ch, skip 2ch

and 1sc, 1sc into each of next 3sc, 3ch, skip 1sc, 1sc into next 5ch arch; rep from * ending last rep in tch, turn.

5th row: 1ch, 1sc into first st, *1sc into next 3ch sp, 3ch, skip 1sc, 1sc into next sc, 3ch, skip 1sc, 1sc into next 3ch sp, 1sc into next sc; rep from * to end, skip tch, turn.

6th row: 1ch, 1sc into each of first 2 sts, *1sc into next 3ch sp, 5ch, 1sc into next 3ch sp**, 1sc into each of next 3sc; rep from * ending last rep at **, 1sc into each of last 2sc, skip tch, turn.

Rep these 6 rows.

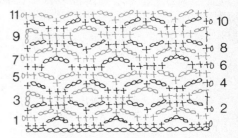

Picot Fan Stitch

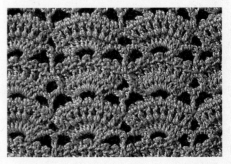

Multiple of 12 sts + 1.
(add 1 for base chain)

1st row (right side): 1sc into 2nd ch from hook, *5ch, skip 3ch, 1sc into next ch; rep from * to end, turn.

2nd row: 5ch (count as 1dc and 2ch), *1sc into next 5ch arch, 8dc into next arch, 1sc into next arch**, 5ch; rep from * ending last rep at ** in last arch, 2ch, 1dc into last sc, skip tch, turn.

3rd row: 1ch, 1sc into first st, skip 2ch and 1sc, *work a picot of [1dc into next dc, 3ch, insert hook down through top of dc just made and sl st to close] 7 times, 1dc into next dc, 1sc into next arch; rep from * to end, turn.

4th row: 8ch, skip 2 picots, *1sc into next picot, 5ch, skip 1 picot, 1sc into next picot, 5ch, skip 2 picots, 1dc into next sc**, 5ch, skip 2 picots; rep from * ending last rep at **, skip tch, turn.

Rep 2nd, 3rd and 4th rows.

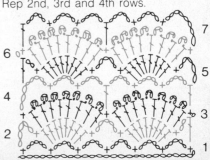

Openwork and Lace Patterns

Crazy Diamond Stitch

Multiple of 12 sts + 1.
(add 1 for base chain)

Special Abbreviation
CRC (Crazy Cluster) = [yo] 3 times, insert hook as indicated, yo, draw loop through, [yo, draw through 2 loops] 3 times, (2 loops on hook), yo, insert hook into center left side of dtr in progress, yo, draw loop through, yo, draw through 2 loops, (3 loops on hook), yo, draw through all loops on hook, 1ch, [yo] twice, insert hook into lower left side of original dtr, yo, draw loop through, [yo, draw through 2 loops] twice, (2 loops on hook), yo, insert hook into center left side of tr in progress, yo, draw loop through, yo, draw through 2 loops, (3 loops on hook), yo, draw through all loops on hook.

1st row (right side): 1sc into 2nd ch from hook, *1sc into next ch, 1ch, skip 4ch, work [1CRC, 2ch, 1CRC] into next ch, 1ch, skip 4ch, 1sc into next ch**, 1ch, skip 1ch; rep from * ending last rep at **, 1sc into last ch, turn.

2nd row: 3ch (count as 1dc), 1dc into first st, *4ch, 1sc into 2ch sp between next 2CRCs, 4ch**, work a V st of [1dc, 1ch, 1dc] into ch sp between next 2sc; rep from * ending last rep at **, 2dc into last sc, skip tch, turn.

3rd row: 6ch (count as 1ttr), 1CRC into first st, *1ch, 1sc into next 4ch sp, 1ch, 1sc into next 4ch sp, 1ch**, work [1CRC, 2ch, 1CRC] into sp at center of next V st; rep from * ending last rep at **, work [1CRC, 1ttr] into top of tch, turn.

4th row: 1ch, 1sc into first st, *4ch, V st into sp between next 2sc, 4ch, 1sc into 2ch sp between next 2CRCs; rep from * ending last rep in top of tch, turn.

5th row: 1ch, 1sc into first st, *1sc into next 4ch sp, 1ch, work [1CRC, 2ch, 1CRC] into sp at center of next V st, 1ch, 1sc into next 4ch sp**, 1ch; rep from * ending last rep at **, 1sc into last sc, skip tch, turn.

Rep 2nd, 3rd, 4th and 5th rows.

Christmas Tree and Bauble Stitch

Multiple of 10 sts + 6.
(add 2 for base chain)

Special Abbreviation

Tree = work 1ttr as indicated, 1ch, 1dtr into base of stem of previous ttr, 1ch, 1tr into base of stem of previous dtr, 1ch, 1dc into base of stem of previous tr, 2ch, 1hdc into stem of previous dc, 1ch, 1dc into stem of previous tr in same place as previous dc, 1ch, 1tr into stem of previous dtr in same place as previous tr, 1ch, 1dtr into stem of previous ttr in same place as previous dtr.

Base row (right side): Skip 2ch (count as 1dc), 3dc into next ch, *skip 4ch, 1sc into next ch**, skip 4ch, 7dc into next ch; rep from * ending last rep at ** in last ch, turn.

Commence Pattern
1st row: 8ch, 1hdc into 3rd ch from hook, 1ch, skip 1ch, 1dc into next ch, 1ch, 1tr into next ch, 1ch, 1dtr into next ch, 1ch, skip 1ch, 1sc and 3dc, 1sc into next st, *1ch, skip 3dc, work 1 Tree into next sc, 1ch, skip 3dc, 1sc into next st; rep from * to end, turn.

2nd row: 4ch (count as 1tr), skip first st, tr4tog/rb round stems of next 4 branches of Tree, *4ch, 1sc into next 2ch sp**, 4ch, tr8tog/rb round stems of 4 remaining branches of same Tree and first 4 branches of next Tree; rep from * ending last rep at ** in tch, turn.

3rd row: 1ch, 1sc into first st, *skip 4ch, 7dc into loop which closed next cluster, skip 4ch, 1sc into next sc; rep from * ending skip 4ch, 4dc into loop which closed half cluster at edge, turn.

4th row: 1ch, 1sc into first st, *1ch, skip 3dc**, Tree into next sc, 1ch, skip 3dc, 1sc into next st; rep from * ending last rep at **, work first half of Tree into last sc, omitting 2ch at top center and ending 1ch, 1hdc into stem of previous dc, turn.

5th row: 1ch, 1sc into first st, *4ch, tr8tog/rf round stems of 4 branches of first Half Tree and first 4 branches of next Tree, 4ch, 1sc into next 2ch sp; rep from * ending 4ch, tr5tog/rf round stems of 4 remaining branches of last Tree and last sc, skip tch, turn.

6th row: 3ch (count as 1dc), 3dc into first st, *skip 4ch, 1sc into next sc**, skip 4ch, 7dc into loop which closed next cluster; rep from * ending last rep at ** in last sc, skip tch, turn.

Rep these 6 rows.

Clover Fan Stitch

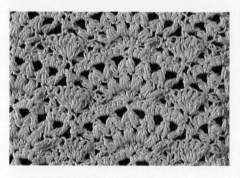

Multiple of 18 sts + 1.
(add 1 for base chain)

Special Abbreviation
CVC (Clover Cluster) = [yo, insert hook, yo, draw loop through loosely] twice as indicated for first leg, (5 loops on hook), and twice more as indicated for 2nd leg, (9 loops on hook), *yo, draw through all except last loop, yo, draw through remaining 2 loops.

Note: For CVC with 1 leg only, omit 2nd leg and complete as given from * to end.

1st row (wrong side): 1sc into 2nd ch from hook, *skip 2ch, 5dc into next ch, skip 2ch, 1sc into next ch; rep from * to end, turn.

2nd row: 3ch (count as 1dc), 2dc into first st, *skip 2dc, 1sc into next dc, skip 2dc and 1sc, work CVC with 1 leg only into next dc, [2ch, 1CVC inserting hook into same place as previous CVC for first leg and into next dc for 2nd leg] 4 times, 2ch, work CVC with 1 leg only into same place as 2nd leg of previous CVC, 1ch, skip 1sc and 2dc, 1sc into next dc, skip 2dc, 5dc into next sc; rep from * ending last rep with only 3dc into last sc, skip tch, turn.

3rd row: 1ch, 1sc into first st, *skip 2dc, 1sc and 1ch, work CVC with 1 leg only into next CVC, [2ch, 1CVC inserting hook into same place as previous CVC for first leg and into next CVC for 2nd leg, skipping 2ch between] 5 times, 2ch, work CVC with 1 leg only into same place as 2nd leg of previous CVC, skip 1ch, 1sc and 2dc, 1sc into next st; rep from * to end, turn.

4th row: 1ch, 1sc into first st, 1sc into each st and each ch to end, skip tch, turn.

5th row: 1ch, 1sc into first st, *skip 3sc, 5dc into next sc, [skip 2sc, 1sc into next sc, skip 2sc, 5dc into next sc] twice, skip 3sc, 1sc into next sc; rep from * to end, skip tch, turn.

Stitch Variations. Abbreviations and Symbols on pages 7 to 15

Openwork and Lace Patterns

Rep 2nd, 3rd, 4th and 5th rows.

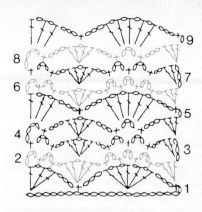

Open Pineapple Stitch

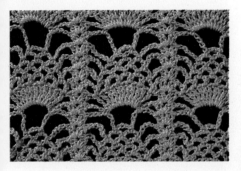

Multiple of 15 sts + 1.
(add 2 for base chain)

Special Abbreviation
DV Stitch = Double V Stitch.

Base row (right side): Skip 2ch (count as 1dc), 2dc into next ch, *7ch, skip 5ch, 1sc into next ch, 3ch, skip 2ch, 1sc into next ch, 7ch, skip 5ch**, work a DV st of [2dc, 1ch, 2dc] into next ch; rep from * ending last rep at **, 3dc into last ch, turn.

Commence Pattern
1st row: 3ch (count as 1dc), 2dc into first st, *3ch, 1sc into 7ch arch, 5ch, skip 3ch, 1sc into next 7ch arch, 3ch**, DV st into sp at center of DV st; rep from * ending last rep at **, 3dc into top of tch, turn.

2nd row: 3ch (count as 1dc), 2dc into first st, *skip 3ch, 11tr into next 5ch arch, skip 3ch**, DV st into next sp; rep from * ending last rep at **, 3dc into top of tch, turn.

3rd row: 3ch (count as 1dc), 2dc into first st, *2ch, skip 2dc, 1sc into next tr, [3ch, skip 1tr, 1sc into next tr] 5 times, 2ch, skip 2dc**, DV st into next sp; rep from * ending last rep at **, 3dc into top of tch, turn.

4th row: 3ch (count as 1dc), 2dc into first st, *3ch, skip 2ch, 1sc into next 3ch arch, [3ch, 1sc into next 3ch arch] 4 times, 3ch, skip 2ch**, DV st into next sp; rep from * ending last rep at **, 3dc into top of tch, turn.

5th row: 3ch (count as 1dc), 2dc into first st, *4ch, skip 3ch, 1sc into next 3ch arch, [3ch, 1sc into next 3ch arch] 3 times, 4ch, skip 3ch**, DV st into next sp; rep from * ending last rep at **, 3dc into top of tch, turn.

6th row: 3ch (count as 1dc), 2dc into first

st, *5ch, skip 4ch, 1sc into next 3ch arch, [3ch, 1sc into next 3ch arch] twice, 5ch, skip 4ch**, DV st into next sp; rep from * ending last rep at **, 3dc into top of tch, turn.
7th row: 3ch (count as 1dc), 2dc into first st, *7ch, skip 5ch, 1sc into next 3ch arch, 3ch, 1sc into next 3ch arch, 7ch, skip 5ch**, DV st into next sp; rep from * ending last rep at **, 3dc into top of tch, turn.
Rep these 7 rows.

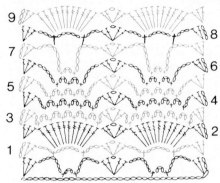

Strawberry Lace Stitch

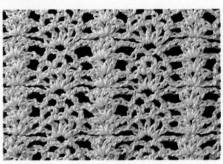

Multiple of 12 sts + 7.
(add 1 for base chain)

1st row (right side): 1sc into 2nd ch from hook, *3ch, skip 5ch, into next ch work a 5 group of 1dc, [1ch, 1dc] 4 times, 3ch, skip 5ch, 1sc into next ch; rep from * ending 3ch, skip 5ch, into last ch work 1dc, [1ch, 1dc] twice, turn.

2nd row: [3ch, 1sc into next ch sp] twice, *1ch, skip 3ch, work a DV st of [2dc, 1ch, 2dc] into next sc, 1ch, skip 3ch, 1sc into next ch sp, [3ch, 1sc into next sp] 3 times; rep from * ending 1ch, skip 3ch, 3dc into last sc, skip tch, turn.

3rd row: 3ch (count as 1dc), 2dc into first st, *2ch, skip 1ch, 1sc into next 3ch arch**, [3ch, 1sc into next 3ch arch] twice, 2ch, skip 1ch, DV st into next ch sp; rep from * ending last rep at **, 3ch, 1sc into tch, turn.

4th row: 4ch, 1sc into next 3ch arch, *3ch, skip 2ch, DV st into next ch sp, 3ch, skip 2ch, 1sc into next 3ch arch, 3ch, 1sc into next 3ch arch; rep from * ending 3ch, skip 2ch, 3dc into top of tch, turn.

5th row: 1ch, 1sc into first st, *3ch, skip 3ch, 5 group into next 3ch arch, 3ch, skip 3ch, 1sc into next ch sp; rep from * ending 3ch, skip 3ch, into tch work 1dc, [1ch, 1dc] twice, turn.

Rep 2nd, 3rd, 4th and 5th rows.

Open Crescent

Multiple of 18 sts + 1.
(add 1 for base chain)

1st row (wrong side): 1sc into 2nd ch from hook, *3ch, skip 2ch, 1sc into next ch, [5ch, skip 3ch, 1sc into next ch] 3 times, 3ch, skip 2ch, 1sc into next ch; rep from * to end, turn.

2nd row: 3ch (count as 1dc), 1dc into first st, *3ch, skip 3ch, 1sc into next arch, 9dc into next arch, 1sc into next arch, 3ch, skip 3ch, 3dc into next sc; rep from * working only 2dc at end of last rep, skip tch, turn.

3rd row: 1ch, 1sc into each of first 2 sts, *1ch, skip 3ch and 1sc, 1dc into next dc, [1ch, 1dc into next dc] 8 times, 1ch, skip 1sc and 3ch, 1sc into each of next 3 sts; rep from * omitting 1sc at end of last rep, turn.

4th row: 1ch, 1sc into first st, *skip 1sc and 1ch, 1dc into next dc, [1ch, skip 1ch, 1dc into next dc] 3 times, 1ch, skip 1ch, work [1dc, 1ch, 1dc] into next dc, [1ch, skip 1ch, 1dc into next dc] 4 times (Crescent completed), skip 1ch and 1sc, 1sc into next sc; rep from * to end, skip tch, turn.

5th row: 6ch (count as 1dc and 3ch), *1sc into 3rd dc of next Crescent, 5ch, skip 1ch and 1dc, 1sc into next ch, 5ch, skip 1dc, 1ch and 1dc, 1sc into next ch, 5ch, skip 1dc and 1ch, 1sc into next dc, 3ch, skip remaining sts of same Crescent, 1dc into next sc, 3ch; rep from * omitting 3ch at end of last rep, skip tch, turn.

Rep 2nd, 3rd, 4th and 5th rows.

Openwork and Lace Patterns

Broomstick Lace

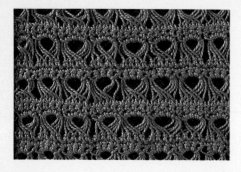

Multiple of 4 sts.
(add 1 for base chain)

1st row (right side): 1sc into 2nd ch from hook, 1sc into next and each ch to end, turn.
2nd row: 1ch, 1sc into first st, 1sc into next and each st to end, skip tch, turn.
3rd row: *1ch, draw loop on hook up to approx height of dtr, keeping loop on hook and not allowing it to change size through yarn slippage, insert hook into next st, yo, draw loop through; rep from * to end keeping all lace loops on hook. (Hint: slip some sts off handle end of hook if they become too numerous.) At end remove all except last lace loop from hook, yo, draw loop through, insert hook under back thread and work 1sc as for Solomon's Knot (see page 11). to lock last lace loop, turn.
4th row: *Always inserting hook through next 4 lace loops together work 4sc; rep from * to end, turn.
Rep 2nd, 3rd and 4th rows.

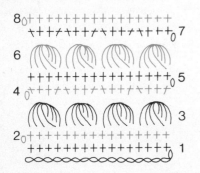

Crossed Lace Loop Stitch

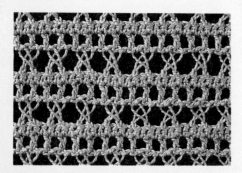

Multiple of 2 sts + 1.
(add 3 for base chain)

1st row (right side): 1dc into 6th ch from hook, *1ch, skip 1ch, 1dc into next ch; rep from * to end, turn.
2nd row: 1ch, 1sc into first st, *1sc into next ch, 1sc into next dc; rep from * ending 1sc into each of next 2ch of tch, turn.
3rd row: *1ch, draw loop on hook up to approx height of tr, keeping loop on hook and not allowing it to change size through yarn slippage, insert hook into next st, yo, draw loop through, sl st into next st; rep from * to end keeping all lace loops on hook. (Hint: slip some off handle end of hook, if they become too numerous.) At end remove all except last lace loop from hook, yo, draw loop through, insert hook under back thread as though for Solomon's Knot (see page 11), but make sl st to lock last lace loop, turn.
4th row: *1ch, skip 1 lace loop, sl st into top of next loop, 1ch, bring forward loop just skipped and sl st into top of it; rep from * ending sl st into top of last loop, turn.
5th row: 4ch (count as 1dc and 1ch), skip 1ch, 1dc into next sl st, *1ch, skip 1ch, 1dc into next sl st; rep from * to end, turn.
Rep 2nd, 3rd, 4th and 5th rows.

Little Pyramid Stitch

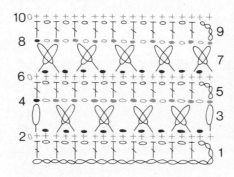

Multiple of 4 sts + 1.
(add 1 for base chain)

1st row (right side): 1sc into 2nd ch from hook, *work a Pyramid of [6ch, 1sc into 3rd ch from hook, 1dc into each of next 3ch], skip 3ch, 1sc into next ch; rep from * to end, turn.
2nd row: 6ch (count as 1dtr and 1ch), *1sc into ch at tip of next Pyramid, 3ch; rep from * ending 1sc into ch at tip of last Pyramid, 1ch, 1dtr into last sc, skip tch, turn.
3rd row: 10ch, skip 1ch, 1sc into next sc, *work Pyramid, skip 3ch, 1sc into next sc; rep from * ending 5ch, skip 1ch, 1dtr into

next ch of tch, turn.
4th row: 1ch, 1sc into first st, *3ch, 1sc into ch at tip of next Pyramid; rep from * ending last rep in center of 10th ch, turn.
5th row: 1ch, 1sc into first st, *work Pyramid, skip 3ch, 1sc into next sc; rep from * to end, skip tch, turn.
Rep 2nd, 3rd, 4th and 5th rows.

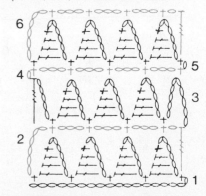

Chevron Lattice

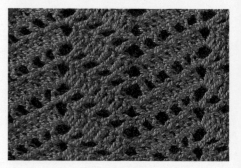

Multiple of 20 sts + 11.
(add 3 for base chain)
Special Abbreviation
Dc cluster: leaving last loop of each dc on hook work 1dc into next ch, skip 3ch, and work 1dc into next ch, then yo and draw through all 3 loops on hook.

1st row (wrong side): 1dc into 6th ch from hook, *[1ch, skip 1ch, 1dc into next ch] 3 times, 1ch, skip 1ch**, work [1dc, 3ch, 1dc] into next ch, [1ch, skip 1ch, 1dc into next ch] 3 times, 1ch, skip 1ch, work a dc cluster over next 1dc, 3ch and 1dc; rep from * ending last rep at **, work [1dc, 1ch, 1dc] into last ch, turn.
2nd row: 3ch (count as 1dc), 2dc into first st, *1dc into next ch sp, [1dc into next dc, 1dc into next ch sp] 3 times**, leaving last loop of each dc on hook work 1dc into next dc, skip dc cluster, work 1dc into next dc and complete as dc cluster, [1dc into next ch sp, 1dc into next dc] 3 times, 1dc into next ch, work [1dc, 3ch, 1dc] into next ch; rep from * ending last rep at **, work dc cluster over next 2 dcs, skip tch, turn.
3rd row: 3ch, skip first 2 sts, 1dc into next st, *[1ch, skip 1dc, 1dc into next dc] 3 times**, 1ch, skip 1ch, work [1dc, 3ch, 1dc] into next ch, 1ch, skip 1ch, [1dc into next dc, 1ch, skip 1dc] 3 times, leaving last loop of each dc on hook work 1dc into next dc, skip 1dc, dc cluster and 1dc, work 1dc into next dc and complete as dc cluster; rep from * ending last rep at **, 1ch, skip 1dc, work [1dc, 1ch, 1dc] into top of tch, turn.
Rep 2nd and 3rd rows.

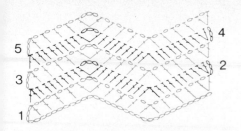

Solomon's Knot

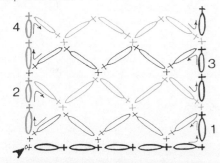

Multiple of 2 Solomon's Knots + 1.
(add 2 Solomon's Knots for base 'chain')

Special Abbreviations

ESK (Edge Solomon's Knot): these form the base 'chain' and edges of the fabric and are only two-thirds the length of MSK's.

MSK (Main Solomon's Knot): These form the main fabric and are half as long again as ESK's.

Base 'chain': 2ch, 1sc into 2nd ch from hook, now make a multiple of 2ESK's (say, 2cm), ending with 1MSK (say, 3cm).

1st row: 1sc into sc between 3rd and 4th loops from hook, *2MSK, skip 2 loops, 1sc into next sc; rep from * to end, turn.

2nd row: 2ESK and 1MSK, 1sc into sc between 4th and 5th loops from hook, *2MSK, skip 2 loops, 1sc into next sc; rep from * ending in top of ESK, turn.

Rep 2nd row.

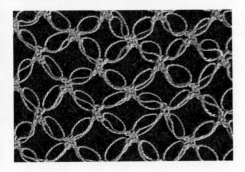

Lacewing Network

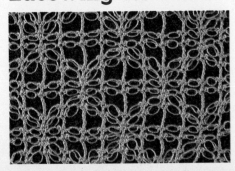

Multiple of 16 sts + 1.
(add 1 for base chain)

Special Abbreviation

SK (Solomon's Knot): loop approx 1.5cm.

Note: You may need to experiment with the number of ch in the base chain and length of loop, or even make the base 'chain' itself out of Knots.

Base row (right side): 1sc into 2nd ch from hook, *1SK, skip 3ch, 1tr into next ch, 1SK, skip 3ch, 1ttr into next ch, 1SK, skip 3ch, 1tr into next ch, 1SK, skip 3ch, 1sc into next ch; rep from * to end, turn.

Commence Pattern

1st row: 3ch, 1sc into 2nd ch from hook, *1SK, skip SK, 1dc into next st; rep from * to end, turn.

2nd row: 6ch, 1sc into 2nd ch from hook, *1SK, skip SK, 1tr into next st, 1SK, skip SK, 1sc into next st, 1SK, skip SK, 1tr into next st, 1SK, skip SK, 1 ttr into next st; rep from * to end, turn.

Rep the last 2 rows once then work 1st row again.

6th row: 1ch, 1sc into first st, *1SK, skip SK, 1tr into next st, 1SK, skip SK, 1 ttr into next st, 1SK skip SK, 1tr into next st, 1SK, skip SK, 1sc into next st; rep from * to end, turn.

7th row: As 1st row.

8th row: As 6th row.

Rep these 8 rows.

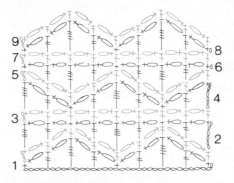

Embossed Flower Network

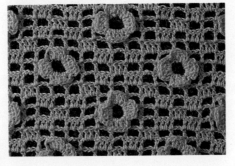

Multiple of 24 sts + 4.
(add 4 for base chain)

Note: When working Embossed Flower always treat the various stitches and threads which form the four sides of the space as if they were the base ring of a Motif, i.e. always insert hook through center of this 'ring' to make stitches.

Base row (right side): 1dc into 8th ch from hook, *2ch, skip 2ch, 1dc into each of next 4ch, [2ch, skip 2ch, 1dc into next ch] 3 times, 1dc into each of next 3ch, [2ch, skip 2ch, 1dc into next ch] twice; rep from * to end, turn.

Commence Pattern

1st row: 5ch (count as 1dc and 2ch), skip 2ch, 1dc into next st, *2dc into next 2ch sp, 1dc into next st, [2ch, skip 2 sts, 1dc into next st] twice, 2dc into next sp, 1dc into next st, [2ch, skip 2 sts, 1dc into next st] twice, 2dc into next sp, 1dc into next st, 2ch, skip 2ch, 1dc into next st; rep from * to end, turn.

2nd row: 3ch (count as 1dc), skip first st, 2dc into next 2ch sp, 1dc into next st, *[2ch, skip 2 sts, 1dc into next st] twice, 2dc into next sp, 1dc into next st, 2ch, skip 2dc, 1dc into next st. Now work Embossed Flower round space just completed, (see note above); with right side facing and working around anticlockwise, work 1sc into corner (top left), down left side work **3ch, 3dc, 3ch, 1sc into next corner** (bottom left); rep from ** to ** 3 more times, omitting sc at end of last rep and ending sl st to first sc, sl st to last dc made of main fabric. Continue working main fabric as follows: 2dc into next 2ch sp, 1dc into next st, [2ch, skip 2 sts, 1dc into next st] twice, 2dc into next 2ch sp, 1dc into next st; rep from * ending last rep in 3rd ch of tch, turn.

3rd row: As 1st row.

4th row: 5ch (count as 1dc and 2ch), skip 2ch, 1dc into next st, *2ch, skip 2 sts, 1dc into next st, 2dc into next 2ch sp, 1dc into next st, [2ch, skip 2 sts, 1dc into next st] 3 times, 2dc into next sp, 1dc into next st, [2ch, skip 2 sts, 1dc into next st] twice; rep from * ending last rep in 3rd ch of tch, turn.

5th row: 3ch (count as 1dc), skip first st, 2dc into next 2ch sp, 1dc into next st, *[2ch, skip 2 sts, 1dc into next st] twice, [2dc into next sp, 1dc into next st, 2ch, skip 2 sts, 1dc into next st] twice, 2ch, skip 2ch, 1dc into next st, 2dc into next sp, 1dc into next st; rep from * ending last rep in 3rd ch of tch, turn.

6th row: 5ch (count as 1dc and 2ch), skip first 3 sts, 1dc into next st. Now work Embossed Flower round space just completed as in 3rd row. Continue working main fabric as follows: *2dc into next 2ch sp, 1dc into next st, [2ch, skip 2 sts, 1dc into next st] twice, 2dc into next sp, 1dc into next st, [2ch, skip 2 sts, 1dc into next st] twice, 2dc into next sp, 1dc into next st, 2ch, skip 2 sts, 1dc into next st. Now work Embossed Flower round space just completed as before; rep from * ending last rep of main fabric in top of tch, turn.

7th row: As 5th row.

8th row: As 4th row.

Rep these 8 rows.

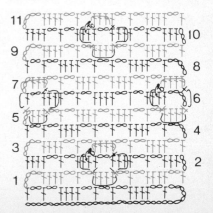

Openwork and Lace Patterns

Offset Filet Network

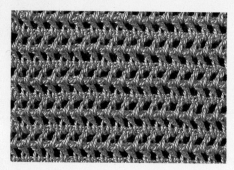

Multiple of 2 sts.
(add 3 for base chain)

1st row (right side): 1dc into 6th ch from hook, *1ch, skip 1ch, 1dc into next ch; rep from * ending 1dc into last ch, turn.

2nd row: 4ch (count as 1dc and 1ch), skip first 2 sts, 1dc into next ch sp, *1ch, skip 1dc, 1dc into next sp; rep from * to tch, 1dc into next ch, turn.

Rep 2nd row.

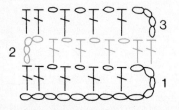

String Network

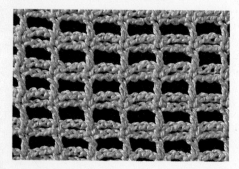

Multiple of 4 sts + 1.
(add 5 for base chain)

1st row (right side): 1dc into 10th ch from hook, *3ch, skip 3ch, 1dc into next ch; rep from * to end, turn.

2nd row: 1ch, 1sc into first st, *3ch, skip 3ch, 1sc into next dc; rep from * ending 3ch, 1sc into 4th ch of tch, turn.

3rd row: 6ch (count as 1dc and 3ch), skip first st and 3ch, 1dc into next sc, *3ch, skip 3ch, 1dc into next sc; rep from * to end, turn.

Rep 2nd and 3rd rows.

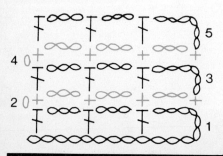

Double Crochet and Popcorn Squares

Multiple of 8 sts + 3.
(add 2 for base chain)

Popcorns occur on both right and wrong side rows. Be sure to push them all out on the right side of the fabric as you complete them.

1st row (right side): 5dc Popcorn into 4th ch from hook, *1dc into each of next 7ch, 5dc Popcorn into next ch; rep from * ending 1dc into last ch, turn.

2nd row: 4ch (count as 1dc and 1ch), skip first st and next Popcorn, 1dc into next st, *2ch, skip 2 sts, 5dc Popcorn into next st, 2ch, skip 2 sts, 1dc into next st, 1ch, skip next Popcorn, 1dc into next st; rep from * ending last rep in tch, turn.

3rd row: 4ch (count as 1dc and 1ch), skip first st and next ch, 1dc into next st, *1ch, skip 1ch, 5dc Popcorn into next ch, 1ch, skip Popcorn, 5dc Popcorn into next ch, [1ch, skip next ch, 1dc into next st] twice; rep from * ending last rep in tch, turn.

4th row: 4ch (count as 1dc and 1ch), skip first st and next ch, 1dc into next st, *2ch, 5dc Popcorn into ch sp between next 2 Popcorns, 2ch, 1dc into next dc, 1ch, skip 1ch, 1dc into next st; rep from * ending last rep in tch, turn.

5th row: 3ch (count as 1dc), skip first st, 5dc Popcorn into next ch, *1dc into next dc, 1dc into each of next 2ch, 1dc into next Popcorn, 1dc into each of next 2ch, 1dc into next dc, 5dc Popcorn into next ch; rep from * ending 1dc into next ch of tch, turn.

Rep 2nd, 3rd, 4th and 5th rows.

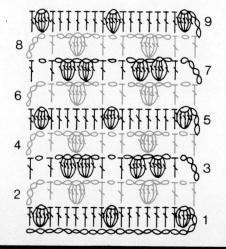

Picot Ridge Stitch

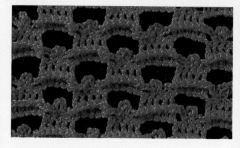

Multiple of 10 sts + 7.
(add 2 for base chain)

1st row (right side): Skip 3ch (count as 1dc), *1dc into each of next 5ch, 3ch, skip 2ch, [1sc, 4ch, 1sc] into next ch, 3ch, skip 2ch; rep from * ending 1dc into last ch, turn.

2nd row: 8ch (count as 1dc and 5ch), skip first st and next 3ch arch, *1dc/rf round each of next 5 sts, 5ch, skip next 3 arches; rep from * ending 1dc/rf round each of last 5dcs, 1dc into top of tch, turn.

3rd row: 6ch, skip first 3 sts, *[1sc, 4ch, 1sc] into next st, 3ch, skip 2 sts, 1dc into each of next 5ch**, 3ch, skip 2 sts; rep from * ending last rep at **, 1dc into next ch of tch, turn.

4th row: 3ch (count as 1dc), skip first st, *1dc/rf round each of next 5 sts, 5ch**, skip next 3 arches; rep from * ending last rep at **, skip next 2 arches, 1dc into tch arch, turn.

5th row: 3ch (count as 1dc), skip first st, *1dc into each of next 5ch, 3ch, skip 2 sts, [1sc, 4ch, 1sc] into next st, 3ch, skip 2 sts; rep from * ending 1dc into top of tch, turn.

Rep 2nd, 3rd, 4th and 5th rows.

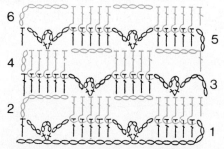

Fancy Picot Stitch

Multiple of 10 sts + 1.
(add 2 for base chain)

1st row (right side): Skip 3ch (count as 1dc), *1dc into each of next 2ch, work a picot of [3ch, insert hook down through top of last st made and sl st to close], [1ch, skip 1ch,

Openwork and Lace Patterns

1dc into next ch, picot] twice, 1ch, skip 1ch, 1dc into each of next 2ch**, 1ch, skip 1ch; rep from * ending last rep at **, 1dc into last ch, turn.

2nd row: 3ch (count as 1dc), skip first st, *1dc into each of next 2 sts, [picot, 1ch, skip next ch and picot, 1dc into next dc] 3 times, 1dc into next dc**, 1ch, skip 1ch; rep from * ending last rep at **, 1dc into top of tch, turn.

Rep 2nd row.

Squares and Ladders

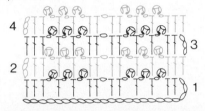

Multiple of 16 sts + 5.
(add 3 for base chain)

Base row (right side): 1dc into 6th ch from hook, *1ch, skip 1ch, 1dc into next ch; rep from * to end, turn.

Commence Pattern

1st row: 4ch (count as 1dc and 1ch), skip first st and next ch, 1dc into next dc, 1ch, skip 1ch, 1dc into next dc, *5ch, skip 5 sts, dc3tog into next dc, 5ch, skip 5 sts, 1dc into next dc, [1ch, skip 1ch, 1dc into next st] twice; rep from * ending last rep in tch, turn.

2nd row: 4ch (count as 1dc and 1ch), skip first st and next ch, 1dc into next dc, 1ch, skip 1ch, 1dc into next dc, *4ch, 1sc into 5ch arch, skip cluster, 1sc into next 5ch arch, 4ch, 1dc into next dc, [1ch, skip 1ch, 1dc into next st] twice; rep from * ending last rep in tch, turn.

3rd row: 4ch (count as 1dc and 1ch), skip first st and next ch, 1dc into next dc, 1ch, skip 1ch, 1dc into next dc, *4ch, 1sc into 4ch arch, 1sc between 2sc, 1sc into next 4ch arch, 4ch, 1dc into next dc, [1ch, skip 1ch, 1dc into next st] twice; rep from * ending last rep in tch, turn.

4th row: 4ch (counts as 1dc and 1ch), skip first st and next ch, 1dc into next dc, 1ch, skip 1ch, 1dc into next dc, *5ch, dc3tog into 2nd of 3sc, 5ch, 1dc into next dc, [1ch, skip 1ch, 1dc into next st] twice; rep from * ending last rep in tch, turn.

5th row: 4ch (count as 1dc and 1ch), skip first st and next ch, 1dc into next dc, *1ch, skip 1ch, 1dc into next st; rep from * ending last rep in tch, turn.

6th row: As 5th row.

Rep these 6 rows.

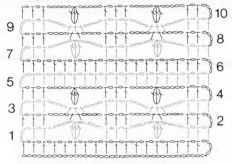

Shell Network

Multiple of 8 sts + 3.
(add 3 for base chain)

1st row (right side): 1dc into 6th ch from hook, *skip 2ch, 5dc into next ch, skip 2ch, 1dc into next ch, 1ch, skip 1ch, 1dc into next ch; rep from * to end, turn.

2nd row: 4ch (count as 1dc and 1ch), skip first st and next ch, 1dc into next dc, *skip 2dc, 5dc into next dc, skip 2dc, 1dc into next dc, 1ch, skip 1ch, 1dc into next dc; rep from * ending last rep in 2nd ch of tch, turn.

Rep 2nd row.

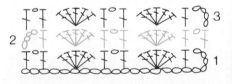

Sieve Stitch

Multiple of 2 sts + 1.
(add 1 for base chain)

Base row (wrong side): 1sc into 2nd ch from hook, *1ch, skip 1ch, 1sc into next ch; rep from * to end, turn.

Commence Pattern

1st row: 1ch, skip 1 st, *2sc into next ch sp, skip next sc; rep from * until 1 ch sp remains, 1sc into last ch sp, 1sc into next sc, skip tch, turn.

2nd row: 1ch, skip 1 st, 1sc into next st, *1ch, skip 1 st, 1sc into next sc; rep from * until only tch remains, 1sc into tch, turn.

3rd row: 1ch, skip first 2 sts, *2sc into next ch sp, skip next sc; rep from * until only tch remains, 2sc into tch, turn.

4th row: As 2nd row.

5th row: 1ch, 1sc into first st, *skip next sc. 2sc into next ch sp; rep from * ending last rep in tch, turn.

6th row: 1ch, skip 1 st, *1sc into next sc, 1ch, skip 1sc; rep from * ending 1sc into tch, turn.

7th row: 1ch, skip 1 st, 1sc into next ch sp, *skip 1sc, 2sc into next sp; rep from * ending skip last sc, 1sc into tch, turn.

8th row: 1ch, 1sc into first st, *1ch, skip 1sc, 1sc into next st; rep from * to end working last st into top of tch, turn.

Rep these 8 rows.

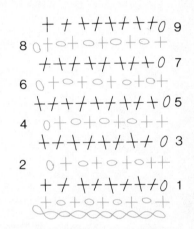

Winkle Picot Stitch

Multiple of 3 sts + 2.
(add 4 for base chain)

1st row (right side): 1sc into 6th ch from hook, *skip 1ch, 1sc into next ch, 3ch, 1sc into next ch; rep from * until 3ch remain, skip 1ch, 1sc into next ch, 2ch, 1hdc into last ch, turn.

2nd row: 4ch, 1sc into next 2ch sp, *[1sc, 3ch, 1sc] into next 3ch arch; rep from * ending [1sc, 2ch, 1hdc] into last ch arch, turn.

Rep 2nd row.

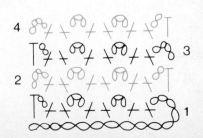

Openwork and Lace Patterns

Half Double Crochet V Stitch

Multiple of 2 sts.
(add 2 for base chain)

1st row (right side): [1hdc, 1ch, 1hdc] into 4th ch from hook, *skip 1ch, [1hdc, 1ch, 1hdc] into next ch; rep from * until 2ch remain, skip 1ch, 1hdc into last ch, turn.

2nd row: 2ch, *skip 2 sts, [1hdc, 1ch, 1hdc] into next ch sp; rep from * to last ch sp, skip 1 st, 1hdc into tch, turn.

Rep 2nd row.

Double Crochet V

Multiple of 2 sts.
(add 2 for base chain)

1st row (right side): 2dc into 4th ch from hook, *skip 1ch, 2dc into next ch; rep from * to last 2ch, skip 1ch, 1dc into last ch, turn.

2nd row: 3ch, *skip 2 sts, 2dc between 2nd skipped st and next st; rep from * to last 2 sts, skip 1 st, 1dc into top of tch, turn.

Rep 2nd row.

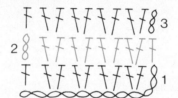

Offset V Stitch

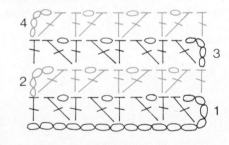

Multiple of 3 sts + 1.
(add 3 for base chain)

1st row (right side): 1dc into 4th ch from hook, *skip 2ch, work a V st of [1dc, 1ch, 1dc] into next ch; rep from * to last 3ch, skip 2ch, 1dc into last ch, turn.

2nd row: 4ch, 1dc into first st, *V st into 2nd dc of next V st; rep from * until 1dc and tch remain, skip 1dc and 1ch, 1dc into next ch, turn.

Rep 2nd row.

Twin V Stitch

Multiple of 4 sts + 2.
(add 2 for base chain)

1st row (right side): 2dc into 5th ch from hook, 2dc into next ch, *skip 2ch, 2dc into each of next 2ch; rep from * to last 2ch, skip 1ch, 1dc into last ch, turn.

2nd row: 3ch, *skip 2 sts, 2dc into each of next 2 sts; rep from * to last 2 sts, skip 1 st, 1dc into tch, turn.

Rep 2nd row.

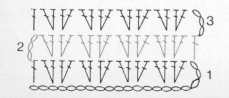

Three-and-Two Stitch

Multiple of 6 sts + 2.
(add 2 for base chain)

1st row (right side): Work a V st of [1dc, 1ch, 1dc] into 5th ch from hook, *skip 2ch, 3dc into next ch, skip 2ch, work a V st into next ch; rep from * to last 5ch, skip 2ch, 3dc into next ch, skip 2ch, 1dc into last ch, turn.

2nd row: 3ch, *skip 2 sts, work 3dc into center dc of next 3dc, work a V st into ch sp at center of next V st; rep from * ending 1dc into top of tch, turn.

3rd row: 3ch, *V st into sp of next V st, 3dc into center dc of next 3dc; rep from * ending 1dc into top of tch, turn.

Rep 2nd and 3rd rows.

Basket Stitch

Multiple of 3 sts + 2.
(add 2 for base chain)

1st row (wrong side): Work a V st of [1dc, 1ch, 1dc] into 5th ch from hook, *skip 2ch, work V st into next ch; rep from * to last 2ch, skip 1ch, 1dc into last ch, turn.

2nd row: 3ch, skip 2 sts, work a Double V st of [2dc, 1ch, 2dc] into ch sp at center of V st, *1ch, skip next V st, work a Double V st into sp at center of next V st; rep from * leaving last loop of last dc of last Double V st on hook and working it together with 1dc into top of tch, turn.

3rd row: 3ch, work a V st into each sp to end finishing with 1dc into top of tch, turn.

4th row: 3ch, 1dc into first st, *1ch, skip next V st, work a Double V st into sp at center of next V st; rep from * until 1 V st remains, 1ch, skip V st, 2dc into top of tch, turn.

5th row: As 3rd row.

Rep 2nd, 3rd, 4th and 5th rows.

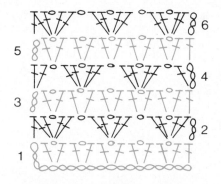

Empress Stitch

Multiple of 18 sts + 1.
(add 3 for base chain)
Notes

Popcorns occur on both right and wrong side rows alternately. Be sure to push them all out on the right side of the fabric as you complete them.

1st row (wrong side): 1dc into 4th ch from hook, *skip 2ch, work a V st of [1dc, 1ch, 1dc] into next ch; rep from * to last 3ch, skip 2ch, 2dc into last ch, turn.

2nd row: 3ch, 1dc into first st, V st into sp at center of next V st, *5ch, skip next V st, 1sc into sp at center of next V st, 5ch, skip next V st**, [V st into sp at center of next V st] 3 times; rep from * ending last rep at **, V st into sp at center of last V st, 2dc into top of tch, turn.

3rd row: 3ch, 1dc into first st, V st into sp at center of next V st, *[3ch, 1sc into next 5ch arch] twice, 3ch**, [V st into sp at center of next V st] 3 times; rep from * ending last rep at **, V st into sp at center of last V st, 2dc into top of tch, turn.

4th row: 3ch, 1dc into first st, V st into sp at center of next V st, *skip next 3ch arch, [5dc Popcorn, 2ch, 5dc Popcorn, 2ch, 5dc Popcorn] into next 3ch arch, skip next 3ch arch**, [V st into sp at center of next V st] 3 times; rep from * ending last rep at **, V st into sp at center of last V st, 2dc into top of tch, turn.

5th row: 3ch, 1dc into first st, V st into sp at center of next V st, *[3ch, 1sc into next 2ch sp] twice, 3ch**, [V st into sp at center of next V st] 3 times; rep from * ending last rep at **, V st into sp at center of last V st, 2dc into top of tch, turn.

6th row: 3ch, 1dc into first st, V st into sp at center of next V st, *[V st into 2nd ch of next 3ch arch] 3 times**, [V st into sp at center of next V st] 3 times; rep from * ending last rep at **, V st into sp at center of last V st, 2dc into top of tch, turn.

Rep 2nd, 3rd, 4th, 5th and 6th rows.

Noughts and Crosses Stitch

Multiple of 2 sts + 1.
(add 3 for base chain)

1st row (right side): 1dc into 6th ch from hook, *1ch, skip 1ch, 1dc into next ch; rep from * to end, turn.

2nd row: 3ch, skip next ch sp, work 2 crossed stitches as follows: 1dc forward into next ch sp, 1dc back into ch sp just skipped going behind forward dc so as not to catch it, *1dc forward into next unoccupied ch sp, 1dc back into previous ch sp going behind forward dc as before; rep from * to end when last forward dc occupies tch, 1dc into next ch, turn.

3rd row: 1ch (counts as 1sc), 1sc into first st, 1sc into next and each st to end working last st into top of tch, turn.

4th row: 4ch (counts as 1dc and 1ch), skip 2 sts, 1dc into next st, *1ch, skip 1 st, 1dc

into next st; rep from * ending last rep in tch, turn.

Rep 2nd, 3rd and 4th rows.

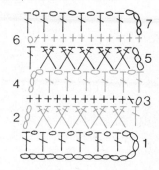

Fantail Stitch

Multiple of 10 sts + 1.
(add 1 for base chain)

1st row (right side): 1sc into 2nd ch from hook, 1sc into next ch, *skip 3ch, work a Fan of [3dc, 1ch, 3dc] into next ch, skip 3ch, 1sc into next ch**, 1ch, skip 1ch, 1sc into next ch; rep from * ending last rep at **, 1sc into last ch, turn.

2nd row: 2ch (count as 1hdc), 1hdc into first st, *3ch, 1sc into ch sp at center of next Fan, 3ch**, work a V st of [1hdc, 1ch, 1hdc] into next sp; rep from * ending last rep at **, 2hdc into last sc, skip tch, turn.

3rd row: 3ch, 3dc into first st, *1sc into next 3ch arch, 1ch, 1sc into next arch**, work a Fan into sp at center of next V st; rep from * ending last rep at **, 4dc into top of tch, turn.

4th row: 1ch, 1sc into first st, *3ch, V st into next sp, 3ch, 1sc into sp at center of next Fan; rep from * ending last rep into top of tch, turn.

5th row: 1ch, 1sc into first st, *1sc into next arch, Fan into sp at center of next V st, 1sc into next arch**, 1ch; rep from * ending last rep at **, 1sc into last sc, skip tch, turn.

Rep 2nd, 3rd, 4th and 5th rows.

Openwork and Lace Patterns

Flying Shell Stitch

Multiple of 4 sts + 1.
(add 1 for base chain)

1st row (right side): Work a Flying Shell (called FS) of [1sc, 3ch, 3dc] into 2nd ch from hook, *skip 3ch, 1FS into next ch; rep from * to last 4ch, skip 3ch, 1sc into last ch, turn.
2nd row: 3ch, 1dc into first st, *skip 3 sts, 1sc into top of 3ch**, work a V st of [1dc, 1ch, 1dc] into next sc; rep from * ending last rep at **, 2dc into last sc, skip tch, turn.
3rd row: 3ch, 3dc into first st, skip next st, *1FS into next sc, skip next V st; rep from * ending 1sc into last sc, 3ch, dc2tog over last dc and top of tch, turn.
4th row: 1ch (counts as 1sc), *V st into next sc, skip 3 sts, 1sc into top of 3ch; rep from * to end, turn.
5th row: 1ch, FS into first st, *skip next V st, FS into next sc; rep from * ending skip last V st, 1sc into tch, turn.
Rep 2nd, 3rd, 4th and 5th rows.

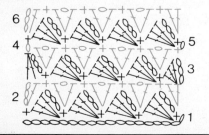

Picot V Stitch

Multiple of 3 sts + 1.
(add 2 for base chain)
1st row (right side): Skip 3ch (count as 1dc), 1dc into next ch, skip 1ch, 1dc into next ch, work a picot of [3ch, insert hook down through top of dc just made and work a sl st], 1dc into same ch as last dc, *skip 2ch, [1dc, picot, 1dc] into next ch; rep from * to last 3ch, skip 2ch, 1dc into last ch, turn.

2nd row: 3ch (count as 1dc), 1dc into first st, *skip 1dc and picot, [1dc, picot, 1dc] into next dc; rep from * to last 2 sts, skip next dc, 1dc into top of tch, turn.
Rep 2nd row.

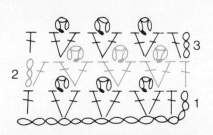

Pebble Lace Stitch

Multiple of 4 sts + 3.
(add 1 for base chain)

Close tr7tog clusters with 1ch drawn tightly, (this does not count as part of following ch loop).
Clusters always occur on wrong side rows. Be sure to push them all out to the back (right side) of the fabric as you complete them.
1st row (wrong side): 1sc into 2nd ch from hook, *2ch, skip 1ch, work tr7tog into next ch, 2ch, skip 1ch, 1sc into next ch; rep from * to last 2ch, 2ch, skip 1ch, 1hdc into last ch, turn.
2nd row: 1ch, 1sc into first st, *3ch, 1sc into next cluster; rep from * ending 1ch, 1hdc into last sc, skip tch, turn.
3rd row: 4ch, skip first hdc and ch, 1sc into next sc, *2ch, tr7tog into 2nd of next 3ch, 2ch, 1sc into next sc; rep from * to end, skip tch, turn.
4th row: 3ch, skip first st and 2ch, 1sc into next cluster, *3ch, 1sc into next cluster; rep from * ending 3ch, 1sc into last 4ch arch, turn.
5th row: 1ch, 1sc into first st, *2ch, tr7tog into 2nd of next 3ch, 2ch, 1sc into next sc; rep from * ending 2ch, skip 1ch, 1hdc into next ch of tch, turn.
Rep 2nd, 3rd, 4th and 5th rows.

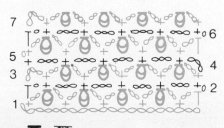

 =

Plain Trellis Stitch

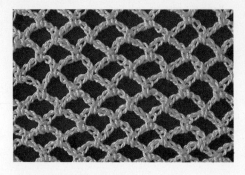

Multiple of 4 sts + 3.
(add 3 for base chain)
1st row: 1sc into 6th ch from hook, *5ch, skip 3ch, 1sc into next ch; rep from * to end, turn.
2nd row: *5ch, 1sc into next 5ch arch; rep from * to end, turn.
Rep 2nd row.

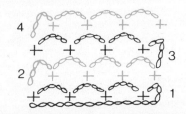

Picot Trellis Stitch

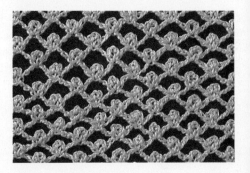

Multiple of 5 sts + 1.
(add 1 for base chain)
1st row: 1sc into 2nd ch from hook, *5ch, skip 4ch, 1sc into next ch; rep from * to end, turn.
2nd row: *5ch, work a picot of [1sc, 3ch, 1sc] into 3rd ch of next 5ch arch; rep from * ending 2ch, 1dc into last sc, skip tch, turn.
3rd row: 1ch, 1sc into first st, *5ch, skip picot, picot into 3rd ch of next 5ch arch; rep from * ending 5ch, skip picot, 1sc into tch arch, turn.
Rep 2nd and 3rd rows.

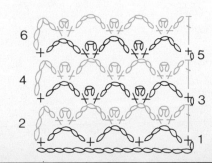

Stitch Variations, Abbreviations and Symbols on pages 7 to 15

Filet Charts

Filet crochet is based on a simple network or 'ground' made of double crochet and chain stitches. Patterns are therefore usually presented in the form of squared charts. Designs of all kinds - flowers, geometric patterns, lettering and even whole scenes - can be created by 'filling in' some of the squares or spaces with dc instead of chain.

Like stitch diagrams, charts are read from the bottom to the top, right side rows from right to left and wrong side rows from left to right. Each open square represents an open space whilst a filled-in square represents a 'block' of stitches. Every row starts with three chain (count as 1dc), bringing you to the correct height and balancing the pattern.

The basis of filet crochet is rectangular. Ideally each space or block should be square, but this is hard to achieve because of variations in tension. Small variations to the ratio between height and width can be made by changing the way you hold the yarn or hook. To test your tension first work a swatch based on sample 'b' below. This is worked so that each open square on the chart represents a space formed by two chain and a double crochet. The other edge of the space is formed by the last stitch of the preceeding space or block or by the three chain at the beginning of the row. When a square is filled the two chain space is replaced by two double crochet making a single block of three double crochet. Each additional block therefore adds three double crochet, so two blocks together (with a space either side), appear as seven double crochet, and three blocks, as ten double crochet.

If you cannot adjust the ratio between height and width sufficiently by changing the way you hold the work it may be necessary to change the size of the blocks and spaces. A space could be reduced to 1ch and 1dc, with a 2dc block (sample 'a'), or enlarged to a 3ch and 1dc space with a 4dc block (sample 'c'). The photographs of the samples show the differences between the three variations.

'b', but whatever your tension look at the other methods as there may be times you would wish to use these purely for their decorative effect.

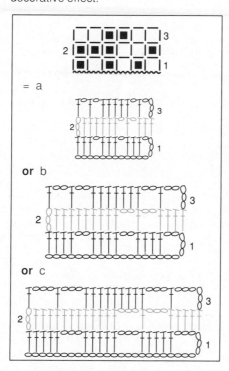

Starting Chain

When working as sample 'b', the number of chain required to start filet crochet is calculated by multiplying the number of squares required by three. Add five chain if the first square to be worked is a space or three chain if the first square to be worked is a block (see diagram 'b above').

To work samples 'a' or 'c', multiply the number of squares by two or four, adding four or six chain for a space and three chain for a block (see diagrams 'a' and 'c').

Lacets and Bars

Variations on blocks and spaces include 'V' shapes known as lacets, and longer chains known as bars.

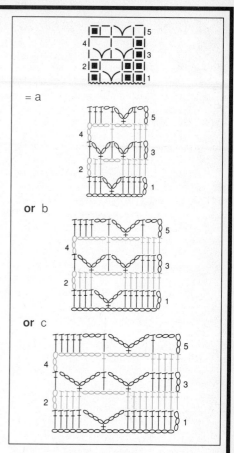

The diagrams above show the stitches and their positioning for each variation.

Increasing and Decreasing

In filet crochet increases are usually made in whole squares rather than stitches. If increases are made at the beginning of rows and decreases at the ends of rows no special techniques are required as the following stitch diagram shows.

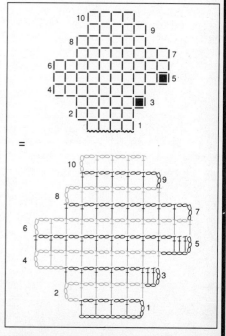

When increases are needed at the end of a row or decreases at the beginning of a row, the following techniques should be used.

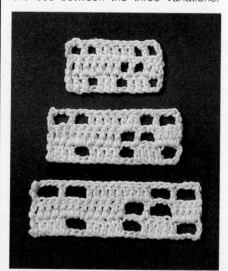
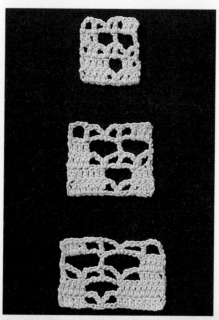

The worked samples in this section have been made following the style of sample

Filet Crochet

To increase a space at the end of a row

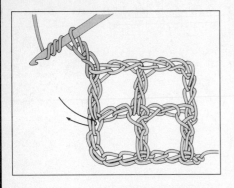

1. Work two chain, then work a double treble into same place as previous double crochet.

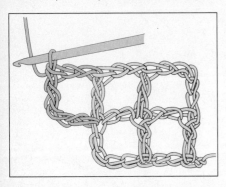

2. The double treble makes the outer edges of the increased space.

To increase a block at the end of a row

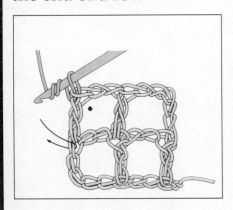

1. Work a treble into same place as previous double crochet.

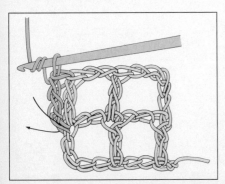

2. Then work [a treble into bottom segment of previous treble] twice.

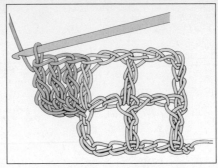

3. Thus making an increased block.

To decrease at the beginning of a row

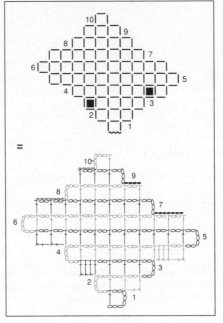

=

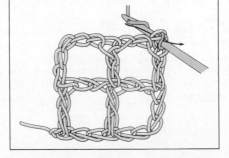

1. Turn work. Slip stitch into top of last double crochet worked, then into each of next two chain (or top of double crochet if last square in previous row is a block) and into top of next double crochet.

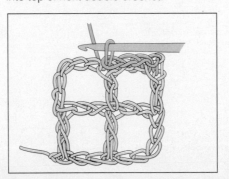

2. Hook is in position to commence row.

Using Filet Patterns

The patterns in this book can be used exactly as they are to produce fabrics with all-over patterns, borders, insertions and motifs. Different effects can be achieved by working the charts downwards or sideways or by repeating or combining designs. Graph paper should be used to plot out any changes.

Key

☐ = Space

▣ = Block

☐ = Bar

☐Y☐ = Lacet

Pressing and Finishing Filet

The feature of Filet which distinguishes it from other styles of crochet is its rectangular appearance. For information on how to press and finish your filet crochet see the general instructions on page 15 but remember, at every stage, to check that all the vertical and horizontal lines of the work are laying at right-angles. After removing the pins and while the work is still quite damp, use your fingertips to gently ease the edges into perfectly straight lines.

Filet crochet is often used for borders, edgings and insertions on items like tablecloths and tray mats. The crochet piece is sewn on to a piece of fabric. Firstly turn under the raw edges to form a hem, and slip-stitch in place. Then whip stitch the crochet piece to the outer fold of the fabric, (see Picture Frame on page 97).

TIP

Larger items, such as curtains and bedspreads, can easily be made in Filet. Work a small piece of alternate blocks and spaces to ascertain the number of blocks and rows to 10cms or 4 inches. From that you can calculate the number of squares you will need in Filet to cover the area you require and this can then be drawn on to graph paper. Any of the designs given in this section can then be added, either singly or in repeats, or you can even design your own exclusive pattern!

Mitre Block

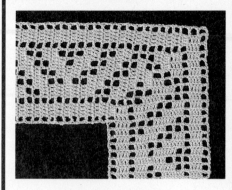

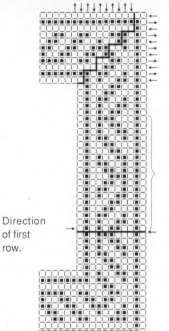

↑↓↑↓↑↑↓↑↓

Rep these 18 rows to adjust length.

Start and finish here.

Direction of first row.

Turning corners

Following chart, work short rows to corner, then turn piece and work into the side of completed stitches.

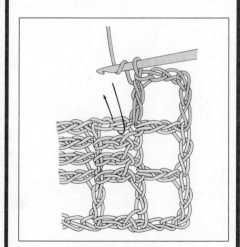

It is important to remember when working a mitered corner that the final row, before changing direction, should be worked towards the the inner edge so that the yarn is in the correct position to turn and work at right angles to the edge.

Join the start and finish together with a neat seam (see page 14).

Space Race

Rep these 2 squares
Rep these 2 rows.

Gull Wings

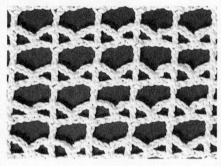

Rep these 2 squares
Rep these 2 rows.

Square Cross

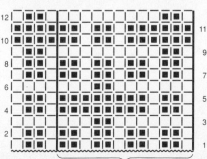

Rep these 12 squares
Rep these 12 rows.

Cross Over

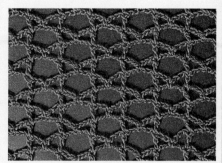

Rep these 4 squares
Rep these 2 rows.

Chequers

Rep these 4 squares
Rep these 4 rows.

Penta Point

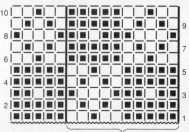

Rep these 10 squares
Rep these 10 rows.

Filet Crochet

Swept Back

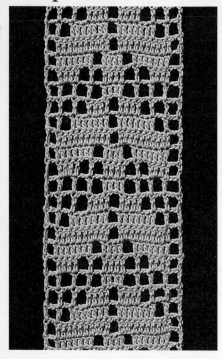

Extra Line

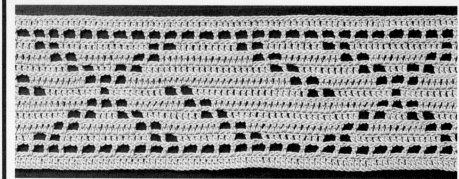

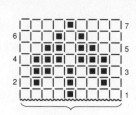

9 squares

Rep 2nd to 7th rows.

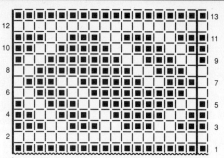

Rep these 17 squares

Sunburst

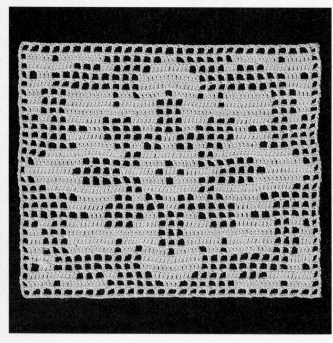

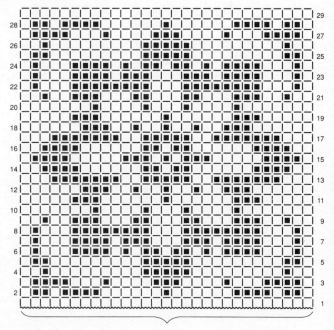

29 squares

Double Hook

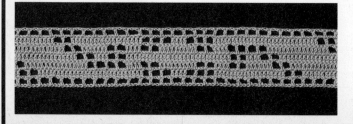

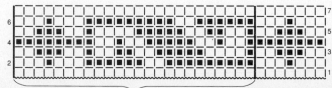

Rep these 24 squares

For more information and key to Filet Symbols see pages 89 and 90

Icicle

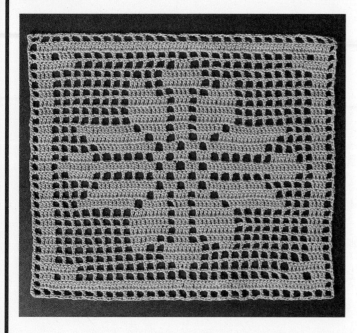

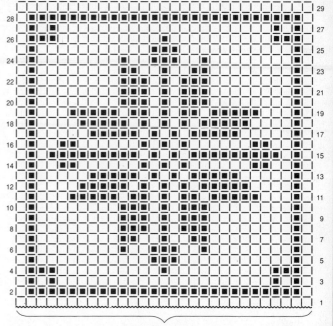

29 squares

Board Games

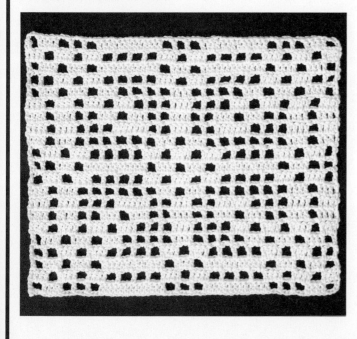

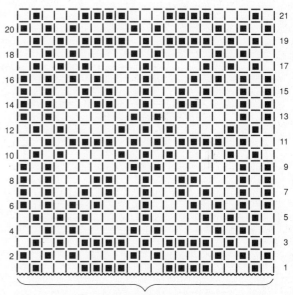

21 squares

Love Birds

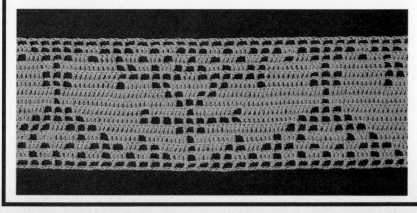

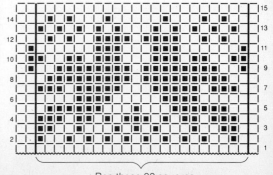

Rep these 22 squares

Filet Crochet

Four Square

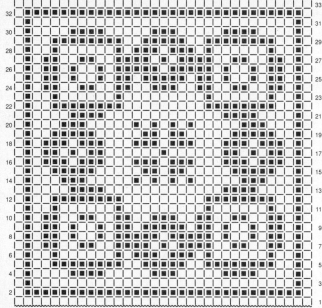

33 squares

Falling Leaves

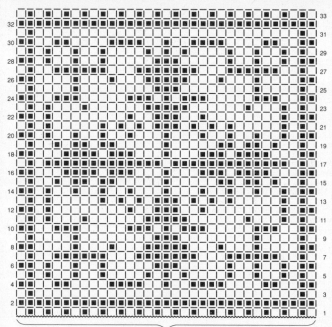

33 squares

Bookmark

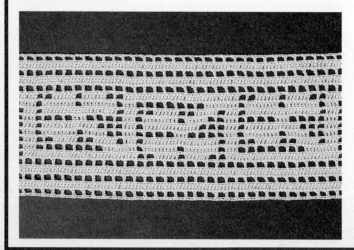

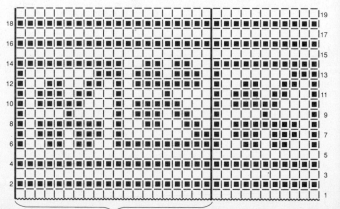

Rep these 20 squares

For more information and key to Filet Symbols see pages 89 and 90

Floral Accent

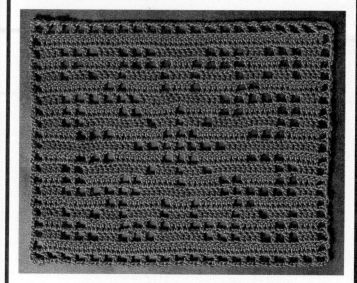

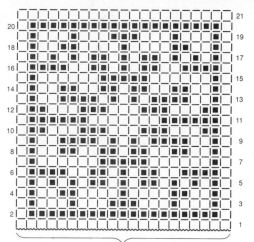

21 squares

Hollow Shape

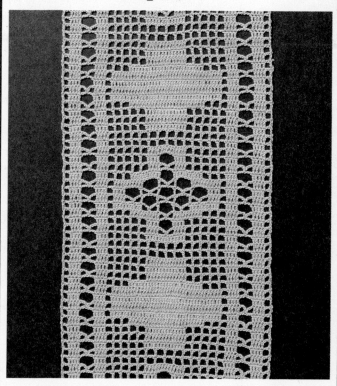

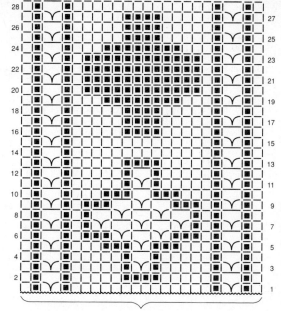

24 squares

Rep these 28 rows.

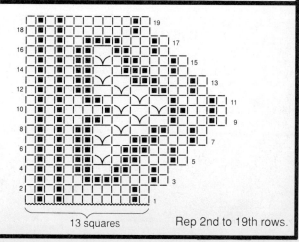

13 squares

Rep 2nd to 19th rows.

Even Border

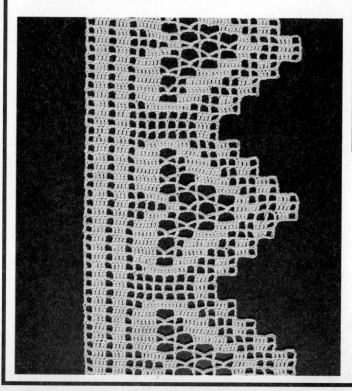

Filet Crochet

Union Flag

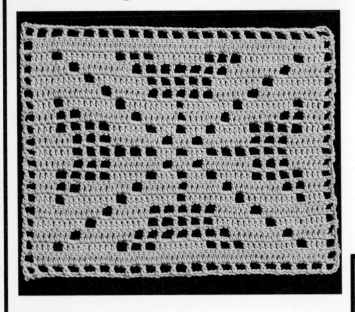

Poppy Seed

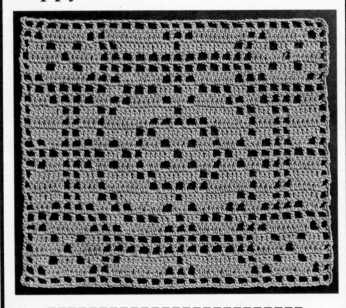

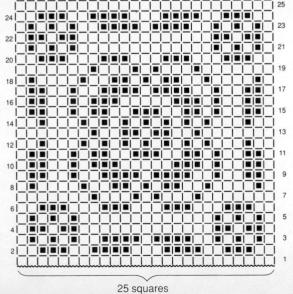

25 squares

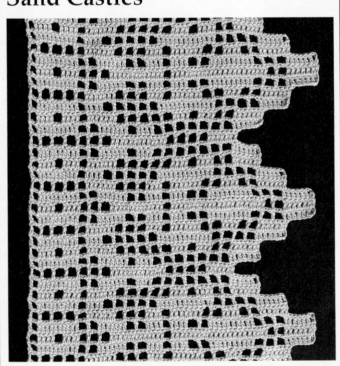

21 squares

Sand Castles

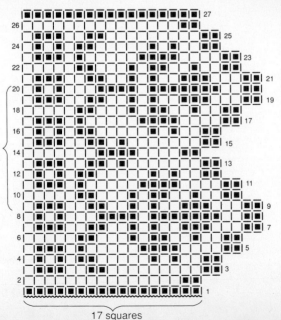

Rep these 12 rows

17 squares

For more information and key to Filet Symbols see pages 89 and 90

Pennants I

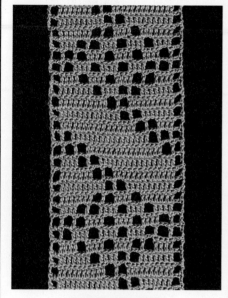

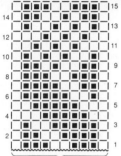

10 squares

Rep 2nd to 15th rows.

Pennants II

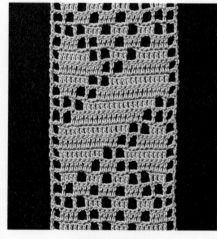

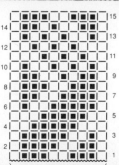

10 squares

Rep 2nd to 15th rows.

Picture Frame

Work first 10 rows of whole diagram, then work the 10 squares of right hand side of 11th row. Continue on right hand side only, finishing with a row as 35th row. Do not turn but make a chain for base of center top (a multiple of 14 + 11 squares). Break yarn, rejoin at X and work left side to match right but finishing on a row as 36th row. Do not turn but continue in pattern across chain already made (taking care that the chain is not twisted), then work 36th row across right side to end. Complete remaining 9 rows.

If preferred, edging may be worked starting and ending at line A with 10 squares, working first row in direction of arrow and making mitered corner at line B (see page 91).

See page 90 for attaching to fabric.

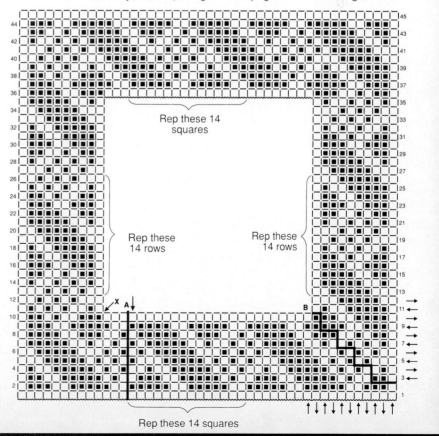

Rep these 14 squares

Rep these 14 rows

Rep these 14 rows

Rep these 14 squares

Filet Crochet

Filet Crochet Lace

☐ = space (2ch)
⌐ = bar
⌣ = lacet
⊡ = block

Greek Key Frieze

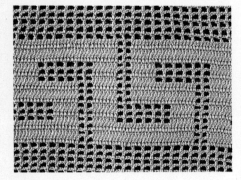

Base Row
Multiple of 3 sts per square + 1
Pattern Repeat = 12 squares

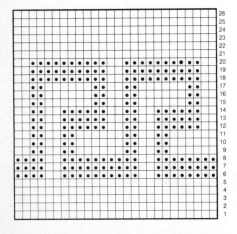

Alternating Tiles

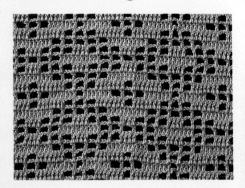

Base Row
Multiple of 3 sts per square + 1
Pattern Repeat = 8 squares

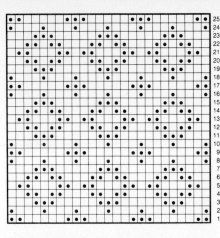

Base Row
Multiple of 3 sts per square + 1
Pattern Repeat = 22 squares

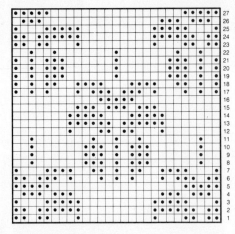

Southern Cross

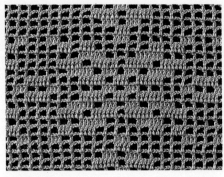

Base Row
Multiple of 3 sts per square + 1
Pattern Repeat = 15 squares

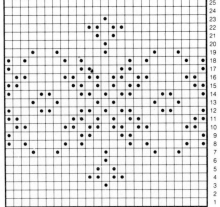

Orchid Blooms

Blocks and Lacets

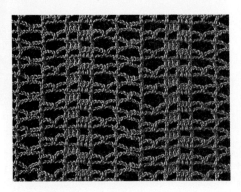

Base Row
Multiple of 3 sts per square + 1
Pattern Repeat = 8 squares wide by 2 squares deep

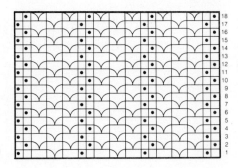

Hint: Larger items, such as curtains and bedspreads, can easily be made in Filet. Work a small piece of alternate blocks and spaces to ascertain the number of blocks and rows to the inch. From that you can calculate the number of squares you will need in Filet to cover the area you require and this can then be drawn onto graph paper. Any of the designs suggested here can then be added, either singly or in repeats, or you can design your own exclusive pattern!

For more information and key to Filet Symbols see pages 89 and 90

Flowerpots

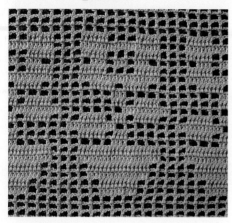

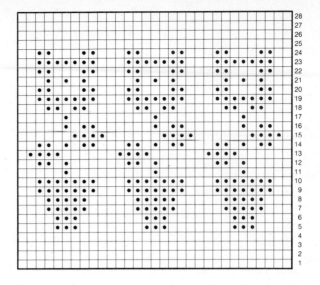

Base Row
Multiple of 3 sts per square + 1
Pattern Repeat = 10 squares

Butterfly

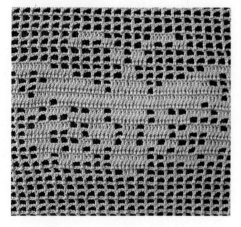

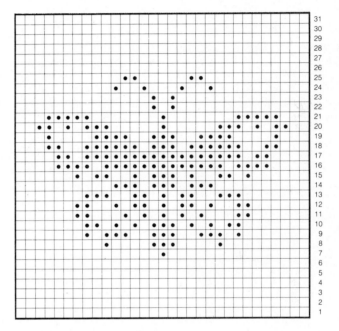

Base Row
Multiple of 3 sts per square + 1
Pattern Repeat = 31 squares

Peace Rose

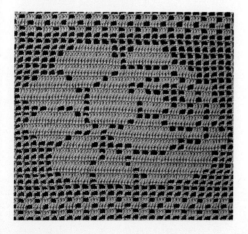

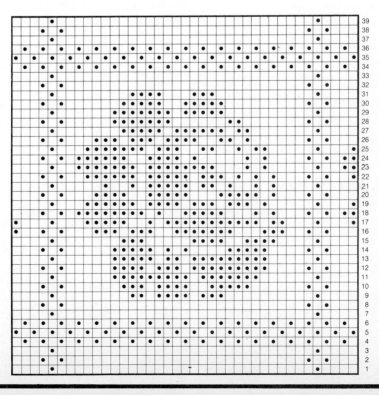

Base Row
Multiple of 3 sts per square + 1
Pattern Repeat = 30 squares

Filet Crochet

Pokerwork

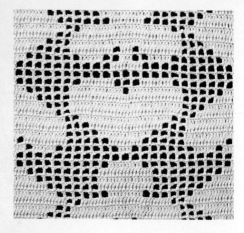

Base Row
Multiple of 3 sts per square + 1
Pattern Repeat = 24 squares wide by 23
squares deep

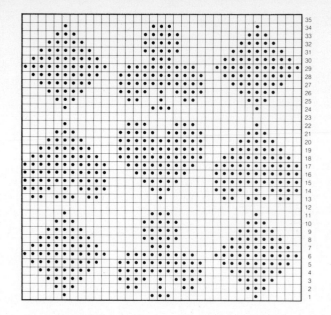

Letterform

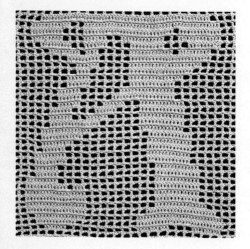

Base Row
Multiple of 3 sts per square + 1

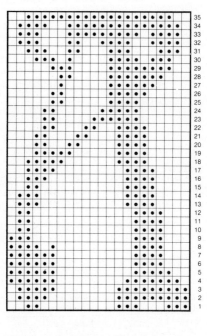

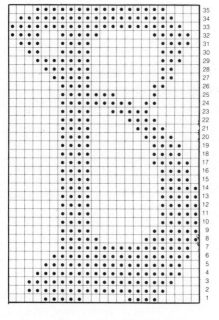

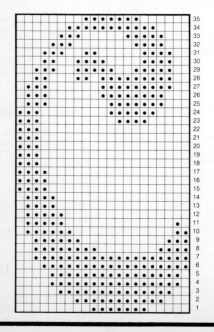

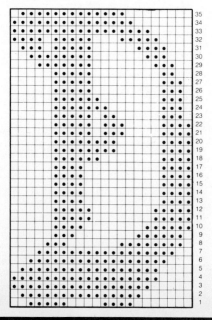

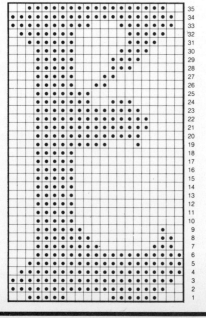

For more information and key to Filet Symbols see pages 89 and 90

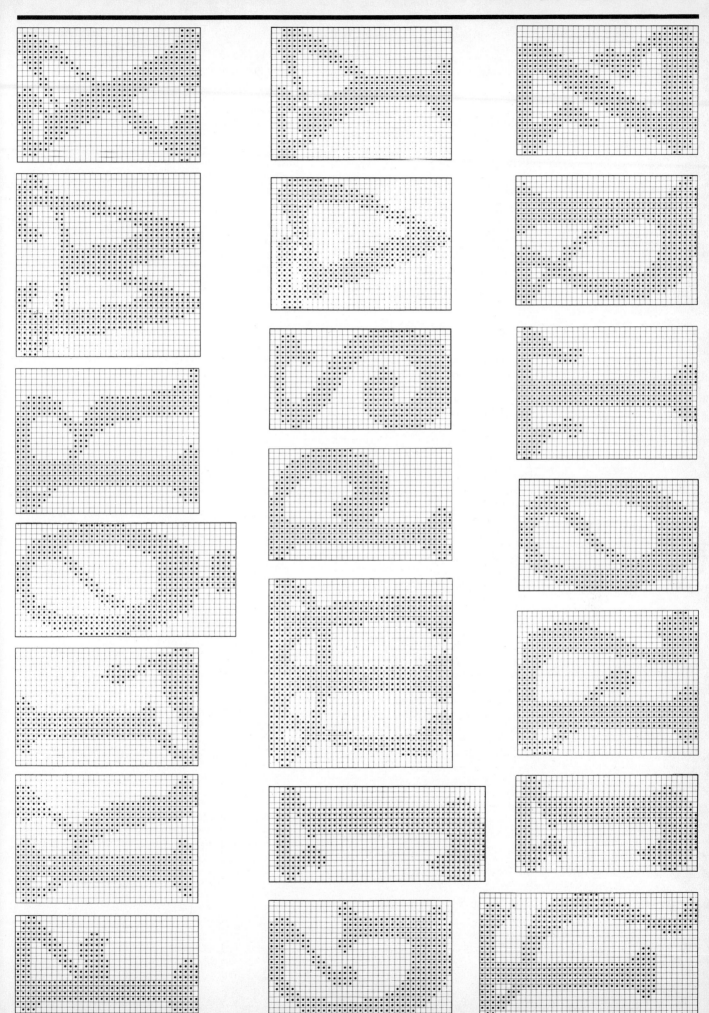

Motifs

Working in Rounds

Most motifs are not worked in rows but are worked from the center outwards in rounds. Unless otherwise indicated do not turn the work between rounds but continue with the same side facing and treat this as the right side of the fabric. The center ring is usually formed by a number of chains joined together with a slip stitch.

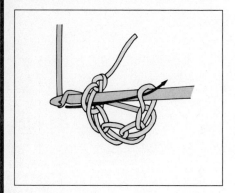

1. Insert the hook back into the first chain made.

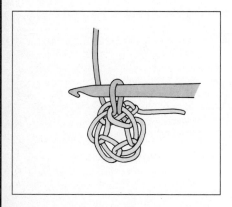

2. Make a slip stitch to join into a ring.

At the beginning of each round one or more chain can be worked to match the height of the following stitches. (This is equivalent to a turning chain).

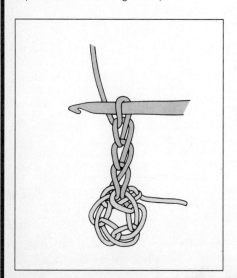

3. When working double crochet three starting chain are required.

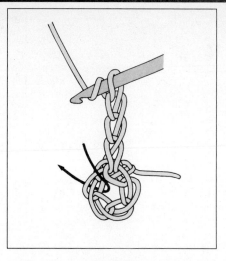

4. The stitches of the first round are worked by inserting the hook into the space at the center of the chain ring. Occasionally the first round is worked into the first chain (Crystal Web).

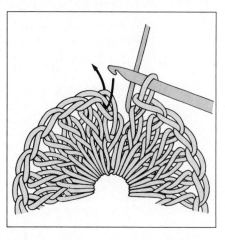

5. When each round is complete insert the hook into the top of the chain or stitch at the beginning of the round and slip stitch together.

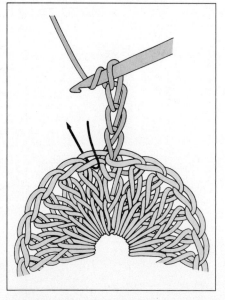

6. When working second and subsequent rounds, unless otherwise stated, insert the hook under the two top loops of the stitches in the previous round.

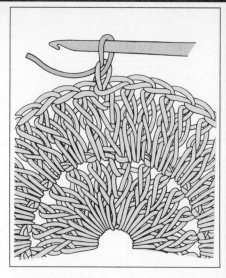

7. After joining final round with a slip stitch, fasten off by making a chain, then cutting the yarn and drawing the end through.

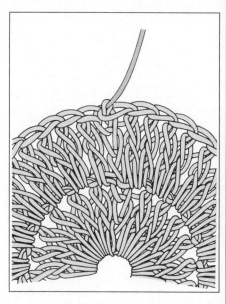

8. Tighten gently to form a knot.

Joining Motifs

Motif Layout

Some motifs such as triangles, squares and hexagons fit together exactly while others leave interesting spaces when joined. These spaces can themselves be a decorative part of an openwork fabric or can be filled in a variety of ways. Smaller spaces can be filled with suitable combinations of chains and stitches and larger ones with small motifs. Most motifs can be joined in more than one way so that any individual motif can form the basis of several different fabric designs. If motifs are worked in different colors they can be laid out to produce patchwork effects. Solid motifs are particularly suitable for working colored patchwork.

Opposite are just a few examples of how motifs of various shapes can be positioned to create interesting patterns.

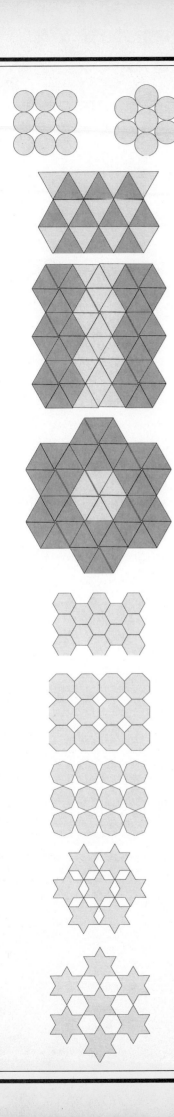

Methods of Joining

Layouts that involve motifs fitting together along straight edges can be joined with a flat seam or by working a row of slip stitch or single crochet through both edges (see page 15). The crochet joins should be done with the right sides of the motifs together so they will be invisible on the right side of the fabric. Alternatively a crochet join can be used as a decorative feature when worked on the right side.

Some designs, particularly those with chain arches or picots round their edges, can be joined to previous motifs during the course of their final rounds. This is done by interrupting the picots or arches at half

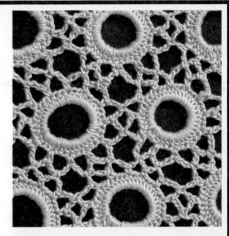

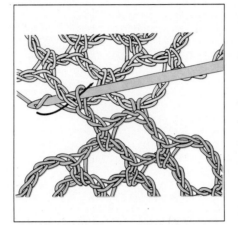

way and slip stitching to the corresponding places on the adjacent motifs.

Spaces between motifs are sometimes filled with small motifs, made and joined in at the same time as they are worked.

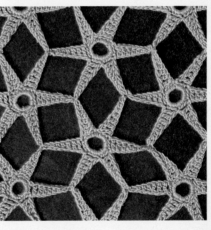

Joined Motifs

We show here a few motifs joined in various ways. The possibilities are infinite and only depend on the shape of the motif and your ingenuity!

Motifs

Traditional Square I

Base ring: 4ch, join with sl st.

1st round: 5ch (count as 1dc and 2ch), [3dc into ring, 2ch] 3 times, 2dc into ring, sl st to 3rd of 5ch.

2nd round: Sl st into next ch, 5ch (count as 1dc and 2ch), 3dc into same sp, *1ch, skip 3dc, [3dc, 2ch, 3dc] into next sp; rep from * twice, 1ch, skip 3 sts, 2dc into same sp as 5ch at beg of round, sl st to 3rd of 5ch.

3rd round: Sl st into next ch, 5ch (count as 1dc and 2ch), 3dc into same sp, *1ch, skip 3dc, 3dc into next sp, 1ch, skip 3dc**, [3dc, 2ch, 3dc] into next sp; rep from * twice and from * to ** again, 2dc into same sp as 5ch, sl st to 3rd of 5ch.

4th round: Sl st into next ch, 5ch (count as 1dc and 2ch), 3dc into same sp, *[1ch, skip 3dc, 3dc into next sp] twice, 1ch, skip 3dc**, [3dc, 2ch, 3dc] into next sp; rep from * twice and from * to ** again, 2dc into same sp as 5ch, sl st to 3rd of 5ch.

Fasten off.

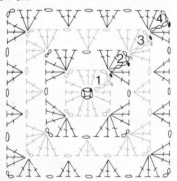

Traditional Square II

Worked as Traditional Square I.
Work 1 round each in colors A, B, C and D.

Double Crochet Square I

Base ring: 4ch, join with sl st.

1st round: 5ch (count as 1dc and 2ch), [3dc into ring, 2ch] 3 times, 2dc into ring, sl st to 3rd of 5ch. (4 groups of 3dc.)

2nd round: Sl st into next ch, 7ch (count as 1dc and 4ch), *2dc into same arch, 1dc into each dc across side of square**, 2dc into next arch, 4ch; rep from * to ** again, 1dc into same arch as 7ch, sl st to 3rd of 7ch (4 groups of 7dc).

3rd round: As 2nd round. (4 groups of 11dc).

4th round: As 2nd round. (4 groups of 15dc).

Fasten off.

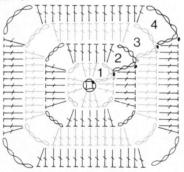

Double Crochet Square II

Worked as Double Crochet Square I.
Work 1 round each in colors A, B, C and D.

French Square

Base ring: 6ch, join with sl st.

1st round: 4ch (count as 1dc and 1ch), [1dc into ring, 1ch] 11 times, sl st to 3rd of 4ch. (12 spaces).

2nd round: Sl st into next ch, 3ch, work hdc3tog into same sp (counts as hdc4tog), *2ch, work hdc4tog into next sp, 3ch, 1tr into next dc, 3ch, work hdc4tog into next sp, 2ch**, hdc4tog into next sp; rep from * twice more and from * to ** again, sl st to top of first cluster.

3rd round: 1ch, 1sc into same place, *2ch, skip next 2ch sp, 4dc into next 3ch sp, 2ch, 1tr into next tr, 3ch, insert hook down through top of last tr and work sl st, 2ch, 4dc into next 3ch sp, 2ch, skip next 2ch sp, 1sc into next cluster; rep from * 3 more times, omitting sc at end, sl st to first sc.

Fasten off.

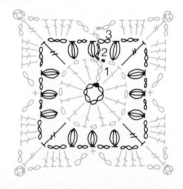

Italian Square

Base ring: 4ch, join with sl st.

1st round: 3ch (count as 1dc), 11dc into ring, sl st to top of 3ch. (12 sts).

2nd round: 3ch, work hdc4tog into same place as 3ch (counts as hdc4tog), *[1ch, work hdc4tog into next st] twice, 5ch**, hdc4tog into next st; rep from * twice more and from * to ** again, sl st to top of first cluster.

3rd round: Sl st into next sp, 3ch, work hdc3tog into same sp (counts as hdc4tog), *1ch, hdc4tog into next sp, 2ch, 5dc into next 5ch arch, 2ch**, hdc4tog into next sp; rep from * twice more and from * to ** again, sl st to top of first cluster.

4th round: Sl st into next sp, 3ch, work hdc3tog into same sp (counts as hdc4tog), *3ch, skip 2ch, [1dc into next dc, 1ch] twice, work [1dc, 1ch, 1dc, 1ch, 1dc] into next dc, [1ch, 1dc into next dc] twice, 3ch, skip 2ch**, work hdc4tog into next sp; rep from * twice more and again from * to **, sl st to top of first cluster.

5th round: 1ch, 1sc into each ch and each st all round, but working 3sc into 3rd of 5 dc at each corner, ending sl st to first sc. Fasten off.

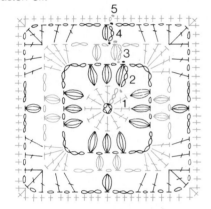

Christmas Rose Square

Base ring: Using A, 6ch, join with sl st.

1st round: 5ch (count as 1dc and 2ch), [1dc into ring, 2ch] 7 times, sl st to 3rd of 5ch. (8 spaces).

2nd round: 3ch, work dc3tog into next sp (counts as dc4tog), [5ch, work dc4tog into next sp] 7 times, 5ch, sl st to top of first cluster. Fasten off.

3rd round: Using B join into same place, 1ch, 1sc into same place, *2ch, working over the 5ch arch so as to enclose it work 1dc into next dc of 1st round, 2ch, 1sc into top of next cluster; rep from * all round omitting sc at end, sl st to first sc.

4th round: Sl st into next ch, 1ch, 1sc into same place, *3ch, 1sc into next sp; rep from * all round omitting sc at end, sl st to first sc.

5th round: Sl st into next ch, 3ch (count as 1dc), [1dc, 2ch, 2dc] into same arch, *2ch, 1sc into next arch, [3ch, 1sc into next arch] twice, 2ch**, [2dc, 2ch, 2dc] into next arch; rep from * twice more and from * to ** again, sl st to top of 3ch. Fasten off.

1, 2 – A   3, 4, 5 – B

Baltic Square

Base ring: 8ch, join with sl st.

1st round: 3ch, 4dc Popcorn into ring (counts as 5dc Popcorn), [5ch, 5dc Popcorn into ring] 3 times, 5ch, sl st to top of first Popcorn.

2nd round: 3ch (count as 1dc), *work [2dc, 2ch, 5dc Popcorn, 2ch, 2dc] into next 5ch arch**, 1dc into next Popcorn; rep from * twice more and from * to ** again, sl st to top of 3ch.

3rd round: 3ch (count as 1dc), 1dc into each of next 2 sts, *2dc into next sp, 2ch, 5dc Popcorn into next Popcorn, 2ch, 2dc into next sp**, 1dc into each of next 5dc; rep from * twice more and from * to ** again, 1dc into each of last 2dc, sl st to top of 3ch.

4th round: 3ch (count as 1dc), 1dc into each of next 4dc, *2dc into next sp, 2ch, 5dc

Popcorn into next Popcorn, 2ch, 2dc into next sp**, 1dc into each of next 9dc; rep from * twice more and from * to ** again, 1dc into each of last 4dc, sl st to top of 3ch. Fasten off.

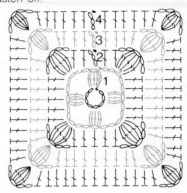

Cranesbill Lace Square

Base ring: 6ch, join with sl st.

1st round: 3ch, dc2tog into ring (counts as dc3tog), [3ch, dc3tog into ring] 7 times, 3ch, sl st to top of first cluster.

2nd round: Sl st to center of next 3ch arch, 1ch, 1sc into same place, [5ch, 1sc into next arch] 7 times, 2ch, 1dc into first sc.

3rd round: *5ch, [dc3tog, 3ch, dc3tog] into next arch**, 5ch, 1sc into next arch; rep from * twice and from * to ** again, 2ch, 1dc into dc which closed 2nd round.

4th round: *5ch, 1sc into next arch, 5ch, [1sc, 5ch, 1sc] into corner 3ch arch, 5ch, 1sc into next 5ch arch; rep from * 3 times, ending last rep into dc which closed 3rd round, sl st to first ch. Fasten off.

Motifs

Rose Square

Base ring: Using A, 12ch, join with sl st.

1st round: 1ch, 18sc into ring, sl st to first sc. (18 sts).

2nd round: 1ch, beginning into same st as 1ch [1sc, 3ch, skip 2 sts] 6 times, sl st to first sc.

3rd round: 1ch, work a petal of [1sc, 3ch, 5dc, 3ch, 1sc] into each of next 6 3ch arches, sl st to first sc.

4th round: 1ch, [1sc between 2sc, 5ch behind petal of 3rd round] 6 times, sl st to first sc.

5th round: 1ch, work a petal of [1sc, 3ch, 7dc, 3ch, 1sc] into each of next 6 5ch arches, sl st to first sc. Fasten off.

6th round: Using B join between 2sc, 1ch, [1sc between 2sc, 6ch behind Petal of 5th round] 6 times, sl st to first sc.

7th round: Sl st into next ch, 3ch (count as 1dc), *[4dc, 2ch, 1dc] all into same arch, 6dc into next arch, [2dc, 2ch, 4dc] all into next arch**, 1dc into next arch; rep from * to **, sl st to top of 3ch.

8th round: 3ch (count as 1dc), 1dc into each dc all round with [3dc, 2ch, 3dc] into each 2ch corner sp, ending sl st to top of 3ch. Fasten off.

9th round: Using C join into same place, 1ch, 1sc into same st as 1ch, *1sc into next st, work a 3ch picot of [3ch, sl st down through top of last sc made] twice, 1sc into each of next 3 sts, work [3ch picot, 1sc into next st] twice, [1sc, 7ch, 1sc] into corner 2ch sp, [1sc into next st, 3ch picot] twice, 1sc into each of next 3 sts, [3ch picot, 1sc into next st] twice, 1sc into next st; rep from * 3 times omitting sc at end of last rep, sl st to first sc.

10th round: Sl st across to top of next 3ch picot, 1ch, 1sc into same picot, *5ch, skip next picot, 1sc into next picot, 5ch, [1sc, 7ch, 1sc] into corner 7ch arch, [5ch, skip next picot, 1sc into next picot] twice, 5ch, 1sc into next picot; rep from * 3 times omitting sc at end of last rep. sl st to first sc.

Fasten off.

Popcorn Wheel Square

Base ring: 6ch, join with sl st.

1st round: 3ch (count as 1dc), 4dc into ring and complete as for 5dc Popcorn, [3ch, 5dc Popcorn into ring] 7 times, 3ch, sl st to first Popcorn.

2nd round: 3ch (count as 1dc), 1dc into next 3ch arch, [9dc into next arch, 2dc into next arch] 3 times, 9dc into last arch, sl st to top of 3ch.

3rd round: 1ch, 1sc into same place as 1ch, 1sc into next st, *into next 9dc group work 1sc into each of first 3dc, skip 1dc, [1hdc, 4dc, 1hdc] into next dc, skip 1dc, 1sc into each of last 3dc**, 1sc into each of next 2 sts; rep from * twice and from * to ** again, sl st to first sc.

Fasten off.

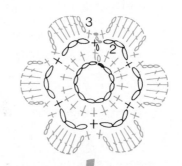

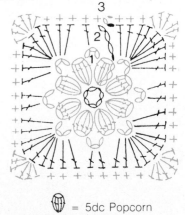

= 5dc Popcorn

Floribunda

Base ring: Using A, 6ch, join with sl st.

1st round: 1ch, 16sc into ring, sl st to first sc. (16 sts).

2nd round: 6ch (count as 1dc and 3ch arch), skip 2 sts, [1dc into next st, 3ch, skip 1 st] 7 times, sl st to 3rd of 6ch.

3rd round: 1ch, work a petal of [1sc, 1hdc, 5dc, 1hdc, 1sc] into each of next 8 3ch arches, sl st to first sc. Fasten off.

4th round: Using B join between 2sc, 1ch, [1sc between 2sc, 6ch behind petal of 3rd round] 8 times, sl st to first sc.

5th round: 1ch, work a petal of [1sc, 1hdc, 6dc, 1hdc, 1sc] into each of next 8 arches, sl st to first sc. Fasten off.

6th round: Using C join into 2nd dc of petal of 5th round, 1ch, 1sc into same place as 1ch, 6ch, skip 2dc, 1sc into next dc, [6ch, 1sc into 2nd dc of next petal, 6ch, skip 2dc, 1sc into next dc] 7 times, 3ch, 1dc into first sc.

7th round: 3ch (count as 1dc), 3dc into arch formed by dc which closed 6th round, *4ch, 1sc into next arch, [6ch, 1sc into next arch] twice, 4ch**, [4dc, 4ch, 4dc] into next arch; rep from * twice and from * to ** again, ending [4dc, 4ch] into last ch arch, sl st to top of 3ch.

Fasten off.

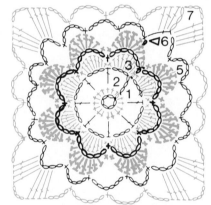

1, 2, 3 — A   4, 5 — B   6, 7 — C

Daisy Cluster Square

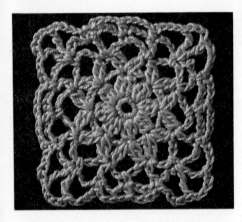

Base ring: Wrap yarn round finger.

1st round: 1ch, 8sc into ring, sl st to first sc. (8 sts).

2nd round: 3ch, dc2tog into first st (counts as dc3tog), [3ch, dc3tog into next st] 7 times, 3ch, sl st to top of first cluster.

3rd round: 3ch, 1dc into first st (counts as dc2tog), *skip 3ch, [dc2tog, 5ch, dc2tog] all into next cluster; rep from * 6 times, dc2tog into next cluster, 5ch, sl st to top of 3ch.

4th round: Sl st into next cluster, 7ch (counts as 1dc and 4ch), [1sc into next 5ch arch, 4ch, skip 1 cluster, 1dc into next cluster, 4ch] 7 times, 1sc into next arch, 4ch, sl st to 3rd of 7ch.

5th round: 1ch, 1sc into same place as 1ch, *4ch, skip 4ch, [1tr, 4ch, 1tr] into next sc, 4ch, skip 4ch, 1sc into next dc, 4ch, skip 4ch, 1hdc into next sc, 4ch, skip 4ch, 1sc into next dc; rep from * 3 times, omitting sc at end of last rep, sl st to first sc.

Fasten off.

Sow Thistle Square

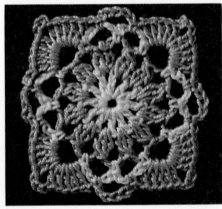

Base ring: Using A, 4ch, join with sl st.

1st round: 4ch (count as 1dc and 1ch), [1dc, 1ch] 11 times into ring, sl st to 3rd of 4ch. Fasten off. (12 spaces).

2nd round: Using B join into sp, 3ch, dc2tog into same sp (counts as dc3tog), [3ch, dc3tog into next sp] 11 times, 3ch, sl st to top of first cluster. Fasten off.

3rd round: Using A join into 3ch arch, 1ch, 1sc into same arch, [5ch, 1sc into next arch] 11 times, 2ch, 1dc into first sc. Fasten off.

4th round: Using B join into same place, 1ch, 1sc into same place, *5ch, 1sc into next arch, 1ch, [5dc, 3ch, 5dc] into next arch, 1ch, 1sc into next arch; rep from * 3 times, omitting 1sc at end of last rep, sl st to first sc. Fasten off.

1 — A   2 — B   3 — A   4 — B

Daisy Wheel Square

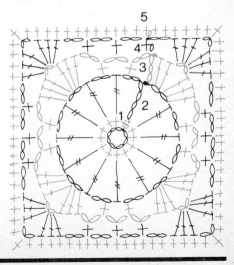

Base ring: 8ch, join with sl st.

1st round: 1ch, 12sc into ring, sl st to first sc. (12 sts).

2nd round: 6ch (count as 1tr and 2ch), skip 1 st, [1tr into next st, 2ch] 11 times, sl st to 4th of 6ch.

3rd round: 5ch (counts as 1dc and 2ch), *[1sc into next sp, 2ch] twice, [3dc, 2ch, 3dc] into next sp, 2ch; rep from * 3 times, omitting 1dc and 2ch at end of last rep, sl st to 3rd of 5ch.

4th round: 1ch, *[1sc into next sp, 2ch] 3 times, [3dc, 2ch, 3dc] into corner sp, 2ch; rep from * 3 times, sl st to first sc.

5th round: 1ch, work 2sc into each sp and 1sc into each st all round, but working 3sc into each corner sp, sl st to first sc.

Fasten off.

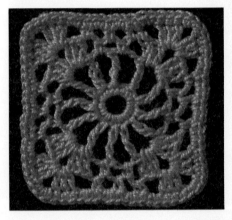

Motifs

Puff Stitch Square

Base ring: 8ch, join with sl st.
Special Abbreviation
Puff st = hdc5tog,
1st round: 2ch, hdc4tog into ring (counts as 1 Puff st), 2ch, work [Puff st, 2ch] 7 times into ring, sl st to first Puff st.
2nd round: 5ch (count as 1dc and 2ch), 1dc into same Puff st, *2ch, [Puff st into next sp, 2ch] twice**, work a V st of [1dc, 2ch, 1dc] into next Puff st; rep from * twice and from * to ** again, sl st to 3rd of 5ch.
3rd round: Sl st into next ch, 5ch (count as 1dc and 2ch), 1dc into same sp, *2ch, [Puff st into next sp, 2ch] 3 times**, V st into next sp at corner; rep from * twice and from * to ** again, sl st to 3rd of 5ch.
4th round: As for 3rd round, but work 4 Puff sts along each side of square.
5th round: As for 3rd round, but work 5 Puff sts along each side of square.
Fasten off.

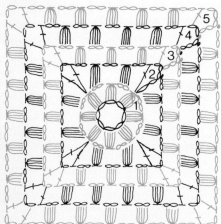

Spanish Square

Base ring: 8ch, join with sl st.
1st round: 1ch, 16sc into ring, sl st to first sc. (16 sts).
2nd round: 1ch, 1sc into same place as 1ch, [7ch, skip 3 sts, 1sc into next st] 3 times, 7ch, skip 3 sts, sl st to first sc.
3rd round: Sl st across to 3rd ch of next arch, 3ch (count as 1dc), 1dc into same place, *[3ch, 2dc] into same arch, 3ch, dc2tog inserting hook into same arch for first leg and into next arch for 2nd leg, 3ch, 2dc into same arch; rep from * 3 times, omitting 2dc at end of last rep, sl st to top of 3ch.
4th round: Sl st into next dc and next ch, 3ch (count as 1dc), 1dc into same place, *[3ch, 2dc] into same arch, 3ch, skip 2dc, 3dc into next 3ch, 1dc into next cluster, 3dc into next 3ch, 3ch, skip 2dc, 2dc into next arch; rep from * 3 times, omitting 2dc at end of last rep, sl st to top of 3ch.
5th round: Sl st into next dc and next ch, 3ch, 2dc into same place, *[3ch, 3dc] into same arch, 6ch, skip [2dc, 3ch, 1dc], 1dc into each of next 5dc, 6ch, skip [1dc, 3ch, 2dc], 3dc into next 3ch arch; rep from * 3 times, omitting 3dc at end of last rep, sl st to top of 3ch.
6th round: 3ch (count as 1dc), 1dc into each of next 2dc, *[3dc, 5ch, 3dc] into next 3ch arch, 1dc into each of next 3dc, 6ch, skip [6ch and 1dc], 1dc into each of next 3dc, 6ch, skip [1dc and 6ch], 1dc into each of next 3dc; rep from * 3 times, omitting 3dc at end of last rep, sl st to top of 3ch.
Fasten off.

Crystal Square

Base ring: 10ch, join with sl st.
1st round: 14ch, [5dc into ring, 11ch] 3 times, 4dc into ring, sl st to 3rd of 14ch.

2nd round: Sl st into each of next 5ch, 3ch (count as 1dc), [2dc, 3ch, 3dc] into same ch arch, *9ch, [3dc, 3ch, 3dc] into next arch; rep from * twice, 9ch, sl st to top of 3ch.
3rd round: 3ch (count as 1dc), 1dc into each of next 2dc, *[3dc, 3ch, 3dc] into 3ch sp, 1dc into each of next 3dc, 4ch, skip 4ch, 1sc into next ch, make a picot of [3ch, sl st down through top of last st], 4ch, skip 4ch**, 1dc into each of next 3dc; rep from * twice and from * to ** again, sl st to top of 3ch.
4th round: 3ch (count as 1dc), 1dc into each of next 5dc, *[3dc, 3ch, 3dc] into 3ch sp, 1dc into each of next 6dc, 9ch**, 1dc into each of next 6dc; rep from * twice and from * to ** again, sl st to top of 3ch.
5th round: 6ch, sl st to 4th ch from hook (counts as 1dc and picot), *[1dc into each of next 4dc, picot] twice, work [3dc, 5ch, sl st to 4th ch from hook, 1ch, 3dc] into 3ch sp, 1dc into next dc, picot, [1dc into each of next 4dc, picot] twice, 4ch, skip 4ch, 1sc into next ch, picot, 4ch, skip 4ch**, 1dc into next dc, picot; rep from * twice and from * to ** again, sl st to top of 3ch.
Fasten off.

Moorish Medallion

Base ring: 6ch, join with sl st.
Special Abbreviation
Ssc (Spike single crochet) = insert hook 2 rounds below st indicated, i.e. into top of 1st round, yo, draw loop through and up to height of current round, yo, draw through both loops on hook
1st round: 1ch, 16sc into ring, sl st to first sc. (16 sts).
2nd round: 1ch, 1sc into same place as 1ch, 1sc into next sc, *[1sc, 9ch, 1sc] into

Stitch Variations, Abbreviations and Symbols on pages 7 to 15

next sc**, 1sc into each of next 3sc; rep from * twice and from * to ** again, 1sc into next sc, sl st to first sc.

3rd round: 1ch, 1sc into same place as 1ch, *skip next 2sc, work [2hdc, 17dc, 2hdc] into next 9ch arch, skip next 2sc, 1sc into next sc; rep from * 3 more times omitting 1sc at end of last rep and ending sl st to first sc.

4th round: 1ch, 1Ssc over first st, *5ch, skip 5 sts, 1sc into next st, 3ch, sl st into 3rd ch from hook, [5ch, skip 4 sts, 1sc into next st, 3ch, sl st into 3rd ch from hook] twice, 5ch, skip 5 sts, 1Ssc over next st; rep from * 3 times omitting Ssc at end of last rep and ending sl st to first Ssc.

Fasten off.

Russian Square

Base ring: Using A, 8ch, join with sl st.

1st round: 6ch (count as 1dc and 3ch), [3dc into ring, 3ch] 3 times, 2dc into ring, sl st to 3rd of 6 ch. Fasten off.

2nd round: Using B join into a different corner sp, 3ch (count as 1dc), 2dc into same corner sp, *1dc/rf round each of next 3 sts**, [3dc, 3ch, 3dc] into next corner sp; rep from * twice more and from * to ** again, [3dc, 3ch] into last corner sp, sl st to top of 3 ch. Fasten off.

3rd round: Using C join into a different corner sp, 6ch (count as 1dc and 3ch), 3dc into same corner sp, *1dc/rb round each of next 3 sts, 1dc/rf round each of next 3 sts, 1dc/rb round each of next 3 sts**, [3dc, 3ch, 3dc] into next corner sp; rep from * twice more and from * to ** again, 2dc into last corner sp, sl st to 3rd of 6ch. Fasten off.

4th round: Using D join into a different corner sp, 3ch (count as 1dc), 2dc into same corner sp, *[1dc/rf round each of next 3 sts, 1dc/rb round each of next 3 sts] twice, 1dc/rf round each of next 3 sts**, [3dc, 3ch, 3dc] into next corner sp; rep from * twice more and from * to ** again, [3dc, 3ch] into last corner sp, sl st to top of 3ch.

Fasten off.

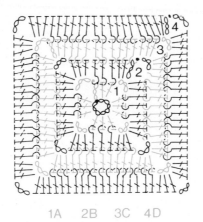

1A 2B 3C 4D

Frozen Star

Base ring: 12ch, join with sl st.

1st round: 1ch, 24sc into ring, sl st to first sc. (24 sts).

2nd round: 6ch, dtr3tog over next 3 sts (counts as dtr4tog), [7ch, dtr4tog over same st as last leg of previous cluster and next 3 sts] 7 times, 7ch, sl st to top of first cluster.

3rd round: 1ch, 1sc into same place as 1ch, *[3ch, skip 1ch, 1sc into next ch] 3 times, 3ch, skip 1ch, 1sc into top of next cluster; rep from * 7 times, omitting sc at end of last rep, sl st to first sc.

4th round: Sl st to center of next 3ch arch, 1ch, 1sc into same arch, *3ch, 1sc into next arch; rep from * to end, omitting sc at end of last rep, sl st to first sc.

5th round: As 4th round.

6th round: Sl st to center of next 3ch arch, 1ch, 1sc into same arch, *[3ch, 1sc into next arch] 4 times, 3ch, skip next arch, work [tr3tog, 5ch, dtr4tog, 4ch, sl st to top of last cluster, 5ch, tr3tog] into next arch, 3ch, skip next arch, 1sc into next arch; rep from * 3 times, omitting sc at end of last rep, sl st to first sc.

Fasten off.

Spider Square

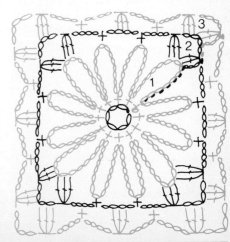

Base ring: 6ch, join with sl st.

1st round: 1ch, [1sc into ring, 15ch] 12 times, sl st to first sc.

2nd round: Sl st along to center of next 15ch arch, 3ch, dc2tog into same arch (counts as dc3tog), *4ch, dc3tog into same arch, [4ch, 1sc into next arch] twice, 4ch, dc3tog into next arch; rep from * 3 times, omitting dc3tog at end of last rep, sl st to first cluster.

3rd round: Sl st into next arch, 3ch, dc2tog into same arch (counts as dc3tog), *4ch, dc3tog into same arch, [4ch, 1sc into next 4ch arch, 4ch, dc3tog into next 4ch arch] twice; rep from * 3 times, omitting dc3tog at end of last rep, sl st to first cluster.

Fasten off.

Motifs

Spiral Pentagram

Base ring: 5ch, join with sl st.

1st round: [6ch, 1sc into ring] 5 times. (Hint: mark last sc of each round with contrasting thread.)

2nd round: [6ch, 3sc into next 6ch arch] 5 times.

3rd round: [6ch, 3sc into next 6ch arch, 1sc into each of next 2sc] 5 times. (5 blocks of 5sc each).

4th round: [6ch, 3sc into next 6ch arch, 1sc into each sc of next block except skip last sc] 5 times. (5 blocks of 7sc each).

Continue as given on 4th round for 3 more rounds finishing with 5 blocks of 13sc each.

8th round: *5ch, 1sc into center of next 6ch arch, 5ch, skip 1sc, 1sc into each sc of next block except last; rep from * 4 more times.

9th round: *[5ch, 1sc into next arch] twice, 5ch, skip 1sc, 1sc into each sc of next block except last sc; rep from * 4 more times.

Continue as given on 9th round for 3 more rounds, but work 1 more 5ch arch in each segment on each round at same time as number of sc in each block reduces, finishing with 6 arches and 3sc in each of 5 segments.

13th round: 5ch, 1sc into next arch, *[3ch, 1sc into next arch] 5 times, 3ch, 1dc into 2nd of next 3sc, 3ch, 1sc into next arch; rep from * 4 more times omitting sc at end of last rep, sl st to first sc.

Fasten off.

2-Color Star

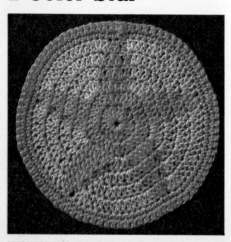

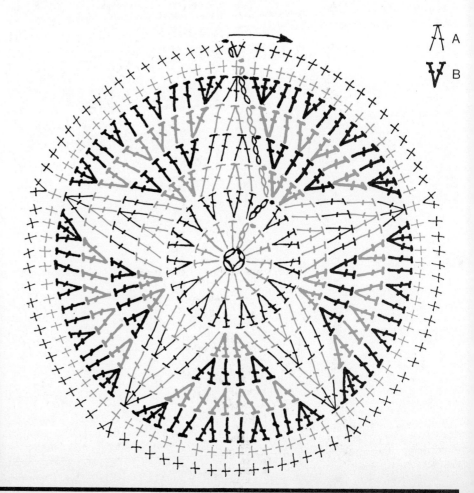

Base ring: Using A, 4ch, join with sl st.

1st round: 3ch (count as 1dc), 14dc into ring, sl st to top of 3ch. (15 sts).

2nd round: 3ch (count as 1dc), 1dc into same place as 3ch, 2dc into next and each dc all round, sl st to top of 3ch. (30 sts).

3rd round: 3ch (count as 1dc), *1dc into next st, dc2tog over next 2 sts, 1dc into each of next 2 sts, change to B, 2dc into same place as last dc with A, 2dc into next st, change to A**, 1dc into same place as last dc with B; rep from * 3 more times and from * to ** again, sl st to top of 3ch.

4th round: 3ch (count as 1dc), *dc2tog over next 2 sts, 1dc into each of next 2 sts, change to B, 2dc into next st, 1dc into each of next 2 sts, 2dc into next st, change to A**, 1dc into next st; rep from * 3 more times and from * to ** again, sl st to top of 3ch.

5th round: 3ch (count as 1dc), *dc2tog over next 2 sts, change to B, 2dc into next st, 1dc into next st, 2dc into each of next 2 sts, 1dc into next st, 2dc into next st, change to A**, 1dc into next st; rep from * 3 more times and from * to ** again, sl st to top of 3ch.

6th round: 3ch, *dc2tog over next 2 sts (counts as dc3tog), change to B, 3dc into next st, [1dc into each of next 2 sts, 2dc into next st] twice, 1dc into each of next 2 sts, 3dc into next st, change to A**, dc3tog over next 3 sts; rep from * 3 more times and from * to ** again, sl st to top of first cluster.

7th round: Continue using A only 1ch, 1sc into same place as 1ch, 1sc into next and each st all round, sl st to first sc, turn.

8th round (wrong side): 1ch, 2sc into same place as 1ch, 1sc into next and each st all round, except 2sc into each of 4 sts corresponding to remaining points of Star, ending sl st to first sc.
Fasten off.

Ridged Hexagon I

Base ring: 4ch, join with sl st.

1st round: 3ch (count as 1dc), 1dc into ring, [1ch, 2dc into ring] 5 times, 1ch, sl st to top of 3ch. (6 spaces).

2nd round: Sl st into next dc and into next ch, 3ch (count as 1dc), *1dc/rb round each of next 2dc**, work a V st of [1dc, 1ch, 1dc] into next sp; rep from * 4 more times and

from * to ** again, 1dc into last sp, 1ch, sl st to top of 3ch.

3rd round: 3ch (count as 1dc), 1dc/rb round each dc and 1 V st into each sp all round, ending with a sl st to top of 3ch. (6 groups of 6dc).

4th round: As 3rd round. (6 groups of 8dc).

5th round: As 3rd round. (6 groups of 10dc
Fasten off.

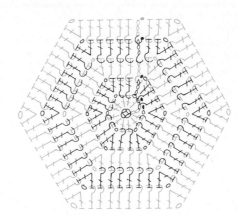

Ridged Hexagon II

Worked as Ridged Hexagon I.
Work 1 round each in colors A, B, C, D and E.

Traditional Hexagon I

Base ring: 6ch, join with sl st.

1st round: 3ch, dc2tog into ring (counts as dc3tog), [3ch, dc3tog into ring] 5 times, 1ch, 1hdc into top of first cluster.

2nd round: 3ch, dc2tog into arch formed by hdc (counts as dc3tog), *3ch, work [dc3tog, 3ch, dc3tog] into next sp: rep from * 4 more times, 3ch, dc3tog into last sp, 1ch, 1hdc into top of first cluster.

3rd round: 3ch, dc2tog into arch formed by hdc (counts as dc3tog), *3ch, work [dc3tog, 3ch, dc3tog] into next sp**, 3ch, dc3tog into next sp; rep from * 4 more times and from * to ** again, 1ch, 1hdc into top of first cluster.

4th round: 3ch (counts as 1dc), 1dc into arch formed by hdc, *3dc into next sp, [3dc, 2ch, 3dc] into next sp**, 3dc into next sp; rep from * 4 more times and from * to ** again, 1dc into next sp, sl st to top of 3ch.

5th round: 1ch, 1sc into same place, 1sc into each dc and each ch all round, ending sl st to first sc.
Fasten off.

Traditional Hexagon II

Worked as Traditional Hexagon I.
Work 1 round each in colors A, B, C, D and E.

Motifs

2-Color Popcorn Hexagon

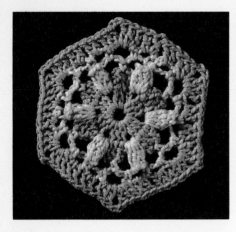

Base ring: Using A, 6ch, join with sl st.

1st round: 3ch (count as 1dc), 2dc into ring, [2ch, 3dc into ring] 5 times, 2ch, sl st to top of 3ch. (6 spaces).

2nd round: 1ch, 1sc into same place, *2ch, 1dc into next dc, 2ch, 1sc into next dc, 1ch, sl st into each of next 2 ch, 1ch, 1sc into next dc; rep from * 5 more times omitting last sc and ending sl st to first sc. Fasten off.

3rd round: Using B, join into 2ch sp, 3ch, 4dc Popcorn into same sp (counts as 5dc Popcorn), *4ch, skip 1sc and 2ch, 1sc into next dc, 4ch, skip 2ch and 1sc, 5dc Popcorn into next sp; rep from * 5 more times omitting last Popcorn and ending sl st to top of first Popcorn.

4th round: 1ch, 1sc into same place, *[3ch, 1sc into next arch] twice, 3ch, 1sc into next Popcorn; rep from * 5 more times omitting last sc and ending sl st to first sc. Fasten off.

5th round: Using A, join into next ch, 3ch (count as 1dc), 1dc into same sp, *[3dc, 2ch, 3dc] into next sp**, 2dc into each of next 2 sps; rep from * 4 more times and from * to ** again, 2dc into next sp, sl st to top of 3ch.

Fasten off.

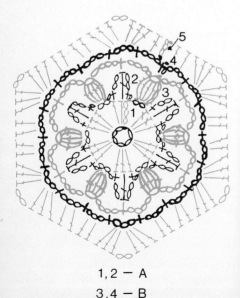

```
1,2 — A
3,4 — B
  5 — A
```

Eastern Star

Base ring: 6ch, join with sl st.

1st round: 1ch, [1sc into ring, 3ch] 12 times, sl st to first sc.

2nd round: Sl st into each of next 2ch, 1ch, 1sc into same 3ch arch, [3ch, 1sc into next 3ch arch] 11 times, 1ch, 1hdc into top of first sc.

3rd round: *6ch, 1sc into next 3ch arch**, 3ch, 1sc into next 3ch arch; rep from * 4 more times and from * to ** again, 1ch, 1dc into hdc which closed previous round.

4th round: *[5dc, 2ch, 5dc] into next 6ch arch, 1sc into next 3ch arch; rep from * 5 more times ending last rep in dc which closed previous round, sl st into next st. Fasten off.

Water Wheel

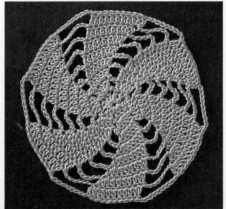

Base ring: 4ch, join with sl st.

1st round: 3ch (count as 1dc), 1dc into ring, [2ch, 2dc into ring] 5 times, 2ch, sl st to top of 3ch.

2nd round: 3ch (count as 1dc), 2dc into same place as 3ch, 1dc into next dc, *3ch, skip 2ch, 3dc into next dc, 1dc into next dc; rep from * 4 more times, 3ch, skip 2ch, sl st to top of 3ch. (6 segments of 4dc and 3ch).

3rd round: 3ch (count as 1dc), 2dc into same place as 3ch, 1dc into next dc, dc2tog over next 2dc, *4ch, skip 3ch, 3dc into next dc, 1dc into next dc, dc2tog over next 2dc; rep from * 4 more times, 4ch, skip 3ch, sl st to top of 3ch.

4th round: 3ch (count as 1dc), 2dc into same place as 3ch, [1dc into next dc] twice, dc2tog over next 2dc, *5ch, skip 4ch, 3dc into next dc, [1dc into next dc] twice, dc2tog over next 2dc; rep from * 4 more times, 5ch, skip 4ch, sl st to top of 3ch.

5th round: 3ch (count as 1dc), 2dc into same place as 3ch, [1dc into next dc] 3 times, dc2tog over next 2dc, *6ch, skip 5ch, 3dc into next dc, [1dc into next dc] 3 times, dc2tog over next 2dc; rep from * 4 more times, 6ch, skip 5ch, sl st to top of 3ch.

6th, 7th and 8th rounds: As 5th round, but adding 1 more single dc in each dc block and 1 more ch in each ch arch on each round.

Fasten off.

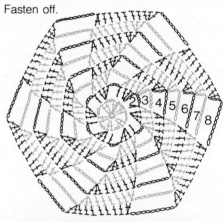

Little Gem

Base ring: Using A, 5ch, join with sl st.

1st round: 4ch (count as 1tr), 2dc into 4th ch from hook, *3ch, 1tr into ring, 2dc into

Stitch Variations, Abbreviations and Symbols on pages 7 to 15

base of stem of tr just made; rep from * 4 more times, 3ch, sl st to top of 4ch.

2nd round: 3ch, dc2tog over next 2dc (counts as dc3tog), *6ch, skip 3ch, dc3tog over next 3 sts; rep from * 5 more times omitting last dc3tog and ending sl st to top of first cluster. Fasten off.

3rd round: Using B join in to center of 3ch arch of 1st round, then so as to enclose 6ch arch of 2nd round work 1ch, 1sc into same place as 1ch, *5ch, 1dc into top of next cluster, 5ch, 1sc into 3ch arch of 1st round at same time enclosing 6ch arch of 2nd round; rep from * 5 more times omitting last sc and ending sl st into first sc. Fasten off.

4th round: Using C join in to same place, 1ch, 1sc into same place as 1ch, *5ch, skip 5ch, 3sc into next dc, 5ch, skip 5ch, 1sc into next sc; rep from * 5 more times omitting last sc and ending sl st into first sc.

Fasten off.

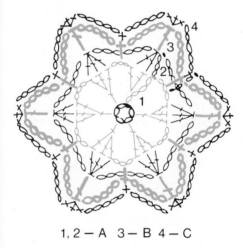

1, 2 — A   3 — B   4 — C

Snowflake

Base ring: 12ch, join with sl st.

1st round: 1ch, 24sc into ring, sl st to first sc. (24 sts).

2nd round: 1ch, 1sc into same place as 1ch, *1sc into next st, work a picot of [3ch, insert hook down through top of sc just made and work sl st]**, 1sc into next st; rep from * 10 times and from * to ** again, sl st to first sc.

3rd round: 8ch (count as 1tr and 4ch), skip Picot, [1tr into next sc between Picots, 4ch] 11 times, sl st to 4th of 8ch.

4th round: 1ch, [5sc into next 4ch arch] 12 times, sl st to first sc.

5th round: 1ch, *1sc into back loop only of each of next 5sc, 15ch, skip 5sc; rep from * 5 more times, sl st to first sc.

6th round: 1ch, *1sc into back loop only of each of next 5sc, 15sc into next 15ch arch; rep from * 5 more times, sl st to first sc.

7th round: Sl st into back loop only of next st, 1ch, 1sc into same place as 1ch, 1sc into back loop only of each of next 2sc, *skip 1sc, [1sc into each of next 3sc, Picot] 4 times, 1sc into each of next 3sc, skip 1sc**, 1sc into back loop only of each of next 3sc; rep from * 4 more times and from * to ** again, sl st to first sc.

Fasten off.

Scallop Flower

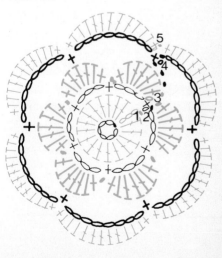

Base ring: Using A, 6ch, join with sl st.

1st round: 3ch (count as 1dc), 17dc into ring, sl st to top of 3ch. (18 sts).

2nd round: 1ch, 1sc into same place as 1ch, *3ch, skip 2 sts, 1sc into next st; rep from * 5 more times omitting last sc and ending sl st to first sc. Fasten off.

3rd round: Using B join in to next ch, 1ch, *work a Petal of [1sc, 1hdc, 3dc, 1hdc, 1sc] into 3ch arch, sl st into next sc; rep from * 5 more times.

4th round: Sl st into each of next 4 sts to center dc of next Petal, 1ch, 1sc into same place as 1ch, *8ch, 1sc into center dc of next Petal; rep from * 5 more times omitting last sc and ending sl st to first sc. Fasten off.

5th round: Using A join in to next ch, 1ch, *work [1sc, 3hdc, 5dc, 3hdc, 1sc] into next arch; rep from * 5 more times, ending sl st into first sc.

Fasten off.

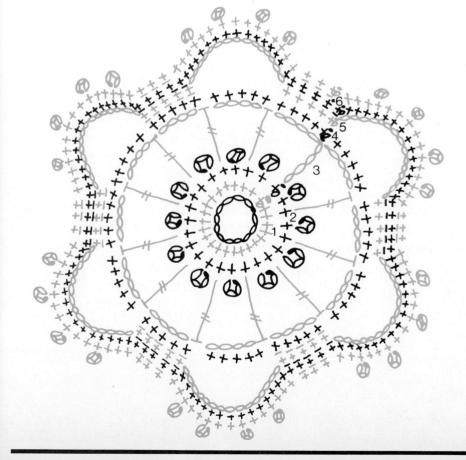

1, 2 — A   3, 4 — B

5 — A

Motifs

Ice Crystal

Rainbow Petal Motif

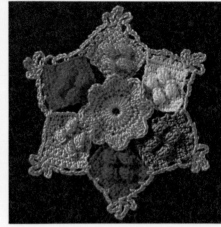

3rd round: 1ch, 1sc into same place as 1ch, *work [1hdc, 1dc, 1tr] into next st, [1tr, 1dc, 1hdc] into next st, 1sc into next st; rep from * 7 more times, omitting sc at end of last rep, sl st to first st. Fasten off.

Star Blocks

Make 6 Star Blocks alike, 1 each in B (Red), C (Orange), D (Yellow), E (Green), F (Indigo) and G (Violet) as follows:

1st Block

Join yarn to back loop of any st in 1st round of Center and make 10ch, turn.

1st row (right side): Skip 2ch (count as 1sc), 1sc into next and each ch to end, turn. (9 sc).

2nd and every alt row: 1ch (counts as 1sc), skip first st, 1sc into next and each st to end working last st into tch, turn.

3rd row: Work as 2nd row but make a 5dc popcorn (to stand out on right side of fabric) on 5th st.

5th row: As 2nd row but making 5dc popcorns on the 3rd and 7th sts.

7th row: As 3rd row.

Work 2 more rows as 2nd row. (10 rows in all). Fasten off.

Remaining Blocks

Skip 3 sts of 1st round of Center and join new yarn into back loop of next st, then work as for 1st Block.

Edging

Making sure all parts of fabric are right side facing, join A at left corner of 1st Block, 1ch, sc2tog over same place as 1ch and right

---

Ice Crystal

Base ring: 6ch, join with sl st.

1st round: 1ch, 12sc into ring, sl st to first sc. (12 sts).

2nd round: 1ch, 1sc into same place as 1ch, [7ch, skip 1sc, 1sc into next sc] 5 times, 3ch, skip 1sc, 1tr into top of first sc.

3rd round: 3ch (count as 1dc), 4dc into arch formed by tr, [3ch, 5dc into next 7ch arch] 5 times, 3ch, sl st to top of 3ch.

4th round: 3ch (counts as 1dc), 1dc into each of next 4dc, *3ch, 1sc into next 3ch arch, 3ch**, 1dc into each of next 5dcs; rep from * 4 more times and from * to ** again, sl st to top of 3ch.

5th round: 3ch, dc4tog over next 4dcs (counts as dc5tog), *[5ch, 1sc into next 3ch arch] twice, 5ch**, dc5tog over next 5dcs; rep from * 4 more times and from * to ** again, sl st to first cluster.

6th round: Sl st into each of next 3ch, 1ch, 1sc into same place, *5ch, 1sc into next 5ch arch; rep from * all round omitting last sc and ending sl st to first sc.

7th round: Sl st into each of next 3ch, 1ch, 1sc into same place, *5ch, 1sc into next 5ch arch, 3ch, [5dc, 3ch, 5dc] into next arch, 3ch, 1sc into next arch; rep from * 5 more times omitting last sc and ending sl st to first sc.

Fasten off.

Center

Base ring: Using A (Blue), 6ch, join with sl st.

1st round: 3ch (count as 1dc), 23dc into ring, sl st to top of 3ch. (24 sts).

2nd round: 1ch, 1sc into same place as 1ch, 1sc into front loop only of next and each st all round, sl st to first sc.

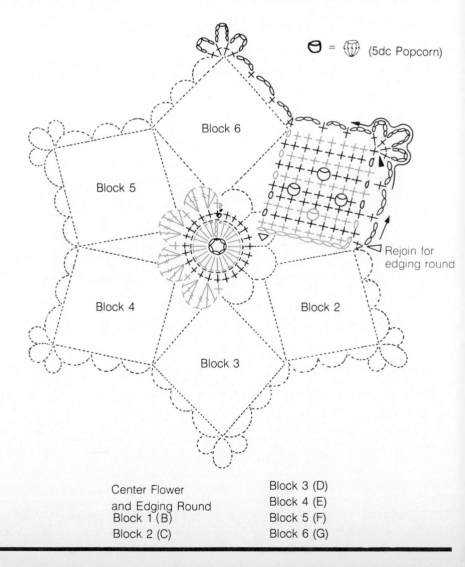

$\bigcirc$ = $\bigoplus$ (5dc Popcorn)

Block 6

Block 5

Block 4

Block 2

Block 3

Rejoin for edging round

Center Flower and Edging Round
Block 1 (B)
Block 2 (C)

Block 3 (D)
Block 4 (E)
Block 5 (F)
Block 6 (G)

Stitch Variations, Abbreviations and Symbols on pages 7 to 15

Mica Motif

corner of 2nd Block, *make 3 arches evenly spaced along edge of Block ending at top corner as follows: [3ch, 1sc into edge] 3 times, work [5ch, 1sc, 7ch, 1sc, 5ch, 1sc] into same corner, work 3 arches evenly spaced as before along next edge of same Block as follows: [3ch, 1sc into edge] twice, 3ch**, sc2tog over left corner of same Block and right corner of next Block; rep from * 4 more times and from * to ** again, sl st to first sc.

Fasten off.

Crystal Motif

Base ring: Using A make 12ch, join with sl st.

1st round: 1ch, 1sc into ring, *work [7ch, 1sc, 4ch, 1dtr, 4ch, 1sc] into ring; rep from * 5 more times omitting sc at end of last rep, sl st to first sc. Fasten off.

2nd round: Join B into top of any dtr, 1ch, 1sc into same place as 1ch, *13ch, skip 7ch arch, 1sc into top of next dtr; rep from * 5 more times omitting sc at end of last rep, sl st to first sc.

3rd round: 1ch, 1sc into each of next 6ch, *3sc into next ch, 1sc into each of next 5ch**, sc3tog over [next ch, next sc and next ch], 1sc into each of next 5ch; rep from * 4 more times and from * to ** again, 1sc into next st, sl st to first sc.

4th round: 1ch, skip first st, 1sc into next st, *1sc into each of next 5 sts, 3sc into next st, 1sc into each of next 5sc**, sc3tog over next 3 sts; rep from * 4 more times and from * to ** again, 1sc into next st, sl st to first sc.

5th round: As 4th round. Fasten off.

6th round: Join C into same place, 1ch, 1sc into same place, *7ch, skip 6sc, work 1dtr, [5ch, 1dtr] 4 times into next sc at tip of star, 7ch, skip 6sc, 1sc into next sc cluster; rep from * 5 more times omitting sc at end of last rep, sl st to first sc.

Fasten off.

Base ring: 6ch, join with sl st.

1st round: 5ch (count as 1dc and 2ch), [1dc into ring, 2ch] 7 times, sl st to 3rd of 5ch. (8 spaces).

2nd round: 3ch (count as 1dc), [4dc into next sp, 1dc into next dc] 7 times, 4dc into next sp, sl st to top of 3ch.

3rd round: Sl st into next st, 3ch (count as 1dc), *1sc into each of next 2 sts, 1dc into next st, 5ch, skip 1 st**, 1dc into next st; rep from * 6 more times and from * to ** again, sl st to top of 3ch.

4th round: 3ch, dc3tog over next 3 sts (counts as dc4tog), *5ch, 1sc into next 5ch arch, 5ch**, dc4tog over next 4 sts; rep from * 6 more times and from * to ** again, sl st to top of first cluster.

5th round: 8ch (count as 1dc and 5ch), *1sc into next 5ch arch, 1sc into next sc, 1sc into next arch, 5ch**, 1dc into next cluster, 5ch; rep from * 6 more times and from * to ** again, sl st to 3rd of 8ch.

6th round: 10ch (count as 1dc and 7ch), skip 5ch, *1sc into 2nd of next 3sc, 7ch, skip 5ch**, 1dc into next dc, 7ch, skip 5ch; rep from * 6 more times and from * to ** again, sl st to 3rd of 10ch.

7th round: 6ch (count as 1dc and 3ch), 1dc into same place as 6ch, *[2ch, 1dc] 3 times into next 7ch arch, 1dc into next sc, [1dc, 2ch] 3 times into next 7ch arch**, work [1dc, 3ch, 1dc] into next dc; rep from * 6 more times and from * to ** again, sl st to 3rd of 6ch.

Fasten off.

1 — A
2, 3, 4, 5 — B
6 — C

Motifs

Astrolabe Motif

Base ring: 4ch, join with sl st.

1st round: 4ch (count as 1dc and 1ch), [1dc into ring, 1ch] 7 times, sl st to 3rd of 4ch. (8 spaces).

2nd round: 1ch, 1sc into same place as 1ch, [3ch, skip 1ch, 1sc into next dc] 8 times omitting sc at end of last rep, sl st to first sc.

3rd round: Sl st into each of next 2ch, 1ch, 1sc into same place as 1ch, [6ch, 1sc into next 3ch arch] 8 times omitting sc at end of last rep, sl st to first sc.

4th round: Sl st into each of next 3ch, 1ch, 1sc into same place as 1ch, [6ch, 1sc into next arch] 8 times omitting sc at end of last rep, sl st to first sc.

5th round: 1ch, 1sc into same place as 1ch, *work [2dc, 4ch, 2dc] into next arch, 1sc into next sc; rep from * 7 more times omitting sc at end of last rep, sl st to first sc.

6th round: Sl st into each of next 2dc and next 2ch, 1ch, 1sc into same place as 1ch, [8ch, 1sc into next arch] 8 times omitting sc at end of last rep, sl st to first sc.

7th round: 1ch, *work a Wave of [1sc, 1hdc, 2dc, 1tr, 2dc, 1hdc, 1sc] into next arch; rep from * 7 more times, sl st to first sc.

8th round: Sl st into each of next 4 sts to tr, 1ch, 1sc into same place as 1ch, [11ch, 1sc into tr at center of next Wave] 8 times omitting sc at end of last rep, sl st to first sc.

9th round: 1ch, work [2sc, 2hdc, 2dc, 4tr, 2dc, 2hdc, 2sc] into next 11ch arch 8 times, sl st to first sc.
Fasten off.

Halley's Comet Motif

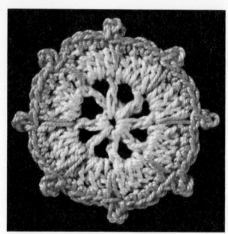

Special Abbreviation

Ssc (Spike single crochet) = insert hook below st indicated 1 row down, i.e. into top of 1st round, yo, draw loop through and up to height of current round, yo, draw through both loops on hook

Base ring: Using A, 4ch, sl st to join.

1st round: 5ch (count as 1dc and 2ch), [1dc into ring, 2ch] 7 times, sl st to 3rd of 5ch. (8 spaces).

2nd round: 3ch (count as 1dc), 3dc into next sp, [1dc into next dc, 3dc into next sp] 7 times, sl st to top of 3ch. (32 sts). Fasten off.

3rd round: Join B into same place, 1ch, 1Ssc over first st, work a picot of [3ch, insert hook down through top of sc just made and work sl st to close], *1sc into next st, 2sc into next st, 1sc into next st**, 1Ssc over next st, picot; rep from * 6 more times and from * to ** again, sl st to first Ssc.
Fasten off.

1, 2 — A
3 — B

Briar Rose

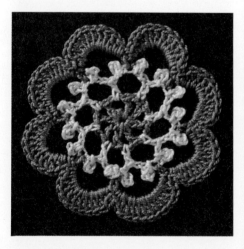

Base ring: Using A, 3ch, join with sl st.

1st round: 5ch (count as 1dc and 2ch), [1dc into ring, 2ch] 7 times, sl st to 3rd of 5ch. Fasten off. (8 spaces).

2nd round: Join B into a sp, 9ch, sl st into 4th ch from hook, 5ch, sl st into 4th ch from hook, 1ch, *1dc into next sp, work a picot of [5ch, sl st into 4th ch from hook] twice, 1ch; rep from * 6 more times, sl st to 3rd ch of starting ch. Fasten off.

3rd round: Join C into 1ch between 2 Picots, 1ch, 1sc into same place as 1ch, *7ch, skip [1 picot, 1dc and 1 picot], 1sc into next ch between picots; rep from * 7

more times omitting sc at end of last rep, sl st to first sc.

4th round: Sl st into next ch, 1ch, *work [1sc, 1hdc, 9dc, 1hdc, 1sc] into next arch; rep from * 7 more times, sl st to first sc. Fasten off.

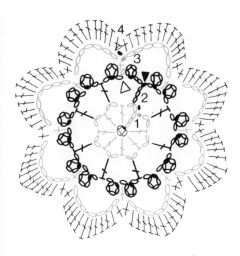

1 — A   2 — B
3, 4 — C

Galaxy Motif

Base ring: 6ch, join with sl st.

1st round: 6ch (count as 1tr and 2ch), [1tr into ring, 2ch] 7 times, sl st to 4th of 6ch. (8 spaces).

2nd round: 2ch, work hdc4tog into next sp (counts as hdc5tog), work [7ch, hdc5tog into next sp] 7 times, 7ch, sl st to first cluster.

3rd round: Sl st into each of next 3ch, 1ch, 3sc into same arch, [9ch, 3sc into next arch] 7 times, 8ch, 1sc into first sc.

4th round: 3ch, dc2tog over next 1sc and next ch skipping sc between (counts as dc3tog), *2ch, skip 1ch, 1dc into next ch, 2ch, skip 1ch, work [1dc, 3ch, 1dc] into next ch, 2ch, skip 1ch, 1dc into next ch, 2ch, skip 1ch**, work dc3tog over [next ch, 2nd of next 3sc and next ch]; rep from * 6 more times and from * to ** again, sl st to top of first cluster. Fasten off.

Sylvan Circles

Base ring: 8ch, join with sl st.

1st round: 3ch (count as 1dc), 31dc into ring, sl st to top of 3ch. (32 sts).

2nd round: 3ch, 1dc into same place as 3ch (counts as dc2tog), 3ch, work dc2tog into same place as last cluster. *7ch, skip 3 sts, work [dc2tog, 3ch, dc2tog] into next st; rep from * 6 more times, 7ch, skip 3 sts, sl st to top of first cluster.

3rd round: Sl st into next ch, 3ch, 1dc into same place as 3ch (counts as dc2tog), 3ch, work dc2tog into same 3ch sp, *7ch, skip 7ch, work [dc2tog, 3ch, dc2tog] into next 3ch sp; rep from * 6 more times, 7ch, skip 7ch, sl st to top of first cluster.

4th round: Sl st into next ch, 3ch, 1dc into same place as 3ch (counts as dc2tog), 3ch, work dc2tog into same 3ch sp, *4ch, 1sc under 7ch arch of 2nd round so as to enclose 7ch arch of 3rd round, 4ch**, work [dc2tog, 3ch, dc2tog] into next 3ch sp; rep from * 6 more times and from * to ** again, sl st to top of first cluster.

5th round: Sl st into next ch, 3ch, 1dc into same place as 3ch (counts as dc2tog), 3ch, work dc2tog into same 3ch sp, *15ch, sl st into 12th ch from hook, 3ch, sl st to top of previous cluster, 6dc into 12ch ring, skip 4ch, sl st to next sc, 8dc into ring, skip 4ch, (inner half of Sylvan Circle completed)**, work [dc2tog, 3ch, dc2tog] into next 3ch sp; rep from * 6 more times and from * to ** again, sl st to top of first cluster.

6th round: *1ch, work [dc2tog, 6ch, sl st to 5th ch from hook, 1ch, dc2tog] into next 3ch sp, 1ch, sl st to top of next cluster, 16dc into 12ch ring (outer half of Sylvan Circle completed), sl st to top of next cluster; rep from * 7 times. Fasten off.

Motifs

Flemish Motif

Base ring: 8ch, join with sl st.

1st round: 1ch, 16sc into ring, sl st to first sc. (16 sts).

2nd round: 12ch (count as 1tr and 8ch), skip first 2sc, [1tr into next sc, 8ch, skip 1sc] 7 times, sl st to 4th of 12 ch.

3rd round: 1ch, *into next 8 ch arch work [1sc, 1hdc, 1dc, 3tr, 4ch, insert hook down through top of tr just made and work a sl st to close, 2tr, 1dc, 1hdc, 1sc]; rep from * 7 more times, sl st to first sc.

Fasten off.

Barnacle Motif

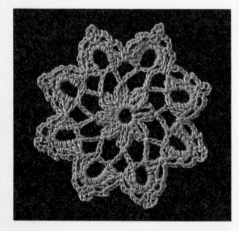

Base ring: 8ch, join with sl st.

1st round: 1ch, [1sc into ring, 3ch. 1tr into ring, 3ch] 8 times, sl st to first sc.

2nd round: Sl st into each of next 3ch and into tr, [12ch, 1dc into 9th ch from hook, 3ch, sl st to top of next tr] 8 times.

3rd round: Sl st into each of next 4ch, 3ch (count as 1dc), *work [1hdc, 7sc, 1hdc] into next 8ch arch, 1dc into next dc, skip last 3ch of same segment and first 3ch of next segment**, 1dc into next ch, (i.e. opposite side of same ch as dc of 2nd round); rep from * 6 more times and from * to ** again, sl st to top of 3ch.

4th round: 1ch, 1sc inserting hook under sl st which joined 3rd round, *3ch, skip [1hdc and 1sc], 1sc into next sc, 3ch, skip 1sc, work [1sc, 4ch, 1sc] into next sc, 3ch, skip 1sc, 1sc into next sc, 3ch, skip [1sc, 1hdc and 1dc]**, work 1sc between 2dc, skip 1dc; rep from * 6 more times and from * to ** again, sl st to first sc.

Fasten off.

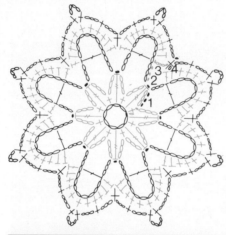

Pulsar Motif

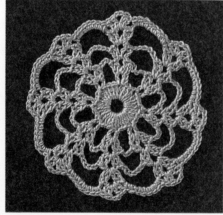

Base ring: 8ch, join with sl st.

1st round: 8ch, sl st into 6th ch from hook (counts as 1dc and picot), *4dc into ring, work a picot of [5ch, insert hook down through top of last dc made and work sl st to close]; rep from * 6 more times, 3dc into ring, sl st to 3rd of 8ch at beg of round. (8 picots).

2nd round: Sl st into each of next 2ch, 3ch (count as 1dc), work [1dc, 2ch, 2dc] into same picot, *4ch, work a DV st of [2dc, 2ch, 2dc] into next picot; rep from * 6 more times, 4ch, sl st to top of 3ch.

3rd round: Sl st into next dc and next ch, 3ch (count as 1dc), work [1dc, 2ch, 2dc] into same sp, *6ch, skip 4ch, DV st into next sp; rep from * 6 more times, 6ch, skip 4ch, sl st to top of 3ch.

4th round: Sl st into next dc and next ch, 3ch (count as 1dc), work [1dc, 2ch, 2dc] into same sp, *8ch, skip 6ch, DV st into next sp; rep from * 6 more times, 8ch, skip 6ch, sl st to top of 3ch.

5th round: Sl st into next dc and next ch, 3ch (count as 1dc), 4dc into same sp, *1sc into each of next 8ch, 5dc into next sp; rep from * 6 more times, 1sc into each of next 8ch, sl st to top of 3ch.

Fasten off.

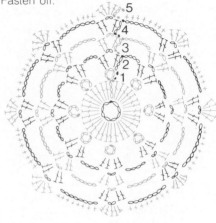

Amanda Whorl

Note: Segments are worked in 4 colors A, B, C and D used successively.

1st Segment

Base ring: Using A 12ch, join with sl st.

1st row (right side): 4ch (count as 1tr), [1tr into ring, 6ch, 1dc into top of tr just made, 1tr into ring] 3 times, 1tr into ring, 2ch, 10tr into ring, turn.

2nd row: Work a picot of [5ch, sl st to 5th ch from hook], ★skip first tr, 1sc into each of next 9tr, change to next color, turn.

2nd Segment

1ch, 1sc into same place as 1ch, 3ch, skip 3sc, 1sc into next sc, 9ch, sl st to first sc to complete joined base ring.

1st row: As given for 1st Segment.

2nd row: 2ch, 1sc into Picot of previous Segment, 3ch, sl st to first ch of row to complete Picot, continue as for 1st Segment from ★.

Work 5 more Segments as 2nd Segment using C, D, A, B and C.

8th Segment

Using D work as for previous Segments,

except also join to 1st Segment during 2nd row as follows: 2ch, 1sc into picot of 7th Segment, 1ch, 1sc into picot of 1st Segment, 2ch, sl st to first ch of row to complete picot, skip first tr, 1sc into each of next 5tr, sl st to 1st Segment, 1sc into each of next 4tr, sl st to 1st Segment. Fasten off.

Center Ring

Using A work inwards round center to make edging as follows: join into any sc, 1ch, 1sc into same place as 1ch, [1sc into next picot, 1sc into side of next sc] 7 times, 1sc into next picot, sl st to first sc.

Fasten off.

1sc into each of next 4dc, *into next 2ch sp work [1sc, 3ch, insert hook down through top of sc just made and work sl st to close, 1sc]**, 1sc into each of next 5dc; rep from * 6 more times and from * to ** again, sl st to first sc.

Fasten off.

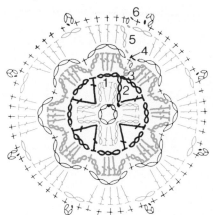

1 — A

2,3 — B

4,5,6 — C

1,2,3 — A

4,5 — B

Starfish

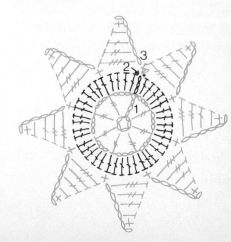

Base ring: 5ch, join with sl st.

1st round: 7ch (count as 1tr and 3ch), [1tr into ring, 3ch] 7 times, sl st to 4th of 7ch. (8 spaces).

2nd round: 3ch (count as 1dc), [4dc into next sp, 1dc into next tr] 7 times, 4dc into next sp, sl st to top of 3ch. (40 sts).

3rd round: 1ch, 1sc into same place as 1ch, *6ch, 1sc into 2nd ch from hook, 1hdc into next ch, 1dc into next ch, 1tr into next ch, 1dtr into next ch, skip 4 sts, 1sc into next st; rep from * 7 more times omitting sc at end of last rep, sl st to first sc.

Fasten off.

Celtic Motif

Base ring: Using A, 6ch, join with sl st.

1st round: Work a Leaf of [3ch, 2dc into ring, 3ch, sl st into ring] 4 times. Fasten off.

2nd round: Join B into same place, 6ch (count as 1dc and 3ch), skip next Leaf, *[1dc, 3ch, 1dc] into sl st, 3ch, skip next Leaf; rep from * twice more, 1dc into next sl st, 3ch, sl st to 3rd of 6ch.

3rd round: 1ch, 1sc into same place as 1ch, *work a Leaf of [3ch, 3dc into next 3ch sp, 3ch, 1sc into next dc]; rep from * 7 more times omitting sc at end of last rep, sl st to first sc. Fasten off.

4th round: Join C into same place, 1ch, 1sc into same place as 1ch, *4ch, skip next Leaf, 1sc into next sc; rep from * 7 more times omitting sc at end of last rep, sl st to first sc.

5th round: 3ch (count as 1dc), 4dc into next 4ch arch, [2ch, 5dc into next arch] 7 times, 2ch, sl st to top of 3ch.

6th round: 1ch, 1sc into same place as 1ch,

Druid Motif

Base ring: Using A, 6ch, join with sl st.

1st round: 2ch, 1hdc into ring (counts as hdc2tog), [3ch, hdc2tog into ring] 7 times, 3ch, sl st to first cluster.

2nd round: Sl st into each of next 2ch, 1ch, 1sc into same place as 1ch, [5ch, 1sc into next 3ch arch] 7 times, 5ch, sl st to first sc.

3rd round: 1ch, [5sc into next 5ch arch] 8 times, sl st to first sc. Fasten off.

4th round: Join B to 3rd of next 5sc, 1ch, 1sc into same place as 1ch, *7ch, skip 4sc, 1sc into next sc; rep from * 7 more times omitting sc at end of last rep, sl st to first sc.

5th round: 1ch, *[4sc, 3ch, 4sc] all into next 7ch arch; rep from * 7 more times, sl st to first sc.

Fasten off.

Motifs

Curlicue Motif

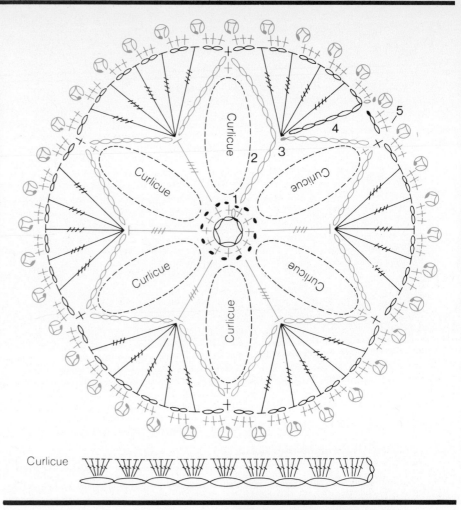

Base ring: 6ch, join with sl st.

1st round: 1ch, 12sc into ring, sl st to first sc. (12 sts).

2nd round: *Work a Curlicue of [12ch, 5dc into 4th ch from hook, 5dc into next and each ch ending sl st into same place as 12ch], sl st into each of next 2sc; rep from * 5 more times omitting 1 sl st at end of last rep.

3rd round: 14ch, *1sc into tip of next Curlicue, 8ch**, 1ttr into sc of 1st round between Curlicues, 8ch; rep from * 4 more times and from * to ** again, sl st to 6th ch of 14ch.

4th round: 8ch (count as 1ttr and 2ch), [1ttr, 2ch] 4 times into same place as 8ch, *skip 8ch, 1sc into next sc, 2ch, skip 8ch**, [1ttr, 2ch] 5 times into next ttr; rep from * 4 more times and from * to ** again, sl st to 6th ch of 8ch.

5th round: 1ch, *3sc into next 2ch sp, 3ch, insert hook down through top of sc just made and work sl st to close; rep from * into each 2ch sp all round, sl st to first sc.

Fasten off.

Curlicue

Lazy Wheel

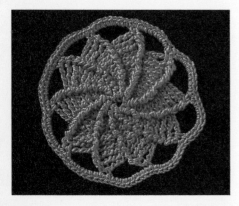

1st Segment

Make 17ch, sl st into 8th ch from hook, 1sc into next ch, 1hdc into next ch, 1dc into next ch, 2dc into next ch, 1dc into next ch, 2tr into next ch, 1tr into next ch, 2dtr into next ch, 1dtr into last ch. Do not turn, but work corded sc back from left to right inserting hook under front loop only of each st, ending sl st into ring.

2nd Segment

Working behind corded sc row into back loop only of next 9 sts of previous Segment work 1sc into first st, 1hdc into next st, 1dc into next st, 2dc into next st, 1dc into next st, 2tr into next st, 1tr into next st, 2dtr into next st, 1dtr into next st. Do not turn, but complete as for 1st Segment.

3rd to 10th Segments

Work as given for 2nd Segment. Fasten off leaving enough yarn to sew 10th Segment to 1st Segment on wrong side.

Edging

1st row (right side): Rejoin yarn at tip of any Segment in corded edge row, 1ch, 1sc into same place as 1ch, [7ch, 1sc into tip of next Segment] 9 times, 7ch, sl st to first sc.

2nd row: 1ch, 2sc into same place as 1ch, *7sc into next arch**, 2sc into next sc; rep from * 8 more times and from * to ** again, sl st to first sc.

Fasten off.

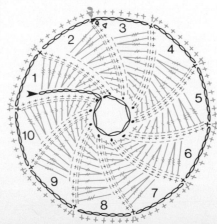

Granite Wheel

Base ring: 7ch, join with sl st.

1st round: 1ch, 12sc into ring, sl st to first sc. (12 sts).

2nd round: 3ch (count as 1dc), 1dc into next sc, *3ch, 1dc into each of next 2 sts; rep from * 4 more times, 3ch, sl st to top of 3ch.

3rd round: Sl st into next dc and next ch, 3ch, hdc2tog into same arch (counts as hdc3tog), 4ch, work hdc3tog into same arch, *4ch, work [hdc3tog, 4ch, hdc3tog] into next arch; rep from * 4 more times, 4ch, sl st to top of first cluster. (12 clusters).

4th round: 1ch, *work [2sc, 3ch, 2sc] into next arch; rep from * 11 more times, sl st to first sc.

Fasten off.

Stitch Variations, Abbreviations and Symbols on pages 7 to 15

Base ring: Using A, 4ch, join with sl st.

1st round: 1ch, 1sc into ring, [4ch, 1dtr into ring, 4ch, 1sc into ring] 4 times omitting sc at end of last rep, sl st to first sc. Fasten off.

2nd round: Join B into same place, 11ch, skip 4ch, 1sc into next dtr, *7ch, skip 4ch**, 1tr into next sc, 7ch, skip 4ch, 1sc into next dtr; rep from * twice more and from * to ** again, sl st to 4th ch of 11ch. Fasten off.

3rd round: Join C into same place, 4ch (count as 1tr), 2tr into same place as 4ch, *1ch, 1sc into next arch, 1ch, work [2dtr, 2ch, 2dtr] into next sc, 1ch, 1sc into next arch, 1ch**, 3tr into next tr; rep from * twice more and from * to ** again, sl st to top of 4ch. Fasten off.

4th round: Rejoin B into same place, 1ch, 1sc into same place as 1ch, 1sc into next and each ch and each st all round, except 3sc into each 2ch sp at corners, ending sl st to first sc. Fasten off.

5th round: Rejoin A into next sc, 6ch (count as 1tr and 2ch), skip first 2sc, *1tr into next sc, 2ch, skip 1sc, 1dc into next sc, 2ch, skip 1sc, 1hdc into next sc, 2ch, skip 1sc, 1sc into next sc, 2ch, skip 1sc, 1hdc into next sc, 2ch, skip 1sc, 1dc into next sc, 2ch, skip 1sc, 1tr into next sc, 2ch, skip 1sc**, 1tr into next sc, 2ch, skip 1sc; rep from * twice more and from * to ** again, sl st to 4th ch of 6ch.

6th round: 1ch, into first st work a trefoil of [1sc, 5ch, 1sc, 7ch, 1sc, 5ch, 1sc], *[2sc into next 2ch sp, 1sc into next st] twice, work a picot of [3ch, insert hook down through top of sc just made and work sl st to close], [2sc into next 2ch sp, 1sc into next st] 4 times, picot, 2sc into next 2ch sp, 1sc into next st, 2sc into next 2ch sp**, trefoil into next st; rep from * twice more and from * to ** again, sl st to first sc.
Fasten off.

Spandrell Motif

Sunflower Motif

Base ring: Using A, 8ch, join with sl st.

1st round: 1ch, 12sc into ring, sl st to first sc. (12 sts).

2nd round: 3ch, 1dc into same place as 3ch (counts as dc2tog), [3ch, dc2tog into next st] 11 times, 3ch, sl st to first cluster.

3rd round: Sl st into each of next 2ch, 1ch, 1sc into same place as 1ch, [4ch, 1sc into next 3ch arch] 11 times, 4ch, sl st to first sc.

4th round: 1ch, *[2sc, 3ch, 2sc] all into next 4ch arch; rep from * 11 more times, sl st to first sc. Fasten off.

5th round: Join B into next 3ch arch, 3ch, dc2tog into same arch (counts as dc3tog), 4ch, dc3tog all into same arch, *[dc3tog, 4ch, dc3tog] all into next 3ch arch; rep from * 10 more times, sl st to first cluster.

6th round: 1ch, 1sc into same place as 1ch, *[2sc, 3ch, 2sc] all into next 4ch arch, skip next cluster**, 1sc into next cluster; rep from * 10 more times and from * to ** again, sl st to first sc.

Fasten off.

1 — A
2 — B
3 — C
4 — B
5 — A

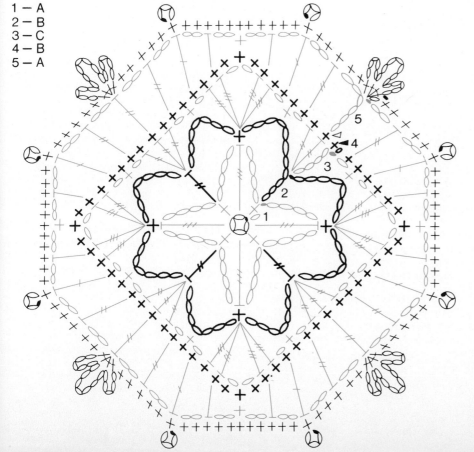

1,2,3,4 — A

5,6 — B

Motifs

Birds Nest I

2nd round: 6ch (count as 1dc, 3ch), 1 popcorn into next dc, 3ch, [1dc into next dc, 3ch, 1 popcorn into next dc, 3ch] 5 times, sl st into 3rd of 6ch at beg of round.

3rd round: 1ch, 1sc into same st as last sl st, 4ch, 1sc into top of next popcorn, 4ch, [1sc into next dc, 4ch, 1sc into top of next popcorn, 4ch] 5 times, sl st into first sc.

4th round: Sl st into first 4ch arch, 2ch (count as 1hdc), into same arch work [1dc, 1tr, 1dtr, 1tr, 1dc, 1hdc], into each of next 11 4ch arches work [1hdc, 1dc, 1tr, 1dtr, 1tr, 1dc, 1hdc], sl st into 2nd of 2ch at beg of round. Fasten off.

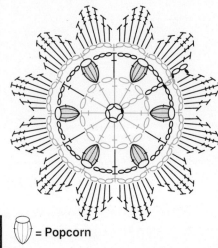

⬭ = Popcorn

Special Abbreviation

Popcorn = work 5dc into next st, drop loop off hook, insert hook into first of these dc, pick up dropped loop and draw through.

Make 5ch, sl st into first ch to form a ring.

1st round: 4ch (count as 1dc, 1ch), work [1dc, 1ch] 11 times into ring, sl st into 3rd of 4ch at beg of round.

Birds Nest II

Work as given for Birds Nest I **but** working 1st and 2nd rounds in A and 3rd and 4th rounds in B.

Six Pack

Special Abbreviation

Bobble = work 5dc into next sc until 1 loop of each remains on hook, yo and through all 6 loops on hook.

Make 6ch, sl st into first ch to form a ring.

1st round: 1ch, work 12sc into ring, sl st into first sc.

2nd round: 3ch, work 4dc into same st as last sl st until 1 loop of each dc remains on hook, yo and through all 5 loops on hook (1 bobble made at beg of round), *5ch, skip 1sc, 1 bobble into next sc; rep from * 4 times more, 5ch, sl st into top of first bobble. Fasten off.

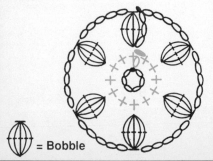

⬭ = Bobble

Flat Disc

Special Abbreviation

Bobble = work 3dc into next st until 1 loop of each remains on hook, yo and through all 4 loops on hook.

Make 12ch, sl st into first ch to form a ring.

1st round: 4ch (count as 1dc, 1ch), into ring work [2dc, 1ch] 11 times, 1dc into ring, sl st into 3rd of 4ch at beg of round.

2nd round: Sl st into first ch sp, 3ch, into same sp work 2dc until 1 loop of each remains on hook, yo and through all 3 loops on hook (1 bobble made at beg of round), 3ch, 1sc into next ch sp, 3ch, [1 bobble into next ch sp, 3ch, 1sc into next ch sp, 3ch] 5 times, sl st into top of first bobble.

3rd round: 3ch, into top of first bobble work [first bobble as at beg of previous round, 2ch, 1 bobble], 1ch, 1dc into next sc, 1ch, into same sc as last dc work [1dc, 1ch, 1dc], 1ch, *into top of next bobble work [1 bobble, 2ch, 1 bobble], 1ch, 1dc into next sc, 1ch, into same sc as last dc work [1dc, 1ch, 1dc], 1ch; rep from * 4 times more, sl st into top of first bobble.

4th round: 3ch, 1 bobble into first bobble as at beg of 2nd round, 2ch, 1 bobble into next 2ch sp, 2ch, 1 bobble into top of next bobble, 1ch, [1dc into next dc, 1ch] 3 times, *1 bobble into next bobble, 2ch, 1 bobble into next 2ch sp, 2ch, 1 bobble into next bobble, 1ch, [1dc into next dc, 1ch] 3 times; rep from * 4 times more, sl st into top of first bobble.

5th round: 3ch, 1 bobble into first bobble as at beg of 2nd round, 2ch, 1 bobble into next 2ch sp, 3ch, 1 bobble into next 2ch sp, 2ch, 1 bobble into next bobble, 1ch, [1dc into next dc, 1ch] 3 times, *1 bobble into next bobble, 2ch, 1 bobble into next 2ch sp, 3ch, 1 bobble into next 2ch sp, 2ch, 1 bobble into next bobble, 1ch, [1dc into next dc, 1ch] 3 times; rep from * 4 times more, sl st into first bobble. Fasten off.

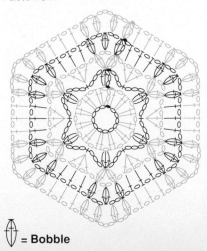

⬭ = Bobble

Stitch Variations, Abbreviations and Symbols on pages 7 to 15

Blue Corner

Special Abbreviations

4dc cluster = work 1dc into each of next 4dc until 1 loop of each remains on hook, yo and through all 5 loops on hook.

4dc bobble or 5dc bobble = work 4dc (or 5dc) into next ch until 1 loop of each remains on hook, yo and through all 5 (or 6) loops on hook.

Make 6ch, sl st into first ch to form a ring.

1st round: 3ch (count as 1dc), work 15dc into ring, sl st into 3rd of 3ch at beg of round.

2nd round: 3ch, 1dc into each of next 3dc, [7ch, 1dc into each of next 4dc] 3 times, 7ch, sl st into 3rd of 3ch at beg of round.

3rd round: 3ch, work 1dc into each of next 3dc until 1 loop of each remains on hook, yo and through all 4 loops on hook (1 cluster made at beg of round), 5ch, skip 3ch, into next ch work [1dc, 5ch, 1dc], 5ch, *4dc cluster over next 4dc, 5ch, skip 3ch, into next ch work [1dc, 5ch, 1dc], 5ch; rep from * twice more, sl st into top of first cluster.

4th round: 1ch, *1sc into top of cluster, 1sc into each of next 5ch, 1sc into next dc, 2ch, 4dc bobble into next ch, 5ch, skip 1ch, 5dc bobble into next ch, 5ch, skip 1ch, 4dc bobble into next ch, 2ch, 1sc into next dc, 1sc into each of next 5ch; rep from * 3 times more, sl st into first sc. Fasten off.

= 4dc cluster

= 4dc bobble   = 5dc bobble

Bermuda Triangle

Special Abbreviations

Popcorn = work 5tr into next ch, drop loop from hook, insert hook from the front into first of these tr, pick up dropped loop and draw through, 1ch to secure.

Picot = make 5ch, sl st into top of dc just worked.

Make 6ch, sl st into first ch to form a ring.

1st round: 6ch (count as 1dc, 3ch), into ring work [1dc, 3ch] 11 times, sl st into 3rd of 6ch at beg of round.

2nd round: 1 sl st into each of first 2ch of first arch, 4ch (count as 1tr), work 4tr into same ch as last sl st, drop loop from hook, insert hook from the front into 4th of 4ch, pick up dropped loop and draw through, 1ch to secure (popcorn made at beg of round), 5ch, 1sc into next 3ch arch, [5ch, skip 1ch of next 3ch arch, 1 popcorn into next ch, 5ch, 1sc into next 3ch arch] 5 times, 5ch, sl st into top of first popcorn.

3rd round: 4ch, into top of first popcorn work [3tr, 5ch, 4tr], 3ch, 1dc into next sc, 1 picot, 3ch, 1sc into top of next popcorn, 3ch, 1dc into next sc, 1 picot, 3ch, *into top of next popcorn work [4tr, 5ch, 4tr], 3ch, 1dc into next sc, 1 picot, 3ch, 1sc into top of next popcorn, 3ch, 1dc into next sc, 1 picot, 3ch; rep from * once more, sl st into 4th of 4ch at beg of round. Fasten off.

= Popcorn

Star Web

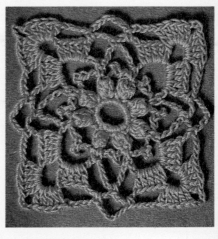

Special Abbreviations

Popcorn = work 5hdc into next sc, drop loop from hook, insert hook from the front into top of first of these hdc, pick up dropped loop and draw through, 1ch to secure popcorn.

Picot = make 3ch, work 1sc into first of these ch.

Make 10ch, sl st into first ch to form a ring.

1st round: 1ch, work 16sc into ring, sl st into first sc.

2nd round: 2ch, work 4hdc into first sc, drop loop from hook, insert hook from the front into 2nd of 2ch, pick up dropped loop and draw through, 1ch to secure (1 popcorn made at beg of round), 2ch, 1 picot, 2ch, [skip 1sc, 1 popcorn into next sc, 2ch, 1 picot, 2ch] 7 times, sl st into top of first popcorn.

3rd round: 1ch, 1sc into same st as last sl st, [9ch, 1sc into top of next popcorn] 7 times, 4ch, 1dtr into first sc.

4th round: Sl st into arch just formed, 3ch (count as 1dc), work 4dc into same arch as last sl st, 4ch, 1sc into next 9ch arch, 4ch, *work [5dc, 5ch, 5dc] into next 9ch arch, 4ch, 1sc into next 9ch arch, 4ch; rep from * twice more, 5dc into same arch as first 5dc, 5ch, sl st into 3rd of 3ch at beg of round.

5th round: 7ch (count as 1dc, 4ch), *1sc into next 4ch arch, 6ch, 1sc into next 4ch arch, 4ch, work [5dc, 3ch, 5dc] into next 5ch arch, 4ch; rep from * 3 times more omitting 1dc and 4ch at end of last rep, sl st into 3rd of 7ch at beg of round. Fasten off.

= Popcorn   = Picot

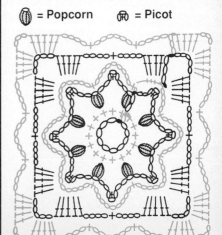

Motifs

Eighty Eight

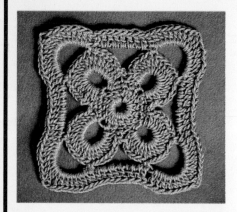

Make 6ch, sl st into first ch to form a ring.

1st round: 3ch (count as 1dc), work 15dc into ring, sl st into 3rd of 3ch at beg of round.

2nd round: 1ch, 1sc into same st as last sl st, 1sc into next dc, *[1sc, 7ch, 1sc] into next dc, 1sc into each of next 3dc; rep from * 3 times more omitting 2sc at end of last rep, sl st into first sc.

3rd round: 1ch, 1sc into same st as last sl st, *into next 7ch arch work [2hdc, 17dc, 2hdc] (1 shell made), skip 2sc, 1sc into next sc; rep from * 3 times more omitting 1sc at end of last rep, sl st into first sc.

4th round: Sl st into each of first 2hdc and 6dc of first shell, 1ch, 1sc into same st as last sl st, 9ch, skip 5dc, 1sc into next dc, *7ch, skip first 2hdc and 5dc on next shell, 1sc into next dc, 9ch, skip 5dc, 1sc into next dc; rep from * twice more, 7ch, sl st into first sc.

5th round: 3ch, *into next 9ch arch work [8dc, 1tr, 8dc], 1dc into next sc, 7dc into next 7ch sp, 1dc into next sc; rep from * 3

times more omitting 1dc at end of last rep, sl st into 3rd of 3ch at beg of round. Fasten off.

Crystal Web

Special Abbreviation

Cluster = work 2dtr into next arch until 1 loop of each remains on hook, yo and through all 3 loops on hook.

1st round: Make 5ch, work 19tr into first ch, sl st into top of 5ch.

2nd round: 8ch (count as 1dtr, 3ch), [1dtr into next tr, 3ch] 19 times, sl st into 5th of 8ch at beg of round. 20 sps.

3rd round: Sl st into first arch, 5ch (count as 1dtr), work 1dtr into same arch as sl st, 6ch, [1 cluster into next arch, 6ch] 19 times, sl st into top of first dtr.

4th round: Work 1 sl st into each of first 3ch of first arch, 1ch, 1sc into same arch as sl sts, [8ch, 1sc into next 6ch arch] 19 times, 4ch, 1tr into first sc.

5th round: 1ch, 1sc into arch just formed, 9ch, [1sc into next 8ch arch, 9ch] 19 times, sl st into first sc. Fasten off.

↑↑↑ = Cluster

Overture

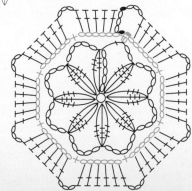

Special Abbreviation

Bobble = work 3dtr into ch until 1 loop of each remains on hook, yo and through all 4 loops on hook.

1st round: Make 6ch, work 2dtr into first ch until 1 loop of each remains on hook, yo and through all 3 loops on hook (bobble made at beg of round), into same ch work [5ch, 1 bobble] 7 times, 2ch, 1dc into top of first bobble.

2nd round: 1ch, work 1sc into arch just formed, 6ch, [1sc into next 5ch arch, 6ch] 7 times, sl st into first sc.

3rd round: Sl st into first 6ch arch, 3ch (count as 1dc), work 5dc into same arch, 3ch, [6dc into next 6ch arch, 3ch] 7 times, sl st into 3rd of 3ch at beg of round. Fasten off.

 = Bobble

Stitch Variations, Abbreviations and Symbols on pages 7 to 15

Wavy Line

Make 10ch, sl st into first ch to form a ring.

1st round: 3ch (count as 1dc), work 23dc into ring, sl st into 3rd of 3ch at beg of round.

2nd round: 3ch (count as 1dc), 1dc into next dc, 2dc into next dc, [1dc into each of next 2dc, 2dc into next dc] 7 times, sl st into 3rd of 3ch at beg of round.

3rd round: 3ch, 2dc into next dc, 2ch, [1dc into each of next 3dc, 2dc into next dc, 2ch] 7 times, 1dc into each of last 2dc, sl st into 3rd of 3ch at beg of round.

4th round: 3ch, 1dc into each of next 2dc, 2ch, 1dc into next 2ch sp, 2ch, [1dc into each of next 5dc, 2ch, 1dc into next 2ch sp, 2ch] 7 times, 1dc into each of last 2dc, sl st into 3rd of 3ch at beg of round.

5th round: 3ch, 1dc into next dc, 5ch, skip 1dc, 1dc into next dc, [5ch, skip 1dc, 1dc into each of next 3dc, 5ch, skip 1dc, 1dc into next dc] 7 times, 5ch, skip 1dc, 1dc into last dc, sl st into 3rd of 3ch at beg of round.

Red Revolver

Make 12ch, sl st into first ch to form a ring.

1st round: 1ch, work 24sc into ring, sl st into first sc.

2nd round: 12ch, skip next sc, 1sc into next sc, turn, *3ch (count as 1dc), 1dc into each of first 7ch of arch, turn, 3ch, skip first dc, 1dc into each of next 6dc, 1dc into top of 3ch**, (first block made). ★Skip next sc on ring, work 1tr into next sc, 8ch, skip 1sc, 1sc into next sc, turn and work from * to ** for next block. Rep from ★ 4 times more, sl st into 4th of 12ch at beg of round.

3rd round: Sl st to top of 3ch at corner of first block, 1ch, 1sc into top of 3ch, 13ch, [1sc into 3rd of 3ch at top of next block, 13ch] 5 times, sl st into first sc.

6th round: 11ch (count as 1dc, 8ch), skip next dc, 1dc into next dc, [8ch, skip 1dc, 1dc into next dc] 14 times, 8ch, sl st into 3rd of 11ch at beg of round. Fasten off.

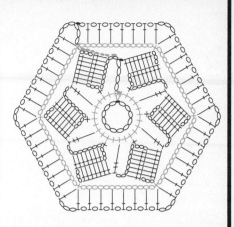

4th round: 6ch (count as 1dc, 3ch), 1dc into same st as last sl st, [1ch, skip 1ch, 1dc into next ch] 6 times, 1ch, *into next sc work [1dc, 3ch, 1dc], [1ch, skip 1ch, 1dc into next ch] 6 times, 1ch; rep from * 4 times more, sl st into 3rd of 6ch. Fasten off.

Low Tide

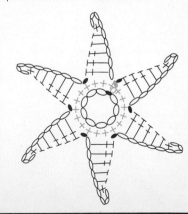

Make 9ch, sl st into first ch to form a ring.

1st round: 1ch, work 18sc into ring, sl st into first sc.

2nd round: 9ch, work 1sc into 4th ch from hook, 1hdc into each of next 2ch, 1dc into each of next 3ch, skip first 3sc on ring, sl st into next sc, *9ch, work 1sc into 4th ch from hook, 1hdc into each of next 2ch, 1dc into each of next 3ch, skip next 2sc on ring, sl st into next sc; rep from *4 times more placing last sl st into same st as sl st of previous round. Fasten off.

Motifs

Flower Web

Special Abbreviation

Cluster = work 1tr into each of next 5tr until 1 loop of each remains on hook, yo and through all 6 loops on hook.

Make 8ch, sl st into first ch to form a ring.

1st round: 9ch (count as 1tr, 5ch), into ring work [1tr, 5ch] 7 times, sl st into 4th of 9ch at beg of round.

2nd round: Sl st into first 5ch arch, 4ch (count as 1tr), work 6tr into same arch, work 7tr into each of next 7 arches, sl st into 4th of 4ch at beg of round.

3rd round: 4ch (count as 1tr), work 1tr into each of next 6tr, 5ch, [1tr into each of next 7tr, 5ch] 7 times, sl st into 4th of 4ch at beg of round.

4th round: Sl st into next tr, 4ch, 1tr into each of next 4tr until 1 loop of each remains on hook, yo and through all 5 loops on hook (1 cluster made at beg of round), 6ch, 1sc into next 5ch arch, [6ch, skip 1tr, work 1 cluster across next 5tr, 6ch, 1sc into next 5ch arch] 7 times, 3ch, 1dc into top of first cluster.

5th round: 1ch, 1sc into arch just formed, [8ch, 1sc into next 6ch arch] 15 times, 4ch, 1tr into first sc.

6th round: 1ch, 1sc into arch just formed, 9ch, [1sc into next 8ch arch, 9ch] 15 times, sl st into first sc. Fasten off.

= Cluster

Watermark

Make 6ch, sl st into first ch to form a ring.

1st round: 3ch (count as 1dc), work 15dc into ring, sl st into 3rd of 3ch at beg of round.

2nd round: 5ch (count as 1dc, 2ch), 1dc into same st as last sl st, *1ch, skip 1dc, into next dc work [1dc, 2ch, 1dc]; rep from * 6 times more, 1ch, sl st into 3rd of 5ch at beg of round.

3rd round: Sl st into first 2ch sp, 3ch (count as 1dc), into same sp work [1dc, 2ch, 2dc], *1ch, into next 2ch sp work [2dc, 2ch, 2dc]; rep from * 6 times more, 1ch, sl st into 3rd of 3ch at beg of round.

4th round: Sl st into next dc and first 2ch sp, 3ch, work 6dc into same sp as last sl st, 1sc into next ch sp, [7dc into next 2ch sp, 1sc into next ch sp] 7 times, sl st into 3rd of 3ch at beg of round. Fasten off.

Teardrops

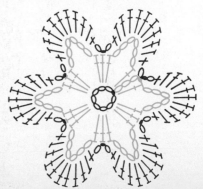

Make 8ch, sl st into first ch to form a ring.

1st round: 3ch (count as 1dc), into ring work 1dc, [6ch, 3dc] 5 times, 6ch, 1dc, sl st into 3rd of 3ch at beg of round.

2nd round: *1ch, into next 6ch arch work [1sc, 1hdc, 7dc, 1hdc, 1sc], 1ch, skip 1dc, 1 sl st into next dc; rep from * 5 times more placing last sl st into 3rd of 3ch at beg of previous round. Fasten off.

Cloister Window I

Make 8ch, sl st into first ch to form a ring.

1st round: 3ch (count as 1dc), work 19dc into ring, sl st into 3rd of 3ch at beg of round.

2nd round: [11ch, skip next dc, sl st into next dc] 9 times, 6ch, 1ttr into sl st of previous round.

3rd round: Sl st into loop just formed, 3ch, into same loop work [2dc, 3ch, 3dc], work [3dc, 3ch, 3dc] into each of next 9 loops, sl st into 3rd of 3ch at beg of round. Fasten off.

Note: After working 3rd round it may be necessary to ease the shells of [3dc, 3ch, 3dc] to center of loop formed in previous round.

Open Slice

Special Abbreviations

Tr2tog = work 2tr into ring until 1 loop of each remains on hook, yo and through all 3 loops on hook.

Cluster = work 3dc into sp until 1 loop of each remains on hook, yo and through all 4 loops on hook.

Make 10ch, sl st into first ch to form a ring.

1st round: 4ch, 1tr into ring, 2ch, into ring work [tr2tog, 2ch] 11 times, sl st into first tr.

2nd round: Sl st into 2ch sp, 3ch, into same 2ch sp as sl st, work 2dc until 1 loop of each remains on hook, yo and through all 3 loops on hook (first cluster made), 3ch, [1 cluster into next 2ch sp, 3ch] 11 times, sl st into top of first cluster.

3rd round: 5ch (count as 1hdc, 3ch), skip first 3ch arch, into next 3ch arch work [1 cluster, 2ch, 1 cluster, 4ch, 1 cluster, 2ch, 1 cluster], 3ch, *skip next 3ch arch, 1hdc into top of next cluster, 3ch, skip next 3ch arch, into next 3ch arch work [1 cluster, 2ch, 1 cluster, 4ch, 1 cluster, 2ch, 1 cluster], 3ch; rep from * twice more, sl st into 2nd of 5ch at beg of round.

4th round: 1ch, work 1sc into same st as last sl st, *3sc into next 3ch sp, 1sc into top of next cluster, 2sc into next 2ch sp, 1sc into next cluster, 5sc into next 4ch arch, 1sc into next cluster, 2sc into next 2ch sp, 1sc into next cluster, 3sc into next 3ch sp, 1sc into next hdc; rep from * 3 times more omitting 1sc at end of last rep, sl st into first sc. Fasten off.

⫰ = Tr2tog   ⩕ = Cluster

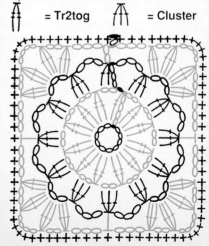

Gear Wheel

Special Abbreviations

Petal = 1ch, 1tr into next sc, 2ch, work 1tr into stem of last tr two thirds of the way down, 2ch, into stem of last tr (two thirds of the way down as before) work [1dc, 2ch] twice, work 1dc two thirds of the way down stem of first tr, 1ch, 1sc into next dc.

3dc bobble = work 3dc into next sc until 1 loop of each remains on hook, yo and through all 4 loops on hook.

Make 8ch, sl st into first ch to form a ring.

1st round: 1ch, work 16sc into ring, sl st into first sc.

2nd round: 3ch, work 2dc into same st as last sl st until 1 loop of each dc remains on hook, yo and through all 3 loops, (1 bobble made at beg of round), [3ch, skip next sc, 1 bobble into next sc] 7 times, 3ch, sl st into 3rd of 3ch at beg of round.

3rd round: 6ch (count as 1dc, 3ch), 1sc into first 3ch arch, 3ch, [1dc into next bobble, 3ch, 1sc into next 3ch arch, 3ch] 7 times, sl st into 3rd of 6ch at beg of round.

4th round: 1ch, work 1sc into same st as last sl st, work 8 petals omitting sc at end of last petal, sl st into first sc. Fasten off.

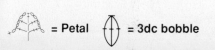 = Petal ⬯ = 3dc bobble

Cloister Window II

Work as given for Cloister Window I working 1 round each in A, B and C.

Motifs

Venetian Star I

Special Abbreviations

Bobble = work 3dc into next st until 1 loop of each remains on hook, yo and through all 4 loops on hook.

Picot = make 3ch, sl st into first of these ch.

1st round: Make 2ch, work 12sc into first ch, sl st into first sc.

2nd round: 3ch (count as 1dc), skip first sc, 1dc into next sc, 3ch, [1dc into each of next 2sc, 3ch] 5 times, sl st into 3rd of 3ch at beg of round.

3rd round: Sl st into next dc and 3ch sp, 3ch (count as 1dc), into same 3ch sp work [2dc until 1 loop of each remains on hook, yo and through all 3 loops on hook (bobble made at beg of round), 3ch, 1 bobble], 7ch, *into next 3ch sp work [1 bobble, 3ch, 1 bobble], 7 ch; rep from * 4 times more, sl st into top of first bobble.

4th round: Work 2 sl sts into first 3ch arch, 1ch, 1sc into same arch, *into next 7ch arch work [6dc, 1 picot, 6dc], 1sc into next 3ch arch; rep from * 5 times more omitting sc at end of last rep, sl st into first sc. Fasten off.

 = Bobble

 = Picot

Venetian Star II

Work as given for Venetian Star I **but** working 1st and 2nd rounds in A, 3rd round in B and 4th round in C.

Speedy Spiral

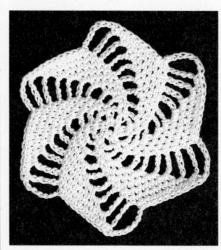

Note: This motif is worked as a continuous spiral, the size can therefore be increased or decreased as required.

1st round: Make 2ch, work 6sc into 2nd ch from hook, sl st into first sc.

Continue in a spiral as follows:
1ch, work 1sc into same st as last sl st, 3ch, [1sc into next sc, 3ch] 5 times, [1sc into next sc, 1sc into next sp, 3ch] 6 times, [skip 1sc, 1sc into next sc, 2sc into next sp, 3ch] 6 times, [skip 1sc, 1sc into each of next 2sc, 2sc into next sp, 4ch] 6 times, [skip 1sc, 1sc into each of next 3sc, 2sc into next 4ch sp, 4ch] 6 times, [skip 1sc, 1sc into each of next 4sc, 2sc into next 4ch sp, 5ch] 6 times, [skip 1sc, 1sc into each of next 5sc, 2sc into next 5ch sp, 5ch] 6 times, [skip 1sc, 1sc into each of next 6sc, 2sc into next 5ch sp, 6ch] 6 times, [skip 1sc, 1sc into each of next 7sc, 2sc into next 6ch sp, 6ch] 6 times, [skip 1sc, 1sc into each of next 8sc, 2sc into next 6ch sp, 7ch] 6 times, skip 1sc, 1sc into next sc. Fasten off.

Four Blade

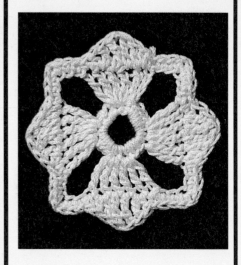

Make 8ch, sl st into first ch to form a ring.

1st round: 1ch, work 16sc into ring, sl st into first sc.

2nd round: 4ch (count as 1tr), work 2tr into first sc, 3tr into next sc, 5ch, [skip 2sc, 3tr into each of next 2sc, 5ch] 3 times, sl st into 4th of 4ch at beg of round.

3rd round: 1ch, 1sc into same st as last sl st, *[1hdc, 1dc] into next tr, 2tr into each of next 2tr, [1dc, 1hdc] into next tr, 1sc into next tr, 1sc into each of next 2ch, 3sc into next ch, 1sc into each of next 2ch, 1sc into next tr; rep from * 3 times more omitting 1sc at end of last rep, sl st into first sc. Fasten off.

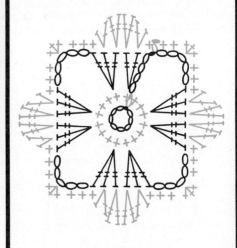

Garland I

Special Abbreviation

Dc2tog = work 1dc into next dc until 2 loops remain on hook, skip 2dc, work 1dc into next dc until 3 loops remain on hook, yo and through all 3 loops on hook.

Make 10ch, sl st into first ch to form a ring.

1st round: 3ch (count as 1dc), work 31dc into ring, sl st into 3rd of 3ch at beg of round.

2nd round: [7ch, skip 3dc, sl st into next dc] 7 times, 3ch, 1tr into same st as last sl st of previous round.

3rd round: 3ch, work 6dc into top of tr, [7dc into 4th ch of next 7ch arch] 7 times, sl st into 3rd of 3ch at beg of round.

4th round: Sl st into next dc, 6ch (count as 1dc, 3ch), *skip 1dc, into next dc work [1tr, 5ch, 1tr], 3ch, skip 1dc, dc2tog, 3ch, skip 1dc, 1sc into next dc, 3ch, skip 1dc, dc2tog, 3ch; rep from * 3 times more omitting 1dc2tog and 3ch at end of last rep, skip 1dc, 1dc into next dc, sl st into 3rd of 6ch at beg of round.

5th round: 1ch, 1sc into same st as last sl st, *3sc into next 3ch sp, 1sc into next tr, 6sc into 5ch arch, 1sc into next tr, 3sc into next 3ch sp, 1sc into top of next dc2tog, 3sc into next 3ch sp, 1sc into next sc, 3sc into next 3ch sp, 1sc into top of next dc2tog; rep from * 3 times more omitting 1sc at end of last rep, sl st into first sc. Fasten off.

 = Dc2tog

King of Siam I

Special Abbreviation

3-Picot Cluster = work 4ch, sl st into first ch, [3ch, sl st into same ch as first sl st] twice.

Make 6ch, sl st into first ch to form a ring.

1st round: 1ch, work 12sc into ring, sl st into first sc.

2nd round: 3ch (count as 1dc), 1dc into same st as last sl st, work 2dc into each of next 11sc, sl st into 3rd of 3ch at beg of round.

3rd round: 1ch, 1sc into same st as last sl st, 1sc into each of next 23dc, sl st into first sc.

4th round: 1ch, 1sc into same sc as last sl st, 5ch, skip 2sc, [1sc into next sc, 5ch, skip 2sc] 7 times, sl st into first sc.

5th round: 1ch, 1sc into same st as last sl st, *into next 5ch arch work [1hdc, 3dc, 3-picot cluster, 3dc, 1hdc], 1sc into next sc; rep from * 7 times more omitting 1sc at end of last rep, sl st into first sc.

6th round: 1ch, 1sc into same st as last sl st, *7ch, 1sc into center picot of 3-picot cluster, 7ch, 1sc into next sc; rep from * 7 times more omitting 1sc at end of last rep, sl st into first sc.

7th round: Sl st into first 7ch arch, 1ch, [work 8sc into next 7ch arch, 3-picot cluster, 8sc into same 7ch arch] 8 times, sl st into first sc. Fasten off.

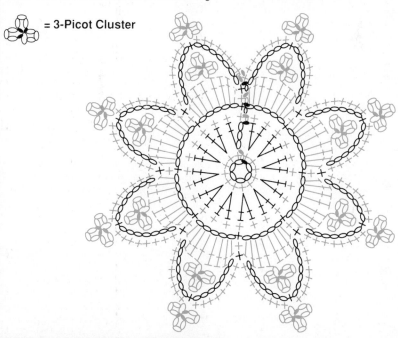 = 3-Picot Cluster

Garland II

Work as given for Garland I **but** working 1 round in each of colors A, B and C, then work 4th and 5th rounds in A.

King of Siam II

Work as given for King of Siam I **but** working 1st, 2nd and 3rd rounds in A, 4th and 5th in B and 6th and 7th in C.

Motifs

Easy Rider

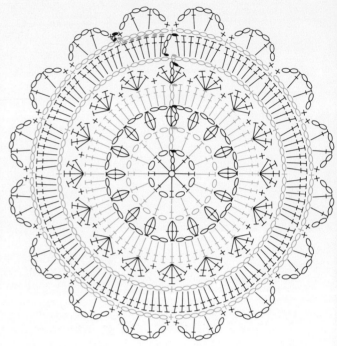

Special Abbreviations

Bobble = work 3dc into next st until 1 loop of each remains on hook, yo and through all 4 loops on hook.

Fan = into next dc work [1hdc, 3dc, 1hdc].

1st round: Make 5ch, work [1dc, 1ch] 7 times into first ch, sl st into 4th of 5ch.

2nd round: 4ch (count as 1dc, 1ch), work 1dc into first ch sp, 1ch, [1dc into next dc, 1ch, 1dc into next ch sp, 1ch] 7 times, sl st into 3rd of 4ch at beg of round.

3rd round: 3ch (count as 1dc), work 2dc into same st as last sl st until 1 loop of each remains on hook, yo and through all 3 loops on hook (1 bobble made at beg of round), 2ch, [1 bobble into next dc, 2ch] 15 times, sl st into top of first bobble.

4th round: 3ch, work 3dc into first 2ch sp, [1dc into next bobble, 3dc into next 2ch sp] 15 times, sl st into 3rd of 3ch at beg of round.

5th round: 3ch, work [1dc, 1hdc] into same st as last sl st, skip 1dc, 1sc into next dc, [skip 1dc, 1 fan into next dc, skip 1dc, 1sc into next dc] 15 times, skip last dc, work [1hdc, 1dc] into same st as sl st at end of previous round, sl st into 3rd of 3ch at beg of round.

6th round: 1ch, 1sc into same st as last sl st, 5ch, [1sc into center dc of next fan, 5ch] 15 times, sl st into first sc.

7th round: Sl st into first 5ch arch, 3ch, work 6dc into same arch as sl st, work 7dc into each of next 15 5ch arches, sl st into 3rd of 3ch at beg of round.

8th round: Sl st into each of first 6dc, 1ch, 1sc between last dc worked into and next dc, 6ch, [skip 7dc, 1sc between last dc skipped and next dc, 6ch] 14 times, skip 7dc, 1sc between last dc skipped and 3ch at beg of previous round, 6ch, sl st into first sc.

9th round: Sl st into first 6ch arch, 1ch, into each of next 16 6ch arches work [1sc, 2ch, 1dc, 2ch, 1dc, 2ch, 1sc], sl st into first sc. Fasten off.

Watercolour

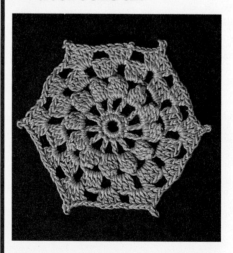

Special Abbreviations

Popcorn = work 5dc into next st, drop loop from hook, insert hook into top of first of these dc, pick up dropped loop and draw through, 1ch to secure popcorn.

Picot = 3ch, sl st into first of these ch.

Make 6ch, sl st into first ch to form a ring.

1st round: 1ch, work 12sc into ring, sl st into first sc.

2nd round: 5ch (count as 1dc, 2ch), skip first sc, [1dc into next sc, 2ch] 11 times, sl st into 3rd of 5ch at beg of round.

3rd round: Sl st into first 2ch sp, 3ch, 4dc into same sp as sl st, drop loop from hook, insert hook into top of 3ch, pick up dropped loop and draw through, 1ch to

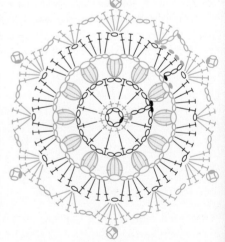

secure (1 popcorn made at beg of round), 3ch, [1 popcorn into next 2ch sp, 3ch] 11 times, sl st into top of first popcorn.

4th round: Sl st into first 3ch sp, 3ch (count as 1dc), 3dc into same sp as sl st, 1ch, [4dc into next 3ch sp, 1ch] 11 times, sl st into 3rd of 3ch at beg of round.

5th round: Sl st into each of next 3dc and into ch sp, 3ch, 3dc into same sp as last sl st, 2ch, into next ch sp work [3dc, 1 picot, 3dc], *2ch, work 4dc into next ch sp, 2ch, into next ch sp work [3dc, 1 picot, 3dc]; rep from * 4 times more, 2ch, sl st into 3rd of 3ch at beg of round. Fasten off.

 = Popcorn   = Picot

Stitch Variations, Abbreviations and Symbols on pages 7 to 15

Octagon Star

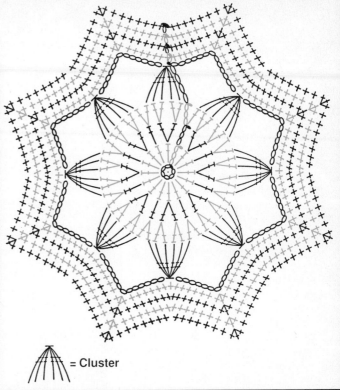

 = Cluster

Special Abbreviation

Cluster = work 1tr into each of next 6dc until 1 loop of each remains on hook, yo and through all 7 loops on hook.

Make 6ch, sl st into first ch to form a ring.

1st round: 3ch (count as 1dc), work 15dc into ring, sl st into 3rd of 3ch at beg of round.

2nd round: 3ch, 2dc into next dc, [1dc into next dc, 2dc into next dc] 7 times, sl st into 3rd of 3ch at beg of round.

3rd round: 3ch, work 2dc into each of next 23dc, 1dc into same st as sl st at end of previous round, sl st into 3rd of 3ch at beg of round.

4th round: 4ch, work 1tr into each of next 5dc until 1 loop of each remains on hook, yo and through all 6 loops on hook (1 cluster made at beg of round), 13ch, [1 cluster over next 6dc, 13ch] 7 times, sl st into top of first cluster.

5th round: 1ch, 1sc into same st as last sl st, *1sc into each of next 6ch, 3sc into next ch, 1sc into each of next 6ch, 1sc into top of next cluster; rep from * 7 times more omitting 1sc at end of last rep, sl st into first sc.

6th round: 1ch, skip first sc, 1sc into each of next 7sc, 3sc into next sc, 1sc into each of next 7sc, [skip 1sc, 1sc into each of next 7sc, 3sc into next sc, 1sc into each of next 7sc] 7 times, sl st into first sc at beg of round.

7th round: 1ch, skip first sc, 1sc into each of next 7sc, 3sc into next sc, 1sc into each of next 7sc, [skip 2sc, 1sc into each of next 7sc, 3sc into next sc, 1sc into each of next 7sc] 7 times, skip next sc, sl st into first sc.

8th round: As 7th round. Fasten off.

Evening Light

Special Abbreviation

3dc bobble or 4dc bobble = work 3 (or 4) dc into next st until 1 loop of each remains on hook, yo and through all 4 (or 5) loops on hook.

1st round: Make 4ch, work 11dc into first of these ch, sl st into 4th of 4ch at beg of round.

2nd round: 3ch, work 2dc into same st as last sl st until 1 loop of each remains on hook, yo and through all 3 loops on hook (3dc bobble made at beg of round), [1ch, 3dc bobble into next dc] twice, 5ch, *3dc bobble into next dc, [1ch, 3dc bobble into next dc] twice, 5ch; rep from * twice more, sl st into top of first bobble.

3rd round: Sl st into first ch sp, 3ch, into same ch sp as last sl st work 3dc until 1 loop of each remains on hook, yo and through all 4 loops on hook (4dc bobble made at beg of round), *1ch, 4dc bobble into next ch sp, 2ch, 5dc into 5ch arch, 2ch, work 4dc bobble into next ch sp; rep

from * 3 times more omitting bobble at end of last rep, sl st into top of first bobble.

4th round: Sl st into first ch sp, 3ch then complete first 4dc bobble as on 3rd round, *2ch, 1dc into 2ch sp, 1dc into each of next 2dc, 5dc into next dc, 1dc into each of next 2dc, 1dc into next 2ch sp, 2ch, 4dc bobble into next ch sp; rep from * 3 times more omitting bobble at end of last rep, sl st into top of first bobble.

5th round: 3ch, *2dc into next 2ch sp, 1dc into each of next 4dc, 3ch, skip 1dc, 4dc bobble into next dc, 3ch, skip 1dc, 1dc into each of next 4dc, 2dc into next 2ch sp, 1dc into top of next bobble; rep from * 3 times more omitting 1dc at end of last rep, sl st into 3rd of 3ch at beg of round.

6th round: 3ch, 1dc into each of next 6dc, *2ch, skip 2ch, 4dc bobble into next ch, 5ch, 4dc bobble into next ch, 2ch, 1dc into each of next 13dc; rep from * 3 times more omitting 7dc at end of last rep, sl st into 3rd of 3ch at beg of round. Fasten off.

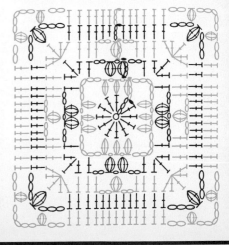

= 3dc bobble   = 4dc bobble

Motifs

Timeclock

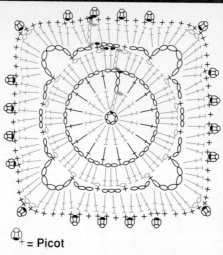

 = Picot

Special Abbreviation

Picot = 3ch, sl st into side of last sc worked.

Make 6ch, sl st into first ch to form a ring.

1st round: 3ch (count as 1dc), work 15dc into ring, sl st into 3rd of 3ch at beg of round.

2nd round: 5ch (count as 1dc, 2ch), [1dc into next dc, 2ch] 15 times, sl st into 3rd of 5ch at beg of round.

3rd round: Sl st into first 2ch sp, 3ch (count as 1dc), work 2dc into first 2ch sp, 1ch, [3dc into next 2ch sp, 1ch] 15 times, sl st into 3rd of 3ch at beg of round.

4th round: Sl st into each of next 2dc, 1ch, 1sc into first ch sp, 3ch, 1sc into next ch sp, 6ch, *1sc into next ch sp, [3ch, 1sc into next ch sp] 3 times, 6ch; rep from * twice more, [1sc into next ch sp, 3ch] twice, sl st into first sc.

5th round: Sl st into first 3ch sp, 3ch, work 2dc into first 3ch sp, into next 6ch arch work [5dc, 2ch, 5dc], *3dc into each of next 3 3ch sps, into next 6ch arch work [5dc, 2ch, 5dc]; rep from * twice more, 3dc into each of last 2 3ch sps, sl st into 3rd of 3ch at beg of round.

6th round: 1ch, 1sc into same st as last sl st, 1sc into each of next 2dc, 1 picot, 1sc into each of next 5dc, into next 2ch sp work [1sc, 1 picot, 1sc], 1sc into each of next 5dc, *1 picot, [1sc into each of next 3dc, 1 picot] 3 times, 1sc into each of next 5dc, into next 2ch sp work [1sc, 1 picot, 1sc], 1sc into each of next 5dc; rep from * twice more, 1 picot, [1sc into each of next 3dc, 1 picot] twice, sl st into first sc. Fasten off.

Fourways

Make 6ch, sl st into first ch to form a ring.

1st round: 3ch (count as 1dc), work 15dc into ring, sl st into 3rd of 3ch at beg of round.

2nd round: 3ch (count as 1dc), 2dc into same st as last sl st, 2ch, skip 1dc, 1dc into next dc, 2ch, skip 1dc, *3dc into next dc, 2ch, skip 1dc, 1dc into next dc, 2ch, skip 1dc; rep from * twice more, sl st into 3rd of 3ch at beg of round.

3rd round: 3ch, 5dc into next dc, *1dc into next dc, [2ch, 1dc into next dc] twice, 5dc into next dc; rep from * twice more, [1dc into next dc, 2ch] twice, sl st into 3rd of 3ch at beg of round.

4th round: 3ch, 1dc into each of next 2dc, 5dc into next dc, *1dc into each of next 3dc, 2ch, 1dc into next dc, 2ch, 1dc into each of next 3dc, 5dc into next dc; rep from * twice more, 1dc into each of next 3dc, 2ch, 1dc into next dc, 2ch, sl st into 3rd of 3ch at beg of round.

5th round: 3ch, 1dc into each of next 4dc, 5dc into next dc, *1dc into each of next 5dc, 2dc into next 2ch sp, 1dc into next dc, 2dc into next 2ch sp, 1dc into each of next 5dc, 5dc into next dc; rep from * twice more, 1dc into each of next 5dc, 2dc into next 2ch sp, 1dc into next dc, 2dc into last 2ch sp, sl st into 3rd of 3ch at beg of round. Fasten off.

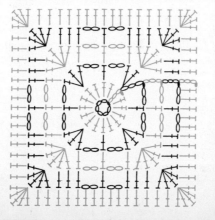

Ship Shape

Special Abbreviation

Bobble = work 5dc into next st until 1 loop of each remains on hook, yo and through all 6 loops on hook.

1st round: Make 6ch and working into first of these ch work [1dc, 2ch] 7 times, sl st into 4th of 6ch at beg of round.

2nd round: 3ch (count as 1dc), work 2dc into same st as last sl st, 2ch, [3dc into next dc, 2ch] 7 times, sl st into 3rd of 3ch at beg of round.

3rd round: 3ch, 1dc into same st as last sl st, 1dc into next dc, 2dc into next dc, 2ch, [2dc into next dc, 1dc into next dc, 2dc into next dc, 2ch] 7 times, sl st into 3rd of 3ch at beg of round.

4th round: 5ch (count as 1dc, 2ch), skip next dc, 1 bobble into next dc, 2ch, skip 1dc, 1dc into next dc, 2ch, [1dc into next dc, 2ch, skip 1dc, 1 bobble into next dc, 2ch, skip 1dc, 1dc into next dc, 2ch] 7 times, sl st into 3rd of 5ch at beg of round.

5th round: 3ch, 1dc into same st as last sl st, 2dc into first 2ch sp, 1dc into top of next bobble, 2dc into next 2ch sp, 2dc into next dc, 2ch, [2dc into next dc, 2dc into next 2ch sp, 1dc into top of next bobble, 2dc into next 2ch sp, 2dc into next dc, 2ch] 7 times, sl st into 3rd of 3ch at beg of round. Fasten off.

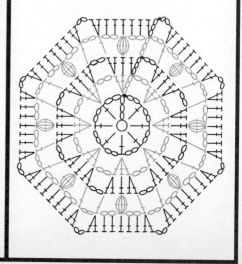 = Bobble

Stitch Variations, Abbreviations and Symbols on pages 7 to 15

Viola

1, 2, 3, 4	—	A
5	—	B
6	—	C
7	—	D
8	—	E

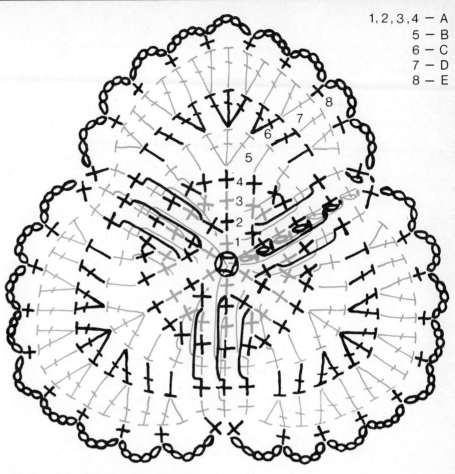

Base ring: Using A, 4ch, join with sl st.

Special Abbreviation

Ssc (Spike single crochet) = insert hook lower than usual (as indicated), yo, draw loop through and up to height of current row, yo, draw through both loops on hook

1st round: 1ch, 6sc into ring, sl st to first sc. (6 sts).

2nd round: 1ch, 2sc into each sc, sl st to first sc. (12 sts).

3rd round: 1ch, 1sc into first st, [2sc into next st, 1sc into next st] 5 times, 2sc into last st, sl st to first sc. (18 sts).

4th round: 1ch, 1sc into first st, [2sc into next st, 1sc into each of next 2 sts] 5 times, 2sc into next st, 1sc into last st, sl st to first sc. (24 sts). Fasten off.

5th round: Using B join into same place, 1ch, then starting in same st as 1ch work *1Ssc inserting hook into base ring, [1Ssc over next st inserting hook to left of last sc, but 1 round higher] twice, 1hdc into next st, 3dc into next st, 1hdc into next st, 1Ssc over next st inserting hook through top of 2nd round, 1Ssc over next st inserting hook through top of 1st round; rep from * twice, sl st to first Ssc. Fasten off.

6th round: Using C join into same place, 1ch, then starting in same st as 1ch work *1Ssc inserting hook between threads of previous Ssc and through top of 1st round, 1Ssc over next st inserting hook between threads of previous Ssc and through top of 2nd round, 1hdc into next st, 1dc into next st, 2dc into next st, 3dc into next st, 2dc into next st, 1dc into next st, 1hdc into next st, 1Ssc over next st inserting hook between threads of 2nd of 5 previous Sscs and 1 round higher; rep from * twice, sl st to first Ssc. Fasten off.

7th round: Using D join into same place, 1ch, starting in same st as 1ch *1Ssc inserting hook between threads of previous Sscs and through top of 2nd round, 1sc into next st, [1hdc, 1dc] into next st, [1dc into next st, 2dc into next st] 4 times, 1dc into next st, [1dc, 1hdc] into next st, 1sc into next st; rep from * twice, sl st to first Ssc. Fasten off.

8th round: Using E join into next st, 1ch, 1sc into same st as 1ch, *[5ch, skip next st, 1sc into next st] 9 times, skip next st**, 1sc into next st; rep from * and from * to ** again, sl st to first sc. Fasten off.

Popcorn Trefoil

Base ring: Using A, 5ch, join with sl st.

1st round: 1ch, 6sc into ring, sl st to first sc. Fasten off.

2nd round: Using B, 1ch, 1sc into same place as 1ch, *3ch, 5dc Popcorn into next st, 3ch**, 1sc into next st; rep from * and from * to ** again, sl st into first sc.

3rd round: 1ch, 1sc into same place as 1ch, *4ch, 2dc into next 3ch arch, dc2tog inserting hook into same ch arch for first leg and into next ch arch for 2nd leg, 2dc into same ch arch, 4ch**, 1sc into next sc; rep from * and from * to ** again, sl st to first sc. Fasten off.

4th round: Using C join into corner cluster, 1ch, 1sc into same place as 1ch, *2ch, skip 2dc, going behind ch arches of 3rd round work [3dc into next ch arch of 2nd round] twice, 2ch, skip 2dc**, 1sc into corner cluster; rep from * and from * to ** again, sl st to first sc. Fasten off.

5th round: Using B join into last 2ch arch of 4th round, 1ch, *[1sc, 1hdc, 1dc] into 2ch arch, 1ch, 1dc into next sc, 1ch, [1dc, 1hdc, 1sc] into next 2ch arch, 1sc into each of next 6dc; rep from * twice, sl st to first sc. Fasten off.

6th round: Using A join into same place, 1ch, 1sc into same place as 1ch, 3ch, 1sc into each of next 2 sts, 3ch, *2sc into next ch sp, 3ch, 3sc into dc at corner, 3ch, 2sc into next ch sp, 3ch**, [1sc into each of next 2 sts, 3ch] 6 times; rep from * and from * to ** again, [1sc into each of next 2 sts, 3ch] 4 times, 1sc into next st, sl st to first sc. Fasten off.

1	—	A	4	—	C
2, 3	—	B	5	—	B
			6	—	A

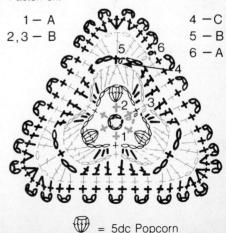

⬦ = 5dc Popcorn

Motifs

Royal Square

Base ring: 16ch, join with sl st.

1st round: 1ch, 24sc into ring, sl st to first sc, (24 sts).

2nd round: 1ch, 1sc into same place as 1ch, *4ch, dtr2tog over next 2 sts, into top of cluster just made work set of 3 leaves as follows: [8ch, 1 quad tr, 7ch, 1sc, 8ch, 1 quin tr, 8ch, 1sc, 7ch, 1 quad tr, 7ch, sl st], 4ch, 1sc into next st of 1st round, 7ch, skip 2 sts, 1sc into next st; rep from * 3 more times, omitting sc at end of last rep, sl st to first sc. Fasten off.

3rd round: Rejoin yarn at tip of 2nd Leaf of next set, in top of 8ch before quin tr work 1ch, 1sc into same place, *2ch, skip quin tr, 1sc into next ch, 5ch, into tip of 3rd Leaf of same set work in same way 1sc just before and 1sc just after quad tr, 7ch, into tip of 1st Leaf of next set work 1sc just before and 1sc just after quad tr, 5ch, into tip of 2nd Leaf of same set work 1sc just before quin tr; rep from * 3 more times, omitting sc at end of last rep, sl st to first sc.

4th round: 1ch, 1sc in same place as 1ch, *3sc into next 2ch sp, 1sc into next sc, 1sc into each of next 5ch, 1sc into each of next 2sc, 1sc into each of next 7ch, 1sc into each of next 2sc, 1sc into each of next 5ch, 1sc into next sc; rep from * 3 more times, omitting sc at end of last rep, sl st to first sc.

5th round: Sl st into each of next 2sc to corner, 4ch (count as 1dc and 1ch), 1dc into same place as 4ch, *[1ch, skip 1 st, 1dc into next st] 13 times to next corner**, [1ch, 1dc] twice all into same place as last dc; rep from * twice more and from * to ** again, ending 1ch, sl st to 3rd of 4ch.

6th round: 4ch (count as 1dc and 1ch), 1dc into same place as 4ch, *[1ch, 1dc into next ch sp] 15 times, 1ch**, [1dc, 1ch, 1dc, 1ch, 1dc] all into next corner st; rep from * twice and from * to ** again, ending 1dc into corner st, 1ch, sl st to 3rd of 4ch.

7th round: 3ch (count as 1dc), 1dc into same place as 3ch, *1ch, [1dc into next ch sp, 1dc into next dc, 1ch, skip 1ch, 1dc into next dc, 1dc into next ch sp, 1ch, skip 1dc] 5 times, 1dc into next ch sp, 1dc into next dc, 1ch, skip 1ch, 1dc into next dc, 1dc into next ch sp, 1ch**, 3dc into corner st; rep from * twice and from * to ** again, ending 1dc into corner st, sl st to top of 3ch.

8th round: 4ch (count as 1dc and 1ch), 1dc into same place as 4ch, *1dc into next dc, [1ch, skip 1ch, 1dc into each of next 2 sts] 13 times to next corner, 1ch**, [1dc, 1ch, 1dc] into same place as last dc; rep from * twice and from * to ** again, ending sl st to 3rd of 4ch.

9th round: 1ch, 2sc into same place as 1ch, 1sc into each ch sp and each dc all round, except 3sc into st at each of next 3 corners and ending 1sc into first corner, sl st to first sc.

10th round: 5ch, dtr2tog all into same place as 5ch (counts as dtr3tog), 2ch, dtr3tog all into same place as last cluster, *5ch, skip 4 sts, dtr3tog all into next st, [5ch, skip 5 sts, dtr3tog all into next st] 6 times, 5ch, skip 4 sts**, [dtr3tog, 2ch, dtr3tog] all into next corner st; rep from * twice and from * to ** again, ending sl st to top of first cluster.

11th round: Sl st to next ch, 8ch, 1sc into 5th ch from hook, 1dc into same 2ch sp, work a picot of [5ch, 1sc into 5th ch from hook], *1dc into next cluster, [picot, skip 2ch, 1dc into next ch, picot, skip 2ch, 1dc into next cluster] 8 times, picot**, [1dc, picot] twice into 2ch sp at corner; rep from * twice more and from * to ** again, ending sl st to 3rd of 8ch.
Fasten off.

Pineapple Square

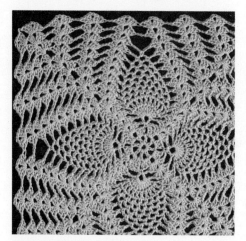

Base ring: 4ch, join with sl st.

1st round: 4ch (count as 1dc and 1ch), [1dc into ring, 1ch] 7 times, sl st to 3rd of 4ch.

2nd round: 5ch (count as 1dc and 2ch), *3dc into next ch sp, 1ch**, 3dc into next sp, 2ch; rep from * twice more and from * to ** again, 2dc into next sp, sl st to 3rd of 5ch.

3rd round: Sl st into next ch, 5ch (count as 1dc and 2ch), 3dc into next sp, *1ch, 1sc into next sp, 1ch**, work a V st of [3dc, 2ch, 3dc] into next 2ch sp; rep from * twice more and from * to ** again, 2dc into next sp, sl st to 3rd of 5ch.

4th round: Sl st into next ch, 5ch (count as 1dc and 2ch), 3dc into next ch sp, *1ch, skip 1ch, work [1dc, 2ch, 1dc] into next sc, 1ch, skip 1ch**, V st into next 2ch sp; rep from * twice more and from * to ** again, 2dc into next sp, sl st to 3rd of 5ch.

5th round: Sl st into next ch, 5ch (count as 1dc and 2ch), 3dc into next sp, *2ch, skip 1ch, 10dc into next 2ch sp, 2ch, skip 1ch**, V st into next sp; rep from * twice more and from * to ** again, 2dc into next sp, sl st to 3rd of 5ch.

6th round: Sl st into next ch, 5ch (count as 1dc and 2ch), 3dc into next sp, *2ch, skip 2ch, 1dc into next dc, [1ch, 1dc into next dc] 9 times, 2ch, skip 2ch**, V st into next

Trefoil Motif

Leaf (make 3 alike)
Base chain: 17ch.

1st row (right side): Skip 2ch (count as 1sc), 1sc into each ch to last ch, work 3sc into last ch for point, then work back along underside of base chain with 1sc into each ch to end, turn.

2nd row: 1ch (counts as 1sc), skip 1 st, 1sc into each st up to st at center of point, work 3sc into center st, 1sc into each st to last 3 sts and tch, turn.

3rd, 4th, 5th, 6th and 7th rows: As 2nd row.

Fasten off.

Stem

Make 22ch (or as required), sl st to center Leaf (2nd) as diagram, work back along base chain in sc and at same time join in side Leaves (1st and 3rd) at, say, 6th and 7th sts as follows: *insert hook through 1st Leaf and base chain, make 1sc, sl st to 3rd Leaf to match; rep from * once more. Continue to end of base chain in sc.

Fasten off.

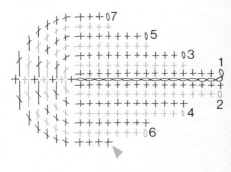

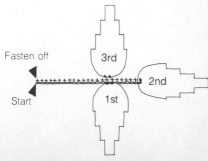

sp; rep from * twice more and from * to ** again, 2dc into next sp, sl st to 3rd of 5ch.

7th round: Sl st into next ch, 5ch (count as 1dc and 2ch), V st into next sp, *2ch, skip 2ch, 1sc into next sp, [3ch, 1sc into next sp] 8 times, 2ch, skip 2ch**, work [V st, 2ch, 3dc] into next sp; rep from * twice more and from * to ** again, 2dc into next sp, sl st to 3rd of 5ch.

8th round: Sl st into each of next 2ch, 5ch (count as 1dc and 2ch), skip 3dc, *V st into next sp, 2ch, skip 2ch, 1sc into next 3ch arch, [3ch, 1sc into next sp] 7 times, 2ch, skip 2ch**, V st into next sp, 2ch; rep from * twice more and from * to ** again, work [3dc, 2ch, 2dc] into next sp, sl st to 3rd of 5ch.

9th round: Sl st into next ch, 5ch (count as 1dc and 2ch), 3dc into next sp, *V st into next sp, 2ch, skip 2ch, 1sc into next 3ch arch, [3ch, 1sc into next 3ch arch] 6 times, 2ch, skip 2ch, V st into next sp**, V st into next sp; rep from * twice more and from * to ** again, 2dc into next sp, sl st to 3rd of 5ch.

10th round: Sl st into next ch, 5ch (count as 1dc and 2ch), V st into next sp, *2ch, V st into next sp, 2ch, skip 2ch, 1sc into next 3ch arch, [3ch, 1sc into next 3ch arch] 5 times, 2ch, skip 2ch, V st into next sp, 2ch**, work [V st, 2ch, 3dc] into next sp; rep from * twice more and from * to ** again, 2dc into next sp, sl st to 3rd of 5ch.

11th round: Sl st into each of next 2ch, 5ch (count as 1dc and 2ch), skip 3dc, *[V st into next sp, 2ch, skip 2ch] twice, 1sc into next 3ch arch, [3ch, 1sc into next 3ch arch] 4 times, [2ch, skip 2ch, V st into next sp] twice**, 2ch; rep from * twice more and from * to ** again omitting 1dc at end of last rep and ending sl st to 3rd of 5ch.

12th round: Sl st into next ch, 5ch (count as 1dc and 2ch), 3dc into next sp, *[V st into next sp, 2ch, skip 2ch] twice, 1sc into next 3ch arch, [3ch, 1sc into next 3ch arch] 3 times, [2ch, skip 2ch, V st into next sp] twice**, V st into next sp; rep from * twice more and from * to ** again, 2dc into next sp, sl st to 3rd of 5ch.

13th round: Sl st into next ch, 5ch (count as 1dc and 2ch), V st into next sp, *2ch, [V st into next sp, 2ch, skip 2ch] twice, 1sc into next 3ch arch, [3ch, 1sc into next 3ch arch] twice, [2ch, skip 2ch, V st into next sp] twice, 2ch**, work [V st, 2ch, 3dc] into next sp; rep from * twice more and from * to ** again, 2dc into next sp, sl st to 3rd of 5ch.

14th round: Sl st into each of next 2ch, 5ch (count as 1dc and 2ch), skip 3dc, *[V st into next sp, 2ch, skip 2ch] 3 times, 1sc into next 3ch arch, 3ch, 1sc into next 3ch arch, [2ch, skip 2ch, V st into next sp] 3 times**, 2ch; rep from * twice more and from * to ** again omitting 1dc at end of last rep and ending sl st to 3rd of 5ch.

15th round: Sl st into next ch, 5ch (count as 1dc and 2ch), 3dc into next sp, *[V st into next sp, 2ch, skip 2ch] twice, V st into next sp, 3ch, skip 2ch, 1sc into next 3ch arch, 3ch, skip 2ch, V st into next sp, [2ch, skip 2ch, V st into next sp] twice**, V st into next sp; rep from * twice more and from * to ** again, 2dc into next sp, sl st to 3rd of 5ch.

16th round: Sl st into next ch, 5ch (count as 1dc and 2ch), V st into next sp, *2ch, [V st into next sp, 2ch, skip 2ch] twice, V st into next sp, 2ch, skip 3ch, 1sc and 3ch, [V st into next 2ch sp, 2ch, skip 2ch] twice, V st into next sp, 2ch**, work [V st, 2ch, 3dc] into next sp, rep from * twice more and from * to ** again, 2dc into next sp, sl st to 3rd of 5ch.

Motifs

Bachelor's Buttonhole

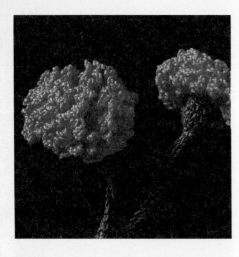

Base ring: Using A, 4ch, join with sl st.
Special Abbreviations
Ldc (Linked double crochet) = insert hook down through horizontal loop round stem of last st made, yo, draw loop through; insert hook as indicated to make st and complete normally.
Note: At beginning of round to make first Ldc treat 2nd ch of starting ch as horizontal loop.
Ldtr (Linked Double Treble) = insert hook down through uppermost of 3 horizontal loops round stem of last st made, yo, draw loop through, [insert hook down through next lower horizontal loop, yo, draw loop through] twice; insert hook as indicated to make st and complete normally.
Note: at beginning of round to make first Ldtr treat 2nd, 3rd and 4th chs of starting ch as horizontal loops.
1st round: 3ch (count as 1dc), 5Ldc into ring, sl st to top of 3ch. (6 sts).
2nd round: 5ch (count as 1dtr), 1Ldtr into first st, [2Ldtr into next st] 5 times, sl st to top of 5ch. (12 sts). Fasten off A.
3rd round: Using B, 1ch, 1sc into each st all round, sl st to first sc.
4th round: As 3rd round.
5th round: 1ch, 2sc into first st, 3sc into each st all round, 1sc into same place as first 2sc, sl st to first sc. (36 sts).
6th round: 3ch (count as 1dc), 2dc into first st, 3dc into each st all round, sl st to top of 3ch, 108 sts. Turn.
7th round (wrong side): 1ch, 1sc into first st, 5ch, *1sc into next st, 5ch; rep from * all round, ending sl st to first sc. (108 arches). Fasten off.

Stem: Rejoin A at underside of flower head into base ring, make 20ch (or as required), 1sc into 2nd ch from hook, 1sc into next and each ch, sl st to opposite side of base ring; now work back down stem in sl st, twisting stem as you go to create interest. Fasten off.

Lace Triangle

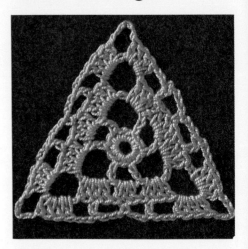

Base ring: Wrap yarn round finger.
1st round: 1ch, 12sc into ring, sl st to first sc.
2nd round: 10ch (count as 1dc and 7ch arch), skip first 2sc, *1dc into next sc, 3ch, skip 1sc, 1dc into next sc, 7ch, skip 1sc; rep from * once, 1dc into next sc, 3ch, skip last sc, sl st to 3rd of 10ch.
3rd round: 3ch (count as 1dc), into next ch arch work [3dc, 7ch, 4dc], *3dc into next ch arch, [4dc, 7ch, 4dc] into next ch arch; rep from * once, 3dc into last ch arch, sl st to top of 3ch.
4th round: 6ch (count as 1dc and 3ch arch), *[4dc, 5ch, 4dc] into next 7ch arch, 3ch, skip 2dc, 1dc into next dc, 3ch, skip 2dc, 1sc into next dc, 3ch**, skip 2dc, 1dc into next dc, 3ch; rep from * once and from * to ** again, sl st to 3rd of 6ch. Fasten off.

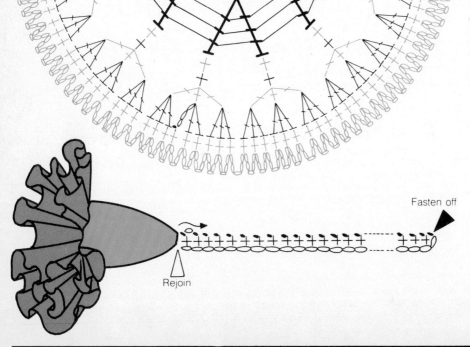

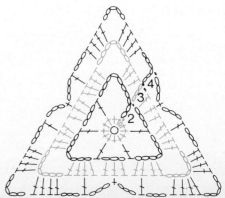

Stitch Variations, Abbreviations and Symbols on pages 7 to 15

Irish Crochet

True Irish crochet is made by first working motifs and then creating a net or mesh background incorporating the motifs and forming the fabric which holds them in position. This is done by placing the motifs in the required position face down on paper or a scrap of fabric and temporarily securing them. The background or filling, is then worked progressively joining in the motifs, after the work is completed the paper or fabric is carefully removed.

Historically crochet is believed to have been introduced into Ireland in the early part of the 19th century by nuns, probably from Italy or France. It was evolved by them and convent-educated girls into an art-form in itself, reaching levels of complexity and delicacy not seen in other styles of crochet work.

Stitches and techniques were developed which are particular to Irish crochet. The use of padding threads which are held at the edge of the work, so that subsequent rows or rounds are worked over them to give a three-dimensional effect is one example, another is the Clones Knot, and both of these are described below.

Because of the difficulty of giving general instructions for the construction of true Irish crochet, and particularly since the various motifs can each be incorporated into almost any crocheted net background, we have simplified the following selection to give you a taste of Irish style crochet.

Padding Threads

Padding threads are used to give a three-dimensional appearance to some Irish crochet motifs. The thread used is usually the same as the thread used for the motif and the number of threads worked over determines the amount of padding. In this book we have usually worked over three thicknesses of thread.

The example below is for padding threads at the beginning of a motif, but they can also be used in other areas of motifs (see Tristar on page 141).

1. Make the required number of chain and join with a slip stitch.

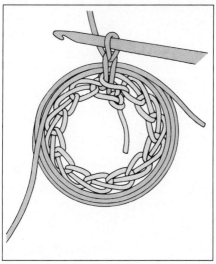

2. Wind a length of thread three or four times around the end of a pencil or finger and hold against the chain.

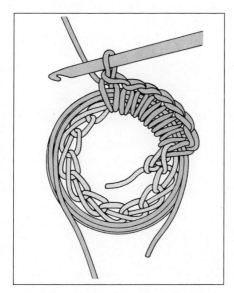

3. The stitches are then worked over the chain and 'padding' threads.

When the motif is complete the ends of the padding thread are pulled through several stitches and cut.

The instructions and diagrams of individual patterns indicate where it is appropriate to use padding threads. On the diagrams the padding thread is indicated with a thicker line.

Working into Base of Stitch

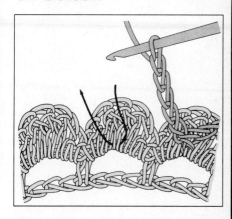

Insert the hook under two strands at the base of the stitch (this is indicated on the diagrams by red arrows see Tea Rose I on page 144). The diagram above shows work viewed from the back.

Clones Knot

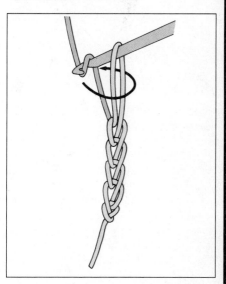

1. Draw up a chain. The length of the chain dictates the size of the Clones Knot.

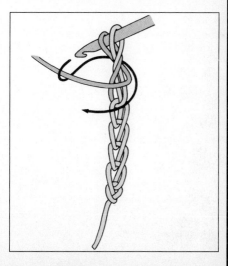

2. Holding chain in place, yarn over. Twist the hook over then under the loop.

Irish Style Crochet

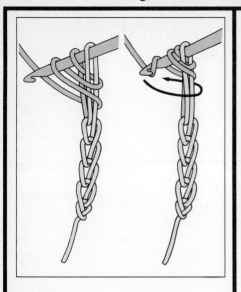

3. Pull the yarn back under the loop with the hook.

4. Repeat steps 2 and 3 until loop is completely covered.

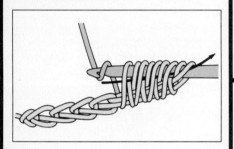

5. Yarn over, draw hook through all the loops.

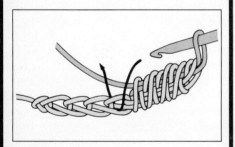

6. Secure knot by working a single crochet into the last chain worked before Clones Knot.

The Clones Knot can be secured in different ways, see individual pattern for instructions.

Filament

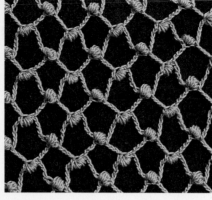

Starting chain: Multiple of 8 sts + 2.

Special Abbreviation

Clones Knot = draw up a chain to required length and hold it in place, *yarn over, twist hook over then under the loop, then pull the yarn back under the loop with the hook; rep from * until the loop is completely covered. Yo, draw hook through all loops on hook. To secure knot work 1sc into last ch before Clones Knot.

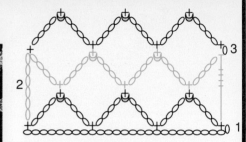

⚓ = Clones Knot

1st row (right side): Work 1sc into 2nd ch from hook, *4ch, 1 Clones Knot, 4ch, skip 7ch, 1sc into next ch; rep from * to end, turn.

2nd row: 10ch (count as 1ttr, 4ch), working behind first Clones Knot work 1sc into sc securing knot, *4ch, 1 Clones Knot, 4ch, 1sc into sc securing next Clones Knot as before; rep from * ending with 4ch, 1ttr into last sc, turn.

3rd row: 1ch, 1sc into ttr, *4ch, 1 Clones Knot, 4ch, working behind next Clones Knot work 1sc into sc securing knot; rep from * to end placing last sc into 6th of 10ch at beg of previous row, turn.

Rep 2nd and 3rd rows.

Chainlink

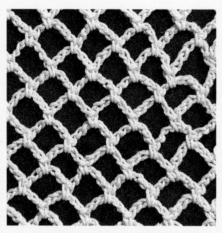

Starting chain: Multiple of 4 sts + 2.

1st row (right side): Work 1sc into 2nd ch from hook, *6ch, skip 3ch, 1sc into next ch; rep from * to end, turn.

2nd row: 8ch (count as 1dtr, 3ch), 1sc into first 6ch arch, *6ch, 1sc into next 6ch arch; rep from * to end, 3ch, 1dtr into last sc, turn.

3rd row: 1ch, 1sc into first dtr, *6ch, 1sc into next 6ch arch; rep from * to end placing last sc into 5th of 8ch at beg of previous row, turn.

Rep 2nd and 3rd rows.

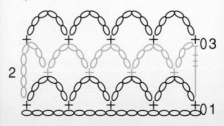

Coathanger

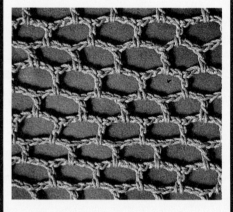

Starting chain: Multiple of 5 sts + 7.

1st row (right side): Work 1dc into 12th ch from hook, *4ch, skip 4ch, 1dc into next ch; rep from * to end, turn.

2nd row: 6ch (count as 1tr, 2ch), 1dc into next 4ch sp, *4ch, 1dc into next 4ch sp; rep from * to end, 2ch, 1tr into 5th ch, turn.

3rd row: 7ch (count as 1dc, 4ch), *1dc into next 4ch sp, 4ch; rep from * to last sp, 1dc into 4th of 6ch at beg of previous row, turn.

Rep 2nd and 3rd rows.

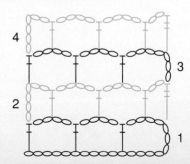

Stitch Variations, Abbreviations and Symbols on pages 7 to 15

Open Diamond

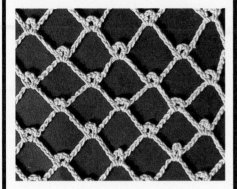

Starting chain: Multiple of 7 sts + 6.

1st row (right side): Work 1sc into 6th ch from hook, 10ch, skip 6ch, *into next ch work [1sc, 4ch, 1sc], 10ch, skip 6ch; rep from * to last ch, into last ch work [1sc, 2ch, 1dc], turn.

2nd row: 11ch (count as 1ttr, 5ch), into next 10ch arch work [1sc, 4ch, 1sc], *10ch, into next 10ch arch work [1sc, 4ch, 1sc]; rep from * to end, 5ch, 1ttr into 3rd of 5ch at beg of previous row, turn.

3rd row: 5ch (count as 1dc, 2ch), 1sc into first arch, 10ch, *into next 10ch arch work [1sc, 4ch, 1sc], 10ch; rep from * to last arch, into last arch work [1sc, 2ch, 1dc], turn.

Rep 2nd and 3rd rows.

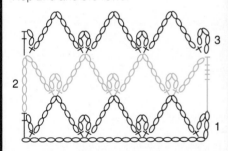

Daisy Time

Special Abbreviation

Dc2tog = work 1dc into each of next 2sc until 1 loop of each remains on hook, yo and through all 3 loops on hook.

Make 6ch, sl st into first ch to form a ring.

1st round: 1ch, work 15sc into ring, sl st into first sc.

2nd round: [3ch, dc2tog over next 2sc, 3ch, sl st into next sc] 5 times placing last sl st into first sc of previous round. Fasten off.

Time Warp

Starting chain: Multiple of 5 sts + 2.

1st row (right side): Work 1sc into 2nd ch from hook, 1sc into each ch to end, turn.

2nd row: 1ch, 1sc into each of first 2sc, *5ch, skip 2sc, 1sc into each of next 3sc; rep from * to end omitting 1sc at end of last rep, turn.

3rd row: 1ch, 1sc into first sc, *5sc into next 5ch arch, skip 1sc, 1sc into next sc; rep from * to end, turn.

Four Petal

Special Abbreviation

Bobble = work 3tr into next sc until 1 loop of each remains on hook, yo and through all 4 loops on hook.

Make 5ch, sl st into first ch to form a ring.

1st round: 1ch, work 12sc into ring, sl st into first sc.

2nd round: *4ch, work 1 bobble into next sc, 4ch, sl st into each of next 2sc; rep from * 3 times more omitting 1 sl st at end of last rep, 7ch, work 1sc into 2nd ch from hook, 1sc into each of next 5ch, sl st into first sc on first round. Fasten off.

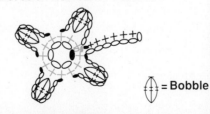

╫ = Bobble

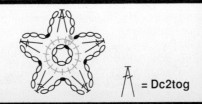

A = Dc2tog

4th row: 6ch (count as 1tr, 2ch), skip first 2sc, 1sc into each of next 3sc, *5ch, skip 3sc, 1sc into each of next 3sc; rep from * to last 2sc, 2ch, 1tr into last sc, turn.

5th row: 1ch, 1sc into first tr, 2sc into 2ch sp, skip 1sc, 1sc into next sc, *5sc into next 5ch arch, skip 1sc, 1sc into next sc; rep from * to last 2ch sp, 2sc into last sp. 1sc into 4th of 4ch at beg of previous row. turn.

6th row: 1ch, 1sc into each of first 2sc, *5ch, skip 3sc, 1sc into each of next 3sc; rep from * to end omitting 1sc at end of last rep, turn.

Rep 3rd to 6th rows.

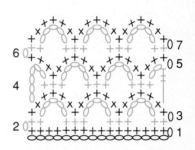

Trellis Stitch

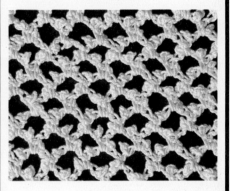

Starting chain: Multiple of 5 sts + 2.

1st row (right side): Work 1sc into 2nd ch from hook, *[4ch, 1sc into 3rd ch from hook] twice, 1ch, skip 4ch, 1sc into next ch; rep from * to end, turn.

2nd row: 9ch (count as 1dtr, 4ch), 1sc into 3rd ch from hook, 1ch, 1sc into center of first arch, *[4ch, 1sc into 3rd ch from hook] twice, 1ch, 1sc into center of next arch; rep from * to end, 4ch, 1sc into 3rd ch from hook, 1ch, 1dtr into last sc, turn.

3rd row: 1ch, 1sc into first dtr, *[4ch, 1sc into 3rd ch from hook] twice, 1ch, 1sc into center of next arch; rep from * to end placing last sc into 5th of 9ch at beg of previous row, turn.

Rep 2nd and 3rd rows.

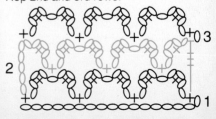

⊕ = 3ch, 1sc into first of these ch.

Irish Style Crochet

Diamond Cluster

3 0 +
1
4
2

Line shows the direction of work for first two rows.

= sl st into next st, [7ch, sl st into same st as last sl st] 3 times.

The starting chain for this pattern forms part of the first row, and continues to form part of the second row.

1st row (right side): Make 16ch, sl st into 8th ch from hook, [7ch, sl st into same ch as last sl st] twice, *23ch, sl st into 8th ch from hook, [7ch, sl st into same ch as last sl st] twice; rep from * the number of times required, (one repeat is shown in the diagram), make 8ch and turn work ready for
2nd row: make 7 more ch, sl st into 8th ch from hook, 7ch, sl st into same ch as last sl st, 7ch, skip next 7ch loop, 1sc into next 7ch loop, *7ch, skip 7ch on previous row, sl st into next ch, [7ch, sl st into same ch as last sl st] 3 times, 7ch, skip next 7ch loop, 1sc into next 7ch loop; rep from * to last 8ch, 7ch, skip 7ch, into last ch work [1 sl st, 7ch, 1 sl st, 4ch, 1tr], turn.

3rd row: 1ch, 1sc into first tr, *7ch, 1 sl st into next sc, [7ch, 1 sl st into same sc as last sl st] 3 times, 7ch, skip next 7ch loop, 1sc into next 7ch loop; rep from * to end, turn.

4th row: [7ch, sl st into first sc] twice, 7ch, skip next 7ch loop, 1sc into next 7ch loop, *7ch, sl st into next sc, [7ch, sl st into same sc as last sl st] 3 times, 7ch, skip next 7ch loop, 1sc into next 7ch loop; rep from * to last sc, 7ch, into last sc work [1 sl st, 7ch, 1 sl st, 4ch, 1tr], turn.
Rep 3rd and 4th rows.

= 3 loop cluster

= Padding thread

Roulette Wheel

Special Abbreviation

3 loop cluster = 7ch, sl st into first of these ch, [6ch, sl st into same ch as last sl st] twice.

Make 8ch, sl st into first ch to form a ring.

1st round: 1ch, working into ring and over

padding threads, work 18sc, sl st into first sc.

2nd round: 6ch (count as 1hdc, 4ch), skip first 3sc, 1hdc into next sc, [4ch, skip 2sc, 1hdc into next sc] 4 times, 4ch, sl st into 2nd of 6ch at beg of round.

3rd round: 1ch, work [1sc, 1hdc, 3dc, 1hdc, 1sc] into each of the 6 4ch arches, sl st into first sc. (6 petals).

4th round: Working behind each petal, sl st into base of each of first 4 sts, [5ch, skip next 6 sts, sl st into base of next dc] 6 times, working last sl st into base of same dc as sl st at beg of round.

5th round: 1ch, work [1sc, 1hdc, 1dc, 5tr, 1dc, 1hdc, 1sc] into each of the 6 5ch arches, sl st into first sc.

6th round: Working behind each petal, sl st into base of each of first 6 sts, [6ch, skip next 10 sts, sl st into base of next tr] 5 times, 3ch, skip next 10 sts, 1tr into base of next tr.

7th round: Sl st into arch just formed, into

same arch work [1sc, 6ch, 1sc], 6ch, *into next arch work [1sc, 6ch, 1sc], 6ch; rep from * 4 times more, sl st into first sc.

8th round: Sl st into each of first 3ch of 6ch loop, into same loop work [1sc, 6ch, 1sc], 6ch, 1sc into next 6ch arch, 6ch, *into next 6ch loop work [1sc, 6ch, 1sc], 6ch, 1sc into next 6ch arch, 6ch; rep from * 4 times more, sl st into first sc.

9th round: Sl st into each of first 3ch of 6ch loop, into same loop work [1sc, 6ch, 1sc], 6ch, [1sc into next 6ch arch, 6ch] twice, *into next 6ch loop work [1sc, 6ch, 1sc], 6ch, [1sc into next 6ch arch, 6ch] twice; rep from * 4 times more, sl st into first sc.

10th round: Sl st into each of first 3ch of first 6ch loop, into same loop work [1sc, 3 loop cluster, 1sc], 6ch, [1sc into next 6ch arch, 6ch] 3 times, *into next 6ch loop work [1sc, 3 loop cluster, 1sc], 6ch, [1sc into next 6ch arch, 6ch] 3 times; rep from * 4 times more, sl st into first sc. Fasten off.

Stitch Variations, Abbreviations and Symbols on pages 7 to 15

Irish Style Crochet

Tristar

2nd round: *1ch, working into next 9ch loop and over **padding threads** work [2sc, 1hdc, 11dc, 1hdc, 2sc], 1ch, sl st into same ch as sl sts of first round; rep from * twice more.

3rd round: Sl st into each of first 9 sts of first loop, [16ch, skip first 8 sts on next loop, sl st into next dc] twice, 16ch, sl st into same dc as last sl st at beg of round.

4th round: 1ch, working over **padding threads**, work 1sc into same dc as last sl st of previous round, 19sc into first 16ch arch, [1sc into same dc as next sl st of previous round, 19sc into next 16ch arch] twice, sl st into first sc. 60sc.

5th round: 8ch (count as 1dc, 5ch), skip next 3sc, [1dc into next sc, 5ch, skip 3sc] 14 times, sl st into 3rd of 8ch at beg of round.

6th round: Sl st into first 3ch of first arch, 1ch, working over **padding threads** work 4sc into first arch, 7sc into each of next 14 arches, 3sc into same arch as first 4sc, sl st into first sc.

7th round: 6ch, [skip next 6sc, sl st into next sc] 14 times, 6ch, sl st into same sc as last sl st of previous round.

8th round: 1ch, into each 6ch arch and over **padding threads** work 2sc, [1 picot, 2sc] 3 times. Sl st into first sc and fasten off.

Special Abbreviation
Picot = make 3ch, sl st into first of these ch.

1st round: Make 10ch, sl st into first ch, [9ch, sl st into same ch as last sl st] twice (3 loops formed).

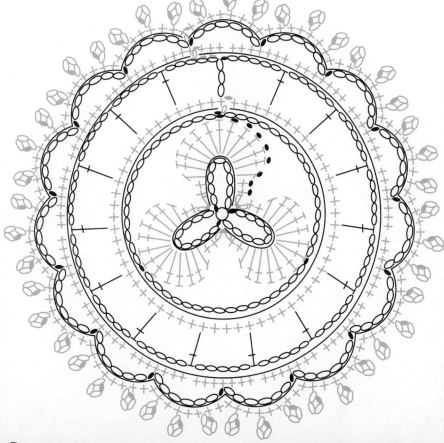

Pin Wheel

Make 6ch, sl st into first ch to form a ring and continue as follows:
1ch, work [1sc, 12ch] 12 times into ring, sl st into first sc. Fasten off.

= Picot   —— = Padding thread

Irish Style Crochet

Magic Circle

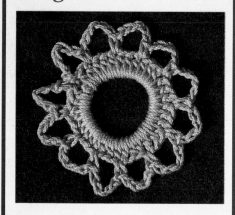

Make 16ch, sl st into first ch to form a ring.

1st round: 2ch (count as 1hdc), work 35hdc into ring and over **padding threads**, sl st into 2nd of 2ch at beg of round.

2nd round: 1ch, work 1sc into same st as last sl st, [5ch, skip 2hdc, 1sc into next hdc] 11 times, 5ch, sl st into first sc. Fasten off.

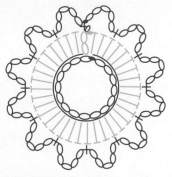

──── = Padding thread

Green Leaf

Special Abbreviation

Picot = make 3ch, sl st into first of these ch.

Make 15ch and work in a spiral as follows:
1sc into 2nd ch from hook, working 1 st into each ch work 1hdc, 3dc, 4tr, 3dc, 1hdc and 1sc, 3ch, then working 1 st into each ch on other side of starting chain work 1sc, 1hdc, 3dc, 4tr, 3dc, 1hdc, 1sc, 1sc into first sc at beg of spiral, 1sc into next hdc, 1 picot, [1sc into each of next 2 sts, 1 picot] 6 times, into 3ch sp at point of leaf work [1sc, 4ch, sl st into 3rd ch from hook, 1ch, 1sc], [1 picot, 1sc into each of next 2 sts] 7 times, sl st into 3ch sp. Fasten off.

Fine Branches

Spring Time

Make 5ch, sl st into first ch to form a ring.

1st round: 1ch, work 10sc into ring, sl st into first sc.

2nd round: 1ch, work 1sc into each sc, sl st into first sc.

3rd round: 2ch (count as 1hdc), skip first sc, work 2hdc into each of next 9sc, 1hdc into first sc, sl st into 2nd of 2ch.

4th round: *2ch, **working into front loop only** of each hdc work 2dc into each of next 3hdc, 2ch, sl st into next hdc; rep from * 4 times more placing last sl st into 2nd of 2ch at beg of previous round. (5 petals made).

5th round: Working behind each petal of previous round and **into back loop** of each hdc on 3rd round, sl st into first 2hdc, *4ch, work 2dtr into each of next 3hdc, 4ch, sl st into next hdc; rep from * 3 times more, 4ch, 2dtr into next hdc, 2dtr into 2nd of 2ch at beg of 3rd round, 2dtr into next hdc, 4ch, sl st into next hdc. Fasten off.

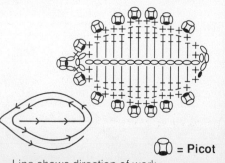

⬡ = Picot

Line shows direction of work.

$\bigvee$ 2dc into **front loop only** of next st. On final round work into back loop only of hdc on 3rd round.

Stitch Variations, Abbreviations and Symbols on pages 7 to 15

Irish Style Crochet

Make 7ch, sl st into first ch to form a ring.

1st round: 1ch, work 16sc into ring, sl st into first sc.

2nd round: 1ch, 1sc into first sc, [5ch, skip 1sc, 1sc into next sc] 7 times, 5ch, sl st into first sc.

3rd round: Sl st into first 5ch arch, 1ch, work [1sc, 5hdc, 1sc] into each 5ch arch to end, sl st into first sc. (8 petals).

4th round: 1ch, working behind each petal work 1sc into first sc on 2nd round, [6ch, 1sc into next sc on 2nd round] 7 times, 6ch, sl st into first sc.

5th round: Sl st into first 6ch arch, 1ch, work [1sc, 6hdc, 1sc] into each 6ch arch to end, sl st into first sc.

6th round: 1ch, working behind each pet-al work 1sc into first sc on 4th round, [7ch, 1sc into next sc on 4th round] 7 times, 7ch, sl st into first sc.

7th round: Sl st into first 7ch arch, 1ch, work [1sc, 7hdc, 1sc] into each 7ch arch to end, sl st into first sc.

8th round: 1ch, working behind each pet-al work 1sc into first sc on 6th round, *[9ch, sl st into 6th ch from hook (1 picot made)] twice, 4ch, 1sc into next sc on 6th round, [13ch, sl st into 6th ch from hook (1 picot made)] twice, 8ch, 1sc into same sc as last sc, [9ch, sl st into 6th ch from hook] twice, 4ch, 1sc into next sc on 6th round; rep from * 3 times more omitting 1sc at end of last rep, sl st into first sc.

9th round: Sl st into each of first 3ch, behind first picot and into next ch of arch between picots, 1ch, 1sc into same arch as sl st, **[10ch, sl st into 6th ch from hook] twice, 5ch, 1sc into corner loop between 2 picots, *[10ch, sl st into 6th ch from hook] twice, 5ch, 1sc into arch be-tween 2 picots; rep from * once more; rep from ** 3 times more omitting 1sc at end of last rep, sl st into first sc.

10th round: Sl st into each of first 4ch, behind first picot and into next 2ch of arch between 2 picots, 1ch, 1sc into same arch between 2 picots, **[10ch, sl st into 6th ch from hook] twice, 5ch, 1sc into next sc at top of loop, *[10ch, sl st into 6th ch from hook] twice, 5ch, 1sc into next arch be-tween 2 picots; rep from * twice more; rep from ** 3 times more omitting 1sc at end of last rep, sl st into first sc. Fasten off.

Irish Style Crochet

Tea Rose I

Make 8ch, sl st into first ch to form a ring.

1st round: 1ch, work 16sc into ring, sl st into first sc.

2nd round: 5ch (count as 1dc, 2ch), skip next sc, [1dc into next sc, 2ch, skip 1sc] 7 times, sl st into 3rd of 5ch at beg of round.

3rd round: Sl st into 2ch sp, 1ch, work [1sc, 1hdc, 1dc, 1hdc, 1sc] into each of the 8 2ch sps, sl st into first sc. (8 petals).

4th round: Working behind each petal, sl st into base of each of next 2 sts, 1ch, 1sc into base of same dc as last sl st, [3ch, skip 4 sts, 1sc into base of next dc] 7 times, 3ch, sl st into first sc.

5th round: Sl st into 3ch arch, 1ch, work [1sc, 1hdc, 3dc, 1hdc, 1sc] into each of the 8 3ch arches, sl st into first sc.

6th round: Working behind each petal, sl st into base of each of next 3 sts, 1ch, 1sc into base of same dc as last sl st, [5ch, skip 6 sts, 1sc into base of next dc] 7 times, 5ch, sl st into first sc.

7th round: Sl st into 5ch arch, 1ch, work [1sc, 1hdc, 5dc, 1hdc, 1sc] into each of the 8 5ch arches, sl st into first sc.

8th round: Working behind each petal, sl st into base of each of next 4 sts, 1ch, 1sc into base of same dc as last sl st, [7ch, skip 8 sts, 1sc into base of next dc] 7 times, 7ch, sl st into first sc.

9th round: Sl st into 7ch arch, 1ch, work [1sc, 1hdc, 7dc, 1hdc, 1sc] into each of the 8 7ch arches, sl st into first sc.

10th round: Working behind each petal, sl st into base of each of next 5 sts, 1ch, 1sc into base of same dc as last sl st, [9ch, skip 10 sts, 1sc into base of next dc] 7 times, 9ch, sl st into first sc.

11th round: Sl st into 9ch arch, 1ch, work [1sc, 1hdc, 9dc, 1hdc, 1sc] into each of the 8 9ch arches, sl st into first sc. Fasten off.

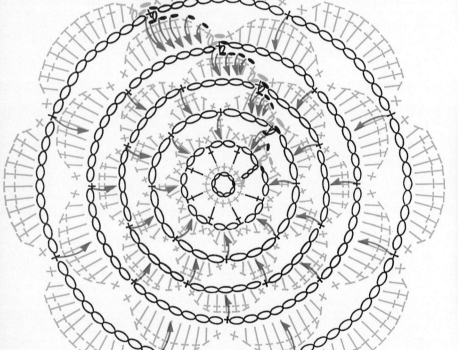

Tea Rose II

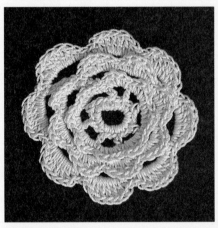

Work as given for 1st to 7th round of Tea Rose I. Fasten off.

Twisting

Starting chain: Any number of sts, plus 3.

Note: Sample photographed has starting chain of 31 sts.

Work 2dc into 4th ch from hook, 3dc into each ch to end. Fasten off.

Stitch Variations, Abbreviations and Symbols on pages 7 to 15

Windmills

Make 6ch, sl st into first ch to form a ring.

1st round: 3ch (count as 1dc), work 17dc into ring and over **padding threads**, sl st into 3rd of 3ch at beg of round.

2nd round: 8ch (count as 1dc, 5ch), [1dc into next dc, 5ch] 17 times, sl st into 3rd of 8ch at beg of round.

3rd round: Sl st into each of next 3ch of first arch, 1ch, into same ch as last sl st work [1sc, 1ch, 1sc], *2sc into 2nd part of arch and 2sc into first part of next arch, into center ch of arch work [1sc, 1ch, 1sc]; rep from * 16 times more, 2sc into 2nd part of last arch, 2sc into first part of first arch, sl st into first sc.

4th round: Sl st into first ch sp, 1ch, into same sp as last sl st work [1sc, 1ch, 1sc], 1sc into each of next 6sc, *into next ch sp work [1sc, 1ch, 1sc], 1sc into each of next 6sc; rep from * 16 times more, sl st into first sc.

5th round: Sl st into first ch sp, 1ch, into same sp as last sl st work [1sc, 1ch, 1sc], 1sc into each of next 8sc, *into next ch sp work [1sc, 1ch, 1sc], 1sc into each of next 8sc; rep from * 16 times more, sl st into first sc.

6th round: Sl st into first ch sp, 1ch, into same sp as last sl st work [1sc, 1ch, 1sc], 1sc into each of next 10sc, *into next ch sp work [1sc, 1ch, 1sc], 1sc into each of next 10sc; rep from * 16 times more, sl st into first sc.

7th round: Sl st into first ch sp, 1ch, work 1sc into same sp as last sl st, 5ch, [1sc into next ch sp, 5ch] 17 times, sl st into first sc.

8th round: 1ch, 1sc into first sc of previous round, 3ch, 1sc into next 5ch arch, [3ch, 1sc into next sc, 3ch, 1sc into next 5ch arch] 17 times, 3ch, sl st into first sc.

9th round: Sl st into first ch of first 3ch arch, 1ch, 1sc into same arch as last sl st, *4ch, 1sc into next 3ch arch; rep from * to end, 4ch, sl st into first sc.

10th round: Sl st into each of first 2ch of first 4ch arch, 1ch, 1sc into same arch as last sl sts, *5ch, 1sc into next 4ch arch; rep from * to end, 5ch, sl st into first sc. Fasten off.

—— = Padding thread

An enlargement of the area within the red frame showing in detail the stitches represented by the dotted lines on the main diagram.

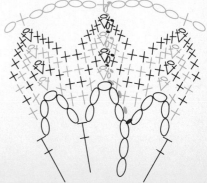

Irish Style Crochet

Solar System

Showtime

Special Abbreviation

Picot = make 3ch, sl st into first of these ch.

Make 10ch, sl st into first ch to form a ring.

1st round: 1ch, into ring work 5sc, 1 picot, [8sc, 1 picot] twice, 3sc, sl st into first sc.

2nd round: 1ch, 1sc into same st as last sl st, *12ch, skip [4sc, 1 picot, 3sc], 1sc into next sc; rep from * once more, 12ch, sl st into first sc.

3rd round: Sl st into first 12ch arch, 1ch, into each of the 3 arches work [1sc, 1hdc, 2dc, 9tr, 2dc, 1hdc, 1sc], sl st into first sc.

4th round: *1ch, 1sc into next hdc, 1ch, [1dc into next st, 1ch] 13 times, 1sc into next hdc, 1ch, sl st into each of next 2sc; rep from * twice more omitting 1 sl st at end of last rep.

5th round: Sl st into each of first [sl st, ch sp, sc and ch sp], 1ch, into same ch sp as last sl st work [1sc, 4ch, 1sc], into each of next 13 ch sps work [1sc, 4ch, 1sc], *1ch, sl st into each of next [sc, ch sp, 2 sl sts, ch sp, sc and ch sp], 1ch, into same sp as last sl st work [1sc, 4ch, 1sc], into each of next 13 ch sps work [1sc, 4ch, 1sc]; rep from * once more, 1ch, sl st into each of last [sc, ch sp and sl st]. Fasten off.

Make 8ch, sl st into first ch to form a ring.

1st round: 1ch, work 15sc into ring, sl st into first sc.

2nd round: 5ch, skip first 3sc, [sl st into next sc, 5ch, skip 2sc] 4 times, sl st into sl st at end of previous round.

3rd round: Sl st into first 5ch arch, 1ch, into same arch and each of next 4 arches work [1sc, 1hdc, 5dc, 1hdc, 1sc], sl st into first sc. (5 petals).

4th round: 1ch, working behind each petal of previous round, work 1 sl st into last sl st on 2nd round, 8ch, [1 sl st into next sl st on 2nd round, 8ch] 4 times, sl st into same st as first sl st at beg of round.

5th round: Sl st into first 8ch arch, 1ch, into same arch and each of next 4 arches work [1sc, 1hdc, 8dc, 1hdc, 1sc], sl st into first sc.

6th round: 2ch, working behind each petal of previous round work 1 sl st into last sl st on 2nd round, 10ch, [1 sl st into next sl st on 2nd round, 10ch] 4 times, sl st into same st as first sl st at beg of round.

7th round: Sl st into first 10ch arch, 1ch, work 15sc into same arch and into each of next 4 arches, sl st into first sc.

8th round: Sl st into next sc, *[4ch, skip 1sc, sl st into next sc] 6 times, turn, work 2 sl sts into first 4ch arch, [4ch, sl st into next 4ch arch] 5 times, turn, work 2 sl sts into first 4ch arch, [4ch, sl st into next 4ch arch] 4 times, turn, work 2 sl sts into first 4ch arch, [4ch, sl st into next 4ch arch] 3 times, turn, work 2 sl sts into first 4ch arch, [4ch, sl st into next 4ch arch] twice, turn, work 2 sl sts into first 4ch arch, 4ch, sl st into next arch and fasten off*. [Turn, skip next 2sc on 7th round, rejoin yarn to next sc and rep from * to *] 4 times.

⊞ = Picot

Stitch Variations, Abbreviations and Symbols on pages 7 to 15

Irish Style Crochet

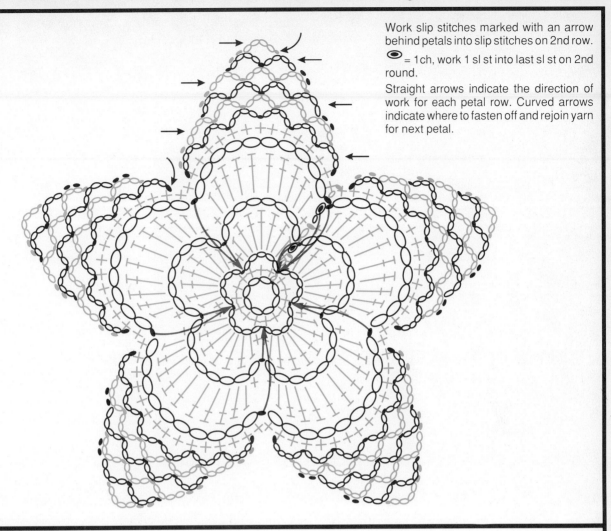

Work slip stitches marked with an arrow behind petals into slip stitches on 2nd row.

👁 = 1ch, work 1 sl st into last sl st on 2nd round.

Straight arrows indicate the direction of work for each petal row. Curved arrows indicate where to fasten off and rejoin yarn for next petal.

Traffic Lights

Make 6ch, sl st into first ch to form a ring.

1st round: 1ch, work 2sc into ring, *13ch, sl st into 6th ch from hook, 3ch, skip 3ch, sl st into next ch, 3ch, sl st into side of last sc worked, work 4sc into ring; rep from * 3 times more omitting 2sc at end of last rep, sl st into first sc. (4 points made).

2nd round: *Into each of first 2 sps on next point work [1sc, 3dc, 1sc], 1sc into top sp of same point, into same top sp work [3dc, 1sc] twice, then working on other side of loop work [1sc, 3dc, 1sc] into each of next 2 sps, 1 sl st into each of next 3sc on first round; rep from * 3 times more omitting 1 sl st at end of last rep.

3rd round: 1ch, work 1sc into same sc as last sl st, *16ch, 1sc into center sc at top of point, 16ch, 1sc into center sc between 2 points on first round; rep from * 3 times more omitting 1sc at end of last rep, sl st into first sc.

4th round: 1ch, *work 1sc into each of next 16ch, 1sc into next sc, 1sc into each of next 16ch, skip 1sc; rep from * 3 times more, sl st into first sc. Fasten off.

147

Irish Style Crochet

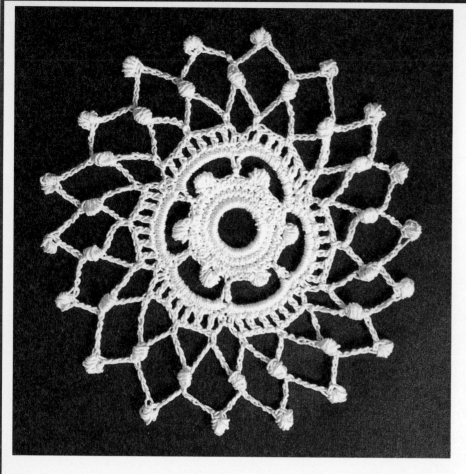

Irish Eyes

Special Abbreviations

Clones Knot = ★draw up a chain to required length and hold it in place, *yarn over, twist hook over then under the loop, then pull the yarn back under the loop with the hook; rep from * until the loop is completely covered. Yo, draw hook through all loops on hook★. To secure knot work 1sc into last ch before Clones Knot.

Sc-Clones Knot = work as given for Clones Knot from ★ to ★. To secure knot work 1sc into last sc before Clones Knot.

Make 18ch, sl st into first ch to form a ring.

1st round: 1ch, working into ring and over **padding threads**, work 36sc, sl st into first sc.

2nd round: 1ch, work 1sc into same st as last sl st, 1sc into each of next 35sc, sl st into first sc.

3rd round: 1ch, work 1sc into same st as last sl st, 1sc into each of next 2sc, *into next sc work [1sc, 1Sc-Clones Knot], 1sc into each of next 5sc; rep from * 5 times more omitting 3sc at end of last rep, sl st into first sc.

4th round: 11ch, skip [first 3sc, 1Sc-Clones Knot, 2sc], sl st into next sc, *11ch, skip [2sc, 1Sc-Clones Knot, 2sc], sl st into next sc; rep from * 4 times more placing last sl st into first sc of previous round.

5th round: 1ch, work 15sc into each of the 6 arches and over **padding threads**, sl st into first sc.

6th round: 1ch, 1sc into next sc, 2ch, 1dc into next sc, [1ch, skip 1sc, 1dc into next sc] 5 times, 2ch, 1sc into next sc, *miss 2sc, 1sc into next sc, 2ch, 1dc into next sc, [1ch, skip 1sc, 1dc into next sc] 5 times, 2ch, 1sc into next sc; rep from * 4 times more, sl st into first sc.

7th round: Sl st into first ch, 1ch, 1sc into 2ch sp, *4ch, 1 Clones Knot, 4ch, skip 3dc, 1sc into next ch sp, [4ch, 1 Clones Knot, 4ch, 1sc into next 2ch sp] twice; rep from * 5 times more omitting 1sc at end of last rep, sl st into first sc.

8th round: Sl st into each ch to first Clones Knot, 1ch, [working behind Clones Knot work 1sc into sc securing Clones Knot, 4ch, 1 Clones Knot, 4ch] 18 times, sl st into first sc. Fasten off.

⟨⟨⟩⟩ = Sc-Clones Knot

⟨⟩ = Clones Knot

—— = Padding thread

Stitch Variations, Abbreviations and Symbols on pages 7 to 15

Anenome

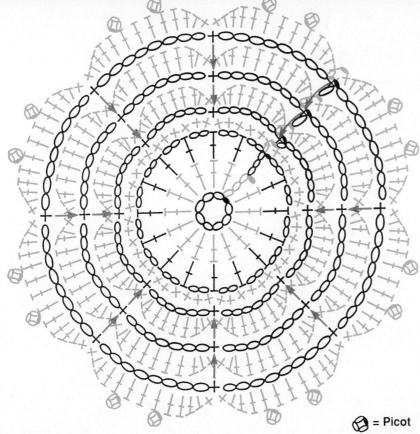

⬡ = Picot

Special Abbreviation

Picot = make 3ch, sl st into first of these ch.

Make 8ch, sl st into first ch to form a ring.

1st round: 3ch (count as 1dc), work 15dc into ring, sl st into 3rd of 3ch at beg of round.

2nd round: 5ch (count as 1dc, 2ch), [1dc into next dc, 2ch] 15 times, sl st into 3rd of 5ch at beg of round.

3rd round: 1ch, work 3sc into each of the 16 2ch sps, sl st into first sc.

4th round: 1ch, work 1sc into same sc as last sl st, *6ch, skip 5sc, 1sc into next sc; rep from * 6 times more, 6ch, sl st into first sc.

5th round: Sl st into first 6ch arch, 1ch, work [1sc, 1hdc, 6dc, 1hdc, 1sc] into each of the 8 6ch arches, sl st into first sc. (8 petals worked).

Trefoil Design

1st round: Make 16ch, sl st into first ch (first loop formed), [15ch, sl st into same ch as last sl st] twice.

2nd round: 1ch, working over **padding threads** work [28sc into next loop, 1 sl st into same ch as sl sts of first round] 3 times.

3rd round: Sl st into each of first 3sc, 1ch, 1sc into same st as last sl st, 1sc into each of next 23sc, [skip 4sc, 1sc into each of next 24sc] twice, 17ch, working over **padding threads** work 1sc into 2nd ch from hook, 1sc into each of next 15ch, sl st into first sc. Fasten off.

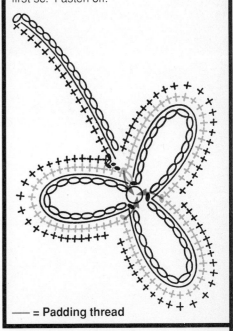

— = Padding thread

6th round: 1ch, working behind each petal of previous round, work 1sc into first sc on 4th round, *7ch, 1sc into next sc on 4th round; rep from * 6 times more, 7ch, sl st into first sc.

7th round: Sl st into first 7ch arch, 1ch, work [1sc, 1hdc, 7dc, 1hdc, 1sc] into each of the 8 7ch arches, sl st into first sc.

8th round: 1ch, working behind each petal of previous round, work 1sc into first sc on 6th round, *8ch, 1sc into next sc on 6th round; rep from * 6 times more, 8ch, sl st into first sc.

9th round: Sl st into first 8ch arch, 1ch, work [1sc, 1hdc, 3dc, 1 picot, 3dc, 1 picot, 3dc, 1hdc, 1sc] into each of the 8 8ch arches, sl st into first sc. Fasten off.

Edgings and Trimmings

Using Edgings

Edgings are self evidently an addition to something which already exists. Household items such as table mats or cloths, handkerchiefs, towels and pillowcases are all enhanced when trimmed with a matching or toning crochet border.

All the written and diagramatic instructions in this section include the starting chain. If you are going to sew the border on to material you need this chain to work into. However in many cases it is preferable to omit the starting chain and work a row of single crochet directly into the folded edge of the fabric (see illustration of Big Top II which has been worked in this way). If the first row of the design is a single crochet row the instructions as given do not need amending. If however this base is not included in the pattern it is recommended that you work a row of firm single crochet on to the folded edge of the material using the same multiple as given for the starting chain.

We have included a few examples of curved versions of some of the edgings (see Crown Edge II opposite). These can be used as collar or neck edgings, or if worked or sewn on to a straight edge they will flute or form a frill.

The direction in which the edging is made can also vary. If a particularly long piece is required, as for example the border for a large table cloth, it may be advisable to choose one which is worked sideways like Flower Group on page 160. The advantage of this is that you can pin or baste the border in position before it is finished, to ensure that the length you have worked is correct.

Loop Line

Starting chain: Multiple of 4 sts + 2.

1st row (right side): Work 1sc into 2nd ch from hook, 1sc into each ch to end, turn.

2nd row: 1ch, 1sc into first sc, *5ch, skip 3sc, 1sc into next sc; rep from * to end, turn.

3rd row: 1ch, 1sc into first sc, *7ch, 1sc into next sc; rep from * to end.

Fasten off.

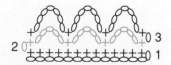

Big Top I

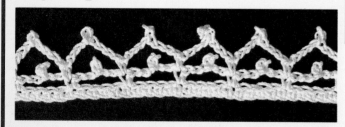

Starting chain: Multiple of 5 sts + 2.

1st row (right side): Work 1sc into 2nd ch from hook, 1sc into each ch to end, turn.

Big Top II

To make edging in rounds, make a starting chain of a multiple of 5 sts + 1 for each side + 1 for each of the 4 corners. Place a marker in last ch (4th corner ch) and in each of the other 3 corner ch. Sl st into first ch to form a ring.

1st round (right side): 1ch, work 1sc into same ch as last sl st, 1sc into each ch to first corner ch, [3sc into corner ch, 1sc into each ch to next corner ch] 3 times, 3sc into last corner ch, sl st into first sc.

2nd round: 1ch, work 1sc into same st as last sl st, *5ch, sl st into 3rd ch from hook, 3ch, skip 4sc, 1sc into next sc; rep from * to next corner, 6ch, sl st into 3rd ch from hook, 4ch, skip 3sc (corner scs), 1sc into next dc**; rep from * to ** 3 times more omitting 1sc at end of last rep, sl st into first sc.

3rd round: 1ch, work 1sc into same st as last sl st, *6ch, sl st into 3rd ch from hook, 4ch, 1sc into next sc; rep from * to next corner, 8ch, sl st into 3rd ch from hook, 6ch, 1sc into next sc**; rep from * to ** 3 times more omitting 1sc at end of last rep, sl st into first sc. Fasten off.

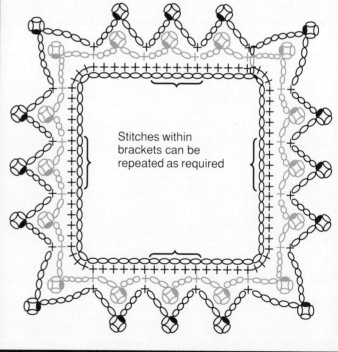

Stitches within brackets can be repeated as required

2nd row: 1ch, 1sc into first sc, *5ch, sl st into 3rd ch from hook, 3ch, skip next 4sc, 1sc into next sc; rep from * to end, turn.

3rd row: 1ch, 1sc into first sc, *6ch, sl st into 3rd ch from hook, 4ch, 1sc into next sc; rep from * to end. Fasten off.

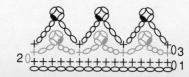

Stitch Variations, Abbreviations and Symbols on pages 7 to 15

Crown Edge I

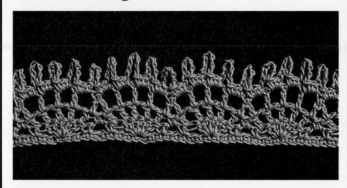

Starting chain: Multiple of 9 sts + 5.

Special Abbreviation

Dc2tog = work1dc into each of next 2dc until 1 loop of each remains on hook, yo and through all 3 loops on hook.

1st row (right side): Work 1sc into 2nd ch from hook, 1sc into each ch to end, turn.

2nd row: 1ch, 1sc into first sc, 2ch, skip 2sc, 1sc into next sc, *skip 2sc, 5dc into next sc, skip 2sc, 1sc into next sc, 2ch, skip 2sc, 1sc into next sc; rep from * to end, turn.

3rd row: 1ch, 1sc into first sc, 2ch, *1dc into next dc, [1ch, 1dc into next dc] 4 times, 1sc into next 2ch sp; rep from * to end omitting 1sc at end of last rep, 2ch, 1sc into last sc, turn.

4th row: 3ch (count as 1dc), [1dc into next dc, 2ch] 4 times, *dc2tog, 2ch, [1dc into next dc, 2ch] 3 times; rep from * to last dc, work 1dc into next dc until 2 loops remain on hook, 1dc into last sc until 3 loops remain on hook, yo and through all 3 loops, turn.

5th row: 1ch, 1sc into first st, 3sc into first 2ch sp, *7ch, 3sc into next 2ch sp; rep from * to end, 1sc into 3rd of 3ch at beg of previous row. Fasten off.

 = Dc2tog

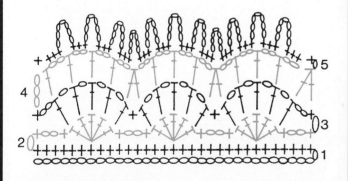

Crown Edge II

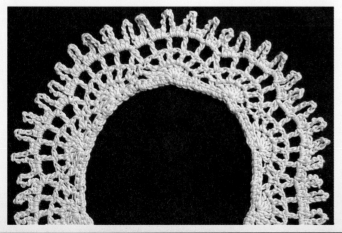

Driftwood

Starting chain: Multiple of 10 sts + 8.

1st row (wrong side): Work 1sc into 2nd ch from hook, 1sc into next ch, 6ch, skip 3ch, *1sc into each of next 7ch, 6ch, skip 3ch; rep from * to last 2ch, 1sc into each of last 2ch, turn.

2nd row: 1ch, 1sc into first sc, *into next 6ch arch work [1sc, 1hdc, 5dc, 1hdc, 1sc], 7ch; rep from * omitting 7ch at end of last rep, work 1sc into last sc, turn.

3rd row: 5ch, skip first 5 sts, work 1sc into next dc, [3ch, 1sc] 3 times into same st as last sc, *3ch, [1sc, 3ch, 1sc] into next 7ch arch, 3ch, skip next 4 sts, 1sc into next dc, [3ch, 1sc] 3 times into same st as last sc; rep from * to last 5 sts, 5ch, sl st into last sc. Fasten off.

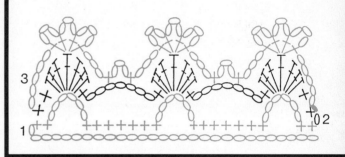

Starting chain: Multiple of 9 sts + 5.

Special Abbreviation

Dc2tog = work1dc into each of next 2dc until 1 loop of each remains on hook, yo and through all 3 loops on hook.

1st row (right side): Work 1sc into 2nd ch from hook, 1sc into each ch to end, turn.

2nd row: 1ch, 1sc into first sc, 2ch, skip 2sc, 1sc into next sc, *skip 2sc, 6dc into next sc, skip 2sc, 1sc into next sc, 2ch, skip 2sc, 1sc into next sc; rep from * to end, turn.

3rd row: 1ch, 1sc into first sc, 2ch, *1dc into next dc, [1ch, 1dc into next dc] 5 times, 1sc into next 2ch sp; rep from * to last 2sc, omitting 1sc at end of last rep, 2ch, 1sc into last sc, turn.

4th row: 3ch (count as 1dc), [1dc into next dc, 2ch] 5 times, *dc2tog, 2ch, [1dc into next dc, 2ch] 4 times; rep from * to last dc, work 1dc into next dc until 2 loops remain on hook, 1dc into last sc until 3 loops remain on hook, yo and through all 3 loops, turn.

5th row: 1ch, 1sc into first st, 3sc into first 2ch sp, *7ch, 3sc into next 2ch sp; rep from * to last 2dc, 1sc into 3rd of 3ch at beg of previous row. Fasten off.

 = Dc2tog

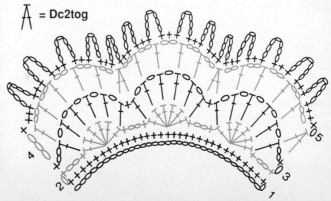

Edgings and Trimmings

Tightrope

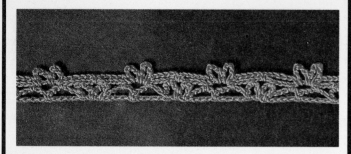

Starting chain: Multiple of 12 sts.

1st row (right side): Work 1sc into 2nd ch from hook, [5ch, skip 4ch, 1sc into next ch] twice, *[5ch, 1sc into next ch] twice, [5ch, skip 4ch, 1sc into next ch] twice; rep from * to end.

2nd row: 6ch (count as 1dc, 3ch), 1sc into first 5ch arch, *3ch, 1sc into next 5ch arch; rep from * to end, 3ch, 1dc into last sc, turn.

3rd row: 1ch, 1sc into first dc, *5ch, skip 1 arch, 1sc into next 3ch arch, into same arch as last sc work [5ch, 1sc] twice, 5ch, skip 1 arch, 1sc into next 3ch arch; rep from * to end working last sc into 3rd of 6ch at beg of previous row. Fasten off.

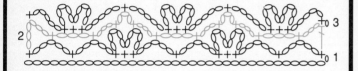

Wide Variety

Starting chain: Multiple of 17 sts + 3.

Special Abbreviation

Bobble = work 3dc into next space until 1 loop of each remains on hook, yo and through all 4 loops on hook.

1st row (right side): Work 1sc into 2nd ch from hook, 1sc into each ch to end, turn.

2nd row: 1ch, work 1sc into each sc to end, turn.

3rd row: 1ch, work 1sc into each of first 8sc, *4ch, skip 3sc, 1sc into each of next 14sc; rep from * to last 11sc, 4ch, skip 3sc, 1sc into each of last 8sc, turn.

4th row: 3ch (count as 1hdc, 1ch), skip first 2sc, 1sc into each of next 3sc, 1ch, into next 4ch sp work [1dc, 1ch] 6 times, skip 3sc, 1sc into each of next 3sc, *3ch, skip 2sc, 1sc into each of next 3sc, 1ch, into next 4ch sp work [1dc, 1ch] 6 times, skip 3sc, 1sc into each of next 3sc; rep from * to last 2sc, 1ch, 1hdc into last sc, turn.

5th row: 1ch, 1sc into first hdc, 2ch, [1 bobble into next ch sp, 2ch] 7 times, *1sc into next 3ch arch, 2ch, [1 bobble into next ch sp, 2ch] 7 times; rep from * to last 3ch, skip 1ch, 1sc into next ch, turn.

Minstrel Gallery

Starting chain: Multiple of 10 sts + 2.

Special Abbreviation

Bobble = work 3dc into next space until 1 loop of each remains on hook, yo and through all 4 loops on hook.

1st row (wrong side): Work 1sc into 2nd ch from hook, 1sc into each ch to end, turn.

2nd row: 5ch (count as 1tr, 1ch), work [1tr, 1ch] twice into first sc, skip 4sc, 1sc into next sc, *1ch, skip 4sc, into next sc work [1tr, 1ch] 5 times, skip 4sc, 1sc into next sc; rep from * to last 5sc, 1ch, work 1tr into last sc, 1ch, into same st as last tr work [1tr, 1ch, 1tr], turn.

3rd row: 1ch, 1sc into first tr, *2ch, into next sc work [1dtr, 2ch] 4 times, skip 2tr, 1sc into next tr; rep from * to end placing last sc into 4th of 5ch at beg of previous row, turn.

4th row: 1ch, 1sc into first sc, *4ch, skip next sp, 1 bobble into next 2ch sp, [3ch, 1 bobble into next 2ch sp] twice, 4ch, 1sc into next sc; rep from * to end. Fasten off.

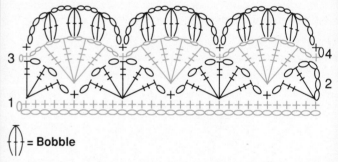

ϕ = Bobble

6th row: 1ch, 1sc into first sc, 2sc into first 2ch sp, 1sc into top of first bobble, 2sc into next 2ch sp, [3ch, 2sc into next sp] twice, 5ch, [2sc into next sp, 3ch] twice, 2sc into next sp, 1sc into top of next bobble, 2sc into next sp, *skip 1sc, 2sc into next sp, 1sc into top of next bobble, 2sc into next sp, [3ch, 2sc into next sp] twice, 5ch, [2sc into next sp, 3ch] twice, 2sc into next sp, 1sc into top of next bobble, 2sc into next sp; rep from * to last sc, 1sc into last sc. Fasten off.

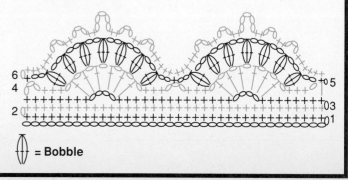

ϕ = Bobble

Stitch Variations, Abbreviations and Symbols on pages 7 to 15

Square Dance

Starting chain: Multiple of 6 sts + 3.

1st row (wrong side): Work 1sc into 2nd ch from hook, 1sc into each ch to end, turn.

2nd row: 3ch (count as 1dc), skip first sc, 1dc into next sc, *1ch, skip 1sc, 1dc into each of next 2sc; rep from * to end, turn.

3rd row: 5ch (count as 1dc, 2ch), 1sc into next ch sp, *4ch, 1sc into next ch sp; rep from * to last 2 sts, 2ch, 1dc into 3rd of 3ch at beg of previous row, turn.

4th row: 1ch, 1sc into first dc, *work 5dc into next 4ch sp, 1sc into next 4ch sp; rep from * to end placing last sc into 3rd of 5ch at beg of previous row. Fasten off.

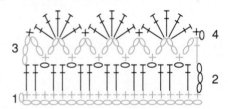

Horizon

Starting chain: Multiple of 6 sts + 3.

Special Abbreviation

Picot = make 3ch, sl st into 3rd ch from hook.

1st row (wrong side): Work 1sc into 2nd ch from hook, 1sc into each ch to end, turn.

2nd row: 5ch (count as 1dc, 2ch), skip first 3sc, 1sc into next sc, work 3 picots, 1sc into next sc, *5ch, skip 4sc, 1sc into next sc, work 3 picots, 1sc into next sc; rep from * to last 3sc, 2ch, 1dc into last sc, turn.

3rd row: 1ch, 1sc into first dc, *8ch, 1sc into next 5ch arch; rep from * to end placing last sc into 3rd of 5ch at beg of previous row, turn.

4th row: 1ch, 1sc into first sc, *11sc into next 8ch arch, 1sc into next sc; rep from * to end. Fasten off.

 = Picot

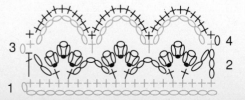

High Rise

Starting chain: Multiple of 16 sts + 2.

Special Abbreviation

Bobble = work 4tr into arch until 1 loop of each remains on hook, yo and through all 5 loops on hook.

1st row (wrong side): Work 1sc into 2nd ch from hook, 1sc into each ch to end, turn.

2nd row: 1ch, 1sc into first sc, *3ch, skip 3sc, 1sc into next sc; rep from * to end, turn.

3rd row: 1ch, 1sc into first sc, 1ch, 1sc into first sp, *3ch, 1sc into next sp; rep from * to last sc, 1ch, 1sc into last sc, turn.

4th row: 6ch (count as 1dc, 3ch), skip first sc, 1sc into next sc, 3sc into next 3ch sp, 1sc into next sc, *6ch, 1sc into next sc, 3sc into next 3ch sp, 1sc into next sc; rep from * to last sc, 3ch, 1dc into last sc, turn.

5th row: 1ch, 1sc into first dc, *4ch, work 1 bobble into next 6ch arch, into same arch as last bobble work [3ch, 1 bobble] twice, 4ch, 1sc into next 6ch arch; rep from * to end placing last sc into 3rd of 6ch at beg of previous row, turn.

6th row: 7ch (count as 1tr, 3ch), *work 1 bobble into next 4ch arch, 3ch, [1 bobble into next 3ch arch, 3ch] twice, 1 bobble into next 4ch arch, 3ch, 1tr into next sc, 3ch; rep from * to end omitting 3ch at end of last rep, turn.

7th row: 1ch, 1sc into first tr, 1ch, [1sc into next arch, 3ch] twice, 4dc into next arch, *3ch, [1sc into next arch, 3ch] 4 times, 4dc into next arch; rep from * to last 2 arches, [3ch, 1sc into next arch] twice, 1ch, 1sc into 4th of 7ch at beg of previous row, turn.

8th row: 1ch, 1sc into first sc, 3ch, [1sc into next 3ch arch, 3ch] twice, skip 1dc, 1dc into each of next 2dc, *3ch, [1sc into next arch, 3ch] 5 times, skip 1dc, 1dc into each of next 2dc; rep from * to last 2 3ch arches, 3ch, [1sc into next arch, 3ch] twice, 1sc into last sc, turn.

9th row: 1ch, 1sc into first sc, work 3sc into each of next 3 arches, 1sc into next dc, 3ch, 1sc into next dc, *3sc into each of next 6 arches, 1sc into next dc, 3ch, 1sc into next dc; rep from * to last 3 arches, 3sc into each of last 3 arches, 1sc into last sc. Fasten off.

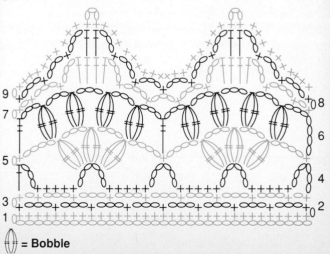

= Bobble

Edgings and Trimmings

Duette

Starting chain: Multiple of 4 sts + 4.

1st row (right side): Work 1dc into 6th ch from hook, *1ch, skip 1ch, 1dc into next ch; rep from * to end, turn.

2nd row: 1ch, 1sc into first dc, *5ch, skip 1dc, 1sc into next dc; rep from * to last dc, 5ch, skip 1dc and 1ch, 1sc into next ch, turn.

3rd row: 1ch, 1sc into first sc, work 7sc into each 5ch arch to end, 1sc into last sc, turn.

4th row: 5ch (count as 1dc, 2ch), skip first 4sc, 1sc into next sc, *3ch, skip 6sc, 1sc into next sc; rep from * to last 4sc, 2ch, 1dc into last sc, turn.

5th row: 1ch, 1sc into first dc, 5ch, 1sc into 2ch sp, into each sp work [1sc, 5ch, 1sc] to end placing last sc into 3rd of 5ch at beg of previous row. Fasten off.

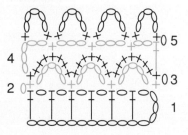

Scissors

Starting chain: Multiple of 9 sts + 4.

1st row (right side): Work 1dc into 4th ch from hook, 1dc into each ch to end, turn.

2nd row: 1ch, 1sc into first dc, 1ch, 1sc into next dc, 9ch, skip 7dc, 1sc into next dc, *3ch, 1sc into next dc, 9ch, skip 7dc, 1sc into next dc; rep from * to end, 1ch, 1sc into top of 3ch, turn.

3rd row: 1ch, 1sc into first sc, 1sc into first ch sp, *5dc into next 9ch arch, 2ch, into same arch as last 5dc work [1sc, 2ch, 5dc], 1sc into next 3ch arch; rep from * to end placing last sc into last ch sp, 1sc into last sc, turn.

4th row: 9ch (count as 1dtr, 4ch), 1sc into next 2ch sp, 3ch, 1sc into next 2ch sp, *9ch, 1sc into next 2ch sp, 3ch, 1sc into next 2ch sp; rep from * to last 5dc, 4ch, 1dtr into last sc, turn.

Half Token

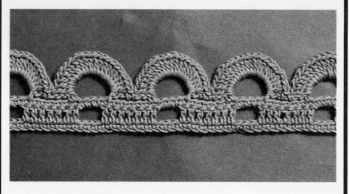

Starting chain: Multiple of 10 sts + 2.

1st row (right side): Work 1sc into 2nd ch from hook, 1sc into each ch to end, turn.

2nd row: 3ch (count as 1dc), skip first sc, 1dc into each of next 3sc, *3ch, skip 3sc, 1dc into each of next 7sc; rep from * to end omitting 3dc at end of last rep, turn.

3rd row: 1ch, 1sc into each of first 4dc, 3sc into next 3ch sp, *1sc into each of next 7dc, 3sc into next 3ch sp; rep from * to last 4dc, 1sc into each of next 3dc, 1sc into 3rd of 3ch at beg of previous row, turn.

4th row: 1ch, 1sc into first sc, 2ch, skip 2sc, 1sc into next sc, 8ch, skip 3sc, 1sc into next sc, *5ch, skip 5sc, 1sc into next sc, 8ch, skip 3sc, 1sc into next sc; rep from * to last 3sc, 2ch, 1sc into last sc, turn.

5th row: 1ch, 1sc into first sc, 19dc into 8ch arch, *1sc into next 5ch sp, 19dc into next 8ch arch; rep from * to last 2ch sp, 1sc into last sc. Fasten off.

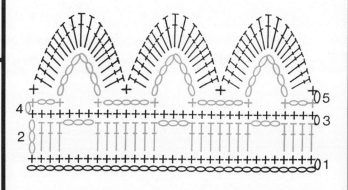

5th row: 3ch (count as 1dc), 5dc into 4ch arch, 1sc into next 3ch arch, *5dc into next 9ch arch, 2ch, into same arch as last 5dc work [1sc, 2ch, 5dc], 1sc into next 3ch arch; rep from * to last arch, 5dc into last arch, 1dc into 5th of 9ch at beg of previous row. Fasten off.

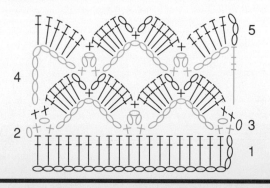

Stitch Variations, Abbreviations and Symbols on pages 7 to 15

Edgings and Trimmings

Shoreline

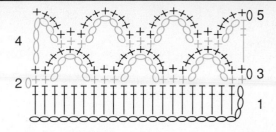

5th row: 1ch, 1sc into tr, 3sc into first arch, 1sc into each of next 3sc, *7sc into next 7ch arch, 1sc into each of next 3sc; rep from * to last arch, 3sc into last arch, 1sc into 4th of 7ch at beg of previous row. Fasten off.

Starting chain: Multiple of 7 sts + 3.

1st row (right side): Work 1dc into 4th ch from hook, 1dc into each ch to end, turn.

2nd row: 1ch, 1sc into each of first 2dc, *7ch, skip 4dc, 1sc into each of next 3dc, rep from * to end omitting 1sc at end of last rep and placing last sc into top of 3ch, turn.

3rd row: 1ch, 1sc into each of first 2sc, *7sc into 7ch arch, 1sc into each of next 3sc, rep from * to end omitting 1sc at end of last rep, turn.

4th row: 7ch (count as 1tr, 3ch), skip 4sc, 1sc into each of next 3sc, *7ch, skip 7sc, 1sc into each of next 3sc; rep from * to last 4sc, 3ch, 1tr into last sc, turn.

Quintet

Starting chain: Multiple of 16 sts + 3.

Special Abbreviation

Cluster = work 2dtr into next st until 1 loop of each remains on hook, yo and through all 3 loops on hook.

1st row (right side): Work 1dc into 4th ch from hook, *1ch, skip 1ch, 1dc into next ch; rep from * to last ch, 1dc into last ch, turn.

2nd row: 3ch (count as 1dc), skip first dc, 1dc into each of next dc, ch sp and dc, 5ch, skip 2 sps, 1tr into next sp, 5ch, skip 2dc, 1dc into next dc, *[1dc into next sp, 1dc into next dc] 3 times, 5ch, skip 2 sps, 1tr into next sp, 5ch, skip 2dc, 1dc into next dc; rep from * to last 3 sts, 1dc into next sp, 1dc into next dc, 1dc into top of 3ch, turn.

3rd row: 3ch, skip first dc, 1dc into each of next 2dc, 7ch, 1sc into next tr, 7ch, *skip 1dc, 1dc into each of next 5dc, 7ch, 1sc into next tr, 7ch; rep from * to last 4 sts, skip 1dc, 1dc into each of next 2dc, 1dc into 3rd of 3ch at beg of previous row, turn.

4th row: 3ch, skip first dc, 1dc into next dc, 7ch, into next sc work [1sc, 5ch, 1sc], 7ch, *skip 1dc, 1dc into each of next 3dc, 7ch, into next sc work [1sc, 5ch, 1sc], 7ch; rep from * to last 3 sts, skip 1dc, 1dc into next dc, 1dc into 3rd of 3ch at beg of previous row, turn.

5th row: 6ch (count as 1dc, 3ch), *skip 7ch arch, work 1 cluster into 5ch arch then [1ch, 1 cluster] 4 times into same arch, 3ch, skip 1dc, 1dc into next dc, 3ch; rep from * to end omitting 3ch at end of last rep and placing last dc into 3rd of 3ch. Fasten off.

〈 = Cluster

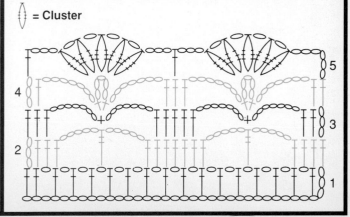

New Dimension

Starting chain: Multiple of 8 sts + 2.

1st row (right side): Work 1sc into 2nd ch from hook, 1sc into each ch to end, turn.

2nd row: 1ch, 1sc into each of first 4sc, into next sc work [1sc, 7ch, 1sc], *1sc into each of next 7sc, into next sc work [1sc, 7ch, 1sc]; rep from * to last 4sc, 1sc into each of last 4sc, turn.

3rd row: 3ch (count as 1dc), skip first sc, *1sc into next sc, 9sc into next arch, skip 3sc, 1sc into next sc, 1dc into next sc; rep from * to end, turn.

4th row: 1ch, 1sc into first dc, *4ch, skip 5sc, into next sc work [1sc, 5ch, 1sc], 4ch, skip 5sc, 1sc into next dc; rep from * to end placing last sc into 3rd of 3ch at beg of previous row, turn.

5th row: 1ch, 1sc into first sc, *3sc into next 4ch arch, 5sc into next 5ch arch, 3sc into next 4ch arch, 1sc into next sc; rep from * to end. Fasten off.

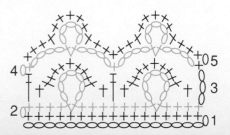

Edgings and Trimmings

Loose Leaf

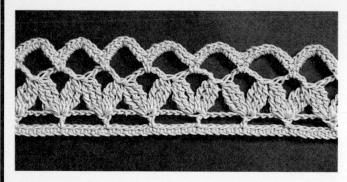

$$\text{\huge }|\!|\!|\!|\text{ = Bobble}$$

Starting chain: Multiple of 6 sts + 2.

Special Abbreviation

Bobble = work 3dtr into next st until 1 loop of each remains on hook, yo and through all 4 loops on hook.

1st row (right side): Work 1sc into 2nd ch from hook, 1sc into each ch to end, turn.

2nd row: 8ch (count as 1dc, 5ch), skip first 6sc, 1dc into next sc, *5ch, skip 5sc, 1dc into next sc; rep from * to end, turn.

3rd row: 6ch (count as 1tr, 2ch), work 1 bobble into first dc, *into next dc work [1 bobble, 5ch, 1 bobble]; rep from * to last dc, into 3rd of 3ch at beg of previous row work [1 bobble, 2ch, 1tr], turn.

4th row: 1ch, 1sc into first tr, *7ch, 1sc into next 5ch arch; rep from * to end placing last sc into 4th of 6ch at beg of previous row, turn.

5th row: 1ch, 1sc into first sc, *9sc into next 7ch arch, 1sc into next sc; rep from * to end. Fasten off.

Far Eastern

Starting chain: Multiple of 9 sts + 5.

Special Abbreviation

Bobble = work 3dtr into sp until one loop of each remains on hook, yo and through all 4 loops on hook.

1st row (wrong side): Work 1dc into 8th ch from hook, *2ch, skip 2ch, 1dc into next ch; rep from * to end, turn.

2nd row: 3ch (count as 1dc), skip next sp, work 1 bobble into next sp, [6ch, 1dc into first of these ch] 3 times, 1 bobble into same sp as last bobble, *skip 2 sps, work 1 bobble into next sp, [6ch, 1dc into first of these ch] 3 times, 1 bobble into same sp as last bobble; rep from * to last sp, skip 2ch, 1dc into next ch. Fasten off.

$$\text{\huge }|\!|\!|\!|\text{ = Bobble}$$

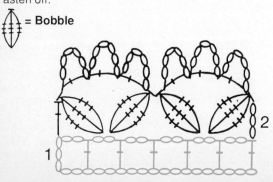

Plough Share

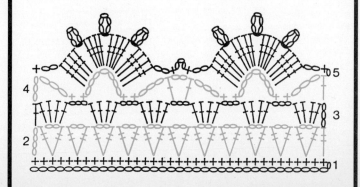

Starting chain: Multiple of 18 sts + 18.

1st row (right side): Work 1sc into 2nd ch from hook, 1sc into each ch to end, turn.

2nd row: 4ch (count as 1tr), *skip next 2sc, work [1tr, 2ch, 1tr] into next sc; rep from * to last 2sc, 1tr into last sc, turn.

3rd row: 3ch (count as 1dc), work 4dc into first 2ch sp, *3ch, skip 1 sp, 4dc into next sp; rep from * to end, 1dc into 4th of 4ch at beg of previous row, turn.

4th row: 6ch (count as 1dc, 3ch), 2sc into first 3ch sp, 7ch, 2sc into next sp, *3ch, into next sp work [1dc, 2ch, 1dc], 3ch, 2sc into next sp, 7ch, 2sc into next sp; rep from * to last 5 sts, 3ch, 1dc into 3rd of 3ch at beg of previous row, turn.

5th row: 1ch, 1sc into first dc, 2ch, into 7ch arch work 4tr and [5ch, sl st into first of these ch, 4tr] 3 times, 2ch, *skip 1 sp, into next 2ch sp work [1sc, 3ch, 1sc], 2ch, into 7ch arch work 4tr and [5ch, sl st into first of these ch, 4tr] 3 times; rep from * to last sp, 2ch, 1sc into 3rd of 6ch at beg of previous row. Fasten off.

Stitch Variations, Abbreviations and Symbols on pages 7 to 15

White Knight I

Starting chain: Multiple of 10 sts + 3.

1st row (right side): Work 1dc into 4th ch from hook, 1dc into each ch to end, turn.

2nd row: 1ch, 1sc into each of first 3dc, *2ch, skip 2dc, into next dc work [2dc, 2ch] twice, skip 2dc, 1sc into each of next 5dc; rep from * to end omitting 2sc at end of last rep and placing last sc into top of 3ch at beg of previous row, turn.

3rd row: 1ch, 1sc into each of first 2sc, *3ch, skip next 2ch sp, into next 2ch sp work [3dc, 2ch, 3dc], 3ch, skip 1sc, 1sc into each of next 3sc; rep from * to end omitting 1sc at end of last rep, turn.

4th row: 1ch, 1sc into first sc, *4ch, skip next 3ch sp, into next 2ch sp work [4dc, 2ch, 4dc], 4ch, skip 1sc, 1sc into next sc; rep from * to end, turn.

5th row: 1ch, 1sc into first sc, *5ch, skip next 4ch sp, into next 2ch sp work [4dc, 2ch, 4dc], 5ch, 1sc into next sc; rep from * to end. Fasten off.

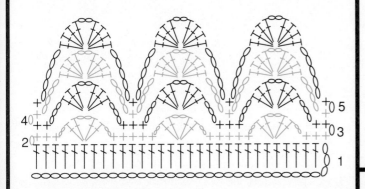

White Knight II

Starting chain: Multiple of 8 sts + 3.

1st row (right side): Work 1dc into 4th ch from hook, 1dc into each ch to end, turn.

2nd row: 1ch, 1sc into each of first 3dc, *2ch, skip 1dc, into next dc work [2dc, 2ch] twice, skip 1dc, 1sc into each of next 5dc; rep from * to end omitting 2sc at end of last rep and placing last sc into top of 3ch at beg of previous row, turn.

Sand Castle

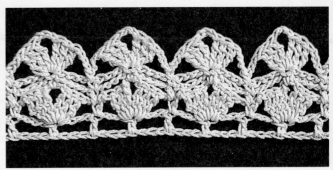

Starting chain: Multiple of 8 sts + 6.

1st row (right side): Work 1dc into 10th ch from hook, *3ch, skip 3ch, 1dc into next ch; rep from * to end, turn.

2nd row: 1ch, 1sc into first dc, *2ch, into next dc work [3tr, 3ch, 3tr], 2ch, 1sc into next dc; rep from * to end placing last sc into 4th ch, turn.

3rd row: 1ch, 1sc into first sc, *5ch, 1sc into next 3ch sp, 5ch, 1sc into next sc; rep from * to end, turn.

4th row: 1ch, 1sc into first sc, *4ch, 1sc into next sc; rep from * to end, turn.

5th row: 1ch, 1sc into first sc, *3ch, into next sc work [3tr, 3ch, 3tr], 3ch, 1sc into next sc; rep from * to end. Fasten off.

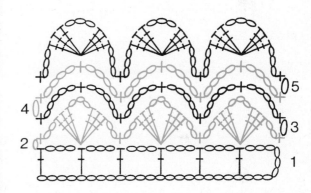

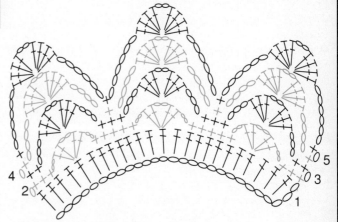

3rd row: 1ch, 1sc into each of first 2sc, *3ch, skip next 2ch sp, into next 2ch sp work [3dc, 2ch, 3dc], 3ch, skip 1sc, 1sc into each of next 3sc; rep from * to end omitting 1sc at end of last rep, turn.

4th row: 1ch, 1sc into first sc, *4ch, skip next 3ch sp, into next 2ch sp work [4dc, 2ch, 4dc], 4ch, skip 1sc, 1sc into next sc; rep from * to end, turn.

5th row: 1ch, 1sc into first sc, *6ch, skip next 4ch sp, into next 2ch sp work [4dc, 2ch, 4dc], 6ch, 1sc into next sc; rep from * to end. Fasten off.

Edgings and Trimmings

Mirabelle

Starting chain: Multiple of 6 sts + 6.

Special Abbreviation

Bobble = work 4dtr into ch until 1 loop of each remains on hook, yo and through all 5 loops on hook.

1st row (right side): Work 1sc into 2nd ch from hook, 1sc into each ch to end, turn.

2nd row: 6ch (count as 1dc, 3ch), skip 4sc, 1dc into next sc, *1ch, skip 1sc, 1dc into next sc, 3ch, skip 3sc, 1dc into next sc; rep from * to end, turn.

3rd row: 1ch, 1sc into first dc, *4ch, skip 1ch, 1 bobble into next ch, 4ch, 1sc into next dc, 1ch, 1sc into next dc; rep from * to end, omitting last ch and sc and working final sc into 3rd of 6ch at beg of previous row. Fasten off.

 = Bobble

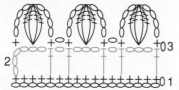

Springtime

Starting chain: Multiple of 11 sts + 3.

Special Abbreviation

Bobble = Work 3dtr into 3ch loop until 1 loop of each remains on hook, yo and through all 4 loops on hook.

1st row (right side): Work 1dc into 4th ch from hook, 1dc into each ch to end, turn.

2nd row: 1ch, 1sc into first dc, *9ch, sl st into 3rd ch from hook, 7ch, skip 10dc, 1sc into next dc; rep from * to end placing last sc into top of 3ch, turn.

3rd row: 5ch, *work 1 bobble into next 3ch loop, 5ch, into same loop as last bobble work [1 bobble, 5ch, 1 bobble], 1dtr into next sc; rep from * to end. Fasten off.

 = Bobble

Long Bows

Starting chain: Multiple of 8 sts + 2.

Special Abbreviation

Triple loop = sl st into next sc, [7ch, 1 sl st] 3 times into same sc.

1st row (wrong side): Work 1sc into 2nd ch from hook, 1sc into each ch to end, turn.

2nd row: 1ch, work 1sc into each sc to end, turn.

3rd row: 1ch, 1sc into each of first 3sc, *9ch, skip 3sc, 1sc into each of next 5sc; rep from * to end omitting 2sc at end of last rep, turn.

4th row: 1ch, 1sc into each of first 2sc, *5ch, 1sc into next 9ch arch, 5ch, skip 1sc, 1sc into each of next 3sc; rep from * to end omitting 1sc at end of last rep, turn.

5th row: 1ch, 1sc into first sc, *5ch, skip 1sc, 1sc into next sc; rep from * to end, turn.

6th row: 1ch, 1sc into first sc, *5ch, work 1 triple loop into next sc, 5ch, 1sc into next sc; rep from * to end. Fasten off.

 = Triple loop

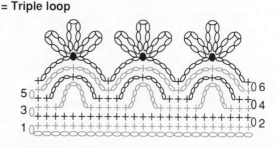

Quadrille

Starting chain: Multiple of 5 sts + 1.

Special Abbreviation

Popcorn = work 4dc into next sc, drop loop from hook, insert hook from the front into top of first of these dc, pick up dropped loop and draw through dc, 1ch to secure popcorn.

1st row (right side): Work 1sc into 2nd ch from hook, 1sc into each ch to end, turn.

2nd row: 4ch (count as 1hdc, 2ch), skip first 2sc, 1sc into next sc, *5ch, skip 4sc, 1sc into next sc; rep from * to last 2sc, 2ch, 1hdc into last sc, turn.

3rd row: 1ch, 1sc into first hdc, 3ch, 1 popcorn into next sc, 3ch, *1sc into next 5ch arch, 3ch, 1 popcorn into next sc, 3ch; rep from * to last sp, 1sc into 2nd of 4ch at beg of previous row. Fasten off.

 = Popcorn

Medal Ribbon

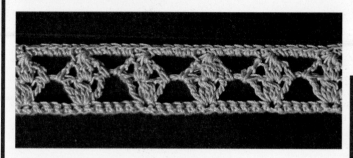

Starting chain: Multiple of 6 sts + 4.

Special Abbreviations

Bobble = work 3dc into next st until 1 loop of each remains on hook, yo and through all 4 loops on hook.

Cluster = work 1tr into next ch sp until 2 loops remain on hook, 3dc into top of next bobble until 1 loop of each remains on hook (5 loops on hook), skip 1ch sp, 1tr into next ch sp until 6 loops remain on hook, yo and through all 6 loops on hook

1st row (wrong side): Work 1sc into 2nd ch from hook, 1sc into each ch to end, turn.

2nd row: 4ch (count as 1dc, 1ch), skip first 4sc, 1tr into next sc, work [1ch, 1 bobble, 1ch, 1tr] into same st as last tr, 1ch, *skip 5sc, 1tr into next sc, work [1ch, 1 bobble, 1ch, 1tr] into same st as last tr, 1ch; rep from * to last 4sc, 1dc into last sc, turn.

3rd row: 6ch (count as 1dc, 3ch), *1 cluster, 5ch; rep from * to end working first tr of each cluster into same ch sp as last tr of previous cluster and omitting 2ch at end of last rep, 1dc into 3rd of 4ch at beg of previous row, turn.

4th row: 1ch, 1sc into first dc, 3sc into first 3ch sp, 1sc into top of first cluster, *5sc into next 5ch sp, 1sc into top of next cluster; rep from * to last sp, 3sc into last sp, 1sc into 3rd of 6ch at beg of previous row. Fasten off.

Keyline

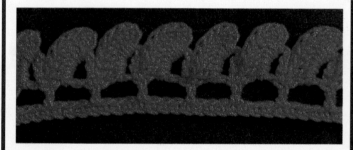

Starting chain: Multiple of 4 sts + 2.

1st row (right side): Work 1sc into 2nd ch from hook, 1sc into each ch to end, turn.

2nd row: 6ch (count as 1dc, 3ch), skip first 4sc, 1dc into next sc, *3ch, skip 3sc, 1dc into next sc; rep from * to end.

3rd row: 1ch, 1sc into first dc, *3ch, 1dc into next sp, 3ch, work 7dc over stem of dc just worked, 1sc into next dc; rep from * to end placing last sc into 3rd of 6ch at beg of previous row. Fasten off.

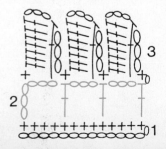

= Bobble

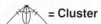
= Cluster

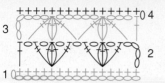

Plant Life

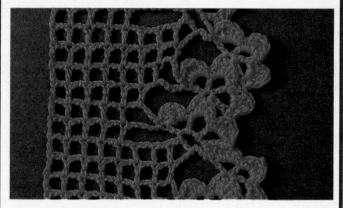

Worked lengthways.

1st row (right side): Make 31ch, work 1dc into 7th ch from hook, [2ch, skip 2ch, 1dc into next ch] 8 times, turn. (9 sps).

2nd row: 5ch (count as 1dc, 2ch), skip first dc, 1dc into next dc, [2ch, 1dc into next dc] 3 times, 5ch, skip next 4 sps, 1dc into next sp, work [3ch, 1dc] 3 times into same sp as last dc, turn.

3rd row: 1ch, 1sc into first dc, into first 3ch sp work [1hdc, 1dc, 1tr, 1dc, 1hdc, 1sc], into next 3ch sp work [1sc, 1hdc, 1dc, 1tr, 1dc, 1hdc, 1sc], into next 3ch sp work [1sc, 1hdc, 1dc, 1tr, 1dc, 1hdc], 1sc into next dc, 5ch, 1dc into next dc, [2ch, 1dc into next dc] 4 times placing last dc into 3rd of 5ch at beg of previous row, turn.

4th row: 5ch (count as 1dc, 2ch), skip first dc, [1dc into next dc, 2ch] 4 times, 1dc into 5ch sp, 7ch, skip first group of 7 sts, work 1dc into tr at center of next group of 7 sts, [3ch, 1dc] 3 times into same st as last dc, turn.

5th row: 1ch, 1sc into first dc, into first 3ch sp work [1hdc, 1dc, 1tr, 1dc, 1hdc, 1sc], into next 3ch sp work [1sc, 1hdc, 1dc, 1tr, 1dc, 1hdc, 1sc], into next 3ch sp work [1sc, 1hdc, 1dc, 1tr, 1dc, 1hdc], 1sc into next dc, 5ch, 1dc into 7ch sp, [2ch, 1dc into next dc] 6 times placing last dc into 3rd of 5ch at beg of previous row, turn.

6th row: 5ch (count as 1dc, 2ch), skip first dc, [1dc into next dc, 2ch] 6 times, 1dc into 5ch sp, 7ch, skip first group of 7 sts, work 1dc into tr at center of next group of 7 sts, [3ch, 1dc] 3 times into same st as last dc, turn.

7th row: 1ch, 1sc into first dc, into first 3ch sp work [1hdc, 1dc, 1tr, 1dc, 1hdc, 1sc], into next 3ch sp work [1sc, 1hdc, 1dc, 1tr, 1dc, 1hdc, 1sc], into next 3ch sp work [1sc, 1hdc, 1dc, 1tr, 1dc, 1hdc], 1sc into next dc, 5ch, 1dc into 7ch sp, [2ch, 1dc into next dc] 8 times placing last dc into 3rd of 5ch at beg of previous row, turn.

Rep 2nd to 7th rows ending with a 7th row.

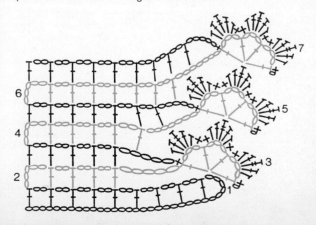

Edgings and Trimmings

Flower Group

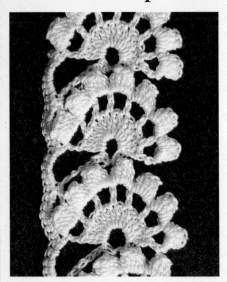

Worked lengthways.

Special Abbreviations

Popcorn at beg of row = 3ch, work 6dc into first sp, drop loop from hook, insert hook from the front into top of 3ch, pick up dropped loop and draw through, 1ch to secure.

7dc Popcorn = work 7dc into next sp, then complete as for popcorn at beg of row inserting hook into top of first of these dc.

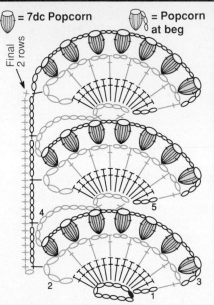

= 7dc Popcorn = Popcorn at beg

Make 10ch and join into a ring with a sl st.

1st row (right side): 3ch (count as 1dc), work 14dc into ring, turn.

2nd row: 5ch (count as 1dc, 2ch), skip first 2dc, 1dc into next dc, [2ch, skip 1dc, 1dc into next dc] 6 times placing last dc into 3rd of 3ch at beg of previous row, turn.

3rd row: Work 1 popcorn at beg of row, [3ch, 1 7dc popcorn into next 2ch sp] 6 times, turn.

4th row: 10ch, skip first 2 sps, work [1sc, 5ch, 1sc] into next 3ch sp, turn.

5th row: 3ch (count as 1dc), work 14dc into 5ch sp, turn.

Rep 2nd to 5th rows until edging is required length ending with a 3rd row. Do not turn work but continue along side edge as follows:

1st Final row: 3ch, 1sc into sp formed at beg of 2nd row of pattern, *5ch, 1sc into sp formed at beg of 4th row of pattern, 5ch, 1sc into sp formed at beg of 2nd row of pattern; rep from * to end, turn.

2nd Final row: 1ch, 1sc into first sc, *5sc into 5ch sp, 1sc into next sc; rep from * to end. Fasten off.

Bandoleer

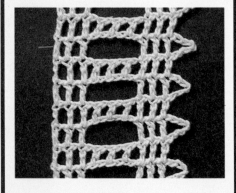

Worked lengthways.

1st row (wrong side): Make 20ch, work 1dc into 6th ch from hook, *1ch, skip 1ch, 1dc into next ch; rep from * to end, turn.

2nd row: 7ch, 1dc into first dc, [1ch, 1dc into next dc] twice, 7ch, skip 3dc, [1dc into next dc, 1ch] twice, skip 1ch, 1dc into next ch, turn.

3rd row: 4ch (count as 1dc, 1ch), skip first dc, 1dc into next dc, 1ch, 1dc into next dc, [1ch, skip 1ch, 1dc into next ch] 3 times, [1ch, 1dc into next dc] 3 times.

Rep 2nd and 3rd rows.

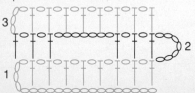

Daisy Chain

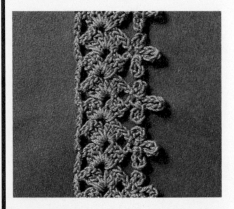

Worked lengthways.

1st row (wrong side): Make 4ch (count as 1dc, 1ch), work 2dc into first of these ch, 2ch, 3dc into same ch as last 2dc, turn.

Saw Tooth

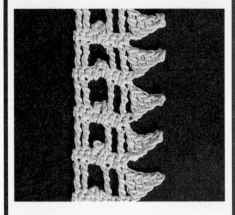

Worked lengthways.

1st row (right side): Make 14ch, work 1sc into 3rd ch from hook, 1hdc into next ch, 1dc into next ch, 1tr into next ch, [1ch, skip 1ch, 1tr into next ch] twice, 2ch, skip 2ch, 1tr into each of last 2ch, turn.

2nd row: 1ch, 1sc into each of first 2tr, 1sc into 2ch sp, 4ch, 1sc into same sp as last sc, 1sc into next tr, 1sc into ch sp, 1sc into next tr, turn.

3rd row: 7ch, work 1sc into 3rd ch from hook, 1hdc into next ch, 1dc into next ch, 1tr into next ch, 1ch, 1tr into next sc, 1ch, skip 1sc, 1tr into next sc, 2ch, skip 2sc, 1tr into each of last 2sc, turn.

Rep 2nd and 3rd rows.

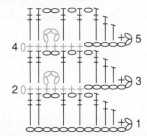

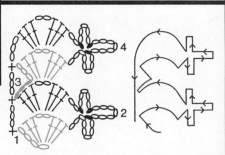

2nd row: 8ch, sl st into 6th ch from hook, 7ch, sl st into same ch as last sl st, 5ch, sl st into same ch as last 2 sl sts, 2ch, 3dc into 2ch sp, 2ch, 3dc into same sp as last 3dc, turn.

3rd row: Sl st into each of first 3dc, 3ch (count as 1dc), 2dc into 2ch sp, 2ch, 3dc into same sp as last 2dc, turn.

Rep 2nd and 3rd rows until edging is required length ending with a 2nd row. Do not turn work but continue along side edge as follows:

Final row: *3ch, 1sc into top of 3ch at beg of next fan, 3ch, 1sc into first sl st at beg of next fan; rep from * to last fan, 1sc into top of 4ch at beg of 1st row. Fasten off.

Stitch Variations, Abbreviations and Symbols on pages 7 to 15

Afghan Crochet

Afghan or Tunisian crochet is worked with a long hook available in the same range of thicknesses as traditional crochet hooks. The hooks are longer than crochet hooks as they are required to hold the loops created on the first (Forward) half of the row before working them off on the return half.

The fabric produced by this technique can be dense and thick. It is important to use a suitable size of hook in relation to the yarn. This is usually at least two sizes larger than would be used when working ordinary crochet with the same yarn.

Each row is worked in two parts. The first or 'Forward' part of the row involves working from right to left and pulling up loops or stitches on to the hook. On the second or 'Return' part of the row these loops are worked off again as the hook travels back from left to right. Afghan crochet is nearly always made without turning, therefore the right side is always facing.

Holding the Hook

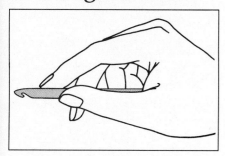

The hook should be held in the center with the hand as shown in the diagram.

Starting Chain

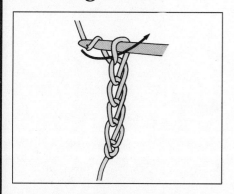

Make the number of chains needed to correspond with the number of stitches required in the first row.

Tip

When working a large piece it is sensible to start with more chains than necessary as it is simple to undo the extra chains if you have miscounted.

Although there are exceptions, Afghan stitch patterns usually begin with the same initial forward and return row - referred to as: **Basic Forward and Return row.**

Forward

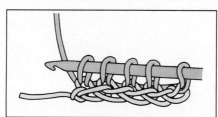

1. Working into back loop only of each chain, insert hook into second chain from hook, yarn over, draw loop through and leave on hook.
2. Insert hook into next chain, yarn over, draw loop through and leave on hook.

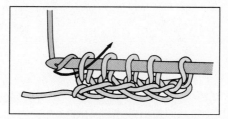

Repeat this in each chain to end. Do not turn.

The number of loops on hook should equal the number of stitches required for first row.

Note: Because the fabric produced in Afghan crochet is usually firmer than in ordinary crochet we recommend that the hook is inserted into the back loop only of the starting chain as this produces a firmer edge.

Return

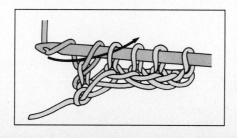

1. Yarn over, draw through one loop. (This chain forms the edge stitch).

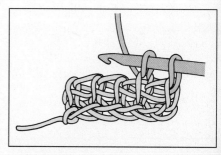

2. Yarn over, and draw through two loops.

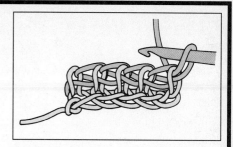

3. Repeat step 2 until one loop remains on hook. Do not turn. The loop remaining on the hook becomes the first stitch of the following row.

The Basic Stitches

These are produced by varying the technique of picking up loops on the Forward row.

Tunisian Simple Stitch (Tss $\uparrow$)

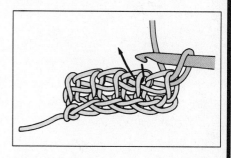

1. Insert hook from right to left behind single vertical thread.

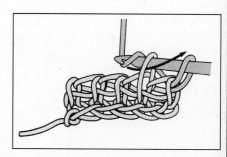

2. Yarn over hook.

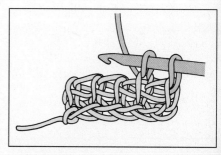

3. Draw loop through and leave on hook. Unless otherwise stated, the hook is always inserted in this way. For example, Afghan half double crochet and double crochet are usually worked from this position.

Afghan (Tunisian) Crochet

Making Afghan (Tunisian) Fabric

Make chain as required and work a Basic Forward and Return row. Generally the single loop on the hook at the end of each Return row counts as the first stitch in the next Forward row and so the first stitch is skipped. (As shown in first diagram for Tunisian simple stitch).

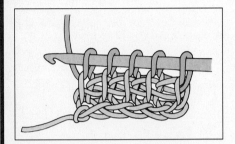

Next row: Pick up loop in each stitch (Tss or as required) including edge stitch.

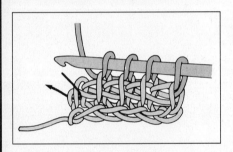

If you require a firmer edge at this end of the row you can work through two loops of the last stitch.
Return as Basic Return row.

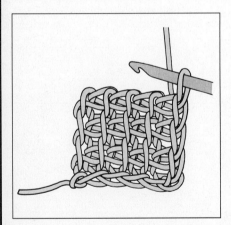

Repeat Forward and Return row as required. It is important to understand how to produce basic Afghan fabric before attempting pattern stitches.

Finishing Off

It is possible simply to finish with a Return row, cutting yarn and threading it through the remaining stitch to secure. However the following method leaves a neater edge and is useful where the Afghan fabric is complete in itself - as for a mat or rug for example.

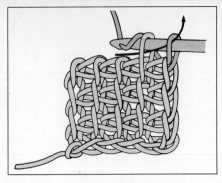

1. Finish with Return row. Insert hook into next stitch, yarn over.

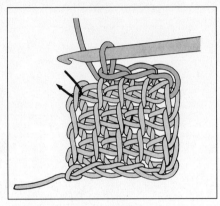

2. Draw through two loops.
Repeat steps 1 and 2 to end. Fasten off remaining loop.
Note: The hook can be inserted as if working Tunisian simple, Tunisian knit or Tunisian purl stitches so that stitches can be finished off in pattern.

Tunisian Knit Stitch (Tks 🎗)

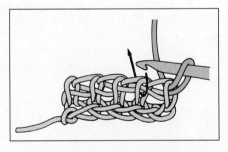

1. Insert hook from front to back through fabric and below chains formed by previous Return row, to right of front vertical thread but to left of corresponding back thread.

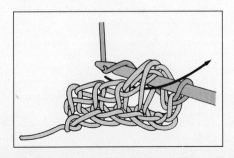

2. Yarn over, draw loop through and leave on hook.

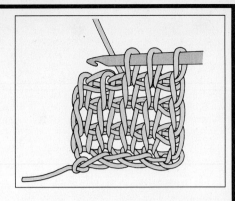

3. Repeat steps 1 and 2 into each stitch to end. At the last stitch of each Forward row work under two loops, return as Basic Return row.

Tunisian Purl Stitch (Tps ～)

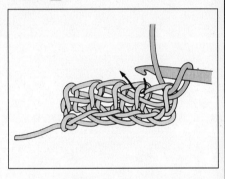

1. Bring yarn to front, insert hook as for Tunisian simple stitch.

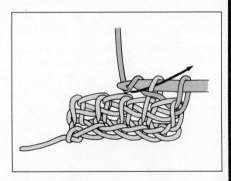

2. Take yarn to back of work and over hook (yo). Draw loop through and leave on hook.

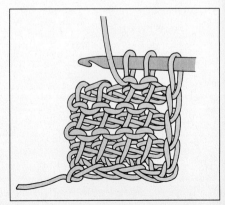

Repeat steps 1 and 2 in each stitch to end, return as Basic Return row.

Afghan (Tunisian) Crochet

Increasing

Inc 1Tss

1. To increase one stitch on a Forward row, insert hook under the back loop between two stitches, yarn over and draw loop through.

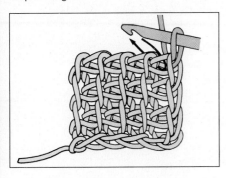

2. Work next stitch in the normal way.

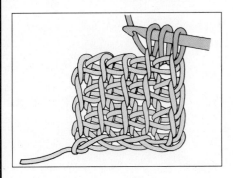

Two loops are to be worked off on Return row.

Decreasing

Tss2tog

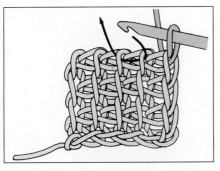

1. To decrease one stitch on a Forward row, insert hook through two stitches.
2. Yarn over and draw through loops. One loop to be worked off on Return row.

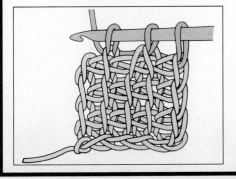

Note: Tss2tog is often worked in conjunction with a yarn over to create a lacy effect. For example:

Yo, Tss2tog

Tss2tog, yo

Two loops are then worked off on the Return row.

Tss3tog

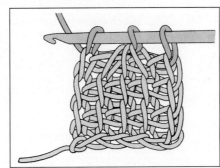

To decrease two stitches on a Forward row work as Tss2tog but insert hook through next three stitches.

Changing Color

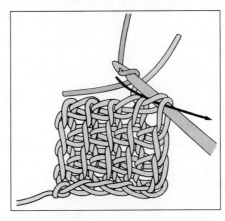

1. When a color change is required at the beginning of a Forward row, yarn over in the new color when two loops remain on the hook at the end of previous Return row.

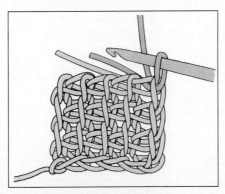

2. Draw through both loops.

To change color at the beginning of a Return row change yarn and continue to work as normal.

Stitch Variations

Tunisian Double Crochet (Tdc)

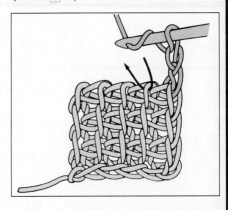

1. Make two chain for the first stitch at beginning of the row. Yarn over and insert hook into the next stitch as if working a Tunisian simple stitch.

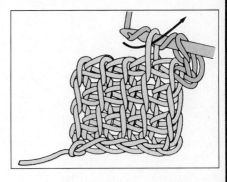

2. Yarn over and draw loop through.

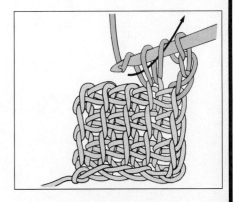

3. Yarn over and draw through two loops on hook.

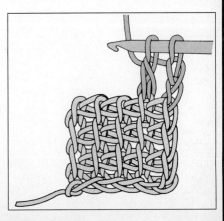

4. Leave remaining loop on hook.

163

Afghan (Tunisian) Crochet

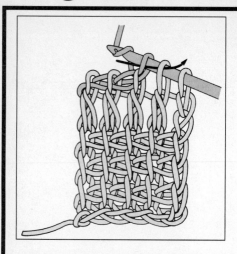

5. Double crochet is completed when Return row is worked.

Tunisian half double crochet (Thdc), Tunisian treble (Ttr), Tunisian double treble (Tdtr) etc. are also used frequently within Afghan patterns. As with Tunisian double crochet these stitches are worked in the same way as for crochet. Refer to introduction on pages 5 and 6 for detailed instructions of how to work these stitches. When working Afghan fabric, unless otherwise stated, the hook should be inserted as if working a Tunisian simple stitch and the stitch then worked as for crochet until one loop remains on the hook. Stitches are completed on the Return row. Turning chains are made at the beginning of Forward rows and are usually one chain less than for ordinary crochet. (Refer to individual pattern instructions).

Working between stitches

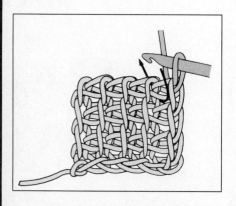

1. Insert hook between vertical loops that form stitches.
2. Yarn over and draw loop through.

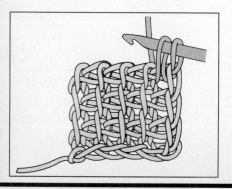

Thdc, Tdc, Ttr etc. can also be worked between stitches.

Tunisian Slipped Stitch (Tsl st ⍌)

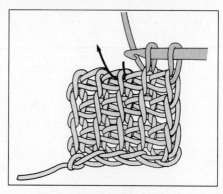

1. Insert hook into stitch as if working Tunisian simple stitch but do not pull yarn through.

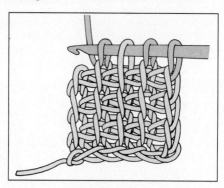

2. Continue working leaving slipped stitch on hook.

Twisted Tunisian Simple Stitch (TwTss ⌇)

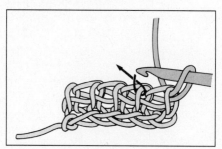

1. Insert hook into stitch from left to right.

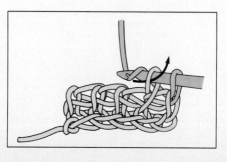

2. Yarn over and draw loop through.

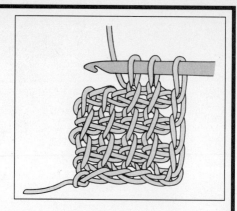

3. Finish stitch with Basic Return row.

Tunisian Bobbles

The following instructions are for a frequently used bobble. However individual pattern instructions should be followed.

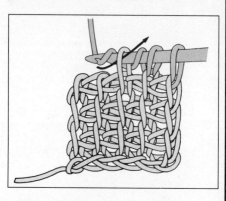

1. Yarn over and insert hook into next stitch as if working Tunisian simple stitch, yarn over and draw loop through.

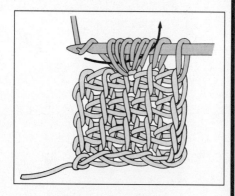

2. Repeat step 1 twice more into same stitch as before.

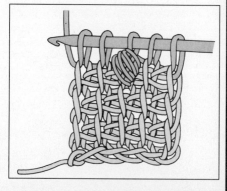

3. Yarn over and draw through all six loops. Remaining loop is worked off on Return row.

Surface Decoration

The evenness of Tunisian simple stitch makes it ideal to add surface decoration. The fabric in the photograph above has been embroidered using cross stitch. The diagram below indicates where to position the crosses in relation to the threads of the fabric.

It is also possible to use many other embroidery stitches in a similar way.

Following Afghan Pattern Instructions

All Afghan patterns are given in the form of written instructions and stitch diagrams. Much of the information about following pattern instructions, pattern repeats, tension etc. given on pages 13 to 15 apply equally to Afghan crochet. The stitch diagrams however are given on a grid where one rectangle represents one stitch worked over a Forward and Return row.

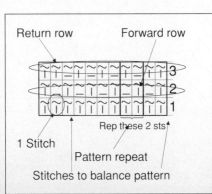

Stitches within dark lines form the pattern repeat. Compare stitch diagrams with written instructions if you have difficulty following the pattern.

Abbreviations and Symbols

Abbreviations

Beg = beginning, **ch** = chain, **dec** = decrease, **inc** = increase, **rep** = repeat, **sp** = space, **st(s)** = stitch(es), **tog** = together, **Tdc** = Tunisian double crochet, **Tdtr** = Tunisian double treble, **Thdc** = Tunisian half double crochet, **Tks** = Tunisian knit stitch, **Tps** = Tunisian purl stitch, **Tsl st** = Tunisian slipped stitch, **Tss** = Tunisian simple stitch, **Ttr** = Tunisian treble, **TwTss** = Twisted Tunisian simple stitch, **yo** = yarn over, **yf** = yarn forward, **yb** = yarn back.

Common Symbols

Note: All symbols represent a completed stitch; the lower part of the symbol is worked on the Forward row where the loops are held on the hook, the upper part (or swash ~) is worked on the Return row when the loops are worked off.

	= Tunisian simple stitch (Tss)
	= Tunisian purl stitch (Tps)
	= Tunisian knit stitch (Tks)
	= Tunisian slipped stitch (Tsl st)
	= Twisted Tunisian simple stitch (TwTss)
	= Tss worked under chain loop and between two vertical loops of previous row
	= Tss worked into back loop only of stitch in previous row
	= Tunisian half double crochet (Thdc)
	= Tunisian double crochet (Tdc)
	= Tunisian double crochet worked between stitches
	= Increase one Tunisian simple stitch (Inc 1Tss)
	= Tunisian simple stitch two together (Tss2tog)
	= Tunisian simple stitch three together (Tss3tog)
	= Make Bobble (MB)
	= Yo, Tss2tog
	= Tss2tog, yo
	= Yo, tss3tog, yo

Tunisian Web

Note: Because this pattern incorporates a slipped stitch it should be worked on a hook which is at least 2 sizes (1mm) larger than usual.

Multiple of 2 sts + 3.

1st row: Using A, as Basic Forward and Return row, changing to B when 2 loops remain at end of return.

2nd row: Using B, with 1 loop on hook, *1Tss into next st, 1Tsl st into next st; rep from * to last 2 sts, 1Tss into each of next 2 sts. Return, changing to A when 2 loops remain.

3rd row: Using A, with 1 loop on hook, *1Tsl st into next st, 1Tss into next st; rep from * to end. Return, changing to B when 2 loops remain.

Rep 2nd and 3rd rows.

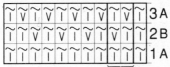

Rep these 2 sts

Close Weave

Multiple of 2 sts + 1.

1st row: As Basic Forward and Return row.

2nd row: With 1 loop on hook, *1TwTss into next st, 1Tss into next st; rep from * to end. Return.

Rep 2nd row.

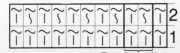

Rep these 2 sts

Afghan (Tunisian) Crochet

Mesh Stitch

Any number of sts.

Note: Check the number of sts after each Forward row. It will be easier to keep the number of sts correct and the edges of the material straight if you take care to alternate the placing of the first Tss, as given on 2nd and 3rd rows.

1st row: As Basic Forward and Return row.

2nd row: With 1 loop on hook, work 1Tss into space between 2nd and 3rd sts, 1Tss into each sp to end, 1Tss into last st. Return.

3rd row: With 1 loop on hook, work 1Tss into sp between first and 2nd sts, 1Tss into each sp to last sp, skip last sp, work 1Tss into last st. Return.

Rep 2nd and 3rd rows.

Rep this stitch

Cover Pattern

Multiple of 2 sts + 3.

1st row: As Basic Forward and Return row.

2nd row: With 1 loop on hook, *1Tps into next st, 1Tss into next st; rep from * to end. Return.

3rd row: With 1 loop on hook, *1Tss into next st, 1Tps into next st; rep from * to last 2 sts, 1Tss into each of last 2 sts. Return.

Rep 2nd and 3rd rows.

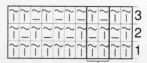

Rep these 2 sts

Masonary Stitch

Multiple of 4 sts + 3.

1st row: Using A, as Basic Forward and Return row, changing to B when 2 loops remain.

2nd row: Using B, with 1 loop on hook, *1Tsl st into next st, work 1Tss into each of next 3 sts; rep from * to last 2 sts, 1Tsl st into next st, work 1Tss into last st. Return, changing to A when 2 loops remain.

3rd row: Using A with 1 loop on hook work 1Tss into each st to end. Return, changing to B when 2 loops remain.

4th row: Using B, with 1 loop on hook, work 1Tss into each of next 2 sts, *1Tsl st into next st, 1Tss into each of next 3 sts; rep from * to end. Return, changing to A when 2 loops remain.

5th row: As 3rd row.

Rep 2nd to 5th rows.

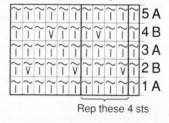

Rep these 4 sts

Buckle Pattern

Note: It is recommended that this stitch is worked using a hook 1 or 2 sizes (0.5mm or 1mm) larger than usual.

Multiple of 2 sts + 3.

Sparkle Stitch

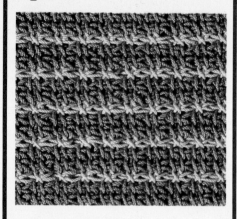

Multiple of 2 sts + 2.

Special Abbreviation

Cross 2 = skip next st, 1Tss into next st, 1Tss into skipped st.

Note: The crossed stitches appear 1 row below the row on which the cross 2 is worked.

1st row: Using A, as Basic Forward and Return row.

2nd row: Using A, with 1 loop on hook, 1Tss into each st to end. Return.

3rd row: Using B, as 2nd row.

4th row: Using A, with 1 loop on hook, *cross 2; rep from * to last st, 1Tss into last st. Return.

Rep 2nd to 4th rows.

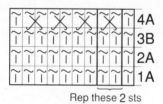

Rep these 2 sts

Special Abbreviation

Sl 1 fwd = yf, insert hook into next st without working it, yb.

1st row: Using A, as Basic Forward and Return row.

2nd row: Using B, with 1 loop on hook, *sl 1 fwd, 1Tss into next st; rep from * to end. Return, changing to A when 2 loops remain.

3rd row: Using A, with 1 loop on hook, *1Tss into next st, sl 1 fwd; rep from * to last 2 sts, 1Tss into each of last 2 sts. Return, changing to B when 2 loops remain.

Rep 2nd and 3rd rows.

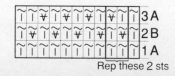

Rep these 2 sts

Stitch Variations, Abbreviations and Symbols on pages 161 to 165

Afghan (Tunisian) Crochet

Platform Stitch

Multiple of 14 sts + 7.

1st row: As Basic Forward and Return row.

2nd row: With 1 loop on hook, work 1Tss into each of next 6 sts, *work 1Tps into each of next 7 sts, work 1Tss into each of next 7 sts; rep from * to end. Return.

3rd to 7th rows: Rep 2nd row 5 times more.

8th row: With 1 loop on hook, work 1Tps into each of next 6 sts, *work 1Tss into each of next 7 sts, work 1Tps into each of next 7 sts; rep from * to end. Return.

9th to 13th rows: Rep 8th row 5 times more.

Rep 2nd to 13th rows.

Roulette

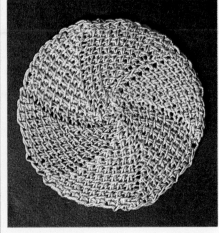

Using A make 12ch.

1st row: With 1 loop on hook, work 1Tss into next ch. Return.

2nd row: With 1 loop on hook, work 1Tss into next st, then work 1Tss into next ch (3 loops on hook). Return.

3rd row: With 1 loop on hook, work 1Tss into each of next 2 sts, then work 1Tss into next ch (4 loops on hook). Return.

Continue working in this manner until all 12ch have been picked up (12 loops on hook). Return, changing color when 2 loops remain.

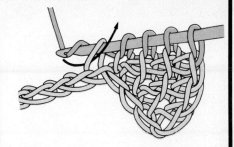

Using B, rep these 11 rows but working into sts of previous color instead of ch. Continue working segments in alternate colors until **6** segments in all have been worked. Fasten off last st.

Join seam.

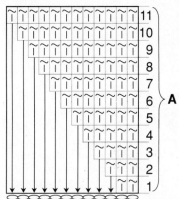

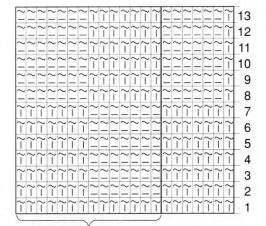

Rep these 14 sts

Cutter Edging II

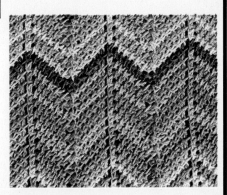

Work as Cutter Edging I **but** working 3 rows in A and 1 row in B throughout **or** using random colors as illustrated below.

Cutter Edging I

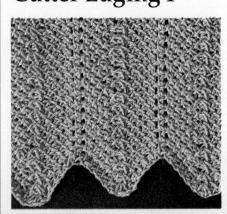

Multiple of 14 sts + 1.

1st row: As Basic Forward and Return row.

2nd row: With 1 loop on hook, *inc 1Tss, work 1Tss into each of next 4 sts, Tss3tog, work 1Tss into each of next 5 sts, inc 1Tss; rep from * to end. Return.

Rep 2nd row.

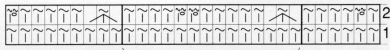

Rep these 14 sts

Afghan (Tunisian) Crochet

Opera Pattern I

Multiple of 2 sts + 3.

Special Abbreviation

 **Long Tdc** (worked on Forward rows) = loosely work 1Tdc into next st 2 rows below.

1st row: As Basic Forward and Return row.

2nd row: With 1 loop on hook, work 1Tss into each st to end. Return.

3rd row: With 1 loop on hook, *1 long Tdc, 1Tss into next st; rep from * to end. Return.

4th row: With 1 loop on hook, *1Tss into next st, 1 long Tdc; rep from * to last 2 sts, 1Tss into each of last 2 sts. Return.

Rep 3rd and 4th rows.

Rep these 2 sts

Opera Pattern II

Work as Opera Pattern I **but** working 1 row each in colors A and B throughout.

Strand Pattern

Multiple of 8 sts + 4.

1st row: As Basic Forward and Return row.

2nd row: With 1 loop on hook, work 1Tss into each of next 3 sts, *work 1Tps into each of next 4 sts, work 1Tss into each next 4 sts; rep from * to end. Return.

Rep 2nd row.

Dual Band

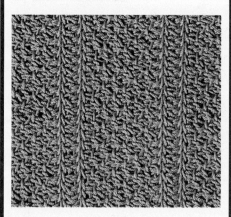

Multiple of 10 sts + 11.

1st row: As Basic Forward and Return row.

2nd row: With 1 loop on hook, 1Tps into next st, 1Tss into each of next 2 sts, *1TwTss into next st, 1Tss into next st, 1TwTss into next st, 1Tps into next st, [1Tss into next st, 1Tps into next st] twice, 1Tss into each of next 2 sts; rep from * to last 7 sts, 1TwTss into next st, 1Tss into next st, 1TwTss into next st, [1Tps into next st, 1Tss into next st] twice. Return.

3rd row: With 1 loop on hook, 1Tss into next st, 1Tps into next st, 1Tss into next st, *[1TwTss into next st, 1Tss into next st] twice, [1Tps into next st, 1Tss into next st] 3 times; rep from * to last 7 sts, [1TwTss into next st, 1Tss into next st] twice, 1Tps into next st, 1Tss into next st, 1Tps into last st. Return.

Rep 2nd and 3rd rows.

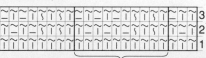

Rep these 10 sts

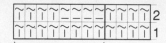

Rep these 8 sts

Kiln Stitch I

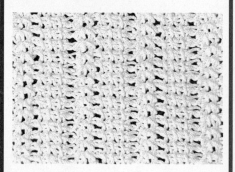

Multiple of 6 sts + 3.

Special Abbreviations

 **Basic Group 3** = first part worked as Basic Forward row, on return row work 1ch, yo, draw hook through 4 loops, 1ch.

Group 3 = on Forward row insert hook under next ch, yo, draw loop through, insert hook into loop over the group 3 on previous row, yo, draw loop through, insert hook under next ch, yo, draw loop through. On Return row work 1ch, yo, draw hook through 4 loops, 1ch.

1st row: As Basic Forward row. Return as follows: Yo, draw hook through 1 loop, [yo, draw hook through 2 loops] twice, *basic group 3, [yo, draw through 2 loops] 3 times; rep from * to end.

2nd row: With 1 loop on hook, work 1Tss into each of next 2 sts, *group 3, work 1Tss into each of next 3 sts; rep from * to end. Return as follows: Yo, draw hook through 1 loop, [yo, draw hook through 2 loops] twice, *group 3, [yo, draw through 2 loops] 3 times; rep from * to end.

Rep 2nd row.

Rep these 6 sts

Kiln Stitch II

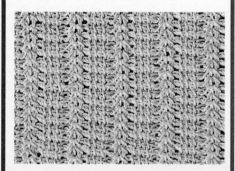

Work as given for Kiln Stitch I **but** working 1 row in A and 1 row in B throughout.

Stitch Variations, Abbreviations and Symbols on pages 161 to 165

Afghan (Tunisian) Crochet

Tunisian Pearls I

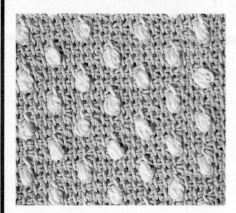

Multiple of 6 sts + 5.

Special Abbreviation

 MB (Make Bobble) = using color B [yo, insert hook into next st, yo and draw loop through] 3 times into same st, yo and draw through 6 loops, see Note.

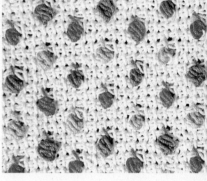

Rep these 6 sts

Note: Pattern is worked in color A on every row. Color B is used for bobbles only and is carried **loosely** across back of work on 2nd and 4th rows. Cut and rejoin color B at beginning of each bobble row.

1st row: As Basic Forward and Return row.

2nd row: With 1 loop on hook, work 1Tss into next st, MB into next st, *1Tss into each of next 5 sts, MB into next st; rep from * to last 2 sts, Tss into each of last 2 sts. Return using A only.

3rd row: With 1 loop on hook, 1Tss into each st to end. Return.

4th row: With 1 loop on hook, 1Tss into each of next 4 sts, *MB into next st, 1Tss into each of next 5 sts; rep from * to end. Return using A only.

5th row: As 3rd row.

Rep 2nd to 5th rows.

Tunisian Pearls II

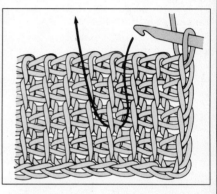

Work as given for Tunisian Pearls I working 1 row of bobbles each in B, C and D.

Tunisian 5 Double Crochet Fan

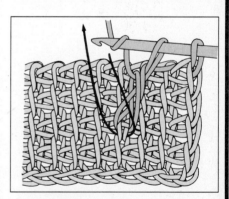

1. Skip two stitches. Loosely work a Tunisian double crochet into the next stitch three rows below (inserting hook as indicated).

Bushel Pattern

Multiple of 10 sts + 7.

Special Abbreviation

5Tdc fan = skip next 2 sts, work 5 **loose** Tdc round stem of next st 3 rows below, skip next 2 sts (see diagrams).

1st row: As Basic Forward and Return row.

2nd row: With 1 loop on hook, 1Tss into each st to end. Return.

3rd and 4th rows: Rep 2nd row twice.

5th row: With 1 loop on hook, work 5Tdc fan, *1Tss into each of next 5 sts, work 5Tdc fan; rep from * to last st, 1Tss into last st. Return.

6th and 7th rows: Rep 2nd row twice.

8th row: With 1 loop on hook, *1Tss into each of next 5 sts, work 5Tdc fan; rep from * to last 6 sts, 1Tss into each of last 6 sts. Return.

Rep 3rd to 8th rows.

2. Loosely work four more Tunisian double crochet into the same stitch.

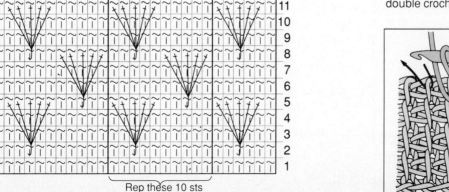

Rep these 10 sts

= 5Tdc fan

3. Skip two stitches and continue working.

Afghan (Tunisian) Crochet

Studio Pattern

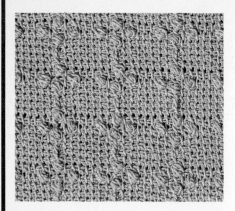

Multiple of 8 sts + 7.

Special Abbreviations

 Long Tdc (worked on Forward rows) = loosely work 1Tdc into vertical loop above bobble 3 rows below.

MB (Make Bobble) = [yo, insert hook into next st, yo and draw loop through] 3 times into same st, yo, draw yarn through 6 loops.

1st row: As Basic Forward and Return row.

2nd row: With 1 loop on hook, work 1Tss into each of next 2 sts, *MB into next st, 1Tss into each of next 7 sts; rep from * to last 4 sts, MB, 1Tss into each of last 3 sts. Return.

3rd row: With 1 loop on hook, *MB into next st, 1Tss into each of next 3 sts; rep from * to last 2 sts, MB, 1Tss into last st. Return.

4th row: As 2nd row.

5th row: With 1 loop on hook work 1Tss into each st to end. Return.

6th row: As 5th row.

7th row: With 1 loop on hook, work 1Tss into each of next 2 sts, *work long Tdc, 1Tss into each of next 7 sts; rep from * to last 4 sts, work long Tdc, 1Tss into each of last 3 sts. Return.

Rep 2nd to 7th rows.

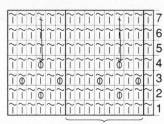

Rep these 8 sts

Twist Stitch

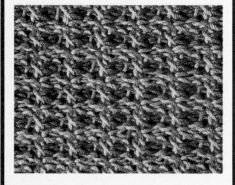

Multiple of 3 sts + 3.

Note: Color is changed after each **Forward** row. Work first ch of each Return row in new color.

Special Abbreviation

Cross 2 = skip next st, 1Tss into next st, 1Tss into skipped st.

Make chain in color A.

1st row: Using color A as Basic Forward row. Using color B Return.

2nd row: Using B, with 1 loop on hook, *1Tps into next st, cross 2; rep from * to last 2 sts, 1Tps into next st, 1Tss into last st. Using A Return.

3rd row: Using A, with 1 loop on hook, *1Tps into next st, cross 2; rep from * to last 2 sts, 1Tps into next st, 1Tss into last st. Using B Return.

Rep 2nd and 3rd rows.

Rep these 3 sts

Cone Pattern

Multiple of 2 sts + 3.

Special Abbreviation

MB (Make Bobble) = work [yo, insert hook into next st, yo and draw loop through] 3 times into same st, yo, draw yarn through 6 loops.

1st row: As Basic Forward and Return row.

2nd row: With 1 loop on hook, work 1Tss into next st, *MB into next st, 1Tss into next st; rep from * to last st, 1Tss into last st. Return.

3rd row: With 1 loop on hook, *MB into next st, 1Tss into next st; rep from * to end. Return.

Rep 2nd and 3rd rows.

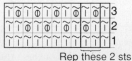

Rep these 2 sts

Spectrum Stitch

Multiple of 3 sts + 2.

Special Abbreviation

 **Long Ttr** (worked on Forward rows) = loosely work 1Ttr into vertical loop of next st 2 rows below.

1st row: As Basic Forward and Return row.

2nd row: With 1 loop on hook, 1Tps into next st, *1Tdc into next st, 1Tps into each of next 2 sts; rep from * to end. Return.

3rd row: With 1 loop on hook, work 1Tss into each st to end. Return.

4th row: With 1 loop on hook, 1Tps into next st, *work 1 long Ttr, 1Tps into each of next 2 sts; rep from * to end. Return.

Rep 3rd and 4th rows.

Rep these 3 sts

Mill Pattern

Multiple of 2 sts + 1.

1st row: As Basic Forward and Return row.

2nd row: With 1 loop on hook, *1Tdc into next st, 1Tps into next st; rep from * to end. Return.

3rd row: With 1 loop on hook, *work 1Tps into next st, 1Tdc into next st; rep from * to end. Return.

Rep 2nd and 3rd rows.

Rep these 2 sts

Stitch Variations, Abbreviations and Symbols on pages 161 to 165

Tunisian Windows

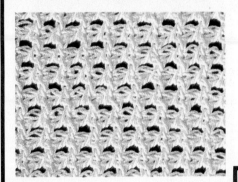

Multiple of 2 sts + 3.

1st row: As Basic Forward and Return row.

2nd row: With 1 loop on hook, *Tss2tog, yo; rep from * to last 2 sts, 1Tss into each of last 2 sts. Return.

3rd row: With 1 loop on hook, *1Tss into next vertical loop, 1Tss under ch loop of next st; rep from * to last 2 sts, 1Tss into each of last 2 sts. Return.

Rep 2nd and 3rd rows.

Rep these 2 sts

Candle Pattern

Multiple of 7 sts + 7.

Special Abbreviation

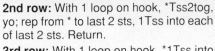 **T3st cable** = skip next 2 sts, work 1Tks into 3rd st, work 1Tks into 2nd st, work 1Tks into first st.

1st row: As Basic Forward and Return row.

2nd row: With 1 loop on hook 1Tps into next st, *1Tks into each of next 3 sts, 1Tps into each of next 4 sts; rep from * to last 5 sts, 1Tks into each of next 3 sts, 1Tps into next st, 1Tss into last st. Return.

3rd and 4th rows: Rep 2nd row twice.

5th row: With 1 loop on hook 1Tps into next st, *T3st cable, 1Tps into each of next 4 sts; rep from * to last 5 sts, T3st cable, 1Tps into next st, 1Tss into last st. Return.

6th to 11th rows: Rep 2nd row 6 times.

Rep 5th to 11th rows.

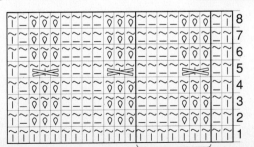

Rep these 7 sts

Diagram only: Rep 2nd to 8th rows.

Tunisian Warp

Multiple of 11 sts + 2.

Note: When working Tss2tog work through diagonal loop of yo of previous row where applicable.

1st row: As Basic Forward and Return row.

2nd row: With 1 loop on hook, 1Tss into each of next 3 sts, [yo, Tss2tog] twice, *1Tss into each of next 7 sts, [yo, Tss2tog] twice; rep from * to last 5 sts, 1Tss into each of last 5 sts. Return.

3rd row: With 1 loop on hook, 1Tss into each of next 3 sts, 1Tss under ch loop of next st, [yo, Tss2tog] twice, *1Tss into each of next 6 sts, 1Tss under ch loop of next st, [yo, Tss2tog] twice; rep from * to last 4 sts, 1Tss into each of last 4 sts. Return.

4th row: With 1 loop on hook, 1Tss into each of next 4 sts, 1Tss under ch loop of next st, [yo, Tss2tog] twice, *1Tss into each of next 6 sts, 1Tss under ch loop of next st, [yo, Tss2tog] twice; rep from * to last 3 sts, 1Tss into each of last 3 sts. Return.

5th row: With 1 loop on hook, 1Tss into each of next 5 sts, 1Tss under ch loop of next st, [yo, Tss2tog] twice, *1Tss into each of next 6 sts, 1Tss under ch loop of next st, [yo, Tss2tog] twice; rep from * to last 2 sts, 1Tss into each of last 2 sts. Return.

6th row: With 1 loop on hook, *1Tss into each of next 6 sts, 1Tss under ch loop of next st, [yo, Tss2tog] twice; rep from * to last st, 1Tss into last st. Return.

7th row: With 1 loop on hook, 1Tss into each of next 7 sts, 1Tss under ch loop of next st, *[yo, Tss2tog] twice, 1Tss into each of next 6 sts, 1Tss under ch loop of next st; rep from * to last 4 sts, yo, Tss2tog, 1Tss into each of last 2 sts. Return.

8th row: With 1 loop on hook, yo, Tss2tog, 1Tss into each of next 6 sts, 1Tss under ch loop of next st, *[yo, Tss2tog] twice, 1Tss into each of next 6 sts, 1Tss under ch loop of next st; rep from * to last 3 sts, yo, Tss2tog, 1Tss into last st. Return.

9th row: With 1 loop on hook, 1Tss under ch loop of next st, yo, Tss2tog, 1Tss into each of next 6 sts, 1Tss under ch loop of next st, *[yo, Tss2tog] twice, 1Tss into each of next 6 sts, 1Tss under ch loop of next st; rep from * to last 2 sts, 1Tss into each of last 2 sts. Return.

10th row: With 1 loop on hook, [yo, Tss2tog] twice, *1Tss into each of next 6 sts, 1Tss under ch loop of next st, [yo, Tss2tog] twice; rep from * to last 8 sts, 1Tss into each of last 8 sts. Return.

11th row: With 1 loop on hook, *1Tss under ch loop of next st, [yo, Tss2tog] twice, 1Tss into each of next 6 sts; rep from * to last st, 1Tss into last st. Return.

12th row: With 1 loop on hook, 1Tss into next st, *1Tss under ch loop of next st, [yo, Tss2tog] twice, 1Tss into each of next 6 sts; rep from * to end. Return.

13th row: With 1 loop on hook, 1Tss into each of next 2 sts, 1Tss under ch loop of next st, [yo, Tss2tog] twice, *1Tss into each of next 6 sts, 1Tss under ch loop of next st, [yo, Tss2tog] twice; rep from * to last 5 sts, 1Tss into each of last 5 sts. Return.

Rep 3rd to 13th rows.

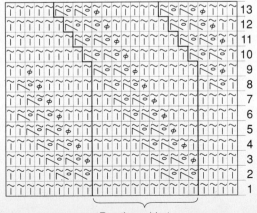

Rep these 11 sts

Afghan (Tunisian) Crochet

Bell Pattern

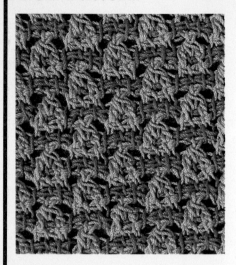

Multiple of 6 sts + 7.

Special Abbreviation

 3 st triangle = on Forward row work 1Tdc into previous st 2 rows below, work 1Tss into next st, work 1Tdc into next st 2 rows below, yo, draw through 3 loops. Return as follows: Yo, draw through 2 loops.

1st row: Using A, as Basic Forward and Return row.

2nd row: Using B, with 1 loop on hook, work 1Tss into next st, *skip 1 st, work 1Tss into next st, skip 1 st, work 1Tss into each of next 3 sts; rep from * to last 5 sts, skip next st, work 1Tss into next st, skip next st, work 1Tss into each of last 2 sts. Return as follows: Yo, draw hook through 1 loop, yo, draw hook through 2 loops, *1ch, yo, draw hook through 2 loops, 1ch, [yo, draw hook through 2 loops] 3 times; rep from * until 4 loops remain on hook, 1ch, yo, draw hook through 2 loops, 1ch, [yo, draw hook through 2 loops] twice.

3rd row: Using A, with 1 loop on hook, work 1Tss into next st, skip next sp, work 3 st triangle, skip next sp,* work 1Tss into each of next 3 sts, skip next sp, work 3 st triangle, skip next sp; rep from * to last 2 sts, work 1Tss into each of last 2 sts. Return as follows: Yo, draw hook through 1 loop, yo, draw hook through 2 loops, *1ch, yo, draw hook through 2 loops, 1ch, [yo, draw hook through 2 loops] 3 times; rep from * until 4 loops remain on hook, 1ch, yo, draw hook through 2 loops, 1ch, [yo, draw hook through 2 loops] twice.

4th row: Using B, with 1 loop on hook, *skip next st, 1Tss under ch loop of next st, 1Tss into next st, 1Tss under ch loop of next st, skip 1 st, 1Tss into next st; rep from * to end. Return as follows: Yo, draw hook through 1 loop, *1ch, [yo, draw hook through 2 loops] 3 times, 1ch, yo, draw hook through 2 loops; rep from * to end.

5th row: Using A, with 1 loop on hook, work 1Tdc into next vertical loop 2 rows below, yo, draw hook through 2 loops, skip next sp, 1Tss into each of next 3 sts, skip next sp, *work 3 st triangle, skip next sp, 1Tss into each of next 3 sts, skip next sp; rep from * to last st, work 1Tdc into

previous st 2 rows below, 1Tss into last st, yo and through 2 loops. Return as follows: Yo, draw hook through 1 loop, *1ch, [yo, draw hook through 2 loops] 3 times, 1ch, yo, draw hook through 2 loops; rep from * to end.

6th row: Using B, with 1 loop on hook, *work 1Tss under ch loop of next st, skip next st, 1Tss into next st, skip next st, 1Tss under ch loop of next st, 1Tss into next st; rep from * to end. Return as follows: Yo, draw hook through 1 loop, yo, draw hook through 2 loops, *1ch, yo, draw hook through 2 loops, 1ch, [yo, draw hook through 2 loops] 3 times; rep from * until 4 loops remain on hook, 1ch, yo, draw hook through 2 loops, 1ch, [yo, draw hook through 2 loops] twice.

Rep 3rd to 6th rows always working Tdc into sts 2 rows below.

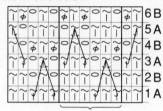

Rep these 6 sts

 = On Forward rows skip 1 st or space, on Return rows work 1ch.

= With 1 loop on hook on Forward row work 1Tss and 1Tdc of 3 st triangle, return as normal.

= On Forward row work 1Tdc of 3 st triangle and 1Tss, Return as normal.

Tunisian Weave

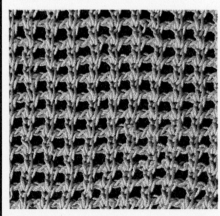

Multiple of 2 sts + 1.

1st row: As Basic Forward and Return row.

2nd row: With 1 loop on hook, 2ch, *skip next st, yo, 1Tks into next st, 2ch; rep from * to end. Return.

3rd row: With 1 loop on hook, 2ch, *skip next sp, yo, 1Tks into upper of 2ch of previous Forward row, 2ch; rep from * to end. Return.

Rep 3rd row.

Spray Pattern

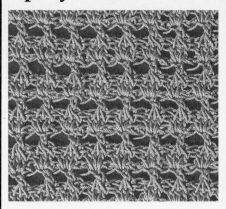

Multiple of 3 sts + 2.

Special Abbreviations

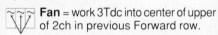 **Fan** = work 3Tdc into center of upper of 2ch in previous Forward row.

Lace 3tog = insert hook through next 3 vertical loops, yo, draw loop through, 2ch (on Return row 1ch, yo, draw hook through 2 loops, 1ch).

Note: Only count sts after 3rd row.

1st row: As Basic Forward and Return row.

2nd row: With 1 loop on hook, 2ch, *Lace 3tog; rep from * to last st, 1Tss into last st, 2ch. Return as follows: Yo, draw hook through 1 loop, 1ch, *yo, draw hook through 2 loops, 2ch; rep from * until 3 loops remain on hook, yo draw hook through 2 loops, 1ch, yo, draw hook through 2 loops.

3rd row: With 1 loop on hook, 2ch, *work 1 Fan; rep from * to last st, 1Tdc into upper ch of last st. Return.

Rep 2nd and 3rd rows.

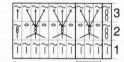

Rep these 3 sts

 = With 1 loop on hook at beginning of Forward row work 2ch. 1 loop to be worked off on Return row.

= Into last st of Forward row work 1Tss, 2ch. On Return row work yo and through 1 loop.

Rep these 2 sts

= With 1 loop on hook at beginning of Forward row work 2ch.

= Skip next st, yo on Forward row, (1 loop to be worked off on Return row).

= 1Tks, 2ch on Forward row, (1 loop to be worked off on Return row). **Note:** On 3rd and every following Forward row work 1Tks into the upper of 2ch of previous Forward row.

Stitch Variations, Abbreviations and Symbols on pages 161 to 165

Index

- A -

Abbreviations and Symbols 15
Basic Symbols used in Diagrams 15
Afghan (Tunisian Crochet) 161-172
Abbreviations and Symbols 165
Changing Color 163
Decreasing 163
Finishing Off 162
Following Afghan Pattern Instructions 165
Forward Row 161
Holding the Hook 161
Increasing 163
Making Afghan (Tunisian) Fabric 162
Return Row 161
Starting Chain 161
Stitch Variations 163
Surface Decoration 165
The Basic Stitches 161
Tunisian Bobbles 164
Tunisian Double Crochet 163
Tunisian Knit Stitch 162
Tunisian Purl Stitch 162
Tunisian Simple Stitch 161
Tunisian Slipped Stitch 164
Twisted Tunisian Simple Stitch 164
Working Between Stitches 164
All-over Patterns 52-63

- B -

Basic Stitches 5
Double Crochet 5
Half Double Crochet 5
Longer Basic Stitches 6
Single Crochet 5
Slip Stitch 5
Treble 6
Basic Stitches 16

- C -

Clusters 19-21

- E -

Edgings and Trimmings 150-160
Using Edgings 150

- F -

Filet Crochet 89-101
Filet Charts 89
Filet Crochet Lace 98
Increasing and Decreasing 89
Symbols Key 90
Lacets and Bars 89
Pressing and Finishing Filet 90
Starting Chain 89
Using Filet Patterns 90

- I -

Introduction 4
About Crochet 4
Chain Stitch 4
Equipment 4
Holding the Hook and Yarn 4
Slip Knot 4
To Start 4
Yarn over (yo) 4
Irish Style Crochet 137-149
Clones Knot 137
Padding Threads 137
Working into Base of Stitch 137

- M -

Making Crochet Fabric 6
Basic Double Crochet Fabric 7
Fastening Off 7
Joining in New Yarn and Changing Color 7
Starting Chain 6
Working in Rows 6
Motifs 102-136
Joining Motifs 102
Working in Rounds 102

- O -

Openwork and Lace Patterns 64-88

- P -

Pattern Instructions 13
Joining Seams 14
Pressing and Finishing 15
Right Side and Wrong Side Rows 13
Shaping 14
Starting Chains and Pattern Repeats 13
Tension (or Gauge) 14
Working from a Diagram 13
Working in Color 14
Patterns for Texture and Color 22-51

- S -

Stitch Variations 7
Bobbles 8
Bullion Stitch 10
Clusters 8
Corded or Reversed Single Crochet 12
Crossed Stitches 9
Groups or Shells 7
Lace Loops 10
Linked Stitches 13
Loop (Fur) Stitch 10
Marguerites (Stars) 12
Picots 9

Placement of Stitches 11
Popcorns 8
Puff Stitches 9
Soloman's Knot 11
Spikes 12
Working Around the Stem of a Stitch 11
Working Between Stitches 12
Working into Chain Spaces 11
Working Under the Front or Back Loop Only 11
Χ Υ and Υ Shapes 9
Stitch Variations 17-18